S0-AIW-562

The Men's Clothing Industry

Colonial Through Modern Times

The Men's Clothing Industry

Colonial Through Modern Times

HARRY A. COBRIN

Fairchild Publications, Inc., New York

Library of Congress Catalog Card Number: 77-77887

Printed in the United States of America

DEDICATED TO THE MEMORY

OF

DAVID DRECHSLER

AND

SIDNEY HILLMAN

two great men who established
the basis for industrial peace
in the industry

Acknowledgments and Thanks

During the many years as Executive Secretary of the Clothing Manufacturers Association of the U.S.A., I met with practically all of the important clothing manufacturers and labor leaders in the Industry. They recounted anecdotes, told me of the history of the Industry as they knew it, and related their own experiences as clothing men. There were literally hundreds of such instances. In addition, while writing this book, I sought and obtained information from members of the Industry who cooperated in a most friendly and helpful manner.

Many thanks to the following:

Richard H. Adler, Joseph & Feiss, Inc.; Leon Armstrong, formerly with Max Udell, Sons & Co.; Arnold Barron, Barron Anderson Co.; Harry Bender, Greater Clothing Contractors of N.Y.; Burt Beck, Amalgamated Clothing Workers of America; Sidney Bender, Greater Clothing Contractors of N.Y.; William Bennet, Market Planning Service, a division of the National Credit Office; Glen Brown, National Association of Wool Manufacturers; William Burston, National Retail Merchants Association; Mrs. H. Carlebach; Joseph and Michael Daroff, H. Daroff & Sons, Inc.; Albert Ettelson, V-Line Clothes; Barclay Ewing, Jacob Reed's Sons; Murray H. Finley, Amalgamated Clothing Workers of America; William B. Flickstein, Philadelphia Clothing Manufacturers Association; Lester Frankenstein, Michaels, Stern & Co.; Milton Fried, Amalgamated Clothing Workers of America; Sylvan Friedman, formerly with J. Friedman & Co.; Harry Frumerman, Amalgamated Clothing Workers of America; Alfred Goldsmith, Louis Goldsmith, Inc.;

Shirley Goldstein, Clothing Manufacturers Association of the U.S.A.; Isidore Grossman, Grossman Clothing Co.; Henry Harris, formerly with Cohen, Goldman & Co.; Walter Hickey, Hickey-Freeman Co.; Louis Hollander, Amalgamated Clothing Workers of America; Ira Horowitz, Amalgamated Insurance Co.; Ruth Jackendorf, Wool Bureau; Robert A. Kaplan, Clothing Manufacturers Association of the U.S.A.; Chester Kessler, Hammonton Park Clothes; Sidney Kraines, Wm. P. Goldman & Bros.; Martin Leibshitz, formerly with Dun & Bradstreet, Inc.; Betty Marr, Joseph & Feiss, Inc.; Albert Mathason, International Association of Clothing Designers; William Mendelsohn, Louis Goldsmith, Inc.; Bernard J. Miller, *Gentlemen's Quarterly;* Nat I. Pincus, P.B.M. Clothes; L. Neville Rieman, Hart, Schaffner & Marx, Inc.; Harry Riemer, formerly with *Daily News Record;* Raymond H. Reiss, Ronthor Reiss Corp.; Mrs. Victor S. Riesenfeld; David Rosenberg, formerly with Cohen, Goldman & Co.; Louis Rothschild, Men's Wear Retailers of America; Abraham Saxe, Men's and Boys' Clothing Manufacturers of New England; Louis Scalise, Howard Clothes; Nathan L. Schwartz, formerly with Julius Schwartz & Sons, Inc.; James J. Shoaff, Amalgamated Insurance Co.; Lew Spaulding, *Boys' Outfitter;* Joel Steinberg, Louis Goldsmith, Inc.; Shirley Trosk, Boys' Apparel Buyers Association; Joseph Szabo, Dun & Bradstreet, Inc.; Deena Wechter, Amalgamated Insurance Co.; Emanuel Weinstein, West Mill Clothes, Inc.; Robert White, National Credit Office.

I am particularly grateful to William Ullman of the Men's Wear Retailers of America for his helpful suggestions, based upon his life long experience as a journalist in our industry.

But, above all, I am greatly indebted to my dear wife, Ella, whose advice, judgment and editorial assistance were of immeasurable aid in preparing this book from start to finish.

HARRY A. COBRIN

Table of Contents

Chapter 1	The Industry Today	3
Chapter 2	From Tailor Shop to Factory	13
Chapter 3	Nationwide Selling Grows	27
Chapter 4	Peace and Prosperity Once More	42
Chapter 5	The Work Force, 1800–1890	60
Chapter 6	The National Association of Clothiers (NAC)	81
Chapter 7	The Two Unions	97
Chapter 8	World War I and Aftermath	113
Chapter 9	Industrial War and Peace	127
Chapter 10	Years of "Normalcy"	146
Chapter 11	Depression and Recovery	162
Chapter 12	From Chaos to Stability	185
Chapter 13	The Industry and World War II	208
Chapter 14	Military Procurement in World War II	223
Chapter 15	The Union and the Manufacturers	233
Chapter 16	The Clothing Manufacturers Association of the U.S.A. (CMA)	256
Chapter 17	The CMA and Further Industry Activities	278
Chapter 18	Merchandising and Sales Trends	299
Chapter 19	The Clothing Workers Today	319
Chapter 20	The Clothing Manufacturers Today	339
Chapter 21	The Clothing Manufacturers of Tomorrow	364

Bibliography 369
Index 372

The Men's Clothing Industry

Colonial Through Modern Times

Chapter 1

The Industry Today

A Unique Industry

"We are meeting today in the spirit of Hillman and Drechsler."

This is the invariable opening statement by spokesmen of labor and management when they first meet to negotiate a new wage agreement. Interpreted by the representatives of the union and the manufacturers, it means that they are meeting as reasonable men who will seek agreement without strife. And since 1937, when industrywide bargaining began, there has been no national strike in the men's clothing industry . . . a remarkable record of labor-management relations in this country!

In explaining this phenomenon, a homely simile quoting a prominent manufacturer, is usually cited: "It's like you are married for thirty years. You get into an argument with your wife. You have a choice, either you make peace with her, or else divorce her. Now, the two sides cannot divorce themselves from each other. So why strike, with money lost in wages and profits? After arguments by both sides, with no punches pulled, each side makes the best deal it can, and gets on with production. It's simple—live and let live, and both are living, not always quietly . . . but at least not at war." It has not always been so. There have been long and bitter strikes, but that is in the past. The industry has matured.

The unique labor-management relationship which exists in the men's and boys' clothing industry was recognized by the New York *Times* in an editorial dated October 10, 1952:

SOUND LABOR RELATIONS

The Clothing Manufacturers Association, now holding its annual convention in this city, has good cause for rejoicing. The relations between the Association and the Amalgamated Clothing Workers have been marked by such harmony and maturity of viewpoint, that no strikes have been reported in the shops of Association members for twenty years.

This long relationship is a natural concomitant of the firm understanding between spokesmen for the Union and the Association that competition in the Industry must be based on efficient operation, and not on a continuing drive for lower wages.

As a result, the sweatshop in Association plants is a thing of the past. These 950 manufacturers, employing 150,000 workers, and producing 90% of all men's and boys' clothing in the country, have as a result of union cooperation, been enabled to devote more attention to improving their product, lowering prices and at the same time increasing wages, shortening hours, and introducing important essential welfare benefits for the employees.

As no industry strike has occurred since 1952, when this editorial appeared, the clothing industry has enjoyed industrial peace for more than 30 years. This is a record probably equalled by few, if any, industries in the United States.

The manufacture of men's clothing has a long history in this country. It is an epic story, depicting the rise of the small hand tailor shops into the mammoth factories of today. There are many other aspects of the industry that are unique, and these shall be detailed in this volume.

The Industry Today

As an important branch of our American economy, the manufacture of clothing has encountered prosperity and depression over the decades, and that story too shall be told. But before we begin our detailed story, let us first define carefully the term clothing, and then evaluate the present status of the industry in American life.

Clothing Means Us . . . Not Them!

Webster's New Collegiate Dictionary defines clothing as follows: "*CLOTHING:* n. Garments in general; clothes; dress; also a covering" . . . This definition is entirely incorrect insofar as the men's clothing industry is concerned. It is correct from the standpoint of pure lexicography, and the layman will refer to clothing when he means any category of apparel worn by men, women or children. But when the noun clothing is used by the manufacturers and retailers of men's suits, topcoats, overcoats, sport coats, and separate trousers, it has a much more restricted meaning. According to trade terms, as customarily understood in the men's apparel industry, all human beings may wear apparel, but all human beings do not necessarily wear clothing.

In the men's apparel industry, garments are classified in the following categories:

Clothing: Men's suits, overcoats, topcoats, sport coats and separate trousers.

Furnishings: Shirts, ties, underwear, socks and pajamas.

Heavy Outerwear: Windbreakers, snowsuits, ski-jackets, and similar items of sportswear.

Work Clothes: Workshirts, overalls, etc. . . .

Rainwear is ordinarily included in the general heading of miscellaneous wearing apparel. The women's and children's wear industry is usually grouped under the heading of ready-to-wear trade, and then is sub-divided into the various categories according to the type of garment.

Within the clothing industry, there never has been any ambiguity as to the proper use of the noun clothing. Because the layman uses the terms apparel and clothing interchangeably, there always has been confusion, particularly when government reports and newspaper stories have mentioned clothing whereas they were actually referring to men's furnishings, women's blouses, or even ladies' girdles. This naturally has raised the hackles of the clothing firms, for it has been their claim that "they had a patent on clothing."

During World War II, when it was necessary to establish clear cut categories of various garments in accordance with regulations issued by the War Production Board (WPB) and the Office of Price Administration (OPA), a special effort was made to define clearly the categories that comprised the men's and boys' apparel industry. After careful study, the term clothing was restricted to usage in accordance with trade custom.

But the Bureau of Labor Statistics (BLS), U.S. Department of Labor, refused to conform to trade usage. A conference was arranged between representatives of the BLS and the Clothing Manufacturers Association of the U.S.A. (CMA). The Bureau officials were adamant in their stand that the nomenclature could not be changed for it would disrupt continuity of reports issued earlier and was against precedent. They quoted liberally the learned Dr. Samuel Johnson and Noah Webster as their authorities. The manufacturers countered this argument by quoting the *Daily News Record*, the industry trade paper as their authority. They minced no words in stating that neither Johnson nor Webster knew anything about the clothing business. After a lengthy discussion, the conference ended in a victory for the *Daily News Record* over Dr. Samuel Johnson and Noah Webster. On July 25th, 1947, the Association issued a victory bulletin to its members, triumphantly headed, "HEREAFTER . . . CLOTHING MEANS US . . . NOT THEM!"

Since that date, there is agreement generally that only men's and boys' suits, topcoats and overcoats, sport coats, and usually separate pants or slacks, are clothing, and nothing else. The New York *Times* continues to be a maverick, for despite industry protestations, it still maintains that Mr. Webster was right, and recognizes no later authority, to the continuing sorrow of the clothing manufacturers.

Are Slacks Clothing?

The separate pants segment of the industry considers itself as part of the industry when merchandising policies are established in retail stores. Nevertheless, these manufacturers stoutly argue that they are separate and apart from the clothing industry when they seek special consideration from government agencies, such as a lower minimum wage for learners, thus giving them an advantage over the regular clothing manufacturers who also produce separate pants. Recently though, slack manufacturers have been cuddling under the wings of the clothing industry to a greater extent than ever, for it has become good business to promote separate slacks and sport coats as a coordinated sales unit.

The reason for this favorable advantage to the separate pants segment of the industry is historic. Prior to World War II, separate dress and sport trousers were usually made of all wool fabrics in northern unionized factories. Southern manufacturers of separate trousers produced pants primarily made of light cotton materials, or else heavy cotton fabrics such as denims. The southern firms always considered themselves to be part of the cotton garment industry, a matter going back to the NIRA days, when they were subject to its Industry Code.

When World War II began, the southern pants manufacturers made large quantities of wool trousers for the military. Having acquired the ability to produce well-made wool trousers, they entered the civilian market after the war, usually manufacturing in non-union shops, where relatively low wages were paid. As a consequence, they competed very successfully with the northern firms who were manufacturing pants in union shops. Today, we find that there is a definite wage differential between the clothing firms in the North and the separate pants firms in the South. In this book, separate pants will be considered as a part of the clothing industry, unless specifically excluded.

The Industry—1969

Today, the clothing industry is an important factor in the economic and social life of our country. Its factories are located from Maine to California, and in the North as well as in the South. The industry employs approximately 120,000 workers in the so-called regular clothing plants and approximately 75,000 workers in the factories producing separate pants. In July, 1969, union employes earned $2.73 an hour in the clothing factories, and the average hourly wage for factory employes in the separate pants factories was $1.97 an hour.

In addition, employes in the unionized shops were beneficiaries of fringe benefits that amounted to nearly 30 per cent of their hourly wage, including life insurance, special industry pensions, health care for self and dependents, vacations, and paid holidays. Non-union workers usually received somewhat lower and fewer benefits.

The clothing industry of 1969 presents a far different picture to the world than its old image of a sweatshop industry, which paid low wages and operated under poor working conditions, an image only too well known in generations past. A prime reason for the improvement in wages, working conditions and welfare benefits was the fact the industry (with the exception of separate pants), was 95 per cent unionized by the Amalgamated Clothing Workers of America. The Amalgamated, led originally by Sidney Hillman, and currently by his successor, Jacob S. Potofsky, has been in the forefront of progressive labor policies which have redounded to the benefit of the clothing industry. The non-union houses necessarily had to follow suit, somewhat reluctantly perhaps, and not so generously at any time in their wage policies and fringe benefits, in order to avoid "dreaded" unionization.

The Economic and Social Importance of the Industry

In recent years, the wholesale dollar value of clothing produced annually by the industry has exceeded two billion dollars. Clearly, the clothing industry is an important factor today in the economic life of our country. In times of war, the production of uniforms for the armed forces has been the prime function and duty of the clothing factories. The record of uniform production during World Wars I and II, the Korean War, and currently the Vietnam War, as detailed in later chapters of this book, will bear out the contention that the men's clothing industry has performed vital and needed services during such times of crisis.

The industry has not merely become a significant economic force in the life of the country, but its leaders, manufacturers and labor officials, have played important roles in national affairs, as well as in their local communities. These men frequently have been called to Washington in order to serve as advisors to the White House, and we cite such men for example, as the late Meyer Kestnbaum of Hart, Schaffner & Marx, the late Sidney Hillman, and Jacob S. Potofsky. Manufacturers and also ACWA officers, have served on numerous government committees. In state and local matters, the activity of both labor and management executives has been outstanding.

It has been the proud boast of the industry that its members have been actively engaged in philanthropic and educational projects in their respective cities. They have served and are serving currently as presidents or directors of hospitals, in practically every city where they are located. Clothing manufacturers and labor representatives as well, have served as trustees on the boards of numerous universities, or else have aided in the founding of nationally prominent educational institutions. As will be told later, Tulane University in New Orleans was endowed by Paul Tulane, a New York clothing manufacturer who owned a retail store in New Orleans. Simmons

College in Boston, received a large sum of money from John Simmons, a Boston manufacturing retailer who started as a tailor. The interest and financial support given by manufacturers as well as by labor in establishing Brandeis University is well known. The Schapiro family of Boston (of the Trimount Clothing Company), has been outstanding as a liberal contributor to this university. Clothing manufacturers and Amalgamated labor leaders have become Fellows of the institution, setting up professorial chairs as well as participating in the building programs.

Certainly, the men's clothing industry has attained national status as a vital economic and social force in this country. It has become a prototype of good labor relations. The executives of labor and management have received due recognition nationally and locally as men of ability and good citizens.

Still Serious Problems to Solve

Admittedly, the industry has made enormous strides as a national institution in recent years, but this is no reason for complacency. Despite the introduction of special machines for use in specific operations, productivity in the clothing factories has not increased to an extent comparable to other American industries. The sewing machine, operated by the worker today, is merely an electric needle which revolves faster in 1969 than it did in 1900. Despite industrial progress, this electric needle still requires constant personal attention with excessive handling time. The industry has yet to experience a fundamental breakthrough in productivity. Until such a revolutionary change occurs, labor costs will represent an unduly high percentage of the total wholesale cost. As wages rise steadily, and this occurs and recurs regularly at each wage settlement, the sales price of the product is affected to a far greater extent than in other industries where labor is relatively a minor cost factor. It is therefore understandable that manufacturers of television sets, refrigerators, and washing machines—items that compete directly for the consumer dollar—can afford to pay substantially higher wages, give large wage increases over the years, and still maintain greater stability in their price structure after such wage boosts than can the clothing industry. A 10 per cent wage increase in the factory of the electronics industry may mean no more than one per cent or two per cent higher cost to the consumer, whereas a similar percentage increase in the clothing industry, where labor represents from 30–40 per cent of wholesale cost, may mean a rise of approximately five per cent or even higher (if we include retail markup) in the sales price of a suit to the consumer. There is a definite danger that the clothing industry, as we know it, is slowly, but surely, pricing itself out of the consumer market to the ultimate advantage of low-priced sportswear.

Until recently, the efforts of the manufacturers to promote fashion and style has had little apparent success. Fashion, as referred to in this book, means a fundamental change in type of garment worn (for example, from suit to sport coat and slacks). This change is influenced by social and economic conditions of the time. Style is more ephemeral, a short term trend, a change within a model, such as the two button suit replacing the three button suit in popularity.

Within the past few years, however, there have been definite signs that the American male, particularly the young man, is becoming style conscious to a far greater extent than previously. Undoubtedly, the promotional program of the American Institute of Men's and Boys' Wear has influenced the trend. In prior years, the average man, young and old, feared to be conspicuous in dress and in appearance. Currently, he seems to glory in emphasizing his individuality. Many men, even those who are middle aged, now sprout wild sideburns, and beards of varying length and design. The garments worn are often "far out" of the ordinary, and frequently these style trends, despite press hoopla, are born and die within one season. But the very fact that clothes of such extraordinary character can be worn publicly, is indicative of the times. It is the outward symptom of the general unrest that has gripped our society, particularly the young in recent years. There is an obvious urge to "break out" in appearance, in dress, or in conduct. We are clearly witnessing a virtual revolution in thought and action which is reflected in clothing as well.

Recently there has been a flurry of interest in styles promoted by foreign designers. Whether these styles, far different from the customary clothing worn by American men, will catch consumer interest, though highly publicized, is as yet uncertain. It is very likely, nevertheless, that such new models will influence American designed clothing for reasons discussed in a later chapter. The basic problem facing the industry with regard to style trends, is whether current consumer awareness of dress, greater now than in prior years, will change buying customs of retailers. This in turn will affect production schedules, so that the entire two seasonal pattern will be subject to change.

This is the industry today, in the year of 1969. The ensuing chapters will tell the story of the struggle to rise in economic strength and community status, a struggle that lasted nearly two centuries. It will recount how the tiny tailoring industry of the 18th century became an industry operating large factories which employ thousands of workers. Many of the larger companies are now publicly owned and are listed on the stock exchanges. Not only clothing manufacturers, but thousands of ordinary stockholders throughout the country now study daily the market quotations of Hart, Schaffner & Marx, Rapid American, Cluett Peabody, Botany Industries, and some dozen or more other dual distributors or conglomerates. The manufacture of clothing has entered the big business stage.

Chapter 2

From Tailor Shop to Factory

The Social and Industrial Revolution

Men's apparel, worn for dress or for special occasions, for centuries required the professional skill of an experienced tailor. Usually, there were frills and extraordinary style features on the garment that only a fully trained craftsman could achieve. The brilliantly colored coats, the velvet vests, the fancy knee breeches of the 17th and 18th centuries, worn by the nobility and by the upper middle classes aping their social superiors, were considered true works of tailoring art. The coats were lavishly embroidered, embellished with lace cuffs, and decorated with highly ornamental buttons. Garments ordinarily made of fine silks or other costly fabrics, could be produced only by highly skilled tailors. Only men with substantial incomes could possibly afford such clothes. The colors were brilliant, for the fabrics were dyed in bright shades such as plum, light blue, and bright green. Because the coat was designed to the contours of the body, the proper cut and final shape of the garment was a matter of concern to the well dressed man. Evidently the twentieth century "British lounge" model, and the current stress on "shape clothing" were no recent innovations.

The importance of elaborate dress during the 18th century might be exemplified by the anecdote told about Dr. Samuel Johnson. Johnson, normally a notoriously sloppy dresser, appeared at Drury Lane Theatre on the opening of his new play in a gay scarlet waistcoat with rich gold lace, a gold embroidered coat, and a handsome Paris wig. In explaining the reason for such attire to James Boswell, his biographer, Johnson sensibly noted that fine clothes are good as a means of producing respect. Clothes then were worn not merely for utilitarian purposes, but also for the purpose of parading wealth or social status. In modern economic terms, such clothing really represented an obvious display of conspicuous consumption, and judging from the alluring advertisements we find in print today, there has been little change in human nature since that date.

This was the period when the nobility of England and France were truly the ruling classes, and were looked upon as the fashion leaders of dress throughout the western world. Tailors in the American colonies drew style inspiration for the benefit of their customers from the specially drawn fashion plates of men's wear sent from London and Paris. The New York patroons possessing thousands of acres, the wealthy Virginia plantation owners, and prominent political leaders of the colonies who copied European modes of dress, had close social, family and business ties across the Atlantic. These classes, representing colonial wealth and power, considered themselves to be the American counterpart of European nobility. They aped Europeans not merely in dress, but as might be expected, they fully approved of the political and social concepts then fashionable overseas.

Yet, at this very time, the western world, including the American colonies, was undergoing a profound social and economic change which had incalculable influence upon every aspect of society. This was the period when the sober, hard-working middle class was gradually assuming economic and political power in Europe, as well as in the colonies. As early as the 1640's, with the success of the Puritan Revolution in England, the prestige of the middle class increased in English society. Thereafter, men in business and in the professions became the models to be followed by their social peers in conduct and dress. The merchant became the prototype throughout the western world of what well dressed men of civic repute and economic substance should wear. The sober broadcloth suits worn by the Puritans became the insignia of an active and serious minded business man. Obviously, an enterprising executive intent upon his work, could scarcely enter his place of business, be it a retail store, counting house, or professional office, arrayed with a plume in his hat, wearing a jacket made of fragile silk, sleeves edged with lace cuffs, and an ornamental sword at his side. Just as the Puritan Revolution in England propelled the middle class to the forefront of English society, so did the French Revolution at a later date cause the nobility to be replaced by the bourgeois as the dominant class in France.

In the histories describing social conditions within the American colonies, we read of constant friction in the seaport towns between wealthy merchants and commoners, for the latter were seeking to gain political concessions which would liberalize the property qualifications that restricted the voting franchise. Greater democratic control of the colonial government was desired. On the frontier, where slavery did not exist, there were numerous disputes between absentee owners of large unsettled tracts of land, and squatters who were seeking free land. It was a time of colonial unrest in the years immediately preceding the Revolution. As might be expected, because of close social and economic ties, many of the wealthy merchants in cities such as New York, Boston and Philadelphia, favored the British cause during the conflict between the mother country and the colonies. After the war, there was a substantial exodus of these wealthy Tories to Canada, to other British colonies, and to England. With the departure of the supporters of

Great Britain, the middle and working classes gained greater political and economic strength in the now independent states. At the same time, their social importance was enhanced because of their improved political status. The revolution was not merely political, but social as well, and because it was social, fashions in men's apparel were profoundly affected.

Usually, the average workman in the towns wore a heavy linen shirt, breeches of striped ticking and a coat of Duroy, which was a type of coarse woven cloth. A leather belt held up the breeches, and a leather apron protected them from wear and tear. Incidentally, according to R. Turner Wilcox in her book, "Five Centuries of American Costume," breeches were made very full without any front opening. This meant, that when signs of wear were obvious on the seat of the pants, it could be turned around completely and worn anew! Prolonging the life of the pants as a result of this style feature seemingly was discarded by later generations with no regrets by pants manufacturers.

The American Revolution naturally had a quieting effect in the matter of dress among those who formerly had followed European fashions. Foreign costume ornaments on clothes were now omitted, and articles of domestic manufacture were favored. Cloth woven in the United States was preferred, and imported fabrics were out of favor. Therefore, when Washington was inaugurated as President in 1789, he was dressed in a suit of fine dark brown broadcloth woven in Worcester, Massachusetts. This was a far cry from the elaborate silk coats of the pre-Revolutionary days worn by the wealthy Virginia planters on dress occasions.

At the very time business and professional classes grew in importance as social arbiters of proper dress in the newly independent colonies, a change in physical living conditions of the population occurred. There was a gradual growth of cities and a steady urbanization of the population. Admittedly, the pace was slow at the start, but with increasing industrialization of production, and a consequent expansion of commerce as the years went by, the population grew rapidly. The growing importance of the business class, numerically and socially, in conjunction with the development of cities, profoundly influenced trends in fashions of men's apparel. This was the opportunity to clothe the city merchant, the storekeeper, the professional man, and their assistants, suitably, and reasonably in a manner which conformed to the new ideals of good taste in dress. The underlying principle of good taste was now utility and not ornamentation, simplicity of garment and not embellishment.

The well-dressed businessman ordinarily wore a claw-hammer tailcoat of dull gray cloth and a waistcoat and breeches usually of somber colors. Despite a common myth that Beau Brummel (1778–1840) stressed excessive styling in dress, according to contemporary reports his influence was towards conservatism in clothes. Interestingly, Brummel introduced as an unusual feature in the mode of living the need for a daily bath with soap and water rather than a deluge of perfume. On the whole, bathing was something of a novelty in the 18th century. It was noted by the French, with some disapproval, that Napoleon and Josephine took daily baths —a method of cleanliness considered entirely excessive. The supposedly old American custom of the weekly Saturday bath came into use only in the late 19th century. In prior times, according to social histories of the period, bathing was not practiced with frequency.

The expansion of the cities during the inception of the Industrial Revolution, meant that many new industries were born, with large numbers employed in newly created occupations. There was an increasing demand for garments suitable for this commercial community. Such clothes had to be reasonably priced in order to meet the needs of the relatively low paid new and expanding white collar class, as well as satisfy the requirements of the higher income groups. Obviously, the tailor who had catered to the wealthy in days past, and to those who had admired and copied their modes of dress, could not readily produce garments styled for this large urban population.

Moreover, men's fashions in clothes were also changing with living conditions, and slowly were undergoing a process of evolution, with relatively minor style features added or discarded from year to year. On the basis of a short term trend, men's clothing seemed to vary slightly each year, but over a longer period, there was a noticeable change. Gradual evolution in men's clothes has continued to be the general practice up to the present, despite recent efforts to create "something new each season."

Undoubtedly, the growth of the men's ready-made clothing industry was the direct result of this urban development. As cities grew in size and number in the last decades of the 18th century, industry grew in proportion. Obviously, broadcloth suits could not be worn daily either by the farmer, the sailor, or the miner, except in church, at weddings, and finally worn at death. To this very day, the ready-made clothing industry has catered primarily to the urban segment of the population. Its core of customers historically has consisted of the middle or white collar class, the city dwellers who wore "tailored" clothing daily during business hours.

Ready-Made Clothing Feasible

With clothing becoming standardized in style, and utilitarian in purpose, methods of production and selling practices changed. Now the garments could be stocked and sold ready-made, for the extreme individuality of style formerly sought by the customer had changed into a desire for conformity. Politicians and other public figures readily saw, as suffrage broadened, the necessity of becoming "one of the people." They quickly discarded the powdered wig and other accoutrements of former attire, because it was to their obvious interest to dress in the same manner as their constituents.

The possibility of producing and selling ready-made clothing in volume, which would be acceptable to the city dweller, was now practical. Tailor shops that previously catered to customers buying elaborately styled garments were suffering a decline in sales, and these tailors were now anxious to regain their lost volume by supplying the needs of the new city dwellers. Therefore, in the eastern seaboard cities, at the end of the 18th century, when former villages had become fair sized cities, custom tailors were beginning to offer ready-made clothing. Of course, for a time they also continued their old practice of taking orders for individually cut garments, but ready-made clothing quickly became the most important item of their sales volume. This then posed the matter of proper nomenclature, for sellers of ready-made clothing could not be considered tailors.

Originally, the term "clothier" described a finisher of wool cloth, but by 1790, it had come to mean a dealer in ready-made clothing. A tailor was defined as one who actually sewed the clothes for men, and this term has retained its usage to this day. The gradual change in name designation as retail selling practices evolved, could be exemplified by following the career of one Adam Chirnside of New York City. In 1790, the New York City directory listed Adam Chirnside, located at 5 Old Slip, merely as a retailer; during the years of 1791–94 he was listed as a tailor and shopkeeper, and in 1795 he was listed as a dealer in ready-made clothes. The successive changes in listing were indicative of the growing importance of ready-made clothing and the need to be known as a seller of such clothes. The term, clothing store, spread to Boston where it made its first appearance in the public notices in 1813, and in Baltimore the first such advertisement was seen in 1819. These clothing stores all carried an inventory of ready-made garments which they had manufactured themselves. The garments were cut on the store premises and then contracted out to tailors who sewed at home. Today we would consider them to be manufacturing retailers.

To meet the needs of the sailors who required city clothes when they entered port, ready made apparel of a lower type and quality was produced. Stores catering to this sailor trade were called "slop shops," and to a degree this correctly described the quality and fit of the merchandise. As might be expected, these shops were located on the eastern seaboard cities, on the streets near the wharfs. In 1800, the slop shops of Boston were to be found on Fish Street and Ann Street (later North Street). In New York City, the slop shops were located on Water and Front Streets, and as the city grew, the stores moved to Cherry Street and Maiden Lane. In Philadelphia they were to be found on Front Street, and in Baltimore on Calvert and Water Streets. Judging from the growing number of such stores in the seaboard cities, this trade was of substantial proportions, growing steadily as our foreign trade expanded. Being enterprising merchants, the owners of the slop shops now sought to expand their sales, for a new class of customer in large numbers had now made its appearance in the cities. There was an excellent opportunity to sell to this growing white collar class who were potential buyers of higher quality garments.

Ready-Made Clothing Market Grows

Therefore, shortly after 1800, the slop shops expanded their operations offering higher priced and better made ready-to-wear clothing; they were "trading up." The population of the cities grew steadily, and the demand for ready-made properly styled garments increased among the apprentices and clerks employed in the factories, in the counting offices and in the stores. The owners of the slop shops had actual retailing experience, and were trained in methods of aggressive selling, with no holds barred. For that reason they forged ahead quickly as the leading retail clothing merchants in their respective localities.

Since Boston was now a fair sized city, ready-made clothing sold well. As an example, Thomas Whitmarsh at 3 Congress Square, previously listed as a tailor, was able to advertise in 1825 that he kept in stock from "5,000 to 10,000 fashionable ready made garments." The center of this ready-made clothing retail trade was Ann Street, and out of a total of 35 stores featuring men's clothing listed in the 1825 Boston directory, 21 such retailers were located on that particular street. But, in reality, most stores were insignificant in size, although a few were fairly large carrying substantial stock similar to those advertised by Whitmarsh. However, the majority was small, poorly lit, shacklike in appearance, with low ceilings. On the whole, they were rather dismal and unsightly. Part of the stock was hung in front of the store, comparable to displays that are found even at this date in the streets on the lower East Side of New York. Nevertheless, due to the initiative of enterprising merchants, changes in retail selling methods and display improved

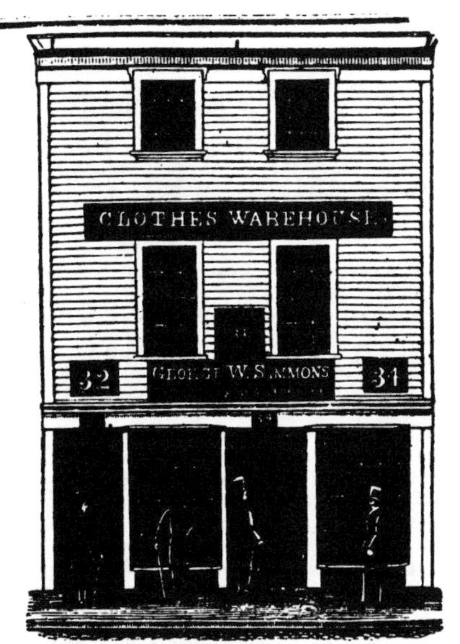

SIMMONS' WHOLESALE AND RETAIL
CHEAP AND FASHIONABLE CLOTH & CLOTHING ESTABLISHMENT.
IO. 32 & 34 ANN STREET—OPPOSITE MERCHANTS' ROW.

T IS WELL KNOWN that this is the CHEAPEST ESTABLISMENT in the city, to purchase any article in the Gentlemen's Furnishing Line, as every variety can be found, from a pair of Gloves to a superfine Dress or FROCK OAT, and at prices that cannot fail to suit the most economical.

RICH SPRING GOODS JUST RECEIVED.

Strangers visiting the city are invited to call before purchasing elsewhere, as they can find every variety of Ready lade Articles, or can have them made to order: Vests and Pants, in urgent cases, ½ days notice; Coat, one day. It is pposed by many that a genteel Coat, Pants or Vest, cannot be made in Ann street. I ask nothing to show my Goods. r to measure and make up any Garment, and if it does not suit the purchaser, and is not 20 per cent less price than

ADVERTISEMENT.
MUNROE'S
CLOTHING & FURNISHING DEPOT
ALFRED MUNROE & Co
THE
LARGEST
Retail
CLOTHING
ESTABLISHMENT
IN THE
UNITED STATES
IS AT
No. 34 MAGAZINE St.,
NEW-ORLEANS.
ALFRED MUNROE & CO., Proprietors.
The immense business done at this establishment, enables the proprietors to be continually offering to their customers A VERY CHOICE VARIETY of new and desirable styles of FASHIONABLE CLOTHING, Gent's Furnishing Goods, &c.
As it would be impossible to enumerate in an advertisement the different articles, suffice it to say, the assortment is complete in every particular, embracing ALL SIZES, for
MEN, YOUTH'S, BOYS AND CHILDREN.
New Goods received by every packet and steamship from New York.
ONE PRICE FOR GOODS——NO DEVIATION.
ALFRED MUNROE & CO.,
34 Magazine Street, corner of Gravier.
EXTENSIVE RETAIL CLOTHING STORE,
No. 441 BROADWAY, NEW YORK.
ALFRED MUNROE & CO., Proprietors.
Persons visiting New York are respectfully invited to call at the above establishment and examine our assortment and styles of FASHIONABLE CLOTHING, embracing all sizes for Men and Boys
The same principles which govern our New Orleans establishment are strictly adhered to
By ALFRED MUNROE & CO., 441 Broadway,
Between Howard and Grand Streets.

Boston Annual Advertiser.

FASHIONABLE CLOTHING.

THOMAS WHITMARSH,

No. 3, CONGRESS SQUARE,

KEEPS constantly for Sale, from 5 to 10,000 Fashionable ready made Garments, comprising every article of apparel appertaining to a Gentleman's Ward Robe. Warranted of the first quality. Adapted to every Climate and Season.

***Also*, as large an assortment of**

SUPERFINE CLOTHS,

CASSIMERES AND VESTINGS,

as can be found in any establishment of the kind in the United States, which will be made to order in a style inferior to none.

quickly, and one of the first to introduce the "new store" look was the Simmons retailing family, one member of which (John) later became the founder of Simmons College for Women in Boston.

John's brother, Cornelius, was listed in the Boston city directory of 1810 as a tailor at 15 Ann Street. By 1815 his listing changed to a slop shop owner. His younger brother, John, had joined him a year previous, and in 1818 John became the owner of his own slop shop at 14 Ann Street. In time, due to his aggressive tactics in selling ready made clothing, John Simmons became very well known and was the most prominent clothing retailer of his time. At his death, he left an estate amounting to nearly two million dollars, which he gave as an endowment to found Simmons College. The members of the clothing industry have continued the practice of John Simmons by endowing and contributing liberally to institutions of higher learning to this very day.

George W. Simmons, son of Cornelius Simmons and a nephew of John Simmons, was born in 1814 in a room above his father's Ann Street store. George W. Simmons was the first retail clothier who made extensive use of newspaper advertising. When he enlarged his store in 1842, he modernized the front, stressing window display rather than continuing the old practice of hanging suits on the outside to attract trade. The remodeled store was now called, somewhat grandiloquently, "Oak Hall," because the woodwork resembled oak. This became the mark of a "high class" store for years to come in men's wear retailing throughout the country. Thus, when John Wanamaker first opened his clothing store in Philadelphia in 1861, it was called Oak Hall too, rather than the actual firm name of Wanamaker & Brown. Simmons used every advertising gimmick then known to man. He threw free overcoats from his rooftop to attract customers, floated toy balloons announcing store sales, and established a mail order department as well. In addition, he also sold at wholesale to retailers throughout the country. As a result of this multiplicity of efforts, his volume zoomed to $500,000 a year, and he was considered to be the leading men's wear retailer of his day.

Another innovator in the retail field, was Colonel Joseph Bennet of Philadelphia. After initially establishing a regular tailoring shop in 1844, he quickly turned to selling ready-made clothes. Extreme and highly imaginative promotion schemes, plus gaudy advertising signs, seemed to pay off even in staid Philadelphia. By 1854, Bennet also built a "Hall" (most likely following the example of Simmons). This Tower Hall, so called because of its height of five stories, accomplished its prime purpose of attracting consumer attention. Bennet advertised widely in every possible media. He also sold wholesale to the stores in other cities, once again following Simmon's example. Incidentally, it was recorded that John Wanamaker started as a boy in Bennet's store in the 1850's, and received his early training there. Because of their outstanding success, Simmons and Bennet established the criteria to be followed throughout the country by later retailers who favored aggressive promotion methods plus lavish advertising in order to sell merchandise. They were the precursors of the "hard sell" in the clothing industry.

A retailer who made his mark in Philadelphia was Jacob Reed, who founded one of the great stores of his city. Reed was apprenticed in 1813 at the age of ten to a tailor. When twenty-one, he obtained his freedom and opened a small shop soon moving to a larger store on Second Street in 1825. Manufacturing ready-made clothing, he sold at retail and wholesale. The store prospered and expanded steadily over the years. In the latter part of the 19th century, it was acknowledged nationally as one of the leading men's clothing establishments of the country. The Reed policy was contrary to the hoopla of Bennet, and was more in keeping with the traditions of Quaker Philadelphia. In truth though, there was a hard core of aggressive salesmanship, stressing quality and service within this seemingly "soft sell" policy. To this very day, the Reed practice of subdued but persistent promotion has been maintained with notable success. Recently, Jacob Reed's Sons has become part of the Hart, Schaffner & Marx chain of clothing stores.

Brooks Bros., which has become synonymous with Madison Avenue, was founded by Henry Sands Brooks, who opened his clothing store in 1818 at the corner of Cherry and Catherine Streets, New York City's retail apparel center. At the time the store opened, it was noted that, "the street dress of gentlemen in 1818 consisted of a blue coat with gilt buttons, white or buff waistcoat with gold buttons, knee breeches of buckskin, buckles and topboots." Spencers, or cloth jackets in cold weather often were worn over the coats, and outerwear "boxcoats," that is "a great-coat with one to seven or more capes buttoned on" were the style. Naturally Brooks featured this apparel in their advertisements. The store grew successfully under the name of H. & D. H. Brooks, until 1855, when it was renamed Brooks Bros. The location of the store changed as the city grew, and better retail shops moved uptown. In 1858, Brooks Bros. opened "magnificent quarters" at Broadway, corner of Grand Street. In their printed store history, Brooks has proudly recalled that one of their customers "undoubtedly the most illustrious was Abraham Lincoln, for whom we made, among other things, an overcoat on the occasion of his second inaugural. The quilted lining of this was embellished (after the fashion of those days) with an embroidered design of an eagle holding in its beak a pennant inscribed, 'One Country, One Destiny.'" Since that time, there has been no doubt that Brooks Bros. has taken a far more conservative means of embellishing its garments. In 1869 Brooks Bros. moved to 14th Street and Union Square; in 1884 to Broadway at the corner of 22nd St.; then to their present location at Madison Avenue and 44th Street in 1915. The steady trend of relocating by the prestige stores from the lower downtown areas to upper Fifth and Madison Avenues was faithfully followed. Currently, Brooks Bros. operates one of the most prestigious men's retail shops in the city, and the Brooks model in men's suits is nationally famous.

By 1840, the first steps in establishing the clothing industry, as we know it today, already had been taken. Manufacturers were expanding production steadily. Ready made garments were accepted by the consumer. Stylish clothing was offered in the attractive retail stores that were opening in many cities. With the country rapidly expanding in area and in population, the manufacture of clothing was on the threshold of fantastic growth. New firms were entering the industry, and the channels of distribution were steadily extending to all of the rapidly settled areas of the country.

The Industry Expands

In addition, government fiscal policy proved to be most helpful to the budding manufacturers. Prior to 1816, the duty for imported clothing was 25 per cent, but the tariff of that year raised the rate to 30 per cent, and in 1828 the rate was further increased to 50 per cent. There was an added duty if the garments came in foreign vessels rather than in American ships. Protected by the government, the industry expanded as the country grew during the decade of 1825–1835. This 50 per cent duty for imported clothing was maintained with slight fluctuations occurring from time to time until the Civil War. By 1860 though, the tariff protective wall was no longer necessary. Because of the growing use of the sewing machine and the consequent rise in productivity of the operators, the former infant industry could well hold its own with foreign competition.

The concurrent development of American worsted and woolen mills directly benefited the domestic clothing firms. Now the clothing manufacturers were able to obtain adequate and satisfactory wool cloth promptly. There was no need to import piece goods which required early buying with deliveries uncertain at best.

As the country grew, the trade in the West and South became important. Interstate commerce began to flourish, although railroads were still in their infancy. Shipments of clothing by sea to the southern states, and through canals such as the Erie to the Great Lakes regions; opened up new and expanding markets. By 1835, New York City had already acquired the reputation of being the nation's leading center for ready-made clothing. In that year, some manufacturers were reported to employ from three hundred to five hundred workers with factory production expanding on a progressively greater scale. Thus, Lewis & Hanford, one of the larger clothing concerns, announced that their cutters had cut 100,580 garments during the winter months of 1848–49, and that their daily production averaged 1,135 garments from November 1, 1848 to July 14, 1849. It should be recalled that such cutting was carried on by means of hand shears and that relatively crude cutting procedures were used. Sizing of garments though, was still haphazard, for there was no recognized industry standard. Admittedly, there was an extensive literature on the subject of proper sizes, but each book or pamphlet recommended a different table of body measurements. Not until the Civil War were standardized body measurements established. Until then, hit or miss sizing bedevilled the industry.

By 1858, the New York Chamber of Commerce was able to report proudly that the New York market produced $40,000,000 worth of clothing at wholesale and that the city was maintaining its position as the largest clothing market in the United States. Nevertheless, Boston, Philadelphia, Newark and Baltimore were also important producers, and in the 1850's, Cincinnati and St. Louis became fairly large manufacturing centers of clothing as well. As the country expanded westward, the cities where clothing was manufactured grew in number, and the industry was in the process of becoming truly national in scope.

Chapter 3

Nationwide Selling Grows

Selling the Retailer

Prior to each season, the clothing manufacturer prepared his line of samples in accordance with industry practice. As new fashions evolved gradually, the "redingote" or riding coat of the English gentry gradually developed into the frock coat or cutaway of the 19th century. In the 1840's, according to R. Turner Wilcox, the silhouette of the man's coat became almost feminine, "with trousers very tight, worn with an elaborate embroidered waistcoat." As men began to wear the frock coat, following Prince Albert's example, black was the favored color. In time, the frock coat became the regular daily raiment for men of substance and was in fact a symbol of social status. Up to the end of the 19th century, it was remarked that many clothing cutters in New York City went to work wearing the frock or cutaway coat, thus publicly stressing their relatively high social standing among clothing workers. Even to the present day, cutters are still considered the "aristocrats" among clothing factory workers, largely due to their limitation in number, special skill and higher wage scale.

Gradually the cut of the coat changed. The silhouette model lost favor. In the 1850's, the short sack coat, without any waist suppression at all made its appearance. Originally it was considered merely as a coat for lounging, rather than to be worn for social or business wear. In time, though, it received consumer acceptance and evolved in the suit jacket we know today. By 1860, the average man might be attired in a "one button sack coat of brown cloth worn with gray cloth trousers, a turned down collar shirt, black silk cravat, and a red velvet waistcoat." He would then be considered a well dressed man belonging to the white collar class. Looking ahead though, the *Mirror of Fashion,* a monthly magazine of the time, noted "that it is now regarded as being in good taste to wear a vest and pantaloons of the same material."

The practice of placing orders through a traveling salesman was almost unknown before 1840, and not fully utilized until the years immediately prior to the Civil War. Since railroads were unimportant as a means of transportation, merchandise was ordinarily shipped by the natural water routes, or if available, by canal, for the roads were poor even in good weather, and frequently impassable during the winter. When retailers undertook to come to the market, they usually figured that four weeks would be devoted for traveling (two weeks each way), and two weeks would be spent actually buying in the market. A few large retailers, situated in distant states, had a resident partner in the East, usually located in New York City, for the prime purpose of purchasing merchandise.

The manufacturers made every effort to induce the stores to visit the market. They mailed cajoling flyers to their accounts. They advertised steadily in the New York papers that circulated out of the city, promising bargains, prompt deliveries, good prices, and the latest models. Moreover, in order to cover fully every means of reaching a reluctant retailer, they even inserted advertisements in the newspapers where their accounts were located, telling the trade of the immense bargains awaiting them when they came to the market. In 1851, F. J. Conant, a prominent New York manufacturer, announced in an advertisement placed in a Savannah newspaper, that "a visit to his place of business at 138 Pearl Street would find a more extensive assortment than formerly, and where the style, make, and materials of the cloaks will be greatly improved and will be sold at about the same low prices as those of last season." Another manufacturer proudly disclosed to his southern accounts his own special system of production for "there are three skillful artists employed in this establishment . . . one to cut coats, one to cut pants, and one to cut waistcoats. Each department is complete in itself." Every advertisement stressed (as might be expected) that the products of that manufacturer were the finest in quality, lowest in price, and styled to suit the fastidious taste of the American male.

Manufacturers began preparing for seasonal visits of the retailers by starting production some four months prior to the buying period, for retailers purchased only from the ready-made inventory available for immediate shipment. The buyers would not place orders from samples for later delivery. Hence, it was economically vital for the manufacturer to sell quickly during this intensive buying period as large a proportion of his ready-made stock as possible. There was always the danger that unsold garments would have to be disposed of at auction, with possible loss. In modern terms, the manufacturer was under pressure to "push hard" when a visiting customer entered his salesroom, or else face the possibility of a forced closeout of his unsold merchandise.

Under the circumstances, when the retailer finally arrived in town, a flock of manufacturers' representatives or agents who were planted in all popular hotels greeted him effusively. The buyer who registered was immediately spotted by the manufacturer's agent, called the "drummer," for he drummed up retailer trade for his employer. If it was at all possible, a smart drummer first checked the credit standing of his prospective customer. Once the financial status of the buyer seemed satisfactory, the drummer used all means to induce the out of town retailer to visit his company's salesroom.

While the drummer's methods of entertaining the customer are not fully described in the literature of the day, in all probability it was not far different from current practices, such as purchase of theater tickets, visits to some "hot spots" perhaps, and invitations to lavish dinners. The rate of commission for drummers usually was two and one-half per cent, so they were also known as the "two and one-half per cent salesmen." If entertainment expenses were paid by the employer, it was likely that the men earned very good salaries.

Credits extended to retailers as to time and method of payment were extremely liberal. The credit system was based upon a merchandising cycle that took at least ten months to complete if and when bills were paid promptly. Retailers received terms of six months, giving a note payable at their local bank. Unfortunately, there was a good chance that the bank itself might become insolvent within that period, because of the "wildcat" banking system prevailing in many of the states at that time. It was therefore understandable that F. J. Conant, the prominent clothing manufacturer, informed his trade that his terms were "six months for approved notes payable at banks in good standing in any part of the country, eight months for city acceptances, or 5 per cent discount for cash." Then, continued Mr. Conant, perhaps hopefully, "the retailer was to be charged 6 per cent per annum" if payments are slow. The crux of all credit terms though, was the financial standing of the bank which had to be checked as well as the financial condition of the buyer.

In turn, the retailer was expected by his own customers to extend credit to them. The stores in rural and semi-rural areas sold their merchandise to farmers or those dependent upon the agricultural interest. Even the prosperity of the dwellers in the larger urban centers was dependent upon demand that ultimately came from the farming areas. The United States was still primarily an agricultural country. So the clothing manufacturer of that day had to watch the credit standing of the retailer who bought the merchandise, of the retailer's bank where the note was to be paid, and the overall condition of the predominant crops grown in the region of his retail account. The life of a credit man had never been an easy one, but it was a particularly difficult task prior to the Civil War.

When the crash of 1837 occurred, with banks failing daily, and numerous retail bankruptcies taking place, manufacturers suffered huge losses. But the United States was growing so rapidly, that these financial crises retarded growth merely for a short period. The country recovered quickly and surged ahead to reach another peak of prosperity in 1857, when, once more, a financial crisis struck the economy.

After experiencing the panic of 1837, the manufacturers had organized a Merchants' Vigilance Association for the purpose of obtaining adequate credit information about their customers throughout the United States. In 1841, Louis Tappan organized the first regular credit agency, calling it the Mercantile Agency. Robert G. Dun became the sole proprietor of the Agency in 1859, and it was known thereafter as the R. G. Dun and Company with credit information systematized and reliable on a nationwide basis. In recent years, due to a merger, the name has been changed to Dun and Bradstreet.

The Expansion of Trade

Despite recurrent crises and substantial credit losses, manufacturers in the different clothing markets expanded their operations throughout the period. It was a time of rapid growth for the United States. In Boston, for example, the firm of Carney and Sleeper prospered so that in 1846, the firm had a net worth estimated at approximately $400,000. The Leopold Morse Company, still well known to this day, began operations at that time by supplying the crews of clipper ships trading in the Far East, but soon turned to selling clothing to the regular Boston trade. As the outstanding manufacturer and retailer of the city, the Simmons family was most active in producing and selling clothing.

In Philadelphia, Colonel Bennet continued as the leading retailer and manufacturer of the day. The firm of F. A. Hoyt and Brother of the city, was well known throughout the country, particularly as a specialist in boys' clothing. On the whole, although Philadelphia did not exceed New York insofar as total market volume or sales to the South was concerned, still it progressed rapidly as a clothing center, catering primarily to the southern trade.

As transportation improved, clothing factories were established in cities far from the seaboard. Now piece goods for manufacture were available from the eastern cities, and shipments of garments could be made to retailers in far distant places. The Erie Canal and the Great Lakes proved to be excellent means of reaching the now growing Midwest. And Rochester, New York was especially well situated for such distribution. It was therefore understandable that in 1824 Meyer Greentree, a recent immigrant from Germany to Rochester, took advantage of the city's location, and began to cut from regular patterns, selling his suits at wholesale. In 1848, Henry Michaels organized his clothing factory in Rochester, and later formed Michaels, Stern & Company, which has continued to this day as a large and flourishing concern. At the time when Michaels first organized his firm, there were already 30 shops in the city making clothing. Blake McKelvey, the historian of Rochester, noted that then "the establishments consisted of a salesroom in front, an adjoining cutting room, and a space above or in the rear for storage. Most of the sewing and trimming was entrusted to workers who finished the garments at home." According to the U.S. Census of 1860, Rochester employed 810 men and 745 women, and the dollar volume for this clothing market was estimated at approximately $500,000 a year, with 42 shops listed as manufacturers.

Going South

The southern trade was the most important interstate sales outlet of clothing for the New York manufacturers, and to a lesser extent, those firms located in Philadelphia, Newark and Baltimore. The Midwest, until the 1840's, was still in the very early stages of settlement, for only country villages and small cities were to be found west of the Appalachians. The Pacific Coast and the adjoining region were beyond the reach of the East, because California and the Southwest were part of Mexico until 1846, and in the Northwest, the international border was still a matter of dispute with Great Britain. Therefore, prior to 1860, garments for the slave trade, better clothing for planters, as well as growing demand for ready-made clothing by the city dwellers in the South, represented 50 per cent or more of total interstate shipments of clothing sent out of New York. Even after the California and the western trade had assumed fair sized proportions during the 1850 decade, the southern trade continued to be of paramount importance to the New York firms.

As already noted, until the country was reasonably developed, serious obstacles were suffered by manufacturers shipping from New York, as well as from other clothing centers. Water transportation was the only feasible means of shipping to the southern cities. This meant that the seaboard towns, such as Charleston, Savannah, Mobile and New Orleans were the receiving centers of garments arriving by packets from the North. The New York manufacturers had a definite advantage as compared with other seaboard clothing markets for they were able to send their merchandise by packets that sailed more frequently and were on a regular schedule to a greater extent than boats going South from the other northern ports. This advantage enabled the New York manufacturer to deliver more promptly and quickly than his competitors shipping from other ports when the need arose.

Once the garments reached a southern city, they might be delivered to a southern retail account directly, who had purchased from the New York manufacturer while on a northern buying trip. Often, though, the garments were sent on consignment to a local auctioneer who offered the merchandise at an advertised auction sale, with retailers of that city and surrounding towns as potential bidders. Retail clothing business flourished in the southern towns, for in 1828 Charleston listed nine specialty clothing stores, and New Orleans boasted of 56 stores specializing in the sale of men's apparel. Retailers who bought directly from manufacturers often supplemented their regular purchases by attending auctions where prices might perhaps be a little less, special lots might be offered, or else they found it necessary to fill in sizes and colors. Reorders were extremely difficult to obtain from the distant northern cities.

Garments made in New York City received wide acceptance in the South. A retail advertisement in a New Orleans paper in 1843 read, "I shall constantly be receiving by every packet from New York, large additions to my present stock, and of the most choice and fashionable styles that the New York market can produce." Another New Orleans retailer announced in 1847 that he was "constantly receiving fine fashionable clothing by every packet from New York." Judging from the advertisements, the very fact that the garments were manufactured in New York had considerable consumer appeal.

The potential possibilities of substantial retail sales were obvious, and the northern clothing houses were determined to garner their full share of both wholesale and retail business. The New York manufacturers were not slow in recognizing that it was more profitable to open their own retail stores in southern cities rather than sell to the independent stores. This gave them a direct and permanent outlet in each area. In addition, such a store served as a salesroom for selling retail accounts in the surrounding territory. Again, the expenses and risk incurred in offering goods by means of auction sales were avoided. The possibilities of making a profit at retail as well as at wholesale were undoubtedly considered by the enterprising manufacturers as well.

By 1830, many New York firms had already established retail outlets in New Orleans, and also in other cities. The clothing manufacturer produced the garments in his New York factory and then shipped them to his southern retail store. New Orleans, as the largest commercial and shipping center of the South, received most attention from the New York manufacturers. Usually, one partner had charge of the New York plant, and another managed the retail store and its related activities, such as selling merchandise in the nearby towns. For example, the firm of Alfred Munroe & Company had their New York plant located at 441 Broadway, and their retail store was situated at 34 Magazine Street in New Orleans. In 1848, Munroe and Company announced that they carried a stock of clothing worth $90,000 in their store, and that they could "fit persons of all sizes, from a man measuring 48 inches to a child." In addition to ready-made garments, a special order service, later known in the industry as made-to-measure, was usually established. Retailers offered to make garments according to measurement of the customer taken in New Orleans, which would then be sent to New York for tailoring.

Another large retail store in New Orleans was owned by the prominent New York clothing firm of Lewis and Hanford (later known as Hanford and Brother). By 1848, this firm, situated in Pearl Street, New York, attained the reputation of being one of the very large distributors in the South. It was reported that they employed nearly 5,000 workers at that time. The company owned several stores in New York and also conducted a large wholesale business. Later, in 1858, John H. Browning formed a partnership with John E. Hanford who had been a member of Lewis & Hanford. The partnership of Hanford and Browning prospered and became a large producer of garments selling to the South and West. This partnership was the predecessor of Browning, King & Company.

However, the outstanding prototype of success in the commercial tie-up of a New York manufacturer with a retail store in New Orleans, was George Opdyke. He was born December 7, 1805 in Hunterdon, New Jersey. After some experience clerking in a retail store, he went to Cleveland in the early 1820's and opened a clothing store there with a partner. The firm was known as Hall and Opdyke. In the opinion of Opdyke there was little prospect of expansion in Cleveland at that time. Thereupon, he and his partner went to New Orleans where they found that clothing was selling at 100 per cent profit. They saw their opportunity and made the most of it. Hall went to New York and opened a clothing factory while Opdyke had charge of the New Orleans store. The firm made $6,000 profit the first year, and progressively higher profits as the business grew. Opdyke made a fortune in this enterprise, and he later retired to become a merchant, an importer, and a banker in

New York. During the Civil War, he was the Mayor of New York City, and highly regarded as an outstanding citizen and an able public official.

Paul Tulane, a native of New Jersey, might be cited as another example of success in this mode of operating a clothing business at that time, namely, a factory in the North, and retail outlets in the South. In 1820, he opened his clothing store in New Orleans. By 1828, he was so successful that he had accumulated $150,000, owning a factory in New York and a large store in New Orleans. In 1882, some five years before he died, Tulane gave two million dollars towards the endowment of an educational institution in New Orleans where he had made his fortune. In appreciation of this large gift, the new institution was named Tulane University.

At this time, Newark, New Jersey was another important manufacturing center of clothing, catering to the southern trade. By 1835, it was reported that 25 clothing factories there were engaged in making garments for the South. They employed 1,591 men, with a total annual output at wholesale of $840,000. The average plant in Newark then employed some 60 workers, and the average dollar volume per firm was $34,000. By 1860, Newark had expanded its production so that the 42 firms there now employed 4,604 workers, and produced clothing annually valued at $2,628,350, or approximately $63,000 per firm. The dollar volume of the market had tripled and the size of the average firm had expanded considerably over the 25 year period.

The northern clothing markets were dominant in the South because of an absence of southern clothing factories. As a general rule, tailoring in the South was considered to be an occupation fit solely for negroes, and was therefore not regarded as a craft suitable for non-slaves. Some few firms actually were started in the South using slave labor in cities such as New Orleans, but these manufacturers did not prosper. Apparently this slave labor, not highly skilled, was not productive to an extent wherein it could compete with the North, even though the negroes received no wages, but only food and shelter. By 1860, the entire South produced less than $3,000,000 in clothing volume, approximately equal to the production of Newark, New Jersey.

Garments were produced in the North for the slave trade as well as for the planter and city trade. Some manufacturers specialized in sewing "negro clothing" which were made of a cheap coarse fabric. Due to productivity and skill, the northern factories, though operating in the low priced clothing field, had no difficulty selling their "negro clothing" to the South where stores regularly advertised such garments for sale. For example, we find in 1826, a Macon, Georgia clothing retailer announcing in the local press the receipt of a "large assortment of negro clothing recently received from the North."

With the outbreak of the Civil War, the entire southern trade collapsed. This was preceded by the panic of 1857, which had already weakened the economic structure of the clothing manufacturers. At that time, they had lost large sums because of retail bankruptcies in the West as well as in the South. With the outbreak of hostilities in 1861, all means of communication were cut off. The New York *Herald* reported that "the falling off in the clothing trade with the South amounts to a complete panic." Retailers in the South immediately cancelled outstanding orders. Southern stores owned by northern firms liquidated their inventories quickly at a great loss. Debts from southern accounts were uncollectable. Many northern manufacturers were wiped out. Others faced possible bankruptcy. The entire clothing industry was in dire financial straits. However, the need for uniforms, which were immediately required in large quantities, meant substantial orders for the panicky industry. Factories reopened once more, and sufficient orders for procurement were received, enabling the manufacturers to survive the crisis and even prosper during the war years.

Going West

With the construction of canals widespread, and the gradual extension of railroads to the West in the 1850's, the clothing industry began to sell and ship goods to the Midwest which was growing rapidly, for villages were becoming cities. New industries were opening factories there. In instances where manufacturers did not open their own stores, the larger retailers in the new cities not merely sold the local trade, but acted as jobbers, selling merchandise to the country stores within their immediate vicinity. With transportation facilities gradually expanded, St. Louis in the 1820's became an important distribution center servicing Missouri and the surrounding states which were being settled rapidly. By the late 1850's, Chicago, which had a population of only 200 in 1833, had become a good sized metropolis, giving evidence that it would soon become a distribution center of great importance. The jobbing trade now grew rapidly, reaching all parts of the Mississippi valley, the Great Lakes region, and eventually the far West. The clothing market that made the most intensive and successful effort to sell these Midwest accounts was Boston, while New York, Philadelphia and Baltimore directed their energies primarily to the South.

Now that northern Ohio was rapidly settled, by 1845 Cleveland was a small prosperous community. Its prospects for the future were far brighter than in the days when George Opdyke left the city for a more profitable site in New Orleans. Recognizing the advantage of its excellent location on the Great Lakes, two dry goods merchants from Meadville, Pennsylvania, namely Koch and Loeb, moved to Cleveland and established themselves as clothing manufacturers. Little did they dream that they were founding the Joseph and Feiss Company, one of the leading clothing firms of the country. After several years, the partnership was dissolved and Koch continued the business, producing ready-made clothing. He cut on the premises, and contracted the sewing out to tailors in accordance with industry custom of the time. The company prospered as population increased in the Midwest, and by 1860, it was becoming one of the largest producers of clothing in the area. Gradually the firm expanded, selling its garments throughout other states. Over the years, there were changes in the partnership and in the corporate name of the organization, with the present name of the Joseph & Feiss Company adopted early in the 20th century. It was the presence of this firm in Cleveland that was the prime cause of establishing that city as one of the important clothing manufacturing centers in the country.

In the 1920's, when the company suffered a decline in volume, a Cincinnati jobber, Felix S. Mayer,. a most dynamic individual, joined the company. He soon became president, reorganized the firm, and established it once more as a prosperous organization. Upon his death in July 1961, he left a well integrated, highly efficient clothing firm. Because Mayer took an old firm and resuscitated the company to its prosperous status, he was frequently called in admiration, Doctor Voronoff, after a physician who reputedly made the elderly youthful again.

Cincinnati, advantageously situated on the Ohio, with excellent water transportation facilities to the nearby states, became a center for clothing manufacturers in the 1830's. In 1850, the firm of Kuhn, Rindskoff & Co. was founded, and out of this company came the founders of the famous New York banking house of Kuhn, Loeb & Co. Cincinnati as a clothing market, expanded to meet the demand of the newly settled states. In 1850, it was estimated that this market produced approximately $4,500,000. A decade later, the clothing dollar volume at wholesale prices had risen by 50 per cent, and 48 wholesale firms were now listed as clothing manufacturers. Cincinnati clothing firms found themselves deeply involved in the effects of the Civil War, for the nearby states were centers of conflict and sales declined in catastrophic proportions. But, as the requirements for uniforms rose, the manufacturers in Cincinnati, as in other clothing markets, managed to survive until peace came in 1865.

An interesting example of the evolution and growth of a clothing factory in the Midwest was the history of J. Capps & Sons, Ltd. of Jacksonville, Illinois. The founder of the company settled there in 1839, coming from Kentucky. With previous training in carding wool, he established a wool carding business. By 1852, Capps had acquired equipment and looms, and began weaving cloth and blankets which were sold to retail stores. There were potential possibilities seen in the sale of trousers to the surrounding retailers. Alert to this opportunity, in 1885 the sons of Capps then began making trousers from the cloth woven in their mills. Their garment business was excellent, so in 1904 they discontinued the sale of wool cloth to retailers, needing all of the fabric for their own use. In June, 1930, the woolen mill discontinued operations and the firm became solely a manufacturer of men's clothing. The firm of J. Capps & Sons Ltd. is highly esteemed for its product, to this day. There are retail accounts on its books that originally bought the wool blankets from the company 100 years ago, and are now buying its regular clothing.

An amusing incident experienced by his company was related by the late Robert Capps. At the time they were weaving wool blankets, they found an extraordinary demand for a special intricate design coming from the Southwest trade. This intrigued them. So they sent a representative there to discover the cause for the great increase in blanket sales, hopeful that they had discovered a new source of business. Their man reported that the Indians in the area were buying the blankets in quantity, and reselling them to the tourists as the genuine hand woven article. "But," continued Capps, "there was one inevitable surprise awaiting these tourists. On each blanket sold by the Indians was a small label, securely sewn on, which noted that it had been woven by J. Capps & Sons, Ltd., of Jacksonville, Illinois."

Another new area for trade expansion was the Pacific Coast. California was annexed in 1846, and with the discovery of gold in 1848, there was a rush of thousands of men seeking overnight fortunes. These fortune hunters needed clothing for traveling, and when they finally arrived on the Coast, they had need of ready-made garments because tailors were scarce. Who would sew suits when he had an opportunity to mine gold? With the price of suits ranging up to $200 in the highly inflated days of the gold rush, retail merchants began ordering from the East in large quantities. New York, Boston and Philadelphia—the important clothing markets located on the seaboard—were able to send garments via the Panama Isthmus, or else ship the clothing around Cape Horn. Following the example set in other sections of the country, the retail stores tended to become jobbers as well as retailers. Eastern manufacturers opened retail outlets on the Coast as well, duplicating their previous practice of distribution they had found so successful in the South.

One enterprising young man however realized that riches could be "mined" by producing clothing in California rather than digging for gold. In 1850, Levi Strauss arrived in San Francisco. By 1853, he organized Levi Strauss & Company, and began to manufacture pants and overalls for miners. His success was immediate, and "Levis" became the national name for his cut of pants. When the Civil War began, there was serious disruption in shipping, for Confederate warships intercepted and captured many of the cargoes that were sent by water to the Pacific Coast. Western trade slumped throughout the years of conflict, and revived only with end of the war.

The years of war between the States created economic chaos insofar as national distribution of clothing was concerned. The South was entirely cut off from its northern sources of supply. Until the latter years of the war, the Confederates controlled large sections of the Mississippi River, which interrupted shipments between the East and the far West. Shipments to the Pacific Coast, as noted, were subject to seizure by the southern warships. Trade was therefore concentrated north of the Ohio River and east of the Mississippi during the conflict. However, this was merely a temporary situation which was reversed once peace came, with free trade possible once more between the States. In 1865, with the war over, the clothing industry looked forward to further expansion in all sections of the country.

Chapter 4

Peace and Prosperity Once More

The Sewing Machine

The invention of the sewing machine revolutionized the system of production in the manufacture of clothing. It created the possibility of establishing regular clothing factories. This, in turn, created the need for adequate financial resources to purchase factory equipment. And, most important, it reduced the need for hand sewing of many operations, thus permitting the employment of semi-skilled sewing operators. Admittedly, the full impact of the sewing machine upon the manufacturing process was not immediate. It took several decades before the introduction of mechanical sewing made itself fully felt in all phases of production and upon the labor force.

While the sewing machine did not receive industry acceptance until the late 1850's, efforts had been made even as early as the

18th century to produce a mechanical device that would supplant hand sewing of garments. In 1790, the first known patent for a sewing machine was issued in England, but it had never been put to practical use. Other patents were issued in the United States and in Austria for machines that stitched garments, but these also were found to be impractical.

The possibility of throwing hand tailors out of work, if and when a sewing machine was ever to be invented, was carefully considered by many. For example, the first American machine to be constructed and entirely practical, was that of the Reverend John Adams Dodge of Vermont, who built the machine in 1818, in order to "lighten the labor of women." But, after he had shown his invention to some journeymen tailors, Dodge explained, "they all seemed to be offended that an attempt should be made to throw them out of work," and so this machine was never patented. The possibility of technological unemployment arose in a more violent form in France. Barthelemy Thimmonier, a Frenchman, secured his patent in 1830 and was the first to produce sewing machines in commercial quantities which were then put to use. By 1841, Thimmonier had 80 machines at work making uniforms for the French Army. Then the hand tailors, in anger, destroyed the mechanical enemy. Not to be daunted, in 1848 he produced additional machines, but they were again destroyed by a mob of workers. Finally, in despair, he escaped from France with a machine model, went to England, patented his invention there in 1849, and obtained a U.S. patent in 1850. By that time though, he was too late to benefit, for more practical machines were already in the field.

In the United States, there were repeated attempts to produce a practical sewing machine for commercial use, but seemingly none was accepted by the garment industry. Then, Elias Howe, Jr. invented his sewing machine, which was registered in the U.S. Patent Office on September 10, 1846. As the story is told, in 1839 Howe, then age 20, while working in a machine shop, listened to an argument wherein a visitor said to his employer, "Why don't you make a sewing machine. I'll insure you an independent fortune." Howe remembered this conversation, and four years later attempted to construct a practical sewing machine. After numerous experiments, in 1845 he built a machine that sewed two suits made of wool cloth. He had proved, by example, that productivity was immensely increased when a tailor sewed the garment on his machine rather than by hand. Still, the Howe machine found no market in the United States. Tailors and seamstresses spurned his invention as impractical. Meanwhile, other inventors interested in creating a practical sewing machine, produced improved models which gradually received acceptance in the garment industries. However, these newer machines had infringed on Howe's patent. The first machine in the needle trades that became really popular was constructed by Isaac Merrit Singer in 1850. Howe then sued Singer for patent infringement and received royalties as a result. After a series of legal battles ensuing between the various patentees, called the "Sewing Machine War," the squabbles of the various inventors were resolved through the organization of the Singer Machine Combination, one of America's first patent pools, which included Howe and Singer. The Combination continued in existence until 1877 when the last of the patents included in the Combination expired.

There was a natural fear that the sewing machine would eliminate the jobs of thousands of men and women. Initially, there was no doubt that, according to contemporary observers, the sewing machine did actually throw many out of work, and did reduce wages. The census of 1860 reported that "the recent introduction of the sewing machine had reduced the number of sewing women, and their sudden displacement in some places may have been injuriously felt." As women learned how to operate these new machines, their productivity increased due to a refined division of labor by breaking down the sewing operations. In time, this temporary chaotic condition in the labor market adjusted itself to the use of the new sewing machine.

The original machines were cumbersome and difficult to operate, and in the first stages of learning, sewed garments at a very slow rate, which caused complaints from operators. They were also expensive, for in the early 1850's, they sold for $100 up to $150 per unit, representing a substantial capital investment. Despite price, and natural prejudice against the new sewing mechanism, the machines grew in popularity. By the end of the 1850's, the sewing machine had received general industry approval. To a great extent, this was due to the extraordinary selling techniques of Isaac M. Singer & Co. Their machines were displayed in attractive showrooms, with girls giving practical demonstrations. Machines were sold on the installment plan. Liberal discounts were given to those who turned in old models, or competitors' models. Sewing machine manufacturers opened up schools in various cities in order to teach operators how to work on the machine. During the twelve months of fall 1858 to fall 1859, more than 37,000 machines were produced. Prices dropped because of mass production, and in 1858 the new models were obtainable for as low as $50.

By 1860, a government survey reported that the popularity of the sewing machine was largely responsible for the revolution that took place in the business structure of the clothing trade, with many small shops merged into large inside shops. Capital investment for the clothing industry as a whole doubled between the years of 1850–1860, but the number of establishments decreased by 11 per cent. When a manufacturer did not have the capital to purchase sewing machines himself, he often required that his operators own their machines, and for the most part this practice spread throughout the industry.

Where factories required individual operator ownership of machines, they were usually purchased on time, or else were rented due to a lack of ready cash. This imposed an additional burden upon the workers whose wages were already low. While the sewing machine did increase production, the short term results for the operators were unfavorable. Their wages did not advance in proportion to greater productivity, and additional expenses were now incurred due to the need to own their machine. In the long run the worker benefited, for over the years wages rose, admittedly all too slowly, and the practice of exploiting the factory operator by compelling him to own his own machine gradually died out.

It was a stroke of good fortune that the sewing machine had come into industrywide use by 1860. The clothing industry was in the doldrums in 1861. The Civil War cut off all trade with the South, while serious dislocations occurred in shipments made to the West and Pacific Coast. It was at this time that the government entered the market, in need of uniforms that had to be produced quickly and necessarily of a standard make with no deviations permitted. With a practical sewing machine available, manufacturers were able to open inside shops where greater division of work was possible, and the quality of the garment could be closely supervised. It also afforded the manufacturers an opportunity to learn the worth of mass production. They now gained experience in managing a fair sized factory by producing garments on a large scale. Such experience would be invaluable for the civilian trade, if only the consumer were assured that mass produced clothing would fit properly. Then the Philadelphia Quartermaster Depot solved this problem for the industry.

It was of obvious importance for the contracting officers at the Philadelphia Quartermaster Depot to have adequate data which disclosed the proportion of sizes to be ordered in purchasing uniforms. Accordingly, Brevet Brigadier General G. H. Crosman, the commanding officer of the Depot, carefully studied the measurements of the millions of recruits entering the Army. Based upon the results of this study, a standard set of body proportions was set up, and this standard became the basis of sizing practice of civilian garments after the War.

The industry had acquired the experience necessary to produce garments in quantity. It was able to offer ready-made clothing in an adequate number of sizes that fit the average man properly. Now the clothing manufacturers were equipped technically to expand production and distribute their garments to all sections of the country.

With Peace Comes Growth

Once the war ended, our country renewed its rapid pace of growth. Railroads soon reached the Pacific Coast and extended their branch lines throughout the Midwest and far West. Mere settlements soon became villages, and shortly thereafter, large cities. The immigrant tide from Europe rose to a flood, bringing into this country millions of young and old who were anxious to make a home for themselves. Accordingly, the clothing industry expanded to meet the increasing demand for ready-made clothes as the table below indicates.

Number of Establishments, Wage Earners, Wages and Value of Product, Men's, Youths' and Boys' Clothing Including Work Clothing Except Shirts, 1849–1889

YEAR	NUMBER OF ESTABLISH-MENTS	WAGE EARNERS (AVERAGE FOR THE YEAR)	WAGES	VALUE OF PRODUCT
1849	4,278	96,551	$15,032,000	$ 48,312,000
1859	4,014	114,800	19,856,000	80,831,000
1869	7,858	108,128	30,747,000	148,660,000
1879	6,166	160,813	45,940,000	209,548,000
1889	4,867	144,926	51,076,000	251,020,000

Source: Bureau of the Census, U.S. Department of Commerce

At the convention of the National Association of Clothiers (then the national organization of manufacturers), held in February, 1915 in Baltimore, William Goldman, President of Cohen, Goldman & Co., of New York, in his day one of the most knowledgeable men in the industry, was the principal speaker. He read a paper entitled, "A History and a Prophecy of the Clothing Trade." Goldman was born in 1863 in Carbondale, Illinois. At 18 he came to New York, forming the firm of Cohen, Goldman three years later and soon became a most successful manufacturer. He was a student of economics, particularly as it affected the clothing industry, and his famous 1925 report proving that the wool market was rigged caused a sharp break in the price of raw wool. As a most articulate man who had his facts at his finger tips, Goldman was considered to be the elder statesman of the industry for many decades. He said in part:

The '70's and the '80's were days of intensive railroad construction; the opening up of the West and Southwest to the settler; the creation of thousands of new communities; the period, too, in which electric light and power first became the handmaiden of all industry, in which factories in countless number in all branches of trade came into being to serve the rapidly increasing population, augmented by millions of high-grade immigrants that flocked to these shores from northern Europe. It was natural that contemporaneously with this great development a large clothing industry should have come into existence.

New Firms Enter the Industry

Enterprising retailers in various sections of the country realized that the possibilities of retail growth in the small towns, where many of them were located, were limited. Only by disposing of the store, by going to a clothing manufacturing center, and by opening a clothing factory could the ambition of the small independent retailer be satisfied. Accordingly, there was an exodus of ambitious store owners to the big city, anxious to enter the manufacturing branch of the industry. There the large profits were to be made. Naturally, not all such owners of retail stores were successful in their new enterprises. At the same time, many of the prominent firms on the roster of the industry today were founded by retailers.

We find that in 1869, Nathan Stein left his clothing store in Geneva, New York and Levi Adler sold his store in Medina, New York, forming the partnership of Stein-Adler in Rochester. At a later date, out of this partnership, two large nationally known concerns arose, namely the Stein-Bloch Company and L. Adler, Bros. & Co. Richard H. Adler, a member of the Adler family is still prominent in the industry. He is currently president of the Joseph & Feiss Company of Cleveland.

Bernard Kuppenheimer was also in the retail clothing business, owning a store in Terre Haute, Indiana. Obviously, the possibilities of growth in Terre Haute during the 1870's were limited. Therefore, Kuppenheimer pulled up stakes, went to the then rapidly growing metropolis of Chicago, and entered the industry there as a manufacturer. In 1876 the firm of B. Kuppenheimer & Co., was organized, and it is still a leading concern, although control of the company recently has passed out of the family.

Of all the diverse immigrant nationalities that entered the United States in the 1850's, the German Jews were most active in entering the men's clothing industry. Moreover, they did not enter the clothing industry as machine operators for they were not factory workers. They were executives who had acquired their industry knowledge either through apprenticeship in Germany, learning about the financial and office management of a clothing concern, or else were retail merchants in the United States who later turned to the manufacture of clothing. The Rosenwald family history exemplifies such German Jews to a remarkable degree.

One of the great sagas in the merchandising history of our country was the rise of Julius Rosenwald of Sears Roebuck fame. The early business life of Rosenwald and his family, while notable for its extraordinary success, was repeated many times over, although to a lesser degree, by his contemporaries in the industry. His rise as a business man is therefore of interest, for he could be considered as a prototype of many manufacturers producing clothing during the latter part of the 19th century.

In 1854, Samuel Rosenwald, the father of Julius Rosenwald, came to the United States from Germany. He started as a peddler, but when in 1857 he married the sister of Hammerslough Bros., prominent clothing manufacturers, he was put in charge of their retail clothing outlet in Peoria, Illinois. For some years, he had charge of various stores for his brothers-in-law in the South and Midwest. Interestingly, the Hammerslough store in Evansville, Indiana, which Samuel Rosenwald managed for a time, was called the "Oak Hall Clothing House," trading on the national fame of the Simmons family business in Boston. In 1861, Samuel Rosenwald moved to Springfield, Illinois (gradually going further West as the country was settled), and opened a store in the name of S. Rosenwald & Co., "the Capitol Clothing House." He was immediately successful, for with the outbreak of the Civil War, Rosenwald sold large quantities of officers' uniforms. By 1868, Rosenwald became the sole owner, continued to prosper, and now called his store "the C.O.D. One-Price Clothier."

Julius Rosenwald, Samuel's son, was born in 1862. He was sent to New York in 1879 to learn the clothing business from his uncles, the Hammerslough Brothers. Starting as a stock boy at $5.00 a week, he supplemented his income by working for Rogers Peet on Saturday nights, earning another $2.00 a week. After some selling experience on the road, in 1884 he entered the retail business in New York with his brother as a partner. When he found that the demand for summer suits was excellent, Rosenwald decided to become a manufacturer. He went into partnership with his brother and a cousin, Julius B. Weil, forming the firm of Rosenwald and Weil in Chicago. Shortly thereafter, Julius Rosenwald organized his own clothing business. When he began selling Sears Roebuck, Rosenwald soon recognized the potential growth of Sears, thereupon he liquidated his own business in 1897 and entered the mail order firm. Thus, the business life of Julius Rosenwald epitomized to a great extent the experience of many clothing manufacturers of that period. They made their first mark as members of the industry, and then turned to other fields notably banking, as Kuhn, politics as Opdyke and Marcus M. Marks, or often entered Wall Street as the Seligman family. The clothing industry was an excellent training ground for many who became nationally known in other fields of activity.

However, there were numerous manufacturers of clothing who felt that their best efforts should not be diverted, so they built organizations that have continued to this day because of enterprise and business acumen. The largest clothing concern in the United States started in 1873 when Harry Hart and Brother opened a retail store on State Street, Chicago. Retailers out of town liked the clothing sold by the Hart Brothers, so they purchased the garments from them for their own stores. That was the beginning of the Hart wholesale business. Expanding their operation in 1879, the Hart Brothers formed a partnership with two brothers-in-law as Hart, Abt and Marx. Later, Abt withdrew, and in 1887, Joseph Schaffner, a distant relative, entered the partnership, with the name now changed to the most famous threesome in the clothing industry, Hart, Schaffner and Marx. The character of business practices inaugurated in that day by this firm was somewhat novel to the industry, such as no cancellations from retailers, selling at only one price whether or not the retailer was a house account, and Hart,

Schaffner and Marx was the first firm to advertise its product on a truly national scale. The partnership prospered to such an extent that it became, in time, the largest concern in the industry. It now owns approximately 200 retail stores in addition to selling its merchandise to thousands of retail accounts. One of the prime reasons for the success of this company has been the absence of nepotism in management, usually a serious flaw in the maintenance of long life for any family firm. As a publicly owned company, with thousands of stockholders, Hart, Schaffner and Marx has shown no signs of old age, rather it is extremely progressive in its selling policies, and is considered to be one of the most efficient clothing firms at the manufacturing, selling and distribution levels.

Another retailer seeking a wider field of activity was David Marks who had opened his clothing store in Schenectady, New York, in 1848. Marks sold the store shortly after the Civil War, came to New York City, and became a clothing manufacturer. The firm of David Marks and Sons was soon a leading concern in the New York market. The outstanding member of this clothing family was Marcus M. Marks, who was the unquestioned national and local leader of the industry for several decades. He was not merely the President of the New York Association of Clothiers, but in 1897 was one of the organizers of the National Association of Clothiers, serving as its president for many years. Marks was articulate and aggressive in promoting and improving the reputation of his industry, which was under a cloud due to sweat shop conditions. He was usually the manufacturers' spokesman and representative before all government agencies. Marks retired from the manufacture of clothing in 1913. In keeping with industry tradition that clothing manufacturers often entered public life after leaving an active business career, in 1914 he was elected President of the Borough of Manhattan, New York City. In that office at the start of World War I, Marks was the first public official to initiate daylight saving in the United States, once more proving his originality and enterprise.

When Charles B. Peet & Co., and Marvin N. Rogers & Co., on November 6, 1874, consolidated to form the Rogers Peet Co., opening their first store on the southwest corner of Broome Street and Broadway in New York City, they founded a nationally famous retail and wholesale business, which has maintained its fine reputation to this day. Actually, the history of this organization can be traced many years prior to 1874, for it was recorded that a John T. Martin of New York began manufacturing clothing in 1838. During the Civil War, Martin, as most clothing manufacturers making uniforms, enlarged his factory to meet this extraordinary demand. Retiring shortly thereafter, Martin turned his business over to his brother, William R. H. Martin and to a brother-in-law, Marvin N. Rogers. In turn, as related, Rogers merged with Peet, who had been conducting a jobbing business in clothing. The merged company sold at wholesale as well as retail, with branch stores gradually opened in New York and other cities. In the early decades of the 1900's Rogers Peet became nationally famous for its imaginative promotional activities. The company recognized the value of appealing specifically to the boys' trade. So ROPECO, a club for boys was organized, all members buying their clothing from the Rogers Peet Co. Badges were issued, and it was a proud lad who pinned one on his lapel. There was a Ropeco magazine that appealed to the youthful customers. The Rogers Peet advertisements in the theatre programs were always timely, often witty, and created a most favorable impression of the store. Its wholesale business, although never large, was highly regarded as to quality of product. Recently, in accordance with current trends, the Cluett, Peabody & Co., primarily a shirt manufacturing corporation, purchased the chain, bringing within its fold this old line organization at a time when Cluett, Peabody had already acquired control of J. Schoeneman, Inc., of Baltimore.

As noted, many of the German Jews who immigrated to the United States after 1848, gravitated to the clothing industry, soon becoming leaders in the field. Thus, Levi Greif, who migrated from Germany in 1851, disposed of his Baltimore retail furnishings store in 1862 in order to become a manufacturer of men's clothing. This was of course, the familiar pattern of advancement from retailing to manufacturing which occurred so often. The company enjoyed steady growth, and when Levi Greif died in 1904, his firm was already considered to be outstanding as a producer of clothing. Greif left the business to his four sons, Simon, David, Leonard and Alvin, who proved to be very able businessmen. The company prospered under the management of the sons and their heirs. For many years, the Greif officers followed a policy of going their own way and they seldom, if ever, participated in industry activity. They held other manufacturers at arm's length, even when the cooperation of all important clothing firms was a necessity. In recent years however, this stand-off attitude of the Greif organization has gradually changed, in belated recognition that what affects all, affects each one, and vice versa. L. Greif & Bro., which had become one of the largest clothing concerns in this country, was controlled by the family until December, 1959 when it was acquired by Genesco, Inc., a conglomerate holding company with interests primarily in the apparel field.

As Baltimore had become an important clothing market, it attracted young men who desired to enter the growing industry. In 1889, Jacob Schoeneman founded his firm, producing wash pants. When his son, Ansel, entered the business in 1897, the company was manufacturing dress pants and golf knickers. In 1910, when Jacob Schoeneman died, he was known throughout the land as the "Pants King." Shortly thereafter, the firm began manufacturing suits. The business acumen of Ansel Schoeneman became legendary in the industry, for his product was so well received by retailers that he allotted merchandise in years when other manufacturers were in desperate need of orders. On October 1, 1955, as noted, the company was acquired by Cluett, Peabody & Co.

In Philadelphia, in 1874, Nathan Snellenberg founded the Snellenberg Clothing Co., housing the wholesale business in the same building where he also conducted a retail store, keeping each business enterprise separately. The firm was ably managed, and by 1900 was considered to be one of the larger companies, not only in Philadelphia, but in the country. In 1924, Louis Goldsmith, who had started as a stock boy 25 years previously, and had risen to become the general manager of the firm, purchased control of the business. The name of the new organization was now known as Louis

Goldsmith, Inc., and it has maintained its position to this day as one of the leading clothing concerns in the United States. Kayser-Roth Corp., acquired control of this manufacturer in February, 1969.

The Jobbers Become Dictators

With the rapid settlement of the country from coast to coast in the post Civil War decades, many clothing manufacturers found that they were in no position to establish readily a national sales force that would enable them to reach directly the thousands of retailers now opening stores in all sections of the country. The average manufacturer in the 1870's did not have the financial resources that would permit him to extend credit on necessarily long payment terms to the multitude of small stores. Again, it took time and a great deal of money (drawing accounts, traveling expenses and sample lines) to establish an adequate sales force that would reach good retailers who could be depended upon to buy regularly from a manufacturer each season. It was obviously easier to sell one account in any one area, whose financial strength was assured, rather than sell to several hundred stores of uncertain credit standing. The local jobber, usually a former store owner, was fully cognizant of current retail as well as wholesale conditions within his particular region, to an extent that no manufacturer, located hundreds or even thousands of miles away, could possibly know. This local jobber had intimate knowledge and was personally acquainted with the owners of stores in the surrounding towns. He knew the special requirements of these retail accounts and he, or his representative, visited the stores in the territory regularly. It was therefore good economics and most feasible for the manufacturer in a far eastern clothing market to sell to one jobber in a region rather than to hundreds of stores.

But the jobber became an economic dictator once he was aware of his growing economic power over the clothing manufacturer. The jobber realized that actually he represented and controlled the equivalent buying power of possibly hundreds of stores. In real terms, the jobber might be compared, to a degree, with the large buying offices of today, except that no manufacturer in modern times would dare risk the future of his business by selling solely to such buying groups. But in the 1870's and the 1880's as well, there was little choice given to the average clothing firm with limited finances, especially if it had just entered the industry. Once the jobber realized his economic strength, in many instances he made full use of it, or rather misuse of it. He imposed prices that permitted only small profits to the manufacturer. The jobber threatened to divert orders if onerous purchase and delivery terms were not granted. Special dating might be asked and extra discounts were often required. The jobber was dictator, and the manufacturers were in danger of becoming no more than contractors who could not afford to lose these large accounts.

All manufacturers recognized the need to break the chains of jobber control. The more substantial firms, in an effort to by-pass the jobber, started to advertise in trade publications in order to reach the far distant retailers. Some manufacturers began to advertise nationally so that consumers would recognize their product. Many manufacturers sent out salesmen regularly, so that direct contact was established between the clothing firm and the retail account. Salesmen now went out on the road each season, acquiring the loyalty of their accounts. This was a valuable asset to any firm, and appreciably weakened the economic power of the local jobber. In turn, the retailers in good financial standing formed buying groups among non-competing stores, establishing direct contact with the manufacturers As a consequence, the jobber found that he was an economic factor only when he serviced the small retailers, granting long terms to those stores who were chronically slow payers and a credit risk at all times. The jobber soon found himself to be merely a marginal supplier, catering to the marginal retailers. Many jobbers recognized that the future portended a gradual elimination of their business. They therefore had the alternative of becoming manufacturers, or else liquidating, and a large number of jobbers, especially in the Midwest, turned to manufacturing. By 1914, the influence of the jobber had declined to relatively minor importance, and by 1940, jobbers practically disappeared as an economic force in the clothing industry.

"Drummers" Become Salesmen

William Goldman, in his historic paper read at the convention of the National Association of Clothiers in Baltimore in February, 1915, noted that in the 1880's and even earlier:

> Clothing, too, was manufactured in advance of its sale; salesmen did not start out until July or August to take fall orders, or until January or February for spring. While there were cheap, medium and fine clothing houses, the majority made a medium grade. There was style in clothing even in those days, but it was a long time coming and a longer time going.
>
> In general, however, the manufacturer, while taking some risk by manufacturing his stock in advance, always had a part of his clientele who bought clothing much as they did bolts of calico or barrels of molasses, and the stores in which it was sold handled it with about as much care as the latter. This made the disposal of the slow-selling stock less difficult than it would be in these days; but it still remained a serious problem for the manufacturer.

This is a far cry from present practice when spring lines open in August, and fall lines open in February, with no goods ordinarily manufactured in advance of orders taken.

The industry merchandising pattern in the years following the Civil War was as follows:

	SPRING SEASON	FALL SEASON
Begin Production	November	May–June
Peak Production	December–February	July–August
Begin to Sell	January–February	July–August
Slow Manufacturing Months	March–April	September–October

The former "drummers" (they retained the name) now became traveling salesmen, for now it had become possible to travel to all sections of the country by rail. Salesmen went on the road each season, their selling trip lasting ordinarily from six weeks to two months. They were usually accompanied by an assistant, whose duties consisted of packing and unpacking the samples which were in half-dozen to a dozen, or even more trunks, acting as a model (a "perfect 38") for the samples when the customers wanted visual presentation and also served as a partner in pinocchle while en route from city to city. In those days, it was the practice to actually show a finished garment for each fabric pattern in the line. This meant an unlimited number of suits had to be carried by each salesman. Selling was made from stock on hand as William Goldman reported.

To hear the former assistants tell their stories now, all salesmen had a hilarious time. Actually, after some probing, it could be seen that the life of the salesman in those days meant many dreary hours of traveling on trains that were either too cold or too hot. There were physical difficulties in moving the heavy sample trunks from town to town, and often hotel arrangements, particularly in the smaller cities, were extremely primitive. Over the years, the Executive Secretary of the Association often heard the older members of the industry talk of the "good old times." One of the most interesting such gabfests occurred prior to a meeting of the Board of Directors in the 1940's, when Meyer Lang of Fashion Park of Rochester, Max Friedman of J. Friedman & Co., of New York, and Julius Morse of Leopold Morse of Boston, recalled the days when they were young. Each man was well over 70 at the time, and they had begun traveling as salesmen at a very early age.

Max Friedman told of the difficulties he encountered while breaking in as a young salesman. He had been desperately anxious to sell a particular account located in a southern Illinois town. The retailer looked at his line with contempt, for it was not Rochester make. Stubbornly determined to sell this account, Friedman offered a low price, long terms, and promised early delivery, but the retailer was unmoved. No one could possibly make a comparable garment as a certain manufacturer located in Rochester. Friedman would not give up. He purchased a suit made by this Rochester manufacturer before he went on his next trip to this Illinois town. He placed a J. Friedman & Co. label on the suit and once more entered the store of this prejudiced retailer. He now offered to sell this sample suit, in any quantity, at $5.00 below the regular price quoted by the Rochester firm. The retailer was still unmoved. In fact, he rejected this sample as badly made, one that fit poorly, and was certain that inferior woolens had been used. Then, as Friedman told the story, in a fury he took scissors, cut the lining open, which exposed the interlining. In accordance with its regular practice, there was the name of the Rochester manufacturer stencilled on the interlining. Friedman then told the store owner of the trick he had played, pointed out the retailer's sheer prejudice, and felt entitled to get an order. The retailer said he would buy Friedman's line only if he got a price concession of $1.00 a suit. Friedman offered 25¢, and after hard bargaining, they settled for 40¢ a suit. "But," he continued, "I got the order," which was his main point. Lang countered by saying that it took price, and not quality, to take the sale away from Rochester.

After further small talk about their adventures and hardships, Lang told of the time he traveled in the Midwest. It was in February, and he was on a train going to a small town. There was just one account there, but a good one. His itinerary called for a one day stop, then to take a train to Chicago where he had an appointment with an important buyer. There was a heavy snowstorm that day. The train crawled. Instead of arriving early afternoon as scheduled, it was ten at night when the train finally pulled in at the station. Not daunted ("I was young then," said Lang), he called the retailer and told him of his predicament. He wanted to show his line, but had to leave next morning for Chicago. Then, according to Lang, when he heard that Fashion Park's line was in town, the retailer got a horse and sleigh, came to the station, and brought Lang and his sample line to his home. For the greater part of the night Lang showed his samples, and the retailer gave a good order. Next morning, after a hearty breakfast, Lang returned to the railroad station via horse and sleigh, going on to Chicago. Lang ended the story by noting that this was a loyal account, and like most men who looked at the past with tinted glasses, he remarked, "That's when you got good merchandise and loyal customers." But Morse was skeptical, pointing out that "for 40¢ a suit the Rochester house lost an account. You call that loyalty?"

That conversation epitomized the experiences of a traveling man in the 1890's, the drive to get the order, the physical hardships endured in travel and the determination to overcome all handicaps. In the 1940's these men were successful in their business life, and highly regarded because of their business acumen and fine human qualities. It was not long after, when these typical representatives of a colorful period of clothing salesmanship passed on.

If a salesman had a regular territory where he was well known, retailers would invite him to spend an evening in the owner's home, and close friendships often resulted. At times, after meeting his customer's family, the salesman perhaps married the retailer's daughter, and settled down to run his father-in-law's store. Many prominent retailers today are descendants of such marriages. Often the salesman advised the store owner what others were buying, what merchandise was selling in the territory, and perhaps he also imparted some information on how other retailers were running their stores. The experienced salesman was a valued contact, highly regarded by his retail accounts.

Commissions were relatively high, ranging up to seven per cent or higher, for a man with a "following" was a valuable asset in building and maintaining the dollar volume of a firm. It could be said that the heyday of the clothing salesman was in the 1890's, when his economic importance and social status reached its peak. Thereafter, new selling methods were gradually introduced which reduced the importance of the traveling man, turning him into the resident salesman, living in his territory, carrying fabric swatches, and not the sample garments in each instance. This eliminated the need for heavy trunks. The romance in selling, partly fact and in greater part highly colored fiction (as told by men who still retell the stories heard from their elders), vanished by 1914 or shortly thereafter. Selling now became a science, and not an exercise in friendship plus mere blarney. The industry was taking its first steps towards introducing greater efficiency in merchandising and distribution.

Chapter 5

The Work Force, 1800-1890

The Immigrants

Until 1850, the clothing industry consisted of custom tailors and manufacturers who, in most instances, were really manufacturing retailers. As noted, the more enterprising firms established their plants on the eastern seaboard with branch stores in large southern cities, and at a later date in the rapidly developing midwestern states and the Pacific Coast. There was no wide national distribution of any manufacturer's line, for modes of transportation were primitive on land, while bulk shipments could be sent only via water. The tailors were ordinarily English, Scotch immigrants, or their descendants. Tailoring (particularly the coat) was a highly skilled craft, for there was little or no division of labor, and a long apprenticeship was required for all who entered the industry. Vests and pants were usually sewn by women, because a minimum of fit was required, and in sewing these garments, merely the ability to use the needle was considered an adequate skill.

However, the total labor cost involved in producing clothes was high relative to the cost of the fabric and total price of the garment. There was consequent economic pressure to train new workers at steadily lower wages and so reduce the proportion of total wages paid for sewing the garment. This could be accomplished only by sub-dividing the operations, so that less skill would be required on the part of each operator. It was a fundamental economic principle which had been generally accepted throughout the western world with the advent of the Industrial Revolution. Division of labor had been widely publicized as an economic fact in 1776 by Adam Smith in his classic "The Wealth of Nations." But we can accept as a likely fact that it was not Adam Smith's world famous treatise that influenced the clothing industry, but sheer economic necessity which forced the manufacturers to seek cheaper means of sewing a garment.

At this very time, because of famine conditions in Ireland during the "hungry forties," a flood of Irish immigrants arrived in the United States. These new arrivals were ordinarily unskilled as tailors, for the overwhelming majority had been engaged in agriculture. Nevertheless, by organizing the factory on the basis of a fine division of labor, and by intensive training (usually during the long hours of a working day), the Irish were soon employed in all of the operating phases of tailoring. When other immigrant nationalities entered the industry in the decades after the Civil War, the Irish, who still remained in the industry, were now employed only in the more highly skilled operations. For a period, the Irish were the majority of cutters and designers in the industry, until they were displaced at a later date by the eastern Jews, and then by the Italians. Nevertheless, in the 1880's, Daniel Edward Ryan, certainly a good Irishman, was the leading designer of his day, styling for Browning King & Co. Until World War I there were still a few Irish clothing designers in the industry.

In 1848, political and economic conditions were at a crisis in Germany. The German immigrants who entered the United States in large numbers were relatively unskilled. They found ready jobs in the clothing industry, soon assuming a dominant position in the factories, replacing the English and Irish operators. Thus, in an 1855 survey made of the industry in New York City, out of a total of 12,609 tailors studied, 6,709 came from Germany, 4,171 came from Ireland, 501 from England, and the balance from some twenty other foreign lands. As already noted, the German Jews who entered the United States in the years following 1848, had been members of the middle class in Europe, and were essentially oriented towards merchandising rather than production, usually obtaining positions in executive capacities.

With religious persecution rampant in Russia and throughout eastern Europe as well, large numbers of Jews in these lands began to emigrate to this country in the 1880's and thereafter. They soon replaced the United Kingdom and Germany as the prime source of foreign labor entering the clothing factories. Unfortunately there was little rapport between the Jews from Germany and those who came from countries further east in Europe. It was not merely a matter of differences in economic conditions, but differences in social status as well. These German Jews looked down upon their lowly co-religionists who arrived at a later date from eastern Europe, even though such immigrants in time also became employers. This social cleavage within the ranks of the religious group who, by 1900, was the majority of employers manufacturing clothing, hampered industrywide cooperation for many years. The detrimental effects were particularly noted in instances when total industry action was necessary such as dealing with labor on an industrywide basis.

The table on page 63 discloses the shift in immigration by country in the decades after the Civil War.

In an analysis of the impact of the flow of immigration upon the industry, and the changes in the racial composition of the factory workers producing clothing, a U.S. Government report in 1916 noted as follows:

From 1899 to 1914 the Hebrews constituted the great majority of the skilled immigrant tailors, being 68.3 per cent of all the immigrant tailors admitted to this country during that period. The next largest immigration was the south Italians, who comprised 12.7 per cent of the total tailors admitted.

Immigration in the United States by Decades
1871–1930

DECADES	TOTAL IN THOUSANDS	PERCENT OF TOTAL ENGLAND	GERMANY	RUSSIA & POLAND	ITALY	OTHER COUNTRIES
1871–1880	2,812	44.4	25.5	1.9	2.0	26.2
1881–1890	5,246	27.9	27.5	5.1	5.9	33.6
1891–1900	3,687	17.6	13.7	16.3	17.7	34.7
1901–1910	8,795	9.8	3.9	20.6	23.3	42.4
1911–1920	5,735	8.5	2.4	16.0	19.3	53.8
1921–1930	4,107	9.2	10.0	7.0	10.1	63.7

Source: Annual Reports of Commissioner-General of Immigration
(Washington 1895 to 1930)

Together, the Hebrews and south Italians furnished the clothing trade, during this period, with 81 per cent, or slightly over four-fifths of all the tailors admitted.

The total immigration of tailors from 1875 to 1898, exclusive of 1896, was 68,587; for 1896 the number was 4,201; and from 1899 to 1914, 300,410; making a grand total of 373,198 tailors admitted to the United States from 1875 to 1914, inclusive.

It must be remembered that during the early years of this immigration clothing manufacturers were dependent to a great extent upon this skilled foreign labor supply.

As newly arrived immigrants, the Jews and the Italians naturally tended to concentrate in the seaboard cities, the ports of their arrival, which were New York, Philadelphia, Boston and Baltimore. The clothing industry needed this immigrant labor, and the newly arrived immigrants needed the jobs. In the Midwest, though, where the first waves of Jewish and Italian immigrants were considerably less in numbers, other nationalities entered the clothing factories. Immigrants of national stocks such as Bohemians, Poles, Lithuanians, and from other lands as well were the dominant groups employed as tailors. Nevertheless, whether the national group came from eastern Europe, or Italy, or from central Europe, the industry labor force was primarily recruited from recent immigrants. In 1880, the Bureau of the Census reported that of 133,756 tailors, (men and women) in the clothing industry, 61 per cent of the total were foreign born. By 1900, the industry expanded so that the total number of workers had risen to 185,400, and the foreign born tailors were now 71 per cent of the factory operators. The increase in the percentage of foreign born employed in the industry in two decades was primarily caused by a heavy Jewish and Italian influx in the shops. Since the 1850's, the clothing industry was known as an immigrant industry, recruiting its work force primarily from recently arrived foreigners. Not until after World War I, when the immigrant flow became a mere trickle, did many American born operators enter the clothing factories.

The fact that the majority of the labor force consisted of immigrants from many lands, speaking diverse languages, influenced greatly the economic and social forces that were to dominate the industry in the years to come. Thus the Irish, who had been in this country for several decades, and who had risen to become the cutters of the cloth, or else were the designers, now lumped all late immigrants as foreigners. They had the utmost contempt for these late arrivals. The many languages spoken by the recent immigrants also fostered the cleavage that now took place between the workers who spoke English (native Americans and Irish) and the later immigrants. As will be related in a later chapter, these racial and cultural differences had a profound effect upon the history of labor relations, and upon the labor organizations within the industry.

The Sweat Shops

Shortly after the Civil War, with ready-made clothing growing in consumer acceptance, production of garments increased rapidly. It was relatively easy now to become a manufacturer and produce clothing. The cutting of the garment merely required a long table for laying out the fabric and a pair of shears. The sewing of the garment was performed by a low priced mechanical device, the sewing machine plus some hand operations. The pressing of the garment required the use of a simple heated iron. Therefore, if labor was available, only a minimum of capital was needed in order to

Woman and Children (Courtesy of ACWA)

open a factory (perhaps only to rent a room) where the garments could be sewed. Nevertheless, some financial resources, even though small, were necessary in order to buy the needed fabrics, the trimmings, pay the workers upon completion of the work and extend credit terms to retail accounts. Under the circumstances, adequate capital, plus trade and bank credit were required. But a knowledgeable manufacturer might reduce his minimum requirements of capital if the garments were sewn off his premises, for the expense of factory rent and ownership of machinery was avoided. In turn, if the workers in the contract shop owned the sewing machines, this reduced the need for substantial investment by the contractor. It was apparent to a potential manufacturer with limited resources (considering his capital), that turning over the work to contractors was most economic and feasible. In addition, when work was sent

New York tenement family making men's trousers.
(© George Eastman House Collections, photo by Lewis W. Hine)

to a contract shop, the burden of general factory supervision and examination of quality in workmanship became the responsibility of the contractor.

The contractor also saw the possibilities of saving his rent, plus his other overhead expenses, if he distributed the garments to operators who worked at home and owned their sewing machines as well. Such economic forces encouraged widespread home work. The contractor became no more than a middle man between manufacturer who had purchased and cut the fabric on his premises, and the worker who sewed and finished the garment at home. At times though, the contractor found it advisable to have the garments sewn in his own factory, giving out the hand work, such as finishing, to home workers. There were obviously many possibilities of combining or dividing the methods of allocating the numerous operations of sewing. Therefore, there were inside shops where garments were cut and also sewn on the premises, contract shops where the garments were sewn after the manufacturer had cut the fabric in his factory, and home workers who sewed the garments parcelled out to them either by the manufacturer directly or by the middleman contractor. In all instances though, regardless of where the garments were sewn, working conditions were hazardous to the health of the operators.

In 1887, the factory inspectors of New York, in their annual report stated as follows:

> The workshops occupied by these contracting manufacturers of clothing, or "sweaters" as they are commonly called, are foul in the extreme. Noxious gases emanate from all corners. The buildings are ill smelling from cellar to garret. The water-closets are used alike by males and females, and usually stand in the room where the work is done. The people are huddled together too closely for comfort, even if all other conditions were excellent. And when this state of affairs is taken into consideration, with the painfully long hours of toil which the poverty-stricken victims of the contractors must endure, it seems wonderful that there exists a human being that could stand it for a month and live. We are not describing one or two places, for there is hardly an exception in this class of manufactories in all New York.

The report also observed:

> Children have never been employed to a great extent in this industry, as their usefulness is limited to a very few operations, like pulling out bastings. Their chief employment then as now appears to have been acting as carriers of goods from the shop to the home and vice versa.

The findings of this government report on child labor were confirmed by Jesse E. Pope in his study of factory conditions in the clothing industry of New York made in the early 1900's. He reported that children were not employed as operators in the inside shops. However, young boys carried the bundles or ran errands in the factory. It was remarked though, that the social and physical surroundings were certainly not conducive to health, nor was this a proper environment for young children. In the tenement shops, children were employed in the minor tasks of sewing, as well as carrying bundles to and from the premises to the manufacturer or contractor. Employment in tenement shops, often living in these

Sweat shop inspection, Sept., 1903 (Courtesy of ACWA)

same rooms as well, was bound to affect the physical and mental health of the young.

A report issued by the U.S. Bureau of Foreign & Domestic Commerce, vividly described home living conditions of the clothing workers in the 1880's as follows:

> The workers, all immigrants lived and worked together in large numbers, in a few small, foul, ill-smelling rooms, without ventilation, water, or nearby toilets. They slept on the unswept floors littered with the work, the work table serving as the dining table as well.
>
> One observer of that time reported that "Conditions were extremely poor, for the houses were unsanitary, lighting poor, atmosphere fetid, and overcrowding endemic." Another observer of the time reported that, "In order to conserve rent, some girls—in one case six—rented a room in which they sewed and slept on the floor on straw beds."

And it was noted by a social worker that "some poor tailors in New York rent a room, occupy a spot themselves, and rent the rest of the room to others, charging 50 cents for seat room for a man, and a girl to assist him; thirty-seven cents for a man alone." Truly, such conditions deserved the public opprobrium and condemnation of the health authorities heaped upon the industry at that time.

Working conditions were thoroughly bad in all clothing markets. The reports already quoted disclosed conditions in New York City. Blake McKelvey, the historian who wrote about the Rochester clothing industry, stated that insofar as manufacturers there were concerned:

> The prosperous times assured large returns that justified the outlays and encouraged the leaders to adopt brand names from their products. But, the lot of the workers was not so rosy. Drawn out of their homes to attend the contractors' machines or those in the big factories, they endeavored to form unions for self protection, but the mounting influx of newcomers from abroad, including many skilled tailors, inundated their ranks and discouraged strike calls. The managers, on the other hand, profited from that influx. Hundreds of Polish or Russian Jews arrived seeking employment. They introduced a new team system, with one tailor, one seamstress, and one assistant working together at specialized tasks on each suit, thus speeding output.
> The pressure for increased production and crowding of many eager workers into the restricted quarters provided by the contractors won these establishments the designation of sweat shops—the public authorities were becoming concerned over sanitary and other health problems and over the schooling of the children . . .

In Cincinnati, the Education Research Bureau issued a report on conditions in that city roundly condemning the clothing plants as unsanitary and castigated homework.

As for Chicago, T. J. Morgan, a trade union official in that city, in 1892 before the U.S. Senate subcommittee investigating the sweating system of that day, testified that Chicago was no exception to "sweating the workers." Morgan stated that:

> Clothing contractors employed men, women and children for not less than 10 hours a day and some up to 18 hours a day, in rooms that were entirely inadequate in size; that about 12 workers on the average worked together in these sweat shops; and in one place on West Division Street, there were 39 girls, 11 men and 12 children in a room that was 10 by 40 feet. This

space was also occupied as living quarters of the contractor where the wife cooked and the family slept on beds made on the floor. Conditions were somewhat better in the inside shops that were owned by manufacturers, for in such instances living quarters were separate and apart from the factory premises.

Charles E. Zaretz, a scholar who wrote on this subject, reported that the sweating system was extreme in Boston, particularly in contract shops. Then, he further noted, that in 1890, nearly 90 per cent of the units made in that city were produced under the contract system.

The sheer misery of the clothing workers throughout the country who sewed garments under frightful conditions, aroused public indignation. State legislative bodies, as well as the U.S. Senate, began to investigate sweat shop conditions which were common throughout the industry. A number of states passed laws in an effort to eliminate the sweat shops. In 1893, the New York State legislature

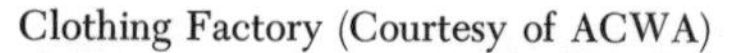
Clothing Factory (Courtesy of ACWA)

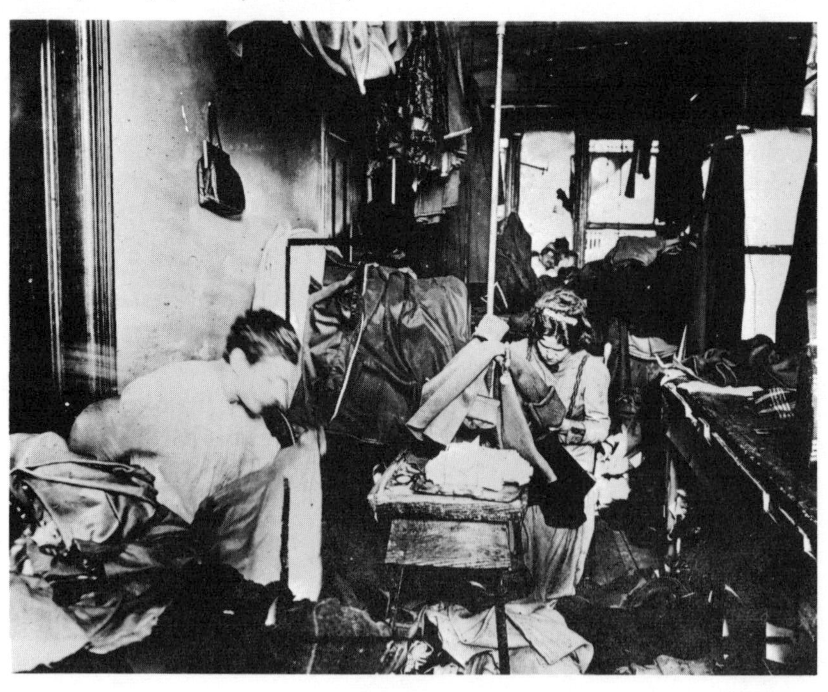

"Bundle Boy" (Courtesy of ACWA)

enacted a law that forbade the manufacture of clothing in any room of a tenement used for eating or sleeping purposes, except by the immediate family living there. This permitted only the members of the family to live and work in their crowded tenement rooms. Peculiarly enough, even such a limited law was considered an act of enlightenment, a sad commentary on conditions at the time. Permits were now required if a tenement was to be used as a factory by the family. In a further effort to stamp out tenement shops, the New York legislature in 1897 entirely forbade all work performed in tenement buildings. Only loft buildings were to be used for manufacture of clothing, but it was reported that "the majority of factories were still in buildings unfit for factory purposes and unsanitary." According to a study made at the time, there were just too many factories and too few inspectors. The New York Factory Laws served as models for legislation in other states where clothing was produced, such as Massachusetts, Pennsylvania and Illinois. Because of legislation enacted by these states, by 1895, working conditions under which clothing was made, showed some slight improvement. These attempts to improve factory conditions were feeble at best, and clothing factories remained subminimum by any decent standard of health and sanitation. The widespread practice of finishing the garments in the workers' homes continued, although condemned by public health authorities. It could not be denied, for the most part, that the clothing industry at the end of the 19th century, was a sweat shop industry of the worst sort.

Long Hours

The following table, compiled by Professor Pope in his study of the clothing industry, discloses the long working week for the clothing workers in the later years of the 19th century.

Pope further noted that the operators often took garments home for two to four hours additional work during the busy season for they were desperate in their need to increase their pay.

Hours a Week—Inside Shops

YEAR	CUTTERS	COAT MAKERS	CLOAK MAKERS	PRESSERS	KNEE PANTS MAKERS	PANTS MAKERS	VEST MAKERS
1883	55–58½		84	84			
1884	55–58½	60–90	84	84			
1885	55–58½	66–96	84	84			
1886	53–54	72–84	84	72			
1887	53	72–84	84	72			
1888	52–53	72–84	84	72–80			
1889	52–53	78–84	84	80–84			
1890	52–53	78–84	72–78	84–96	60		
1891	54–56½	72–84	84	84–96	69–71	84–108	80

In 1886 the cutters struck for an eight hour day, but compromised on a nine hour day. Although accurate statistics were not available, it was generally estimated that home workers worked 72–108 hours a week. (Eighth annual report of the New York Bureau of Labor.)

Low Wages

Once semi-skilled men and women could be employed in the sewing of the garment due to a sub-division of the operations, the trained tailor who was an experienced craftsman was no longer needed. The wage level in the clothing industry declined according to students of that period. Wages became mere subsistance wages, scarcely sufficient for the workers to exist and maintain the physical ability to perform their tasks. While actual wage statistics were meager prior to 1850, it was known at the time that tailors were able to earn about a dollar a day as a minimum, with some earning as high as $1.50 a day in the inside shops. Hours, of course, were uncounted. In 1857, the New York Chamber of Commerce stated that clothing cutters were receiving up to $15 a week; tailors and pressers averaged $9 a week in the factories. As the workers were employed for no longer period than eight months a year due to the slack seasons, the cutters actually earned about $455 a year or $9 a week, and the tailors and pressers earned about $310 a year or $6 a week. Women usually made about two-thirds of the wages received by the male workers, and (according to the New York Chamber of Commerce) young girls were reported to be earning about $150 a year. The Massachusetts Bureau of Labor reported that in 1860, women who worked in clothing factories earned $6.32 a week as basters; the operators $5.53; and the finishers $4.56 a week. According to this same Massachusetts survey, the working day in the inside factories usually ranged from ten to fourteen hours, and the work week consisted of six full days.

Based upon an eight month employment during a year, the annual earnings of the clothing workers were computed as follows according to the Massachusetts Bureau of Labor:

	Years		
	1860	*1872*	*1878*
Men cutters	445.44	635.20	512.00
Men pressers	293.44	513.60	328.96
Women basters	202.24	248.64	206.72
Women operators	171.20	151.68	146.56
Women finishers	145.92	151.68	146.56

The clothing workers in the New York market were receiving comparable annual earnings according to Professor Pope. Wages rose from 1860 to 1872, for the country was then prosperous. There was a sharp reduction of factory wages thereafter, for the panic of 1873 depressed wages generally to a marked degree, and by 1878, the wage scale had not yet returned to the former levels of the pre-depression years.

When the family, usually consisting of four or more people, worked as a unit at home, the entire family (hours unlimited) earned from $20 to $25 a week. After the 1873 panic, according to a study made by U.S. Government agencies, the total family income declined to a mere $15 to $20 a week, truly a starvation wage.

The Task System

The task system widely used was the ordinary method of production. It had been introduced in New York City in 1879–1880, and until 1895 was the usual basis of piece-work payment. This system of production was described and denounced in *Trade Unionism and Labor Problems* by Professor John R. Commons, the famous educator and historian of trade unionism, as follows:

> Under some of these contract shops there developed, especially in New York City, what was known as the "task system." Workers in the shops were organized in teams; an operator, a baster, and a finisher made a team; and it was found that three teams could keep two pressers busy. The making of eight or nine coats was considered a day's work for a team; and each member of the team felt that he must hustle to keep up with the other members, else his whole team fell behind—just the way you feel when you're passing bean bags down a line.
>
> The men were paid by the "task."
>
> Through this division of labor and rush of work, the task shops were able to work at a much lower price than the journeyman tailor; the "task shop," for example, would make a coat for $1.50 for which the tailor would receive $2.50 in the dull season and $5.00 in the busy season.
>
> And now see what happened next. Workers kept on coming into the cities and when a dull season or a dull year came there were a great many more workers than there were jobs. The contractor, possibly himself one

of the team, wanted to get the work from the manufacturer, and so he would offer to make the coats at a cheaper price. Then he would tell his men that instead of lowering wages he would ask them to do one more coat in a day's work.

And so the amount of work in the task increased from year to year—15 coats, 18 coats and even 20 coats, being required of a team to make a day's work. The men could not complete more than 4½ or 5 tasks a week. Do you see that this meant only 4½ or 5 days' pay? They worked longer hours, sometimes 12 to 18 hours a day, and at the utmost speed—yet came out a day's pay short.

Obviously, the task system of piece-work payment combined with the team method of production lent itself to extreme exploitation of the workers. Because of the evils connected with the unscrupulous methods used by some employers in computing piece-work earnings, the very principle of wage payments made in accordance with the number of garments sewn rather than hours worked, was considered by the economically weak employees to be sheer exploitation. The principle of piece work payments became anathema in the minds of the factory operators, for it was closely associated with the hated task system. Only after there was assurance by a strong union that the worker would receive a fair rate of piece work pay, jointly agreed upon by union and management, with no gimmicks permitted that would reduce the rates arbitrarily by the employer, did the workers willingly accept piece work rather than hourly wages in the sewing rooms.

Section Work

The aggregate of operations performed by the team of three was gradually subdivided for the purpose of increasing productivity in the inside shops. By 1895, the bundle system of production had been introduced whereby one or more workers performed a single operation only. Then the bundle of garments (with that operation completed) was passed on to the next group or section of workers who sewed the subsequent operation. In that way, the cut parts of the garment were progressively taken from one operating section to the next one, until the entire garment was completed. The introduction of this section work was really an elaborate refinement in division of labor. In time, the sewing of the coat alone was broken down into approximately 150 separate operations.

As might be expected, section work was bitterly opposed by the operators, for it eliminated the skilled tailor, the mainstay of the team system. He was now replaced by semi-skilled sewers. Section work was first introduced in Boston by English tailors, and when New York factories followed suit, it was known as the "Boston System." This method of production accelerated the use of the semi-skilled workers, who were now recruited from the flood of newly arrived immigrants. By hiring recent arrivals as sewing machine operators, wages were kept low, for job applicants were always greater in number than the need. The factory employes in the clothing industry found themselves in an economic trap. They needed the wages desperately. They could not leave their jobs easily, for the only language they spoke was a foreign one that was understood only by their friends in the shop and at home. They had little or no skill except as sewers of a single operation in a clothing factory. At the same time, wages were low, hours long and factory conditions decidedly unhealthy. Frustrated, the workers in all clothing markets repeatedly rebelled in an effort to better their unhappy state.

Early Labor Unrest

Even during the early years of the 19th century, there was constant labor unrest in the clothing industry, with sporadic strikes, lockouts, and repressive court action frequent. No regular labor organization was able to attain during the period any permanent status, or permanently improve the conditions of labor. Thus the tailors in Baltimore struck in 1795, 1805, and again in 1807 in an effort to raise wages. Although the workers were persistent, they did not succeed in establishing any organization that was more than ephemeral. Their many efforts to improve their lot had no lasting effect.

The strike of the Buffalo tailors in 1824 disclosed a temporarily stable labor organization that was capable of calling a work stoppage. The Buffalo *Emporium* of December 25, 1824 reported the strike and its consequences:

On Monday last, all the Journeymen tailors of the Village had what they call a turnout for higher wages. They presented to their employers bills of the prices which they should demand in the future for their labor, which not being allowed by their employers, they all left the shops, so that the tailoring business was entirely at a standstill.

On the next day, several of the delinquents were brought before Court of Special Sessions of which our first Judge was a member and put upon their trial for conspiracy. The assembling of the Journeymen, the forming of the bill of prices which were considerably advanced, their combination and agreement that they should all leave their employment in case their demands were not complied with, and that each should bear a proportion of the expenses incident to the turnout were proved on part of the people. . . . A similar custom among the Journeymen to coerce the refractory was proved to exist throughout the United States. The Jury found the defendants guilty, and they were fined two dollars each.

Labor discontent was widespread in all clothing markets. In 1827, we find that 24 journeymen tailors were charged with conspiracy before the Mayor's Court in Philadelphia. The tailors had really organized a union as we know it now, although it was then called a "Benevolent Society." This union compelled the employers (the "Masters") to sign a "bill of pieces" which would apply for a year, and the piece work rates of each garment type were listed. Extra features on the garment were priced as additional labor costs. The closed shop was enforced, and strikebreakers in times of trouble received short shrift. The initial cause of the 1827 strike was a dispute over piece rates. Because of the dispute, the workers in a shop who had voiced dissatisfaction were discharged. Soon their fellow workers in that shop stopped sewing, demanding the reinstatement of the discharged employes. The struck shop was picketed. There was violence if and when a strikebreaker appeared. The owners promptly charged the workers with conspiracy, complaining that due to hindrance by the pickets, the strikebreakers were unable to sew. At the trial, the Court seemingly held mainly with the journeymen tailors. The jury brought in a verdict of guilty on one count only, that of conspiracy to secure the reinstatement of the discharged men. This verdict was appealed and later the entire case was dropped. Parenthetically, strikers of later years in the clothing industry might have received excellent primary lessons from the Philadelphia journeymen tailors in ways to call a strike, picket a shop and browbeat strikebreakers.

Records show that in the New York market, a tailors' union existed as early as 1806, but the first recorded strike by that union was in 1819, called for the purpose of protesting the employment of women by the custom tailoring employers. In turn, by 1825, the women tailors in the city organized their own union and then asked for higher wages! Not until 1833 did the tailors demand a raise in pay. They were now organized as the Union Trade Society of Journeymen Tailors. The strikers wrote to tailors in other cities pleading that they stay away from New York and so avoid becoming strike-breakers. However, the number of available women in New York capable of replacing men at low wage scales soon broke the strike.

Following the regular pattern of future labor relations for decades to come, the same union that lost the New York strike in 1833, called another strike during the busy season in October 1835. The "Masters" caved in, granting higher pay, for they needed the garments during the seasonal rush. Then in January, 1836, a relatively slow month, the tables were turned. Now wages were reduced by the employers to the former level. The outraged workers left the shops again. Violence erupted with great bitterness displayed on both sides. The employers now organized a "Society of Master Tailors in the City of New York." They declared that the strikers were "subversive of the rights of individuals, detrimental to the public good, injurious to business, and restrictive of our freedom of action." This could be well considered the prototype for generations to come, of later name calling used in the industry during labor troubles. The strike continued however, and in June, 1836, the leaders were arrested, tried for combination and conspiracy, found guilty and fined. The strike collapsed. Shortly thereafter, the panic of 1837 caused another reduction of wages and the union disappeared entirely from the scene.

During 1835 and 1836, local tailor unions were formed in Cincinnati, St. Louis and other cities of the Midwest. However, with business conditions depressed in 1837, these small and weak organizations folded. Not until 1850 were New York tailors organized once more on an industry basis. Each nationality and each skill within the industry had already established its own union, such as the American tailors, the German tailors, the English tailors, the custom tailors, the cutters, etc. Each organization was supposedly interested solely in the particular ethnic or craft group that comprised its membership. Then, in 1850, all of these small unions united in order to ask for a general wage increase, and as might be expected, the demands were turned down. Thereupon, the workers walked out in July, 1850. The majority of employers granted the demands for higher wages, because July was a busy month, although one prominent manufacturer roared, "I'll be damned if I will surrender," which again indicated that the years may roll on, but the words never change. Obviously encouraged by the show of united strength, all of the separate tailors' unions in New York merged to form the General Trades Union in 1853. However, the severe panic of 1857 created widespread unemployment and the union disappeared, a victim of the depression.

Labor unrest continued to smolder in Philadelphia after the 1827 labor dispute. According to a contemporary observer, the tailors went on strike in 1844. After a few days out, the strikers won a wage increase. Three years later, a government report noted that there had been a long strike in Philadelphia, lasting from June to October of that year, and once more, wages were increased.

Wages see-sawed regularly, going up in the busy season and dropping in the slow months. Unions were strong when there were orders and disappeared when production was slack. The actual condition of the workers, though, showed no real improvement, and dissatisfaction was rife throughout all clothing markets.

Before 1891, whatever local tailor unions did exist from time to time, were affiliated with the Knights of Labor, a catch-all national labor federation which had been founded in 1869 by a Philadelphia clothing cutter named Uriah Stephens. As for practical results of such early unions, in his study of the clothing industry, Professor Pope concluded that the actual "influence of the unions upon conditions in the industry was practically nil up to 1890." Nevertheless, times were ripe for a national organizing effort by clothing workers. In 1891, they succeeded in finally forming a union that had the superficial promise of accomplishing their long sought aims.

Chapter 6

The National Association of Clothiers (NAC)

Industry Conditions in the 1890's

The panic of 1893, as might be expected, was a period of liquidation. Many manufacturers went bankrupt. Those who feared to lose their already depleted capital retired. Some went into banking, a favorite field for former clothing men, or else sought to enter another industry. It was a time when many manufacturers felt that the men's clothing industry had no future, was doomed to permanent stagnation and poor profits. It was no place for a man of enterprise and ambition. The feeling that "all was lost" was to occur regularly whenever economic conditions turned sour in the industry. "There were better ways to make a living," was the cry that persisted in decades to come.

Undoubtedly conditions were very bad for a time. In the years immediately following the panic, men's suits were offered at $5.50, $6.00 and $6.50 each. The smaller firms with low overhead, worked on a minimal profit, thus forcing the larger houses to compete and for some years to suffer losses. By 1898 though, with McKinley as President and a war with Spain stimulating the economy, there was a reversal in sentiment throughout the industry.

Now prices rose, so that suits were offered at $10. Such high prices created a sensation in the industry. Style was promoted and stressed rather than price. Better fabrics were used and hand tailoring operations were introduced as an added feature in the better garments. With business improving, many new firms went into business, bringing new ideas of merchandising and new model changes. By 1900, the clothing industry was on solid ground once more. The deep pessimism which prevailed in the early 1890's suddenly had changed to exuberant optimism. As usual, the industry showed its resiliency, bouncing back stronger than ever after each setback.

Formation of the Association

In 1884 the first national organization of clothing manufacturers was formed. It was called the National Clothiers Association of the United States and was primarily interested in retail credit problems. Due to evident internal dissension, however, it had merely one year of life. No further efforts were made to form a national association until twelve years later.

Today there are few, if any, who remember the powerful National Association of Clothiers (NAC), founded in 1897, an association of clothing manufacturers that lasted approximately a quarter of a century. This organization had a profound influence in establishing policies and precedents that determined industry trends during that period. Practically every important clothing manufacturer in the United States was a member. Every clothing market of any size was represented at the annual conventions which were very social at times, although business affairs were of course paramount. The activities of the NAC during its heyday centered around such matters as retail credits, retail relations, mill relations, and other subjects of usual industry concern. Regularly, the clothing manufacturers encountered difficulty as the federal or state governments enacted new laws, or issued new regulations affecting the production of clothing. In the later years of the organization, the rising power of labor was of increasing concern.

In many of the clothing markets there had been local associations of manufacturers for some years. According to the Rochester historian, McKelvey, in 1883 the manufacturers in Rochester formed a Clothiers Association in order to "standardize their procedures and improve the quality of the product." However, this Clothiers' Association had been ineffective in dealing with the market labor problems which had become acute by 1890. Therefore, the Rochester Clothiers Exchange was organized to replace the former association. Henry Michaels of Michaels, Stern & Co., became its first president, and Sol Wile, a lawyer, was elected secretary. The Exchange, as might be expected, opposed unionization by the clothing local of the Knights of Labor. It also dealt with typical industry matters such as selling practices, retail credit and retail relations. Wile was an enterprising secretary, for he was not only a prime force in organizing the National Association of Clothiers, but in 1898 he sent a letter to 4,500 retailers, inviting them to a style show which was to be held in Rochester that spring, promising to pay half of the round trip fare. That at least, was one retailer "fringe benefit" that did not take hold, probably to the relief of manufacturers in other markets.

Another prominent local organization was the Clothiers Association of New York, which had been organized in 1887. The most important reason for its founding was the need for securing reliable and detailed information on retail credit and adequate protection of the manufacturers against store failures. While there were only scattered reports available about other market organizations, we know that by 1897 there was an association of clothing firms in Baltimore, and in the trade press, news items disclosed that there were also local clothing associations in Chicago, Philadelphia and Boston.

By the end of the 19th century, the manufacturers had come to realize once more that a national association of clothing manufacturers was a necessity, just as labor had recognized the need for a national labor union. There were mounting national problems such as the tariff, and congressional investigations affecting the industry were frequent. It was also evident to the average manufacturer that retail credits and control of bankruptcies could best be handled by a national organization. Then, in the January 20, 1897 issue of the *Clothiers and Haberdashers Weekly,* under the prominent headline of "EXTRA," the industry read the following:

ORGANIZED

THE MANUFACTURING CLOTHIERS OF THE
COUNTRY FORM AN ASSOCIATION.

An Earnest and Businesslike Convention—
Officers Chosen and Rules Adopted—
The Two Days' Session Followed by a
Banquet at the Savoy Hotel.

The business sessions were held in the Broadway Central Hotel, New York City, and Mr. Samuel Rosenthal of Strouse Bros., Baltimore, as the permanent chairman, stressed the necessity of a national organization. He then mentioned some of the industry problems:

> . . . The greatest evils, according to Mr. Rosenthal, are long credits, excessive dating and cancellations of orders. The last named abuse inflicts untold hardship upon both the clothing houses and their salesmen who take the orders. If the sellers should adopt a determined attitude upon this question, the buyers would be taught a needed lesson . . .

At this initial national meeting there were delegates present from New York, Rochester, Baltimore, Cincinnati, Syracuse, Boston, Chicago and Philadelphia. Although St. Louis, Milwaukee and Buffalo sent no delegates, they authorized others to represent them. There were representatives present from Alfred Benjamin and Co., David Marks & Sons, S. J. Nathan & Son and Company all of New York; Michaels, Stern & Company, Stein-Bloch Co., Wile & Brickner, all of Rochester; Strouse and Bros., L. Greif & Bro., Schloss

Bros. & Co., Isaac Hamburger & Sons, all of Baltimore; Mayer, Scheuer & Co., Bloom, Cohen & Co., M. & L. S. Fecheimer & Co., all of Cincinnati; Peavy & Bros., Burton, Mansfield & Co., all of Boston; Kuhn, Nathan and Fischer of Chicago; Blumenthal Bros., and Fleisher Bros., of Philadelphia. In all, there were delegates from thirty companies present. Out of this number, only four concerns have remained in business, under their name or a merged name.

Throughout the two day convention, the New York delegates steadily reiterated that their purpose in favoring a national association was "credits and the protection of creditors against failures." They were adamant that relations between employers and employees "should be left to the discretion of the local associations." The dreaded topic of labor was not to be discussed at any meeting, and the New York position received majority approval. For some years to come, the labor problem, even though it was in the minds of many at all times, might not be placed on the agenda at a convention. With that understanding, the National Association of Clothiers, a federation of the important local markets was formed, and it was to become the official industry spokesman for the next twenty-five years.

Incidentally, as though highlighting the cause for worry about retail credits and failures at the time, in the very same issue of the *Clothiers' & Haberdashers' Weekly* announcing the formation of the national organization, these two news reports were to be found:

J. E. RICHDALE'S SUICIDE

CLEVELAND, OHIO, Jan. 20—J. E. Richdale, clothier, of Kent, Ohio, committed suicide this morning by cutting his throat. The deed was committed while he was in bed, and he died at 5 o'clock. He had inflicted upon himself sixteen wounds.

FAILURE IN COLORADO

MAX BLOOSTON ASSIGNS TO A. REYNOLDS
Liabilities, $10,000

VICTOR, COL., Jan. 20—Max Blooston, clothier and haberdasher, assigned last week to A. Reynolds, his principal creditor, who held a mortgage for $6,000 on his stock of goods.

The total liabilities are estimated at $10,000 and the assets at $14,000.

The Association Conventions

There were annual conventions of the national association, and during the years of 1898, 1899 and 1900, there were news items of meetings held in Philadelphia, Baltimore and Rochester. The first really detailed report of the organization's activities was a lengthy news article about the New York meeting held in February, 1901. The annual banquet, the climax of the convention, was a black tie gala affair held in Sherrys. The importance of the dinner could be judged by the presence of the Governors of New York and Maryland, as well as prominent city officials. The interesting and beguiling program for the evening, as reported by the conscientious *Clothiers' & Haberdashers' Weekly*, listed ten toasts. The speech that followed each toast was printed in its entirety. So the guests had opportunities to drink to:

"Our Association"
"The Wholesale and Retail Clothing Industry"
"The State of New York"
"The State of Maryland"
"The City of New York"
"The State Senate"
"Ideal Politics"
"Organization"
"The New York Trade Center"
"The Relation of Government and Politics to Business"

After each toast, a lengthy speech followed, cluttered up by gaudy flowers of classic literature, sonorous cliches, and windy turns of phrase. The opening remarks of Marcus M. Marks are cited as an example of the oratory inflicted that evening. Said Marks, "Tonight we emerge from our retirement because we feel it is time we send our great message to the business world. We have a pure jewel of wonderful brilliancy, which will, we trust, serve to light our brothers in other trades, on their business paths . . ." etc., etc. Incidentally, his message was simply an announcement that he thought factories should move to the suburbs and so relieve tenement overcrowding.

Undoubtedly, a good time was had by all. It is questionable, though, whether such a bout of drinking and speechmaking could be endured by the clothing manufacturers of today. In truth, the present breed now seems to have difficulty listening to an eloquent discourse for a mere fifteen minutes duration. There must have been lusty clothing men in those days! Or else they were deaf, or perhaps the toasts lulled them into a euphoria of "let 'em talk." In the early 1900's, the manufacturers were not interested in "taking a message" away from the banquet table, a prevalent flaw in current dinner arrangements of today. Then, the guests merely took away a full load of liquor, an earful of speeches and the latest parodies pointing up the quirks in our industry. It was fun, for at this dinner they sang verses such as:

"THE PSALM OF THE CLOTHIER"
(*Melody, "Auld Lang Syne"*)

Not clothiers all, who with us sit,
Our jovial feast to share,
Still brothers all, since fate decrees
That each one clothes must wear.
And though each wears a sober coat
Of cut that suits him best,
"'Tis not the coat that makes the man",
It's trousers and the vest.

No sweat shops mark our garments brands,
The laws we strive to keep,
If man is "brother to the ox",
We're "cousins to the sheep".

Our trials, disappointments, too,
We try to bear with grace,
And though styles change and goods come back,
Still wear a pleasant face.
And though our goods we sometimes get
When six long months have sped,
And get the cash a twelvemonth late,
We smile and go ahead.

We rise superior to each flout
Of fickle fortune's hand,
With shoulder firm to shoulder pressed,
United still we stand.

But despite all efforts to hear not and see not, labor problems were coming to the forefront in many of the clothing markets. Therefore, the subject was finally brought out in the open at the following year's convention in Baltimore. It was generally agreed that if and when labor troubles arose, the need for mediation, conciliation and arbitration were useful procedures. Still, the core of labor troubles, unions and strikes, was taboo and not to be discussed. In preference, the delegates reverted to the familiar subjects of retail returns, retail cancellations and retail failures. During one session, the Rochester market reported that its cancellations were seven and one-half per cent of orders taken, and returns were three and one-half per cent of shipments. The New York market followed by reporting that its cancellations were higher, being eight and one-half per cent of orders taken, and returns were also higher, for they were five and one-half per cent of shipments. In view of such statistics, it was not to be wondered that retail relations were matters of prime concern.

The National Labor Bureau

But by 1903, the annual convention, which was then held in Chicago, could no longer ignore the labor situation on a national level. There had been a serious strike in Rochester led by the United Garment Workers of America. Although the union was beaten, the manufacturers had suffered a substantial loss of production and deliveries to stores were delayed for many weeks. Thereupon, a resolution was unanimously passed which stated in part:

> . . . Resolved, that this convention recommend to the local association of each city that it endeavor to establish a labor bureau for consideration of any action upon labor questions affecting the clothing manufacturers of that city.
>
> Membership in such labor bureau shall be voluntary and all manufacturers of clothing shall be eligible thereto, subject to reasonable regulations as to character and responsibility.
>
> The board of directors or executive committee of such labor bureau shall have authority to pass upon all differences between labor organizations

and members, and all members of such labor bureau shall pledge themselves to abide by the unanimous decision of such board or executive committee.

The said labor bureau of such city shall be the integral parts of a national labor bureau, to be known as the "National Labor Bureau of Clothing Manufacturers of America . . .

The formation of this National Labor Bureau was to profoundly affect labor relations in our industry for many years to come. Membership in the local labor bureau was voluntary. Legally, the National Bureau was to be a separate organization not affiliated with the already established National Association of Clothiers. Actually, the conventions of both were held simultaneously, for they were spiritually and in practice, one and the same group. In 1904, at the convention held in Philadelphia, the constitution of the National Labor Bureau was formally adopted, the preamble of which read in part as follows:

. . . CONSTITUTION OF A PROPOSED NATIONAL LABOR BUREAU OF CLOTHING MANUFACTURERS

PREAMBLE

The clothing manufacturers of the United States, desiring to organize a Labor Bureau for the purpose of improving the conditions of manufacture, do declare the following principles as the basis and aim of their organization:

First. The closed shop is an un-American institution. The right of every man to sell his labor as he sees fit, and the freedom of every employer to hire such labor, are given by the laws of the land, and may not be affected by affiliations or non-affiliation with any organization whatever . . .

The Bureau Wars on Labor

This announcement of an open shop policy was a declaration of war against organized labor as represented by the UGWA. At the annual convention held in New York the following year, it was reported by the National Labor Bureau that the New York manufacturers had posted notices in their factories informing the workers they would pursue, hereafter, an open shop policy. A strike of six weeks followed. The union lost the strike. Henceforth, the New York market, for all practical purposes, was largely an open shop city until the great strike of 1913.

The comprehensive report of the New York Labor Bureau to the national body was of utmost historic interest in showing the attitude of management towards labor in the early 1900's:

> . . . The first market to take affirmative action after the organization of the association was New York, where the declaration of principles was printed and posted in shops of its members.
>
> The labor organization of its employees, known as the United Garment Workers of America, affiliated with the American Federation of Labor, unwisely and without justification, claimed to consider this action as a challenge to and an attack upon unionism, and ordered a strike in the shops of all the members of the New York association. The American Federation of Labor, through its president, sought conferences and arbitration through this national association.
>
> Your president and executive committee, however, recognized that there could be no compromise of the position taken by the New York association in favor of the "open shop;" that it was essential that the attempts of the union to force upon members the closed or union shop should be finally and decisively overthrown, and that the national association should not be involved in a contest which for the time being was directed against the New York market alone, and which it was to the interest of the national organization should be confined to that market until terminated.
>
> The New York association established a labor bureau and set to work with energy and promptness to replace its striking employees. It ignored the union, and throughout the strike took no action and issued no statement open to criticism as tending to irritate the former employees of its members of their union organization . . .

A strike had likewise been called in Chicago when the principle of the open shop had been announced, and this strike was also lost.

Mr. Sol Wile, the Rochester lawyer and secretary of that local market association, had been appointed National Commissioner of the Bureau. Because of his activity throughout the industry, within a year he was able to report that there were local labor bureaus in Chicago, Baltimore, New York, Philadelphia, Rochester, Cincinnati and St. Louis. One of the functions of the local labor bureau was to set up an employment office for the clothing workers of the market. This was to be a clearing house for applicants seeking jobs in the area. While it was perhaps an efficient employment office for "situations wanted" or "help wanted" in each market, it was also possible and even probable, that such a bureau could at times become an organ for blacklisting workers who had been, or currently were, out of favor with any member of the bureau. We do know that the bureau was engaged in strikebreaking, for in 1910, the Secretary of the National Labor Bureau reported the following incident at the Baltimore convention:

> . . . Recently, in the city of St. Louis, a clothing manufacturer became involved in industrial strife. Not then a member of either the local or National Association, they sought a conference of the commissioner. They were advised to place their business and factory upon the open shop basis and become members of the local association, and were told that the National Association would gladly lend them assistance. This they did.
>
> Under the direction of the National President, the Chicago Association and its bureaus were placed at their disposal and considerable aid was given them by supplying work people and in other material ways, tending much toward bringing the difficulties to a conclusion. Representatives of this establishment came to Chicago a number of times for conferences with the commissioner, and he visited St. Louis at their request. This is an illustration of the result of cooperation through the National Association . . .

Other Association Activities

But while labor problems were now in the forefront, retail relations were still of paramount importance, for we read of a pamphlet on cancellations prepared by the association which was sent to 18,000 stores. This pamphlet warned the retailers that the manufacturers would not accept unjustified cancellations. If a retailer was condemned by the association for returning goods unfairly, he was to be notified that he had better mend his practices, or else association members would no longer sell him. The secretary of the National Association proudly reported that 64 retailers had already been so warned. What happened to these 64 delinquents was not disclosed, but the hope was expressed that it might have some effect for the time being. Judging from reports in subsequent years, the impact of the pamphlet and other threats were short lived, for we continue to read of "unfair retailers," "unjust returns" and "cancellations of orders" without any reduction of vehemence at later conventions.

But all was not work and no play at these annual conventions. The Clothiers Association of New York acted as a bountiful host to the visiting delegates of the national convention dinner on April 5, 1905, which was held at Delmonicos. As usual, it was quite a party. William Goldman of Cohen, Goldman & Co., was chairman of the arrangements committee. The spirit of the evening can be best described by reading some of the so-called resolutions presented for adoption at the affair as printed on their menu card:

. . . THE COMMITTEE ON RESOLUTIONS

begs to report as follows:

RESOLVED: that when one of our members sells a customer a bill of $5,000 and makes him an allowance of $6,000 for advertising expense, he should retire from the clothing trade and go into the advertising business and give away clothing.

RESOLVED: that instead of chloroforming men over 60 years of age, Dr. Osler would confer a greater blessing to mankind if he would find the germ of cancellitis and, when found, chloroform the canceller irrespective of age.

RESOLVED: that our members organize a Universal Express Company and charge for outgoing packages four times as much as for incoming packages so that we can at least be sure of a profit as Clothing Manufacturers . . .

At the conclusion of the evening, the following parody was sung during the song fest:

Tune: Auld Lang Syne

. . . With cloth one twenty-five a yard
And linings seventeen,
When fabrics run in stripes and plaids,
With just a tinge of green.
When strikes are apt to happen, and
Put business "on the bum",
Who'll tell me quickly just how wide
Will next year's trousers come? . . .

Oh - Oh - Oh -

Mill Relations

The relationship between manufacturers and mills was an uneasy one for many years. The largest company, the American Woolen Company, was arrogant and had an obvious contempt for the industry. At the Boston Convention in 1907, Marcus M. Marks, the national President, reported that a committee of clothing manufacturers had asked President Wood of the American Woolen Company to meet with them on a matter of complaints against mill practices (details were not given). Woods refused to do so. The delegates expressed indignation and their resentment was obvious, with threats openly made that the mill will lose good will. It had become a matter of history that the American Woolen Company seldom changed its tactics, for during the period of World War II, some forty years later, the attitude of this mill toward the clothing industry followed in spirit the 1907 policy initiated by Wood of "damn the customers." As told in a later chapter, such a consistent point of view was properly rewarded by the disappearance of the mill, once manufacturers had an opportunity to purchase freely from other sources.

Since the woolen and worsted industry as a whole (apart from the American) had expressed the pious hope for better relations in 1908, a Committee of Fourteen was appointed, seven from each side, to cooperate in establishing "satisfactory relations between the two trades." In 1967, using approximately the same phraseology, the Clothing Manufacturers Association of the U.S.A., voted at a directors meeting to do just that thing. During the interval of 59 years, periodically and regularly, as detailed in the latter portions of this volume, there were frequent recurrences to "do something about the mills." Joint conferences were held which led to the soothing words by both parties to "elevate the industry," "we must establish cooperation," and recently, introducing modern jargon, "we must communicate better." Actually, as of 1967, although both sides met for the purpose of "cooperation" at such a recent date, insofar as true cooperation is concerned, conditions show minor change since 1908.

Jeremiah G. Hickey as Toastmaster

One of the outstanding toastmasters at these annual banquets was Jeremiah G. Hickey of Hickey-Freeman Co., a most lovable as well as an extremely able businessman. He lived to a fine old age, so that several generations of younger men knew him well, revered him for his knowledge, and enjoyed his friendship. It was at the 1908 banquet that Hickey led the guests in singing the following:

To the tune of
"IN THE GOOD OLD SUMMER TIME"

In the spring and summer line
Of nineteen hundred and nine,
We got our orders early
And we shipped our goods on time.
Of plaids and checks . . . in new effects,
In worsteds and cashmeres fine,
We'll soon begin to hustle in
Our fall and winter line . . .

followed by—

"WAITING AT THE CHURCH"

There I was waiting at the store
Waiting at the store . . . looking out the door,
There I stood from one till after four,
Oh, how it did excite me!
All at once I got a note instead,
I opened it and read,
And this is what he said,
"I can't get away to buy your goods today,
Because your line don't suit me".

At this convention, it might be said that hope springs eternal, for when "retail labels" was on the agenda, a motion was passed as follows:

. . . Resolved by the National Association of Clothiers in a convention assembled on March 3, 1908, that starting with the fall season of 1908, all customers' labels, hangers, customers' size tickets, sleeve tickets and special buttons *shall be furnished by the customer at his own expense.* That the sewing on of such labels, tickets and buttons shall be charged to and collected from the customer at a uniform rate to be determined and made known by the National Board of Directors . . .

This resulted in an unusually lengthy and heated discussion. Max Friedman of J. Friedman & Co., was appointed chairman of the committee to implement this resolution. Some five decades later, when manufacturers were now paying for the labels themselves, the problem of label costs was still a "hot" subject. Representatives of J. Friedman & Co., at a meeting of the Clothing Manufacturers Association were still vehement about the excessive expense of providing labels to retailers, and directors were still appointing a committee to study the subject. Obviously, there were times when solutions to industry problems moved somewhat slowly.

The 1911 Convention and Later

The Atlantic City Convention held June 5–6, 1911, was strictly business. The songs, the many toasts, and the accompanying speeches were eliminated. The Labor Bureau was now fighting hard for the open shop. The manufacturers had received a report about the great strike taking place in Chicago, where the workers had requested union recognition and the closed shop. Needless to say, the delegates were bitterly opposed to the demands of the union.

At the same time, there were cordial wishes expressed for a new Retail Clothiers Association, which was to be formed, now known as the Menswear Retailers of America. The hope (to be repeated many times in the future) that this would lead to better cooperation between manufacturer and retailer was duly voiced and recorded in the minutes.

It was at this 1911 convention that a prominent manufacturer from Baltimore, a Mr. Samuel E. Reinhard, prepared a paper on fabric weights which makes interesting as well as amusing reading today. He said in part:

. . . Fall weights should never be taken or accepted by any of the clothing manufacturers that are under 16 ounces in weight. The idea of buying goods, and the mill manufacturer forcing on us goods that only in weight are 12, 13, 14 and 15 ounces for fall or winter use is wrong.

To illustrate this fact, I lost a bill this season. The customer was in a large town and here is what he said: "Mr. Reinhard, I will positively not buy goods of this light weight fabric; it is a shame to present such weights to a retail merchant; why the light weights I have carried over weigh 11 and 12 ounces. I might as well run off my light weight stock for my spring usages . . .

By 1913, in some markets, the labor problem had once more reached crisis proportions. The President reported that the National Labor Bureau was informed by the local markets that they would handle their labor matters individually. They definitely did not want the National Labor Bureau to interfere. This was a serious development, indicating that the labor situation was becoming acute in certain clothing centers. There was no doubt now that the bureau had lost the confidence of many members, for it had been too inflexible in its opposition towards unions. This was the first symptom of a portending crackup in the anti-union front by the association.

With the outbreak of war in 1914, conditions changed radically. Labor was now becoming unionized. Piece goods were difficult to obtain. Retailers were desperately anxious to buy. Gradually, the industry was trying to face up to new conditions and shed its former prejudices. Although the manufacturers could not foresee the future, we know now that the industry was on the verge of a fundamental change due to the war and its after effects. Present methods of merchandising and selling would soon become obsolete. For a time, the low priced manufacturing retailers would loom as an awesome threat. A new union was to make rapid progress organizing the clothing factories within a year. The demands of war would shortly bring orders for thousands of uniforms, government restrictions and wild inflation. Unknown to itself, the clothing industry was facing a most uncertain future.

Chapter 7

The Two Unions

A National Union Is Formed

With the increased use of the sewing machine, the inside shops gradually grew in relative importance within the industry. Now manufacturers were able to sell to the jobbers and even to retailers on a national basis to a greater extent. Because widespread distribution was feasible, there was growing inter-market competition between the manufacturers located in the numerous clothing centers of production. Wages could not be increased readily in any one clothing market without seriously handicapping the local firms whose costs had now become greater than the costs of their competitors in the other markets. If labor wanted higher wages in any one area, and wanted these manufacturers to pay such increased wages without losing their competitive position, a national union of tailors was a necessity. Such a union, it was reasoned, could then impose a national scale of wages. This would eliminate the possibility of any one market underselling the other markets due to lower labor costs. As a consequence, repeated efforts to form a national union were inevitable after the Civil War.

By 1865, political conditions returned to normal once more, and the economy showed clear signs of prosperous growth. Thereupon, local union representatives from seven cities (New York, Washington, Worcester, Troy, Cincinnati, Louisville and Philadelphia) met in the latter city in August, 1865, for the purpose of organizing a national tailors union. This industrywide labor organization called the "Journeymen Tailors National Trade Union," held annual conventions until 1872 when it expired quietly. Another national union had been organized in 1871, perhaps to succeed the organization about to fold shortly. This new union lasted only until 1877 when it also disappeared. Between the years of 1877 and 1883 there was no national tailors organization, although there were a number of local unions in the clothing markets that periodically called strikes and sought higher wages. On the whole, though, they had little economic strength and made no effective impact on the industry.

At this time, there was a sharp division within the ranks of the clothing workers, for the highly skilled custom tailors would not accept as equals the semi-skilled shop operators. The organization of a true national union of all clothing workers was therefore stymied. Considering themselves apart from the others in the industry, the custom tailors organized the Journeymen Tailors' National Union in August, 1883. It still functions today as a branch of the Amalgamated Clothing Workers of America (ACWA). The influence of the Journeymen Tailors organization was relatively minor at the time, for it was formed purely as a craft union, was conservative in its ideology, and in practice barred factory operators who were the overwhelming majority of clothing workers. Such a union could not attract the shop operators even had it desired to do so, since the recently arrived immigrants were much more radical in their economic philosophy and more aggressive in labor policy. Many of the factory workers had become socialists. They favored an industrial union that would accept as members all employed in the industry regardless of craft. Hence, the Journeymen Tailors' National

Union had little appeal for the sewing machine operators. But the desire, and even the need for an all inclusive national clothing union persisted throughout the years. Then, in 1886, the clothing workers of New York City, formerly affiliated with the Knights of Labor, organized the Tailors' National Protective Union which lasted until 1891, when the first truly national clothing union was organized, the United Garment Workers of America (UGWA).

The original impetus for the national organization came from the Jewish workers in New York. They had become socialists as a result of their rapid disillusionment of a dream that the streets of the new world were "paved with gold." The low wages, the long hours and the unsanitary working conditions created extreme unrest among the New York clothing workers. As a result, strikes were periodic, occurring each busy season. Following the industry practice, wage increases were won in the busy months, but regularly reduced in the dull months. At this time, the United Hebrew Trades, an organization formed by East Side radicals to encourage unionization of workers in all industries, actively promoted the idea of a national clothing workers trade union. All employed in the industry, regardless of craft, were to be members. The clothing workers readily agreed that the time was now ripe for the formation of a national union. Accordingly, in April, 1891, with delegates from all of the important clothing markets present, the United Garment Workers of America was formed. Unfortunately, the seeds of dissension were planted at the very inception of the organization, for the elected national officers were American born and conservative in philosophy and action. In time, they were to be more interested in selling union labels than in improving the lot of the members. In opposition, the majority of the membership was radical in its point of view, favoring aggressive action against the employers and demanding that a dynamic organizing policy be carried out at all times. With the national officers (the Americans) entrenched in power, and a restless and dissatisfied membership (the foreigners) seeking power, it was inevitable that conflict would ensue, resulting in an eventual schism within the organization.

Early Disunity in UGWA

The newly organized United Garment Workers of America (UGWA), as already noted, was composed of two clearly disparate elements. The east European Jews, who sparked the formation of the union favored the ideology then prevalent on the East Side. On the other hand, the national officers of the union, the Americans who spoke English fluently, followed the general labor policy of the already conservative American Federation of Labor. The radical majority of the union membership (estimated to be at least 60 per cent of the total) was completely at odds with those in power.

It was to be expected, in the nature of the circumstances, that the national officers, in seeking to insure steady organization income, would evolve the idea of selling labels to those manufacturers who considered the union label as an added sales inducement for their product. Regular clothing manufacturers who were already organized, saw no reason for purchasing this label because consumers showed little interest in any insignia indicating that the suit was union made. As the UGWA was authorized by the A.F. of L. to seek membership not only within the clothing industry, but in the overall and shirt trades as well, the national officers found greater potential opportunities in selling labels to the latter two trades. The purchasers of overalls and work shirts were, most likely, workmen and the union label on these garments was thought to enhance sales appeal.

It is very likely that another reason why the national union concentrated its organizing efforts among the overall and shirt trades was the fact that the factories producing such garments were frequently located in the Midwest where the operators were usually of native American stock. Any increase in such membership would strengthen the hands of the American national officials in their power struggle with the foreigner clothing locals. As it happened, the Midwest organizing campaign was not too successful. Therefore, the clothing workers remained as the dominant majority of the membership.

A matter of intense frustration to the clothing locals was the relative neglect of unionizing their branch of the industry. There was no letup in their seething anger at this lackadaisical policy. Breakaway unions were formed by some unhappy workers in New York City as early as 1893, but they made no headway. Even though such rebel locals folded quickly, the bitterness that had originally caused insurgency did not abate. Still, if the union was to attain any financial stability, it was necessary to acquire a steady income. This was particularly important to the national office if the membership rolls were to be restricted by a calculated discouragement in the growth of the clothing locals. Therefore, as very practical men who had a product to sell, they sought supplemental income which would not be dependent upon dues from members. This would release the national office from dependence upon membership good will. As the product to sell was the union label, the UGWA engaged in an extensive and expensive campaign among consumers, using tactics which would be currently characterized in the advertising field as the hard sell. The circular on the following page is typical of the Union's somewhat sensational method of appeal.

Such circularizing and advertising were extremely distasteful to the radical clothing locals. It was severely criticized by them at their meetings as a waste of money which could be used to better purpose for organizing the non-union clothing workers.

Early Wage Negotiations

Totally inexperienced in labor-management relations, there was little finesse in dealing with the bosses during the 1890's when wage negotiations took place. It was simply a matter of handing a "take it or leave it" order to the manufacturers and their contractors. The printed union demand for a contract can hardly be called diplomatic, or even tactful under any circumstances, nor was it intended as such at the time.

When the contract was formally agreed upon, after mutual recriminations of the most violent sort, with personal abuse substituting for reason, the actual terms were relatively concise. The contract detailed hours of work, method of paying wages weekly,

III. Agreement between a manufacturer and District Council No. 1, United Garment Workers of America.

THIS AGREEMENT made and entered into this — day of ——— 1902, by and between ————— party of the first part, and District Council No. 1 United Garment Workers of America a voluntary association, party of the second part.

Witnesseth as follows:—

That in consideration of One (1) Dollar lawful money of the United States of America each party to the other in hand paid, and in consideration of their promises mutually interchanged, and of these presents, it is hereby mutually agreed by and between the parties hereto:

I. That all garments of any kind and description manufactured by them are to be made by persons affiliated with the party of the second part and no others, and that all the contractors doing work for said party of the first part shall employ only members in good standing of the party of the second part, and the following conditions shall be observed in all shops conducted by the said contractors to-wit:

A. The hours of work in any one week shall not exceed 56.

B. The wages of the employees to be paid on the last working day of each week.

C. The rate of wages shall be according to the schedules hereto attached, and made part of this agreement.

II. The party of the first part is to withdraw any work from any contractor, not observing the conditions and covenants hereinbefore set forth, and also to withhold any and all work from them.

III. The party of the first part hereby undertakes and guarantees to become liable and to pay any and all wages that may be due the employees of the contractor whom they employ on such work as performed on garments of the party of the first part. Said guarantee to be limited to one week's wages, providing the party of the first part is notified of any default of such contractor on the day following the ending of the week's work.

IV. The party of the second part is to furnish any and all help that they may have on their Application Books to the contractor employed by the party of the first part as well as to the party of the first part directly. Such furnishing of help to be without any compensation to the party of the second part.

This agreement is to be binding upon the parties hereto for the period of one (1) year from date hereof.

In witness whereof the parties hereto have set their hands and seals the day and year first above written.

(L. S.)

District Council No. 1
United Garment Workers of America.
By
Sec'y (L. S.)

I. Communication sent with a view to prevent the usual strike.

District Council No. 1 of the United Garment Workers of America A. F. of L.

W. Chuck, Secretary

Office
99 Norfolk St

New York, July 7th 1902

GENTLEMEN:—

Our Unions are now ready with their demands for the coming year, and should you desire to comply with same, before any action is taken, we would like you notify us, on or before July 15th, 1902.

Respectfully yours,
W. Chuck, Sec'y
District Council No. 1.

P. S.—Our representative will be present at Room 116, Bible House Building, 8th Street, to furnish you with all the necessary information.

II. Weekly Wage Prices.

CHILDREN JACKET MAKERS—SCALE OF PRICES—UNIONS LOCAL 10 & 155—UNITED GARMENT WORKERS OF AMERICA
[1902]

Baisted Work

Operators, Seventeen (17) Dollars per week and upwards
Baisters, Sixteen (16) Dollars per week and upwards
Baisters Helpers, Twelve (12) Dollars per week and upwards
Fitters, Sixteen (16) Dollars per week and upwards
Lining Makers, Thirteen (13) Dollars per week and upwards
Bushlers, Thirteen (13) Dollars per week and upwards
Pressers, Fourteen (14) Dollars per week and upwards
Assistant Pressers, Eleven (11) Dollars per week and upwards
Under Pressers, Eleven (11) Dollars per week and upwards

Unbaisted Work

Operators, Seventeen (17) Dollars per week and upwards
Pocket Tackers, Fourteen (14) Dollars per week and upwards
Lining Makers Eleven (11) Dollars per week and upwards
Coat Stitchers, Thirteen (13) Dollars per week and upwards
Trimming Makers, Eleven (11) Dollars per week and upwards
Sleeve Makers, Eight (8) Dollars per week and upwards
Pressers, Fourteen (14) Dollars per week and upwards
Assistant Pressers, Eleven (11) Dollars per week and upwards
Under Pressers, Eleven (11) Dollars per week and upwards

Representative Circulars Sent Out by Trade Unions to Arouse Public Opinion.

TO THE PUBLIC.

Attention,

What assurance have you that the ready-made garments you wear were not made in disease-infected tenement house sweat shops, and that you are not liable to be stricken with disease through the germs which lurk in such goods?

It is well-known that a large proportion of clothing is still made under such conditions. Repeated exposures have been made in the daily papers of the extent to which clothing is manufactured in prison under unhealthy conditions and for the benefit of private contractors to the detriment of free labor.

The organized garment workers have issued an official label to be attached to Clothing, Cloaks, Shirts and Overalls, as a guarantee of being made by fair labor in clean shops.

Reduced Size.

Fac-simile [ISSUED BY AUTHORITY — UNITED — AMERICA — UNION MADE — 7041144] of Label.

By giving your preference for goods so labeled you will be protecting your own health and encouraging a more humane system of labor.

The leading labor and reform organizations of the United States and Canada have endorsed this label and a number of large manufacturers in various cities have already adopted it.

Demand this Label from the Retailer.
Don't Wait for others to Act First.
Use your Patronage for a Good Cause.

N. B.—You will find this linen label attached by the machine stitching to the inside of the breast pocket of the coat, the inside of the buckle strap of the vest and on the lining waist band of the pants. On overalls the labels are printed on Gummed Paper and are Consecutively Numbered.

rate of wages, plus the proviso that called for a closed union shop.

In some instances wages were listed in the contract while at other times, the union merely printed the minimum wages which ought to be paid, supposedly handing over the list to the manufacturers. It was reported at the time that the true minimum in most categories was considerably less than the printed schedule which represented merely a forlorn hope of "what it should be, not what it really is." Even the approved wage list revealed an extremely low hourly level, for the weekly wages that were listed were based upon a 56-hour week.

An Apathetic Union

Shortly after its formation, the UGWA made some inroads in the Rochester market with the toleration of the manufacturers, who felt that the new union would perhaps be more reasonable than the Knights of Labor local. The Knights were under a cloud because their officers had been indicted recently for extortion from the manufacturers. Unhappy about factory conditions, and beginning to feel strong economically, the newly organized UGWA locals called a strike in 1895. The union requested prompt payment of wages by the contractors and no arbitrary reduction of the wage scale by manufacturers. The union also tried the strike tactic of calling for a boycott of Rochester-made clothing by the A.F. of L. unions, but the boycott failed to materialize. Finally, a compromise settlement was agreed upon with the assurance of a 55-hour week thereafter, and a promise that weekly wages would be paid promptly by contractors. The union was now discredited as a bargaining agent, because in the opinion of the membership this was a disastrous settlement. So the UGWA disappeared from the Rochester market for a time. With no active labor body in the city to oppose them, the employers promptly repudiated the wage agreement, announcing that as of January, 1896, the work week would be increased to 58 hours, and that there would be wage cuts ranging from 10 per cent to 25 per cent, effective immediately. There was no overt reaction on the part of the disheartened workers. Conditions in the shops did not appreciably improve insofar as sanitation and safety standards were concerned. In 1911, some sixteen years later, during the New York State Senate investigation of Rochester factory conditions, it was found that many clothing plants, particularly the smaller ones, were still dirty and unsanitary, that the wages paid were still low, and the hours worked were still excessively long.

Rochester though, was not the sole offender by any means. Clothing workers throughout the country were suffering from irregular employment, long hours and employment in poorly lit and badly ventilated shops. According to the U.S. Commissioner of Labor in his report on men's clothing, dated August 8, 1910, he noted that as late as that very year the per cent of employes earning less than $5.00 a week was approximately 35 per cent of all clothing workers.

The Commissioner also reported at that time, that in the larger clothing markets, the proportion of male employes earning $12.00 or less was:

Baltimore	81.6%
Philadelphia	72.5%
Chicago	65.4%
New York	65.3%
Rochester	56.9%

And he noted that the hours of work for men and women were 54¼ per week, and for children 44.5 hours a week.

As for homeworkers, the Commissioner reported that the average weekly wages earned were:

Baltimore	$2.24
Philadelphia	2.88
Chicago	4.35
New York	3.61
Rochester	4.14

In face of these conditions, the listless attitude of the UGWA in organizing the clothing industry was frustrating and maddening to the workers. They were ready to revolt against their plight that seemingly caused such little concern to their national union officers. It needed only a spark to set off an explosion in any single market.

The Strikes

In Chicago, on September 22, 1910, due to a relatively minor dispute about piece rates in the Hart, Schaffner & Marx factory, a strike ensued. It quickly spread throughout the city, and some 40,000 tailors joined the walkout, because at that time Chicago was the second largest market in the United States. There were arrests and violence. Two strikers were killed. There was national publicity. Yet, the UGWA national officers assumed a stand-offish attitude towards this spontaneous uprising. Due to the efforts of Joseph Schaffner, the head of Hart, Schaffner & Marx, a settlement was arranged effective January 14, 1911. Schaffner was a man of liberal leanings, and he was truly shocked when he learned of the causes for his workers' dissatisfaction. The essential clause in the settlement that made it a landmark in labor agreements, was the establishment of an arbitration committee of three to consider and adjust all worker grievances, even though no formal union recognition was granted by the company. With no support from their union, the Chicago strikers in the other clothing plants of the city lost heart and returned to work.

Sidney Hillman, later to become the outstanding leader of the clothing workers in this country, was appointed to represent the Hart employes in matters of grievances. Hillman also became the business agent of the Chicago local of the UGWA. At that time, he had been employed as a cutter at Hart's, and, admits his most admiring biographer, "a damn poor cutter at that." Hillman was born in Russia and migrated to the United States in 1907. After a succession of jobs, one of which was stock clerk at Sears Roebuck that paid $8 a week, he joined Hart's in 1909 as an apprentice cutter, receiving a starting salary of $6 a week. After a year, his salary was raised to $8 a week, and then to $12. When the Hart strike occurred in 1910, Hillman was only 23 years old. But this young man, who spoke English poorly, showed extraordinary leadership qualities. He displayed the intuitive ability to lead the workers of diverse nationalities to victory over the largest and most prosperous clothing concern in the city. It was an extraordinary performance of labor statesmanship for such a young man. Even more remarkable, considering his youth, was his spirit of moderation once victory had been won, and his seeming ability to get along not merely with his fellow workers, but with management as well. Young Hillman impressed people as a hard driving, very intense individual, deadly serious in his chosen task. He recognized the limited economic strength of his side, so he dealt realistically with the diverse problems encountered in his new position. Incidentally, one of his great admirers and supporters was a young woman who had been an outstanding leader in the Hart strike, named Bessie Abramowitz, who later became his wife.

Hillman, as an aggressive business agent, ordinarily obtained every single advantage that could possibly be secured for his members, but he did not ask for "pie in the sky" which could not, under any circumstances, be granted by management. Perhaps his tactics would now be called brinksmanship, but Hillman, ever cautious, never went over the cliff. As a business agent for the union, and representing the Hart workers in matters of dispute, Hillman was afforded an invaluable opportunity to gain experience as a practicing union officer. Therefore, when the clothing workers had need of a leader who was to head their newly organized union of clothing workers in 1914, they turned to him as the man best suited for the position.

Nor was Chicago the only market that had become disillusioned with UGWA leadership. As already mentioned, there had been discontent in New York ever since the UGWA was organized. Unhappy and frustrated, there was a continuous series of strikes in New York, usually localized in one or more shops. These strikes ordinarily occurred during the busy season. After a short strike, the workers would obtain a token wage increase which would then be promptly rescinded during the succeeding slow months. It was said that working conditions and wages see-sawed seasonally, from bad to worse. In 1904, when the National Association of Clothiers had announced that their factories hereafter would be run on an open shop basis, the workers went on strike for six weeks. The strike was lost, and the union became merely a shadow of its former self. In

1907, the New York tailors again struck, but the UGWA officials refused to support them. The strikers were defeated once more, with a resultant increase in antagonism towards their national union.

In 1911, utterly disheartened because of a lack of interest displayed by the UGWA officials, the more progressive minded leaders in the union called a national conference for the purpose of creating an organization that would stimulate union activity. At this meeting, which was held in Philadelphia on May 11, 1911, a Tailors' Council was formed, with 89 delegates present from New York, Chicago, Philadelphia, Boston and Newark. The Council, as formed, was actually an insurgent faction within the UGWA, and the national officers realized that they were now confronted with a serious threat of rebellion by the majority of the membership. In haste, they agreed to conduct an organizing campaign in the clothing industry. As events turned out, they once more dragged their feet to a considerable degree. It is very probable, based upon their later action rather than formal policy statements, they foresaw a potential danger to their authority if the membership of the radical tailors was increased by the pending drive on non-union shops. So they talked big, issued belligerent statements that breathed fire, but did little if anything of a concrete nature.

However, the New York Brotherhood of Tailors, which would be considered nowadays to be a joint board in current union parlance (a grouping of market locals), would not be put off. They were determined to unionize their market, whether or not the national office favored such a course. Isaac Goldstein, an organizer of great ability, headed this campaign to unionize New York, and he was assisted by young Louis Hollander, who early displayed the qualities of leadership that eventually made him the New York market manager. Once more the workers were aroused to strike. In December, 1912, over 50,000 tailors left the shops, demanding higher wages, a 50-hour week with overtime pay, and no tenement house work permitted. As usual, the UGWA sought ways and means of settling the strike quickly, if necessary, without the consent of the strikers. A hasty and unsatisfactory agreement of a sort was made by the national office with the manufacturers' association, but this was promptly repudiated by the strikers. Finally, a settlement was reached in March, 1913, giving a $1.00 wage increase to the strikers, reducing hours to 52 a week after January, 1914, with the cutters' work week thereafter to be 48 hours. The workers were entirely dissatisfied with the wage settlement, for it was deemed insufficient, and the weekly hours were still excessive. As might be expected, the UGWA bore the brunt of this condemnation by the New York members. Additional coals were thus heaped upon the already smoldering fires of resentment and frustration. Because factory conditions were also bad in other markets, there were simultaneous strikes in many other clothing centers, resulting in weekly hours reduced a little, usually conforming to the pattern set in the New York market.

The Schism

The two largest clothing markets, New York and Chicago, were now ready to rebel. Likewise, there was widespread dissatisfaction in the locals of all clothing markets due to apathetic national union leadership. Knowing the temper of the clothing workers, the national officers of the union deemed it the better part of discretion to hold the annual convention in Nashville, Tennessee. This would assure good attendance by their supposedly loyal supporters among the overall and shirt delegates whose factories were located in the Midwest. Though the eastern clothing locals objected vehemently because of distance and the expense of traveling to Tennessee, their dissent was overruled. And when the Nashville convention was finally held in October, 1914, the New York clothing locals were barred as delegates on the specious claim of unpaid dues. The real cause for such high-handed action was obviously an effort to maintain control of the delegates by the national officers.

Thereupon, after a heated debate, the clothing locals that remained left the convention floor under the leadership of a fiery young man from Chicago named Frank Rosenblum, who later rose to become general secretary-treasurer of the Amalgamated Clothing

Workers of America. In a separate hall, the now united clothing locals voted that they were the rightful representatives of the union, claiming that the national officers had usurped the authority of the membership in order to control the union. In December, 1914, after legal maneuvers of some months, a separate union was formed: the Amalgamated Clothing Workers of America (ACWA), consisting of the seceding locals. Thereupon, the ACWA elected Sidney Hillman as its president because of his outstanding leadership in the 1910 Hart strike and his conduct thereafter as a business agent of the UGWA local.

With the election of the 27-year old Hillman as president, a new element of union thought, action and procedure, not previously present in the labor affairs of the clothing industry made itself felt, and eventually gained dominance within the union. Joseph Schlossberg, as an outstanding leader of the eastern clothing locals, was elected general secretary-treasurer. Because the organizing convention of the newly-formed union was held in New York City, the ideology then prevalent among the New York clothing workers was inserted in the preamble of the Constitution as the underlying philosophy of the infant union. The preamble was strictly socialist in thought, stressing the class struggle, and concluded with the ringing sentence that "the industrial and inter-industrial organization built upon the solid rock of clear knowledge and class-consciousness will put the organized working class in actual control of the system of production, and the working class will then be ready to take possession of it." This epitomized the ideals and hopes of the eastern clothing workers who were avid readers of radical newspapers and followers of such intellectuals as Morris Hillquit, Abraham Cahan and Meyer London, all prominent in the Socialist party.

With the advent of the very young Hillman as president though, a new, entirely pragmatic approach to labor-management relations was introduced. Hillman felt that the capitalist system was here to stay for a long time at least, and so talk of taking over the system of production was mere wishful thinking. Incidentally, when this preamble was called to the attention of some manufacturers many years later, they wryly smiled, saying, "who else controls production in our industry today but the union, socialism or no socialism?" If, as Hillman saw it, the capitalist system was here for a long time, then it was necessary to obtain better working conditions for the members immediately, without any delay. Therefore, it was good sense to seek and wrest from the employers the best possible settlement at the moment. Once this had been achieved, then it was advisable to strive for even better contract terms at a later date when economic conditions were perhaps more favorable. It was a most prosaic approach. It did not promise a new heaven in the near future when the class struggle would produce the inevitable national crisis that would allow the proletariat to take possession of the factories as prophesied in the ACWA preamble. In fact, at the ACWA convention of 1922, the Socialist preamble was dropped since Hillman found it embarrassing, even harmful at times, in conducting the affairs of the union. Because of this preamble, the ACWA members were painted as wild-eyed bolsheviks by anti-union employers during the red scare of the 1920's.

And in good time, Hillman did get results in the form of higher wages, shorter hours, unemployment insurance for workers, plus other fringe benefits which are recorded in the later chapters of this volume. Gradually, the Chicago group of leaders, the pragmatists, triumphed ideologically in the Amalgamated. Their realistic philosophy was accepted. Hillman, Rosenblum, Potofsky, Levin, Kroll, Weinstein and Block, as well as others from Chicago, were the national officers, or else became the managers of local markets in Cincinnati, Philadelphia, Allentown and Chicago. The Baltimore market was led by Hyman Blumberg (in later years executive vice president), a shrewd, combative leader of quick intelligence and great integrity. His sharp wit and his physical courage, which were combined with a winning personality, won the admiration of Hillman who always respected a man of guts plus brains. It was of prime importance to the Chicago group that Blumberg, always the realist, as the leader of the Baltimore market, support Hillman's policy of studied moderation. The socialist faction that stressed ideology at all times, even at the expense of practicality, gradually grew weaker in influence within the Amalgamated, although the idealism that gave the heart to the union remained in the form of extended social benefits to the members and their dependents. Over the years, due to retirement or death, the vocal socialist element in the Amalgamated gradually disappeared.

ACWA—A National Union

In analyzing the structure of the Amalgamated and its consequent impact upon the conduct of the union, it must be kept in mind that clothing was produced in many important markets throughout the country, and that no one market, not even New York, represented more than 30–40 per cent of the industry total. Therefore, no single market could impose a decisive influence upon the policies of the national office. In political jargon, the power of the locals in the various markets was relatively weak, and the power of the national office was far greater than any one local market. When the union began acquiring members in the shirt and outerwear fields, with only a small number of such plants within the areas where clothing was made, the influence of the individual locals was further diluted. In direct proportion, as national dispersion of the membership spread, the central office of the ACWA attained authority over the separate market locals. This authority became nearly overwhelming with Hillman as president, for his administrative ability was highly regarded, and he had no peer in labor-management matters. Therefore, the philosophy of Hillman, within a short time, permeated all divisions of the ACWA. His stress upon realism based upon an actual appraisal of economic facts found acceptance among the membership, especially when this mode of procedure brought satisfactory labor settlements. It can be said that this realistic approach to all union problems as exemplified by Hillman's philosophy, has governed the ACWA to this day.

Once the Amalgamated was formed, attention then turned to completely organizing the important markets. It was a difficult task, for union finances were low and the UGWA sniped at any ACWA effort to do so. The A.F. of L. strongly supporting the United Garment Workers, refused to recognize the Amalgamated as the legal union for clothing workers, seriously handicapping the ACWA in its relations with other unions.

Still, strikes had to be called and settled. They were often lost as in Chicago and Boston. But slowly, due to persistance, the ACWA made progress. World War I had begun. Economic conditions were changing rapidly, Hillman was astute enough to grasp the impact of the war on the American economy and on the clothing industry specifically. He took advantage of the growing need for workers in the clothing factories now that the flow of immigration had stopped. With business excellent, the manufacturers were very willing to settle their labor differences so as to maintain production. When the country entered into a war economy in 1917, Hillman and his associates, realizing their opportunity, were ready to take full advantage of this entirely new situation. They sought to strengthen the ACWA by increasing the membership. They made demands upon employers that working conditions be improved and wages raised. They preferred peaceful settlements if possible, but were ready to strike if necessary. The employers were now confronted by a relatively powerful national union that had not existed prior to 1915, and the question arose, how would labor-management relations fare in the clothing industry if and when peace came?

Chapter 8

World War I and Aftermath

World War I Begins

When World War I was declared on July 28, 1914, the clothing business was in the doldrums. The rebellion of the unionized workers against their national officials was brewing. The "sellout" by the UGWA of the Chicago strike in 1910, and the more recent New York strike of 1913, as the members viewed it, was recalled with bitterness that would shortly reach a boiling point. The manufacturers were finding business rather poor and profits were meager, for it was clearly a buyer's market. Certainly, the entire industry was unprepared, economically or psychologically, for the profound change that was pending in the business and social structure of our country as a consequence of the War. An outbreak of hostilities of the magnitude that took place in 1914 had not occurred since the days of Napoleon. Moreover, at that time, because of poor and slow means of communication, there was only limited contact between the United States and Europe. That European war, therefore, had relatively little impact on our country during its many years of conflict. Even when, in 1812, we did declare war against Great Britain, fighting was of a restricted nature with most engagements at sea. But the conflict in 1914 meant that the most powerful countries of Europe were battling with armies of millions on either side, merely five days travel from our shores. Never having experienced such a cataclysm, the American people, including the clothing industry, could not readily comprehend the real effect such a war might have on our country. It had never happened before, and there was no past experience as a basis for planning future action. Because the United States was understandably unaware of what "big-time" war might mean to the social and economic life of a country, we followed a policy of business as usual, trying to formulate day to day plans when conditions warranted change. Without any long-range program of government intervention, American industry, including the clothing manufacturers, found itself buffeted by enormous economic pressures that were hardly understood at the time. Certainly, the shortages and eventual glut that created an economic upheaval, lifting the price index far beyond reason, then forcing prices into a trough of near bankruptcy, seemed supernatural and not an act of man. Actually, the wild gyrations of prices could have been controlled, but the authorities just did not know how to do it. When, a generation later, and a generation unfortunately wiser, the United States entered World War II, the necessity of price stabilization was recognized immediately and thereafter maintained with some degree of success.

It was to be business as usual for the clothing manufacturers in 1914, except for initial minor annoyances caused by the war, such as concern about overseas shipments of raw wool for the American mills. In October, labor entered into a legal tangle because of the complete schism within the UGWA at the Nashville convention. Not until December 28, 1914, when the Amalgamated Clothing Workers of America (ACWA) was formally launched in Webster Hall, New York, was there truly a clothing union in existence. Few thought then that this new union, within a few years, would acquire enormous influence and exert great power in labor-management affairs.

The industry was still somewhat bewildered by the impact of the war even in 1915, and uncertain about the future significance of the newly formed ACWA. Since our country was neutral, the interests of the clothing manufacturers centered primarily about the perennial problems confronting them; namely getting orders, making the orders stick and producing the garments for the orders. At the annual convention of the National Association of Clothiers, held in New York in February, 1915, Mr. Louis M. Myers of Springfield, Illinois, the first president of the National Association of Retail Clothiers (now the Menswear Retailers of America), which had been organized the previous year, was a guest speaker. He spoke on the safe and ever popular topic of manufacturer-retailer cooperation for the edification of the clothing delegates and was loudly applauded. Similar addresses on the same subject, by manufacturers as well as retailers, with a minimum of change in phrasing and a minimum of concrete results, were to be repeated for generations to come.

It was at the 1915 convention that Jacob L. Freeman, one of the founders of Hickey-Freeman Co., read a lengthy paper to his fellow manufacturers on reasons why manufacturers were unable to deliver orders on time. His address might be considered the granddaddy of all future addresses on this subject. Mr. Freeman talked for a considerable time on the undeniable value of industry cooperation. Then, warming up, he delineated every single step that followed the sale to a retailer, castigating stores that bought late, attacking the custom of revising an order once given and condemning the frequency of a partial cancellation of the order. Yet, Mr. Freeman pointed out, the retailer demanded early delivery. The problem of mill delivery and all the heartaches of production were then set forth in painful detail. In fact, not one of the many agonizing hours that were usually spent by a manufacturer who endeavored to fill an order promptly was spared this audience. According to reports, they listened with sympathy and complete agreement. Finally, Mr. Freeman offered a simple solution for this complex problem. "The remedy," he concluded, "is a campaign of education among all branches of the industry, which would result in standardized delivery dates." This obvious solution was not controversial. Thereupon a committee was appointed to meet with retailers in order to finally resolve the bothersome matter of revision of orders, cancellations and timely delivery. The committee did meet with the retailers the following year, and after the joint conference, hope was expressed that all such problems were now settled for all time. Yet, this very subject of "deliveries" was again on the agenda, with some slight modifications when the manufacturers and retailers met jointly fifty years later and then again voted to meet further on this subject. Based upon the most recent solutions offered during the conferences held in 1967 and in 1968 as well, Mr. Freeman's topic of discussion, "deliveries," will continue to be a matter of industry concern for some time to come.

Shortages and Wild Inflation

With shortages of all fabrics making themselves felt once the United States had entered the war on April 6, 1917, the United States Council of National Defense inaugurated a campaign on December 15, 1917 to conserve the piece goods to be used during the fall, 1918 season. In order to effect a savings of cloth, the Commercial Economy Board of the Council had sent a questionnaire to the trade for the purpose of ascertaining what style features could be eliminated from current models. Based upon information received from the manufacturers in January, 1918, the Council recommended that the number of models be reduced, that the coats be shorter in length, that the double breasted models be eliminated, that vests be discontinued and that reworked wool be substituted for virgin wool which was needed for the armed forces. In essence, the style features and model modifications recommended were similar to the style simplification orders issued in World War II. However, in 1918 the Council merely requested cooperation, with no punitive action taken against offenders who declined to conform. It was an appeal to patriotism, and reports were that 95 per cent of the industry obeyed the government request. For the spring, 1919 season, new recommendations restricting styles were issued.

The Federal government did not establish an agency for price control such as occurred in World War II, but merely issued statements that deplored rising prices, denounced profiteers and threatened legal action. In the later stages of the inflationary period, there were a few indictments, but there was more publicity about the matter than results. No practical steps were taken to control high prices. Nor were steps taken to ration goods that were in short supply. It was free enterprise running wild in a time of crisis.

Soon the industry was busy producing uniforms. Because military needs required large quantities of cloth and absorbed a substantial proportion of mill and garment productive capacity, the demand for civilian clothing was greater than supply. There was a real shortage of clothing. Something had to give—it was the price level which exceeded all bounds of reason. A basic serge cloth, # 9613-1, sold by the American Woolen Company, showed the following price trend during those years of inflation:

YEAR	PRICE	% OF INCREASE
1914	$1.075	—
1916	1.375	28%
1918	3.125	191%
1920	4.125	283%

The Hickey-Freeman Company, plagued with problems that confronted all manufacturers, issued a "Fact" pamphlet to its accounts, justifying the increase in prices, and detailing the ever rising costs in the components of the garment:

The fabric cited as an example in the pamphlet
was
"Fulton Serge" # 3194:

In Fall 1915—the cost was $1.50 a yard
In Fall 1919—the cost was $3.50 a yard
In Fall 1920—the cost was $5.50 a yard

There had been an increase of 266 per cent within the five year period!

Then, in order to show that the price increase was not merely in wool goods, the firm listed the following data:

TRIMMINGS	1915	JAN., 1920	% OF INCREASE
Alpaca per yard	$ .35	$ 1.15	228%
Sleeve lining	.18	1.00	455%
Canvas	.16	1.15	619%
Silk sleeve lining	1.15	4.50	291%
Sewing silk per lb.	5.70	22.50	295%

And, as a final clincher, Hickey-Freeman then listed the increase in wages:

(a) Weekly wages in a coat shop, December, 1914, were $12.25 for a 50-hour week, or 24.5 cents an hour.

(b) By December, 1919, weekly wages had risen to $31.50 with a 44-hour week in effect—so that hourly earnings were now 71.6 cents—or an increase of 192 per cent.

(c) The firm then pointed out that retail prices had gone up 135 per cent during this period.

With textile prices rising to extraordinary heights, and labor costs going up, the wholesale price of clothing rose steadily. Business was booming at a fevered pace. For example, one reporter noted, "before the war the average cost of a suit of clothes was about $20—for the next spring (1920) it will be over $60 which means prices will range from $40 to $85—The $40 suit will be the cheapest grade of ready-to-wear suit put out by a reliable dealer—In New York City the show windows of retailers are full of suit prices from $50 to $75 and up to $100—Higher priced suits are easily sold." One clothing manufacturer predicted publicly that those who prophesied "unheard of prices to the consumer for next spring may have the right dope."

The peak year of rampant prices and booming business was 1919. The Rochester manufacturers, with a well-organized association in their market, announced a Buyers Market Week to be held in October, 1919, when all lines would be opened, and the retailers were invited to visit Rochester. The buyers were numerous and heavy orders were placed. As a result, the trade press reported that the customary road trips by salesmen would be curtailed.

At the year's end, statements of unusual optimism were made by leaders in the industry, predicting still higher prices and even larger orders for 1920. Max H. Friedman of J. Friedman & Company, president of the Clothing Manufacturers of New York, looked forward to 1920 with great confidence. Mortimer Adler of L. Adler Brothers & Company, Richard Feiss of the Joseph & Feiss Company, and Ludwig Stein of B. Kuppenheimer & Company, assured retailers in the trade press of steady and continued prosperity. These men, highly successful in business, just could not grasp the fact that they were in the midst of a wild price spiral which was bound to result in eventual disaster, for they had never before encountered such inflation. Unknown to themselves, they were the victims of titanic economic forces out of control.

Catastrophe!

But there were storm clouds gathering on the horizon. Consumers were tending to shy away from the purchase of suits that sold at highly inflated prices. The executive secretary of the retail association issued a statement that store inventories were 25 per cent above normal, which was promptly denounced by manufacturers as "destructive publicity" and inconsistent with the facts. Shortly thereafter, the press began printing a series of stories about excess profiteering in the clothing industry. The National Association of Clothiers, as a spokesman of the industry, urged the U.S. Department of Justice to bring unconscionable profiteers to a speedy trial. On February 2, 1920, representatives of the manufacturers, the retailers and the union met with government officials who were concerned with the high cost of clothing. At the conclusion of the meeting, a statement was issued on behalf of all industry representatives, indignantly denying profiteering. The statement then complained that the industry had become an object of unfair publicity, and assurances were now given to the public that prices were based upon fair value, that prices would not decline and therefore the consumer should have no reluctance to buy clothing now.

Despite these brave words, which were hailed as "constructive" and "statesmanlike," all was not well. The headlines of the *Daily News Record* of February 17, 1920, stated in bold type, "Situation Calls for Caution." Retailers were urged not to speculate, for supply was approaching demand and that consumer prices would reach a peak in 1920. Such comment could not be considered as constructive news, so industry reaction was bitter. Even William Wood, president of the American Woolen Company, who had refused to meet with manufacturers some years previously, now deemed it advisable to address the convention of the National Association of Clothiers. He showed himself to be "one of the boys," really a part of the industry, for his subject was "Our Allied Industries." This was somewhat of a belated recognition on the part of Wood that the clothing manufacturers were his customers whose good will and business might be sorely needed in days to come.

In order to overcome the unfavorable publicity of profiteering then heaped upon the clothing industry, it was proposed to raise a fund of $60,000 to explain current price levels and counteract undesirable news stories. However, the manufacturers deemed it advisable to get retail cooperation first and then raise the money. The consumers though, were not the only ones who were now wary of the climbing clothing prices. The store buyers themselves were now beginning to balk at placing orders for future delivery. Thereupon, the manufacturers rushed all goods on order to their accounts for the purpose of avoiding refusal of delivery. Soon the long dreaded threat of possible cancellations was being bruited about in the showrooms. This was a fearful subject to broach when manufacturers met informally. Gratefully, all were reassured when Mr. John Moody, the president of Moody's Investors' Service, hailed as an "optimistic economist," informed the industry that "he did not expect any serious financial situation during the year." Regardless of the worth of his prediction, Moody was enthusiastically applauded as a "constructive influence" (a phrase much used in times of business stress). Further confirming that all would be well, Mr. Louis B. Tirin, secretary of the Manhattan Shirt Company, announced that "silk shirts may be high—$20 or $25, or higher" in 1920. He was referring to single shirt prices!

Then the salesmen went on the road. The *Daily News Record* reported on March 13, 1920, that there was a feeling that "it's too good to last." There was watchful waiting for the possible dreaded change. The markets were tense. The trade press reports caused further anxiety about the coming months. According to news items, Rochester feared a slump in orders. The tailors-to-the-trade, selling directly to consumers, were lowering prices in order to push sales, which was a clear indication of growing consumer resistance to high prices. According to credit men, retail collections were slowing down, for store sales were declining. But the credit men, although usually pessimistic, now foresaw merely a slight depression, followed by rapid recovery—so said news reports. It was obvious that there must be no rocking of the boat at such critical moments, according to the *Daily News Record*, for manufacturers held large inventories. This was followed by a dire warning that shortly smaller manufacturers might be forced to cut prices in order to raise cash.

Reports from all sections of the country disclosed that Easter business was bad. The weather, as usual, was blamed for "it resembled Christmas not spring," and Sam Weider, a shrewd credit man, told the trade reporter on March 25, 1920, that "there is pessimism in New York." Shortly thereafter, the price structure of clothing began to crumble, for the financially weaker firms were now cutting prices. At the end of March, the price decline became an avalanche. Consequently, there was wide apprehension expressed about fall prices when the lines would open. At this time of stress, the industry was confronted by an unforeseen threat. During April, 1920, overall clubs were being formed throughout the country in an effort to fight high clothing prices. It became fashionable for top executives to boast that they were wearing overalls as business garb. Hillman, in an interview, hopefully dismissed this threat to the industry as a "harmful fad." Since consumers felt that this fad was harmful only to prices, it spread throughout the country. In the trade paper, the weather also received daily blame for the ever mounting inventories among retailers and manufacturers.

Still striving to sell, Rochester held another market week in April, 1920. At the very time when retailers were there to buy, the *Daily News Record* informed these visiting buyers that overalls and not suits were selling. To put it mildly, this was considered a stab in the back, and roundly denounced as "destructive." It was then that the Rochester Exchange discovered that a form of industry sabotage was taking place at its very doorstep. New York competitors had secretly hired hotel rooms in Rochester, offering goods at extremely low prices to the buyers who came to the Market Week. The comment of the Rochester manufacturers with regard to the "intruders" probably could not be printed verbatim in a business paper of respectable standing.

There was little understanding that the after effect of wild inflation was bound to be excessive deflation. Except for those who were infants during the Civil War and the succeeding deflation of 1873, no one in 1920 had ever lived through such a period. Moreover, during the 1861–1873 years, inflation and deflation did not take place within a short space of years, nor were the peaks and valleys as extreme as in the 1915–1920 period. Following industry belief that soothing words were always balm in times of trouble, words of optimism, of hope and of cheer were considered to be the proper and specific prescription to drive away bad news. So on April 14, 1920, Mr. William Goldman, as dean of the industry, informed the trade paper that "I do not believe that there will be any general recession of prices in clothing in 1920." But, he continued, in order to safeguard his future reputation as the outstanding industry economist, he believed that "there may be readjustments in material prices and some drop."

On that very day, as if to prove that wages must only go up regardless of economic disaster, the manager of the Baltimore market announced that a demand for a wage increase in his market would be made on May 1. Some time before, the cutters in the New York market had already informed their employers that they wanted a $9 per week increase. "Utterly impossible," was the reaction of the manufacturers who were in no mood to think of still higher wages.

Now the need for publicity was once more raised, but the reason for reaching the consumer was somewhat different. It was not a matter of denying higher prices any longer. It was the necessity of inducing men to buy clothing at any price. The National Association of Clothiers stated that a fund of $150,000 should be raised, and advertisements should be placed in papers, "prepared by doctors of psychology with national and international reputations." It was felt that these ads, written by men learned in the psychology of consumer buying, would perhaps reverse the downward trend. In view of bad business though, the industry judged that this was not the time to raise money and so enlighten the consumer on the advisability of buying clothing at once.

Business conditions were tottering on the brink. When, on May 4, 1920, John Wanamaker announced that he would reduce all prices 20 per cent, the axe fell! The bottom seemed to drop out of the price level and a mood of hysteria gripped the industry. Wanamaker's clothing buyer reported that manufacturers were offering garments at sharply reduced prices, up to 25 per cent below the former prices. By July, 1920, the return of goods exceeded 25 per cent of shipments. Cancellations of orders were high and mounting. Unemployment in the factories increased at an alarming rate. In turn, the woolen mills reported that the manufacturers' cancellations were growing in volume. In an effort to unload inventories, manufacturers now announced publicly their price cuts, with Strouse Brothers of Baltimore reducing suits from $5 to $8 a garment. The firm was promptly denounced by competitors in the *Daily News Record* as a "destructive element." Then they likewise cut prices even further. The deflation was now assuming catastrophic proportions, and the manufacturers were confronted with financial ruin.

Once more, William Goldman felt the need for offering his soothing reassurances to the now-hysterical manufacturers. On May 25, 1920, Goldman called a meeting of the larger New York houses. Such firms as J. Friedman & Company, Samuel Rosenthal & Company, Cohen and Lang, Schwartz & Jaffee, Bashowitz Brothers, Light & Schlesinger and Heidelberg & Wolfe were present. There were admonitions "not to rock the boat," "have a cool heart," and "conditions were fundamentally sound," and the meeting adjourned.

As a further blow to the already-damaged image of the textile and clothing industries, two days later the American Woolen Company, the largest domestic mill, was indicted for profiteering, with the assistant U.S. Attorney saying that its profit in 1920 was from 300–400 per cent greater than in 1919! This was sensational news. Of equal importance, but no longer sensational, or even news, was the announcement that retailers were still reducing prices.

By June 1, 1920, it was obvious that there would be no retail buying for fall. Stocks in stores were still top heavy, and the value of the inventories declining daily. This placed many manufacturers in a precarious financial position. They had large quantities of fall piece goods on hand. Finished garments filled their racks, and prices of piece goods and clothing were falling day by day. There was no seeming escape from a pending catastrophe for the industry.

Efforts to Stabilize Prices

It was then that Moe Levy, an East Side New York City retailer of some prominence, proposed to save the manufacturers who were carrying excessive inventories. He hired Madison Square Garden in order to run a colossal sale of garments where the manufacturers might offer their clothing direct to the consumers. Due to the promotion methods of Levy, coupled with his advertising copy, this sale had the atmosphere of a circus rather than a sale of clothing. Certainly, Levy did not understate the possible savings to the consumer. On that basis, in June, 1920, the stocks of 25 manufacturers were offered to the public at cut-rate prices. It was estimated that Levy sold three million dollars worth of spring, 1920 garments during the event. The other retailers in the city were less than enthusiastic at this hoopla affair, for it established low price levels for their own garments. Similar "Garden" sales were held in other cities with slight success because the wild excitement engineered by Levy was lacking.

Despite setbacks, the industry had to continue its operations. The fall, 1920 season admittedly had been lost; now the spring, 1921 season loomed and lines would be opened shortly. Would the new prices offered be far lower than last season, and most important, would they hold? Would retailers buy anything? To answer these questions, in June, 1920, a committee of retailers met with a corresponding group of manufacturers in Atlantic City. The manufacturers were Eli Strouse of Strouse Brothers; Ludwig Stein of Kuppenheimer; Samuel Weil of Stein-Bloch; William Goldman of Cohen, Goldman; David Kirschbaum of Kirschbaum's; Paul Feiss of Joseph & Feiss; Jeremiah G. Hickey of Hickey-Freeman; Max Friedman of J. Friedman & Company; and others. An agreement was reached whereby manufacturers guaranteed that their fall prices would not be reduced before November 15 for suits and December 15 for overcoats. If prices were reduced prior to that date, the retailer was to receive a rebate for goods already shipped. Colonel Fred Levy of Louisville, Kentucky, president of the retail organization, in an expansive mood, announced, "Confidence has been restored. Business relations between manufacturers and distributors have been stabilized." A publicity campaign was to be inaugurated informing the consumer that "prices are honest," which caused skeptics to ask, what were they before?

Then on July 9, 1920, Kirschbaum's announced a price reduction despite the Atlantic City meeting, and despite a letter to retailers sent on June 14, 1920, in which the firm guaranteed prices for the future. It was at this time that a special U.S. attorney named Howard Figg, decided that this was the time to attack the clothing industry for "guaranteeing prices" in order to protect profits. This raised the blood pressure of the manufacturers and the retailers who were at the very moment taking substantial inventory losses. Mr. Figg was asked in no uncertain terms, "where are the profits?" Nevertheless, Mr. Figg's publicity did not encourage consumer buying.

Now, because of a lack of orders, clothing factories and mills began to shut down completely. The New York manufacturers realized that their market had been hurt because of the Madison Square Garden sale which created ill will among retailers nationally. Therefore, they announced a stag dinner to be held for their retail accounts in Brighton Beach. The dinner was excellent. The retailers enjoyed the evening. Still, complained their New York hosts, the buyers placed no orders but went home immediately thereafter.

Not until September 13, 1920, did the American Woolen Company partly reopen its mills, simultaneously announcing that piece goods prices were lower. Spring buying for 1921 was still poor. The after effects of the so-called November guarantee were bad, for retailers held off buying until the November date, waiting for the expected drop in prices. Michaels, Stern announced one-third off as of November 1, two weeks before the deadline. L. Adler & Brothers announced a 40 per cent reduction as of November 15 and other firms announced similar markdowns. Spring lines opened at sharply reduced prices with Society Brand informing its accounts that suits for spring, 1921, would be $11 below fall, 1920. One large company wrote to its accounts that the suit they sold for spring, 1920 at $32.50, which they had increased for the fall, 1920 season to $37.50, would now be offered at the bargain price of $25 for spring, 1921.

With a bitter strike taking place in New York, which had closed down the largest market, and factories operating elsewhere at reduced capacity, the industry gradually disposed of its inventories. Losses had been heavy, bankruptcies were numerous. It was a lesson that the industry never forgot, for when World War II began, the Clothing Manufacturers Association was in the forefront in favoring immediate strict price controls, coupled with a regulation that allocated piece goods on the basis of priorities.

Chapter 9

Industrial War and Peace

The National Industrial Federation

Industrywide bargaining in the clothing industry was first attempted in 1919. It had become apparent to the clothing manufacturers that the Amalgamated had secured a strong hold on the important clothing markets of New York, Chicago, Baltimore, Rochester and Boston, and maintained a slippery foothold in the other cities, such as Philadelphia, Cleveland and Cincinnati. The National Labor Bureau, which had been organized with the blessing and sponsorship of the National Association of Clothiers to deal with labor problems, had outlived its usefulness. The past history of the Bureau revealed a consistent anti-union bias. It had stressed the need for the "open shop." It had encouraged the blacklisting of pro-union workers, and it had actively organized strikebreaking forays. With such a record, the Bureau could not readily function as an organization that would gain the future confidence of the Amalgamated. Therefore, a new organization was desirable for the purpose of dealing with labor on a national basis, since the ACWA had become the national union of the clothing workers.

In view of such circumstances, and to counterbalance the now growing power of the ACWA, in 1919, at the January convention of the National Association of Clothiers, it was resolved to establish a separate organization that would deal solely with national labor matters. The constitution of this new organization, called the National Industrial Federation of Clothing Manufacturers, gave its officers "the authority to bind the participating manufacturers to any agreement with the Amalgamated Clothing Workers of America, and to make rules and regulations governing the industrial relations between management and workers. It shall be responsible for establishing an industrial government with all necessary organization of administrative, judicial and legislative functions to stabilize wages, hours, standards of efficiency and all conditions of employment." The membership of the Federation was to consist of the market associations already in existence, and individual manufacturers in instances where there was no local organization. The New York, Chicago, Baltimore, Rochester and Boston Associations joined immediately, and individual manufacturers in other cities likewise became members. The Federation therefore represented the overwhelming majority of unionized shops, and the prospects for national bargaining seemed bright. Yet the trials and tribulations of this nebulous organization which lived a life of frustration and futility for approximately two years, disclosed the pitfalls that were to be avoided in the future if collective bargaining on a national scale were to succeed.

As the declared purpose of the Federation was national bargaining, basic industrywide standards and procedures had to be agreed upon. It was essential to agree upon a formula revising the current wage scale that would be acceptable to all markets and to the union. Surprisingly, some markets naïvely joined the Federation in the hope that the level of the wage scale to be agreed upon as the industry standard would be the lowest paid in any market. Naturally, the union could not accept such a proposal for wage negotiations. In turn, the ACWA suggested that all markets be brought up to the highest levels then existent in any single market. The mere fact that such proposals could even be offered by either side clearly proved that labor and management had no understanding of true national bargaining, and were somewhat unrealistic in thinking that their opponents would possibly accept any drastic change in the wage scales. Therefore, at the first joint meeting of the two parties, which was held in Rochester in September, 1919, no national agreement could be reached, and the matter of wages was left to bargaining within the individual markets.

In view of the inability to bargain nationally, which had been the prime purpose of the Federation, the constitution of the organization was revised. It now became merely an advisory body for the employers in the separate markets. A Professor W. E. Hotchkiss was appointed as executive director. He was to function as a liaison between the markets and also between the markets and the union. With no power except to advise, Hotchkiss, a man of good will, was hampered in his efforts to actually perform any service for the industry. Several times he met with the local association executives separately. He also called together all markets for the purpose of arriving at a common policy as a group. After such industrywide conferences, the markets went their own ways, signing individual contracts after bargaining as a market with the respective locals of the ACWA. In matters of dispute, Hotchkiss tried to act as a mediator between the ACWA and local management. This was illogical because he was an employe of the manufacturers and so regarded by the union. Hotchkiss even presented economic data before the arbitrator in Rochester on behalf of the manufacturers when they endeavored to obtain a reduction in wages. He therefore lost any chance, if there ever had been such a possibility, of establishing a basis of personal rapport with the union. By July, 1920, Hillman publicly stated that in all forthcoming wage negotiations he would deal solely on a local basis which completely cut the ground from under the Federation.

A showdown, revealing the weakness of the Federation, occurred when the New York market faced the possibility of forcing a lockout in December, 1920. The New Yorkers sent representatives to Rochester, met with Hotchkiss and sought his support for the forthcoming struggle with labor. Hotchkiss refused to support them, for the Rochester and Chicago markets had declined to assist New York, and he disclosed that they were planning to make separate settlements with the ACWA. This meant that New York firms would be shut due to the lockout, while their competitors in other markets would be working, filling orders that might normally go to New York. When the New York market was turned down, it resigned from the Federation, and shortly thereafter the latter disappeared from the scene.

Ostensibly, the Federation failed as an organization because no practical formula had been devised which established a method of revising wages nationally without seriously upsetting the competitive position of the individual markets. Still, there was a more fundamental cause for the failure of industrywide bargaining. The manufacturers had been unionized for only a short number of years. What assurance was there that the ACWA would not disappear soon, for unions had come and gone in the past? In 1920, there was lack of realization by the manufacturers that the ACWA was here to stay, that it could not be destroyed and that they would have to deal with this union in the years to come. As we shall see, there was an influential group in the New York market which felt that the ACWA could be destroyed. Now that the war was over, government support for unions had been withdrawn, and the industry was in a generally depressed state. The union also lacked experience in national bargaining. It was suspicious of motives if and when manufacturers made any proposals for a settlement of disputes. In addition, the ACWA was as yet weak in several important markets, and so it was in no position to bargain on a truly national scale. Realistically, it was too early in the history of labor-management relations in the clothing industry for national bargaining. A longer period of gradual acquaintance was necessary, and more frequent day to day dealing between employer and union was needed before mutual confidence could be established. A more extended period of engagement, as it were, was essential before the two parties were ready for a marriage in the form of an industrywide agreement.

It was in June, 1921, after the long New York strike had been settled, that the officers and directors of the National Association of Clothiers met in New York City and passed a resolution disbanding the Association. According to Irving Crane, executive secretary, this action was decided upon because of the resignation of the New York market from the national organization. It will be recalled that the New York manufacturers had resigned from the National Industrial Federation in a huff when Hotchkiss, as director of the Federation, refused to aid the market in its forthcoming labor dispute. During this prolonged struggle between the New York firms and the ACWA, the other markets, members of the Federation, kept their factories running, taking considerable business away from the New York firms. Such action did not increase good will between the New York manufacturers and the rest of the unionized markets. This bitterness and suspicion between the markets continued for many years to come. So that labor difficulties might not hamper the regular activities of the National Association of Clothiers, the New York group was asked to resign from the organization. However, this act weakened the national association, for with the loss of the largest market, it was no longer a truly national group. Thereupon, it voted to dissolve as an association. So the once-powerful National Association of Clothiers, founded in 1897, disappeared. The industry had lost its national spokesman, for the association which had conferred frequently with mills and with retailers, was no more. The NAC also had been the recognized organization in dealing with the government in matters affecting the industry. Its disappearance was deeply felt as the years went by, for the men's clothing industry was now without a voice in matters of national concern. Not until the days of the NRA, when a national association had become a necessity in the writing of an industry code, was a national organization of clothing manufacturers formed once more.

The Watershed

Nineteen hundred twenty-one was the year of decision for the industry insofar as labor relations were concerned. After the long New York dispute of 1921, when the union emerged victorious, the stability and permanence of the ACWA never was threatened seriously. Now a new element—the power of union labor—had to be considered in any determination of future labor policy. It truly was a watershed for the industry. Now the manufacturers changed from an antagonistic group which hopefully wished the union to disappear, to an employer group that recognized the union was here to stay, and in matters affecting labor-management relations must be reckoned with. But it took a strike that lasted six months, with no holds barred, before the ACWA was truly acknowledged as a permanent force in the industry.

The previous chapter detailed the wild inflation of clothing prices in 1919 and the consequent deflation that followed. When the bottom fell out of the price level, the manufacturers realized that their costs of materials and labor were too high. The consuming public had refused to buy overpriced clothing. Therefore, the clothing houses promptly stopped purchasing materials and shut down their plants. In order to conform to the newly reduced wholesale price levels, all items of cost had to be lowered. The woolen mills, finding themselves in the same position as the clothing manufacturers, and confronted with highly inflated costs, also shut their plants, reopening them only after inventories had been depleted and factory wages sharply reduced. This was done on a unilateral basis for there were no unions of any strength in the woolen mills, and the price of piece goods soon declined to realistic levels. But the clothing manufacturer found that while his piece goods costs were now lowered, the most important item of cost, labor, could not be reduced without the consent of the ACWA. And readjustments were necessary if business was to revive after the cataclysm of 1920.

It was generally admitted that labor costs in New York City had increased to a far greater extent than in the other markets. One of the reasons for this excessive wage rise was the fact that the majority of garments made in New York were produced in contract shops. As a manufacturer could obtain his fantastically high prices from retailers without any difficulty in the years of 1915–1920, selling all that could be produced, it was desirable for each firm to garner all available production facilities. Therefore, New York manufacturers competed for the services of contractors. They offered large bonuses in order to entice contractors away from competitors. Consequently, contractor prices soared steadily. In turn, the contractors offered wage increases to their operators in order to prevent the workers from leaving, or else strove to hire additional operators at any price in order to expand production. As for the manufacturers who owned inside shops, they found themselves compelled to give their employes comparable wage increases offered by contractors so that their own work force might not be depleted. By June, 1920, with the inflation bubble already burst, manufacturers belatedly realized that New York labor costs were far out of line with existing wage rates in other markets, even though the national wage level itself was highly inflated. To cite one example, according to the Bureau of Labor Statistics, the hourly earnings of women basters had risen 87 per cent for the country as a whole from 1914 to 1919, whereas the hourly earnings of such women basters in New York had increased 126 per cent. The Government data revealed that in all of the operations in sewing a garment, the hourly earnings were far higher in New York than the national average, and that during the years of inflation such labor costs had risen more rapidly than in other clothing markets.

It was well known that most of the out of town markets operated on a piece work basis, so that earnings conformed to actual computed costs, while the New York factories operated on a weekwork basis. According to the New York manufacturers, their true costs were far higher than even the hourly earnings disclosed. They felt that productivity was relatively lower in New York than in the other clothing centers, although no data supporting this contention were ever given. However, it is certain that the New York firms were convinced that their labor costs were too high, far higher than in other markets, and they were determined to bring this wage level in line with their competitors.

The New York situation had not gone unnoticed in high union circles. By the end of 1919, Hillman himself had evidently realized that a very serious labor problem was brewing in the city because work performed was paid on an hourly basis rather than on a piece work basis. It was therefore desirable that wages be computed differently. Yet, due to the unhappy experience in the past, when the workers had been outrageously exploited under the task system (which was a haphazard type of piece work payment), the New York locals were adamantly opposed to any form of piece work. It was not merely a matter of economics, but high emotion and bitter remembrances of employer exploitation in the sweat shops. Therefore, when Hillman, at the 1920 ACWA convention held in Boston, proposed a compromise solution, namely, "a week work system with standards of production," a storm of protest broke out from the New York delegates. They stoutly opposed Hillman's compromise. The trade press reported that Hillman had to "lay it on the line" as a practical vote of confidence before the convention reluctantly agreed to accept his resolution. Blumberg's address favoring the proposal, recounting Baltimore's experience, was a factor in the passage of the resolution.

Hillman could go no further with his membership. The New York locals would accept "standards of production" under protest, but no piece work. Nevertheless, the New York manufacturers were entirely dissatisfied with such a compromise. They wanted piece work, and in addition wanted the right of employe discharge, the ability to change contractors at will, plus any and all practices that were included in other market agreements. Such a demand by the manufacturers was obviously unrealistic, for the union leaders could not obtain local membership consent even if the national leadership accepted the demands of the manufacturers. It was clear that the clothing manufacturers were seeking a cause for industrial strife and not a settlement. The manufacturers persisted. Hillman stood firm, and the employers locked out the workers on December 6, 1920.

A bitter industrial strife of six months ensued. As the struggle continued, violence erupted. Both sides suffered financially. There were law suits aplenty, with manufacturers unsuccessfully seeking injunctions from the courts. No doubt this was a life and death struggle in the New York market between management and labor. The officers of the manufacturers association blatantly favored the "open shop" and wanted no union whatsoever. As this was the time of the "red scare," the president of the National Association of Retail Clothiers, Andreas Burkhardt of Cincinnati, decided that it would be good patriotism and perhaps better publicity to yell "bolshevik" at the ACWA. He actually toured the country, smearing the union with the red label in every speech and was wildly applauded in certain circles. Burkhardt tried desperately to help the manufacturers, but his practical value was questionable at best. He merely muddied the waters with wild accusations that disclosed his possession of a most vivid imagination and a complete lack of facts. After the strike was settled, Burkhardt returned to the quiet life of a Cincinnati retailer, with the satisfied conscience that he had done his best to save his country and the clothing industry from the New York reds. Meanwhile, during all this turmoil, the unionized markets proceeded to fill all retail orders that were being lost by New York firms. By June, 1921, the end was in sight. The bitter enders among the New York manufacturers seceded from their association, and the peace party gained control. The settlement provided for the application of "standards of production" in establishing weekly wages, and such wages were to be reduced 15 per cent from the high levels prevailing before the strike. The New York market had suffered a grievous hurt, for retailers, of necessity, had to seek new sources of supply during the strike, and many never bought again from New York in the quantities previously purchased.

The true significance of this union victory could not be properly evaluated at the time. But upon reflection, this strike settled once and for all time, the bare fact that the ACWA could not be destroyed as an organization. It was here to stay. In the days to come there would be strikes in other markets, but they would be for the purpose of organizing non-union shops. Significantly, the unionized shops stayed union.

With the most important markets of New York, Chicago and Rochester fully unionized, it was a matter of time and persistance before the other clothing areas in the country became unionized. Philadelphia proved to be a particularly hard nut to crack. B. Kirschbaum & Company, the largest concern in the city, used every weapon in the arsenal of strikebreaking tactics. A group of the larger firms in that city banded together on the basis of "one for all, all for one" in holding off the ACWA. After many discouraging efforts, Philadelphia was finally unionized in 1929, and the south Jersey plants soon fell in line.

In Cincinnati, the labor situation was out of the ordinary because the largest firm in the city, a made-to-measure house, was owned by Arthur Nash, nationally known as "Golden Rule" Nash. He injected a strong religious element in the entire running of his business and in his relations with his employes. Nash opposed the unionization of his plants not merely on business grounds, as an ordinary employer might, but also upon the basis of his religious beliefs. Then, by some quirk of his mind, certainly not based upon the usual logic or economic force that ordinarily caused a reluctant employer to accept the union, Nash decided that it was right and proper to have his workers join the Amalgamated. Whether Hillman's reasoning won Nash over, or whatever the cause, is unknown, but Nash himself called the workers together and asked them to join the ACWA. After some opposition, they agreed. Thus, the boss himself did the organizing! It was remarked later on, that Hillman missed a good man when he did not hire Nash immediately as a business agent.

So it went. Gradually, step by step, the ACWA spread throughout the country, organizing the factories. By 1929, the union could look forward to a continued growth of membership, maintaining a relatively harmonious relationship with the manufacturers in most markets. Suddenly, in 1930, the depression struck the industry with the force of a hurricane. There was wide unemployment. Manufacturers went bankrupt, or else liquidated their businesses. Union membership declined sharply. Only with the advent of the NRA in 1933, when new life was breathed into the near bankrupt industry, did the ACWA take hold once more as a powerful union.

The Local Associations

As labor organized in the separate markets, local associations of manufacturers were formed—if they were not already in existence—to deal primarily with the union on a local basis. Such associations that already had been organized prior to the 1920's for the prime purpose of dealing with retail matters, now assumed the additional function of handling local labor problems.

Rochester, as noted, had been the first market to organize a local association that enjoyed a degree of permanence. Although the first Rochester organization was formed in 1883, it was in 1890 that the successor group, the Rochester Clothiers Exchange, proposed to deal specifically with labor as well as all other matters affecting the manufacturers. The Rochester Exchange was affiliated with the National Association of Clothiers at the time, and so kept in touch with the national industry problems as well as local matters. The Exchange was doubtless the most active and enterprising of all local organizations in the country during the 1890's and throughout the early decades of the 1900's. It dealt successfully with labor problems to such an extent that at a later date, it was cited nationally as an example of excellent labor-management relations. Undoubtedly, this was due to the able leadership on the part of manufacturers by men such as Max L. Holtz and Jeremiah G. Hickey, while the labor manager of the market, Abraham Chatman, (also a vice president of the Amalgamated), considered the welfare of the workers at all times, but also recognized the need for establishing a proper relationship with management. The Exchange has continued as a most active organization to this day.

New York City posed a difficult problem both to labor and to management. Due to the large number of firms in the city, and a corresponding large number of contractors, coupled with frequent conflict of interests, the possibilities of any one local organization representing the manufacturers on labor matters were remote. After the formation of the National Labor Bureau, the local Clothiers Association of New York, shied away from any labor matters. In turn, as the market became unionized, the Bureau was pointedly asked not to intervene in New York affairs due to its anti-union reputation. As for the National Industrial Federation, it served merely as an advisory body, supposedly set up to offer expert advice on labor matters, but practically, its efforts were futile, although well-meant.

Since the unionized New York men's clothing manufacturers needed an organization to deal with the ACWA on a market basis, they established the American Clothing Manufacturers Association. In 1919, the Associated Boys Clothing Manufacturers merged with the men's group, and the Clothiers Association of New York also joined the newly formed organization now called the Clothing Manufacturers Association of New York. A year previous, with the war still going on, the larger firms in New York who had no prior dealings with the union, were practically forced as manufacturers of military uniforms to enter into relations with the ACWA due to pressure from the government. Thereupon they organized the Clothing Trade Association, becoming an affiliate of the expanded, new association which now included all segments of the unionized manufacturers in the city. Nevertheless, the members of the Clothing Trade Association, although associated with the larger group, had no desire to maintain a permanent relationship with the union, for they considered themselves parties of a "shot gun" marriage. It was this group of manufacturers that spearheaded the New York labor dispute in 1920–1921. When the strike was lost, they resigned from the larger association. The now-weakened Clothing Manufacturers Association of New York signed a two-year agreement with the union in 1920 and at the end of that time dissolved, with no New York market organization of manufacturers in existence for the time being. Incidentally, those members of the Clothing Trade Association who remained in business were eventually unionized.

But regardless of labor difficulties and disputes, retail credits, returns and bankruptcies were still urgent matters requiring constant attention. Therefore, the manufacturers who had been members of the dissolved association reorganized as the Associated Clothing Manufacturers of New York, stressing retail credit problems as its prime activity, with the understanding that labor matters were to be excluded as a function of the organization. Isidore Grossman of Grossman Clothing Company was elected president of this new association. Even at that early date, Grossman showed a flair for leadership and displayed his unselfish interest in the welfare of the industry.

Upon the dissolution of the Clothing Manufacturers Association of New York noted previously, there was no local market organization to deal with labor until 1924, at which time there was a strike of some 40,000 workers. To remedy this situation, on June 25, 1924, the New York Clothing Manufacturers Exchange was formed by William P. Goldman, Julius H. Levy, Charles D. Jaffee, Charles Douglis, Jacob Eisner, David Hoffman and their counsel, David Drechsler of Drechsler & Leff. This small nucleus of men, in forming a local organization in New York, profoundly influenced the clothing industry for more than forty years, as individuals and collectively.

Wm. P. Goldman, the "father of the Exchange," was the head of Wm. P. Goldman & Brothers and served for many decades as an important officer of the Exchange. When, in 1933, the Clothing Manufacturers Association of the United States of America was formed, he became a director, and later was treasurer of that association. During his long life, Wm. P. as he is known, has shown himself to be a kindly, warm-hearted and empathetic man. He has always intuitively understood the problems of others, as individuals or as members of the industry. A little-known incident may be recounted which will indicate the calibre of the man. Years ago, he met a young fellow endeavoring to sell zippers to the manager of his Brooklyn factory. As a matter of courtesy, he invited the budding salesman to return to New York in his car. While driving to New York, Wm. P. remarked that the suit worn by his guest was of relatively poor quality and workmanship. In the opinion of Wm. P., it was not the proper garb to interview clothing manufacturers. The young fellow replied that as his income was small, he could not afford more expensive clothes. Nothing further was said until they reached the New York offices of Wm. P. Goldman & Brothers, when Wm. P. invited the young man up to his showroom. He then ordered one of his assistants to fit the visitor with two suits, and charge them to Wm. P.'s account. That young man later became a prominent publisher, and this is merely one of the many stories he recounts to indicate the character of Wm. P.

Julius H. Levy was a boys' clothing manufacturer who became the first president of the Exchange and later served as its executive secretary for nearly three decades. Levy was an extremely able administrator and initiated numerous services rendered to the New York membership.

Charles D. Jaffee, also a boys' clothing manufacturer, succeeded Levy as president, and headed that organization, when in 1928, it was successful in finally substituting piece work for week work in the New York market. As head of the Exchange, Jaffee was active in establishing an unemployment fund for union employes. Jaffee served as president until his death in 1938, when he was succeeded by Isidore Grossman who had been the president of the Clothing Manufacturers Association of New York prior to its merger with the Exchange in 1927. Grossman showed himself to be reasonable and understanding in labor-management relations. Under his presidency, the New York market was soon acknowledged as the largest and most potent force in the industry. In later years, the ability of Grossman was recognized nationally when he was elected vice-president of the Clothing Manufacturers Association, after serving as a director for many years. Emanuel Weinstein, of West Mill Clothes, followed Grossman as president of the Exchange, serving as a director of the national organization as well. Weinstein was recently succeeded by Herman Soifer of Brookfield Clothes as president of the Exchange, which had changed its name to the New York Clothing Manufacturers Association.

The lawyer, David Drechsler of Drechsler and Leff, counsel to the new organization, who was one of the founders of the Exchange, was quickly recognized by all as a man of outstanding character combined with a most brilliant mind. At the time of the founding of the Exchange, Drechsler was forty-one years old, handsome in appearance, charming in manner, and a very successful attorney. Drechsler was born in Russia, came to this country as an infant, attended City College, and in 1904, obtained his law degree from New York University. His first clients were clothing manufacturers, and he knew all phases of the industry intimately. Drechsler won recognition quickly as the intellectual leader of the New York group, and when the national association was formed in 1933, his law firm was named as counsel. Drechsler, a religious and learned man, applied the wisdom of the Talmud to all his daily problems. His knowledge, understanding of human nature and practical approach to labor problems impressed prominent men in all walks of life. He acquired an extensive practice in the hotel industry, the shirt industry and in many other fields, but the clothing industry was nearest to his heart throughout his life. Drechsler's poise amidst the most excitable moments in labor negotiations was extraordinary and of considerable importance in concluding satisfactory wage settlements.

The public testimonials given to Drechsler in his lifetime were many, yet he was a most simple man. His office was bare of furniture, the walls empty except for a portrait of his mother, and the floor uncarpeted. It was told that once a prominent Fifth Avenue retailer came to see Drechsler on an important matter. He had been informed that only a man such as David Drechsler could well advise him. Therefore, when this fastidiously dressed retailer, with a white piping edging his vest, opened the door of Drechsler's office his face showed amazement. Was this the office of the famous labor lawyer? Drechsler looked up from his table, for he never used a desk, saw the look of surprise on the visitor's face, and said, "You are wondering what sort of a lawyer I am. Am I a lawyer who cannot afford a better office, or am I so good that I don't give a damn. Well, I'll tell you that I am so good and don't give a damn." The man became his fervent admirer and client. During World War II, the clothing industry felt that Drechsler had served it far beyond his regular duties. He was offered a large sum of money, but he refused to accept any amount in addition to his annual retainer. Thereupon, a special fund was collected to establish a memorial in Israel, commemorating the name of his dead son.

Sidney Hillman recognized the ability of David Drechsler as a labor negotiator early in their relationship as the respective leaders of labor and management. Hillman also realized that Drechsler was not opposed to unionism as such, but believed in a live and let live philosophy, striving at all times to obtain the best possible terms for the employers. In matters of personality and human relations, there was a close similarity between Hillman and Drechsler. They were both extremely serious minded, entirely devoted to their lives' work be it union or law, men who lived private lives of Spartan simplicity, and who were actually very emotional and warm hearted despite their seeming outward austere manner. Therefore, it was no surprise that they took to each other, having a very high regard for each other's ability and integrity. It was Drechsler and Hillman who planned and worked together to establish the foundation for lasting industrial peace between labor and management. They were the two great men of the industry.

Under the leadership of Henry J. Ettelson, a man of driving determination, a small group of manufacturers met in March, 1921, and planned the organization known today as the Philadelphia Clothing Manufacturers Association. William B. Flickstein, then a very young man, was elected as the executive secretary, and he has continued to serve in this capacity to date. The stated purpose of the organization was to "foster, protect and promote the welfare and interest of persons engaged in the business of manufacturing clothing." Its initial activity was to handle matters relating to retailers, such as credits and insolvencies. When the entire market was unionized in 1933, under the leadership of Charles Weinstein, the association entered into a collective bargaining agreement with the ACWA. Labor and management were most interested in developing Philadelphia as a clothing center, and both sides recognized that industrial peace was a prime necessity if such an aim was to

Henry J. Ettleson
(Courtesy of the Ettleson Family)

be achieved. With Weinstein and Ettelson as the respective heads of the local union and the association, a mutually satisfactory relationship was established so that there has been no strike of clothing workers in the city since the first collective bargaining agreement was signed.

As president of the association, Ettelson had the active cooperation of the membership in all industry matters. With the support of Louis Goldsmith of Louis Goldsmith, Inc., Nathan Pincus of Pincus Brothers, the Daroffs of H. Daroff & Sons, and other leading clothing executives, the Philadelphia Clothing Manufacturers Association became not merely an important economic factor in the life of the city, but was also recognized as an industry that was actively involved in all welfare programs within the community, regardless of creed or race. Particularly notable in philanthropic endeavors, locally and nationally, was Samuel H. Daroff of the Daroff clothing family. He was suitably honored after his death

Isidore Grossman
(Courtesy of the CMA)

in 1967, when a building, which was devoted to philanthropic work, was dedicated in his memory.

When Ettelson retired in 1950, after having served as president for 29 years, Michael Daroff of H. Daroff & Sons succeeded him. In turn, Joseph Seitchik of W. Seitchik & Sons became his successor. Recently, Albert Ettelson, a son of Henry J. Ettelson, was elected president of the association. As Philadelphia became the second most important market, the activities of the organization widened under the administrative supervision of Flickstein. It now extended its activities to include matters affecting transportation, military procurement, and all regulations that affected the business of the members. Flickstein, an outstanding executive secretary, was indefatigable in creating special services for the manufacturers.

Yet, despite active local organizations in the important clothing markets of Rochester, New York and Philadelphia, there were many clothing centers where there was no association of clothing firms.

In such instances, the manufacturers were not organized to deal with the local union on a collective bargaining basis, nor safeguard the interests of their market if and when state or local regulations might be enacted that affected the production of clothing. But of paramount importance, there was no national association that might deal with labor or government on an industrywide basis. There was no national spokesman for the industry. The men's clothing industry was truly fragmented, with no collective point of view on any matter. There was need for a national association of clothing manufacturers.

Chapter 10

Years of "Normalcy"

Manufacturers Become Retailers

It will be recalled that manufacturers in pre-Civil War days often owned retail outlets in cities distant from the factory, opening stores in the South and on the Pacific Coast. It was dual distribution in its infancy. With the extraordinarily rapid expansion of railroads shortly after the Civil War and the emergence of jobbers in the large cities throughout the country, manufacturer-owned stores disappeared. Now it was the jobber, buying from the clothing manufacturers, who performed the services of warehousing and selling to retailers within a given area.

But the prospect of a clothing firm owning stores, which guaranteed assured outlets for its production, was the dream of many manufacturers. After 1920, conditions became ripe once more for the manufacturers to enter the retail field. Clothing concerns had found that the credit standing of many retailers had been impaired following the war because of inventory losses that had occurred during the deflation. Hence, there was need to seek new and additional retail outlets. Also, in the 1920's, as a result of excessive optimism during the inflationary period, the manufacturers were burdened with large stocks of clothing that had to be sold at heavy losses. Manufacturer-controlled retail stores would have been an excellent means of siphoning off this inventory. As for selling only to well rated stores that had weathered the economic turmoil, when such stores bought at all, they demanded special prices and extra terms. A ready answer for a manufacturer in such a quandary was to open his own clothing outlets, preferably going into partnership with a store owner who provided the practical retail experience.

The expediency of a manufacturer owning stores was one of the many subjects discussed by William Goldman in his notable address made in 1915, at the convention of the National Association of Clothiers. He deprecated the advantages of such a business arrangement when he said:

> . . . We will, no doubt, continue to see efforts made by organizations to manufacture clothing and distribute it at retail. We have had examples of this sort in the past, none of which has been significant as pointing the way to this method of marketing clothing. Theoretically, the possibility of great savings in overhead at the wholesale end has always had much lure to the clothier's imagination, but practically there is much in the way of its success. A successful organization of this kind would have to be composed of able manufacturers and retailers capable of directing a large number of stores . . .

While Goldman changed his mind in later years, for his firm opened the Broadstreet chain in 1927, at the time of his address, he undoubtedly expressed the views of many manufacturers that "the shoemaker should stick to his last."

However, conditions in the industry had changed radically between the years of 1915 to 1920. When the business climate worsened in 1920 because of deflation, some firms considered Goldman's strictures regarding manufacturer-owned stores as no longer applicable. Shortly thereafter, a number of clothing firms became manufacturing retailers (producing for their own stores only), and others became dual distributors (producing for their own stores but selling to independent stores as well).

The clothing houses that became manufacturing retailers usually were small or medium sized concerns, with a limited retail distribution at best. Therefore, there was little risk when they stopped selling independent stores. However, the nationally advertised clothing manufacturers with thousands of retail customers, could not readily give up selling to these accounts. Under these circumstances they went into retail store ownership in a limited way. They bought either a few local chains which assured a guaranteed distribution absorbing part of their total output, or else they opened new stores in areas where business prospects were excellent, but where they had no retail accounts. This was the real beginning of the extensive dual distribution in its modern form, later to grow into a matter of industry concern, and since discussed with more heat than light.

In keeping with the times, independent store owners also felt the urge to expand, to become "merchants" rather than mere retailers. They took their savings, or borrowed freely, or secured revolving credit terms from their merchandise suppliers, really a form of long term loans, and opened additional stores. Such branches were staffed and supervised ordinarily by relatives. In many instances, the founders of these businesses were far more able than their successors, a frequent occurrence in the industry. Consequently, when business conditions turned bad in the 1930's, too often such chains liquidated, although there were some family chains that continued to prosper and expand, thanks to the able management of the heirs. As a group though, family chains were important retailers within their localities, but few acquired national economic stature.

As clothing chains of all types prospered and proliferated in the 1920's, *Men's Wear Magazine* noted that by 1929 there were 286 men's wear chains, and their sales accounted for 22.7 per cent of total men's and boys' apparel volume. The outstanding group showing the most rapid growth was the manufacturing retailer promoting relatively low priced clothing. It was during this period that Richman Bros., expanded nationally, specializing in $22.50 suits. Crawford Clothes, headed by Joseph Levy, opened many branches in the East, and Kappel, Marks and Langeman started the Howard chain. Bond Stores, sparked by Barney Rubin, grew to become one of the largest of the men's wear specialty chains. All featured the $22.50 suit, though some carried a lower priced line as well. These manufacturing retailers were successful because they were headed by individuals truly gifted in production, merchandising and selling, who saw their opportunity and made the most of it.

It was to be expected that such rapid growth by the manufacturing retailers would alarm the makers of low priced clothing who were selling to the independent stores. Predictions were frequently and loudly made that the average clothing manufacturer and independent retailer as well were doomed to extinction. With distribution and selling costs reduced to a minimum, who could withstand the powerful manufacturer retailer setup? How could an independent store offer competitive values?

Pessimists had a field day. Then, in the course of a few years, with the retirement or death of the founders, many chains folded, merged, or merely continued to mark time. As noted, the initial success of the chains was due to the ability and enterprise of the founders. When these men left the scene, it was extremely difficult to replace them. The inbred method of business succession—nepotism—had always been pervasive throughout the industry. Hence, it naturally spread to chain store operations as a matter of course. The second generation followed the policies of the founders as best they could, but the verve and "extra push" were usually lacking. As a group, although there were exceptions, the manufacturing retailers reached their peak by 1929, and then merely continued as retail outlets. Their threat to the existence of the independent manufacturer and the retailer receded, and the relative industry importance of the manufacturing retailers declined considerably. Within time, due to economic conditions, the single price store was forced to introduce higher priced lines as well. Concurrently, the independent clothing manufacturers reacted to the threat of the manufacturing retailers by stressing volume production, offering clothing at prices that permitted retailers to sell merchandise competitively. So another "danger" to the industry passed.

Periodically, the industry was to be threatened by new merchandising methods that would, according to many, inevitably bring about the extinction of the independent manufacturers and retailers. The expansion of mail order houses, the growth of chains such as J. C. Penney, the initial impact of the discount houses, and numerous other merchandising innovations, have all seemed to endanger the immediate future of the independents. These alarming changes have been regular and frequent. But the most important ingredient of a successful operation within the industry, always has been the initiative and ability of the individual who headed the clothing enterprise, be he manufacturer or retailer. There never has been a dearth of such persons in the industry, and there is every likelihood that a new crop will appear each generation. It can be reasonably expected that new firms will rise, new stores will be opened, and many will grow to importance within a few years, competing successfully with the established firms. In an effort to acquire the skill and knowledge of these new men, the established companies may even merge with their younger competitors. Time will pass and the cycle will probably repeat itself. That has been the history of the industry.

Clothing firms that became dual distributors naturally expanded on a much more restricted scale than the manufacturing retailers. Hart, Schaffner & Marx, Cohen, Goldman & Company and L. Greif & Bro., either opened stores or else purchased some of their outstanding retail accounts. But such controlled stores represented merely a small proportion of the firm's total production. The extraordinary growth of the dual distributors was to occur a generation later, after the second World War.

It was in 1928, in keeping with the feverish tempo of the times, that a combination of extraordinary size was formed. It was a vertical merger of leading retail clothing stores throughout the country, headed by the manufacturing firms of Fashion Park and Stein Bloch. Stores of national prominence such as the Hub in

Chicago, Juster Brothers in Minneapolis, R. B. Baker in Cleveland, and other well known retailers were members of the combine. The spark plug of this somewhat heterogeneous group was Dan Lipmann, then associated with Fashion Park. This prestigious organization had a short life, for the depression soon came. When Lipmann resigned as head of the organization in 1933, the trade paper announced the final disintegration of Fashion Park Associates. According to reports at the time, the depression was merely the catalytic event that brought about the combination's inevitable demise. There had been a lack of proper planning in centralized merchandising and sales policy. There were consequent divergent views which caused internal confusion. Perhaps, if the stock market collapse and the depression that followed had not occurred in 1929, permitting a longer period for assimilation, the combine might have coalesced into a well-knit chain headed by a nationally known manufacturing concern. With the breakup of the associates, the stores resumed their independent status, while Fashion Park Clothes retained ownership of Weber & Heilbroner, continuing its special relationship with Finchley as well. Thus, the experience of dual distribution in the 1920's varied from fairly satisfactory results to financial disaster. Primarily, the reason for failure and the reason for success as always, was management, or more bluntly, who was the boss.

From the standpoint of sheer economics, the growth of chains when properly capitalized, was a sensible trend. There were obvious savings in overhead costs by a manufacturing retailer; dual distributors were assured a proportion of their total volume; the independent retail chains found that centralized buying meant greater purchasing power. Yet each chain, large and small, was handicapped by its Achilles' heel, namely, the need to establish a self-perpetuating management team that would have the drive, the knowledge and the practical experience possessed by the founders of the organization. When retail business proved disappointing in 1929, declining catastrophically in the years immediately following, the crucial test came. Most of the chains in all categories described, found that they were burdened with high rent leases, that much of their capital was tied up in fixtures and that credit terms tightened. Able management now proved its worth merely by surviving during the long depression years. Many chains went bankrupt. Others made settlements with their creditors and continued on a reduced scale. Few survived unscathed. But those chains that still remained in business by 1933, had established their right to continue. They had proven their durability to exist in times of extreme stress.

Tailors-To-The-Trade

During World War II, an official in one of the government agencies welcomed a prominent clothing manufacturer, who was a tailor-to-the-trade, with the cheery greeting, "Oh, I know you, your garments sell in every barber shop." This was supposedly a humorous remark made without any probable intent to denigrate this branch of the industry, yet it did indicate the obvious fact that in the 1940's, tailors-to-the-trade often sold their garments in most unusual retail outlets. Made-to-measure clothing was truly sold everywhere and in every type of store that might conceivably cater to the male customer.

The usual tailor-to-the-trade firm, or made-to-measure house (the terms are interchangeable), was generally defined by the industry, and later by the Federal Trade Commission, as a specialty clothing firm that cut a single garment according to exact measurements of a consumer who had ordered that garment from a retail outlet serviced by the manufacturer. As already noted, there had been some sporadic made-to-measure sales in pre-Civil War days between southern stores and northern manufacturers. But it was only in the later decades of the 19th century, when the tailors-to-the-trade had expanded their method of servicing merchant tailors, that they were recognized as an important branch of the clothing industry.

In prior years, the average country merchant tailor purchased some fabric ends from a woolen jobber in a nearby city, subscribed to a trade publication that featured sketches of the more recent clothing styles, and with this limited selection of material and model, the tailor shop offered its wares to the local trade. The handicaps of meager inventory and restricted style selections were overcome by the small town merchant when he acquired a tailor-to-the-trade franchise. He now received, without charge, an elaborate style book with sketches (often in color), of the latest clothing models, plus a book of fabric swatches which included a wide variety of materials. Sometimes both books were combined as one. Now the merchant tailor had no need to carry any inventory of woolen piece goods or trimmings. Once an arrangement had been made with the wholesale made-to-measure firm, the tailor merely acted as a sales agent. He took the measurements of his customer who had selected the fabric, sent this information to the tailoring house located in a distant city, and delivered the finished garment to the consumer when it arrived from the factory.

Because roads were less developed in the South than in other sections of the country, and cities far between, the average man living in a southern village or small town usually bought his clothes from the local merchant tailor. Since the made-to-measure houses offered a service that appealed especially to a small tailor shop, the manufacturers concentrated their greatest efforts in the South, where sales possibilities were best. Of course, they also sent elaborate brochures outlining their services throughout all sections of the country. The country merchant tailor saw his doom. As a realist, he was not long in substituting the tailor-to-the-trade book for his very limited stock of woolens.

These wholesale tailoring houses were located most frequently in Chicago, Cincinnati and Baltimore. Surprisingly, in the large ready made clothing centers of the Northeast, such as New York, Philadelphia and Rochester, the made-to-measure business never really took hold. The sole exception was the International Tailoring Company in New York (there was also a branch in Chicago), which became by far the largest concern of its type in the industry. Competition for accounts was intense. The average merchant tailor, and later the regular clothing retailer, were flooded each season with offers to accept the latest style and swatch books free. Special prizes, free suits and other inducement gimmicks were used in desperate efforts to secure new accounts or keep the old ones. In a desire to sell every possible outlet in a town, the tailoring houses used several trade names. It was therefore possible for many merchants in any locality to be offering actually the same line with merely different names printed on the cover of the style book. For that reason, an accurate count of the made-to-measure houses in the early years of the trade was haphazard at best, because one wholesale tailoring house might conduct its business under some half-dozen trade names. It was generally known though, that by 1900, there were literally hundreds of tailoring firms in the industry, although most of them were small, operating with very limited capital. The larger firms, entirely ethical in methods of doing business, suffered from the disreputable practices of many fly-by-night houses who entered and left the industry at short notice. Some tailoring houses did not actually cut individual orders separately, but rather trimmed a garment already cut in quantity, so that it coincided, as best it might, with the individual measurements received. Such devious and unethical practices for a time gave a black eye to the industry. Not until local Better Business Bureaus and later, the Federal Trade Commission, took action, did such free-wheeling firms disappear from the scene.

Expanding their activity in the early 1900's on the wave of general prosperity, the tailoring houses made considerable inroads in the ready made clothing business. This especially affected those houses selling to the country trade, particularly in the South where clothing usually was sold in the small towns by the general store. While the individual stores were small accounts, nevertheless the aggregate of this small town business was considerable. It became a common practice for these general stores to substitute the tailors' books for their own limited stock of ready made clothing. They found it a more profitable method of catering to their customers because no capital was tied up in inventory, a most important consideration to the small retailer.

In that manner, tailors-to-the-trade offered strong competition to the ready made clothing manufacturers. The relative importance of the tailoring houses could be accurately gauged in the 1920's, at a time when they reached their apex of activity, because the Bureau of the Census data were available in detailed form for the first time.

% of Total Industry's Suit Production Manufactured By Tailors-To-The-Trade

YEAR	% OF TAILOR-TO-THE-TRADE PRODUCTION
1924	17.6%
1925	15.3%
1926	19.0%
1927	19.5%
1928	21.5%
1932	17.0%
1933	16.5%

As to the relative number of tailoring concerns compared to the industry total of all firms making men's clothing, the Bureau of the Census reported as follows:

YEAR	% OF TAILORING FIRMS COMPARED WITH TOTAL CLOTHING FIRMS REPORTING EACH JANUARY IN YEARS LISTED
1924	20% of total
1925	17% of total
1926	22% of total
1927	21% of total
1928	21% of total
1932	19% of total
1933	19% of total

The peak years of activity for the made-to-measure industry were 1926 through 1928. The years of depression naturally affected the tailoring houses as it did other manufacturers. However, even when business conditions in ready made clothing revived, the tailors-to-the-trade continued to show a steady drop in dollar volume and in number of firms. While in 1933 it was reported that 129 made-to-measure concerns sent in their figures regularly to the Bureau of the Census, during World War II, no more than 75 such firms could be counted by the Clothing Manufacturers Association (CMA) in its industrywide survey. The tailors-to-the-trade had never organized a national association for they were great individualists, and it was not until the CMA was formed in 1933 that the tailors-to-the-trade were finally affiliated with any national group. Their importance as a branch of the industry was duly recognized at the time, and even today, although their numbers have been reduced considerably, the tailoring houses have special representation on the CMA board of directors and on all special committees affecting their interests.

During the second World War, the tailoring houses that were still in business prospered, as did the other branches of the industry. However, once the war ended, the fundamental economic weakness that had become increasingly apparent even prior to 1940, resulted in a widespread and rapid reduction in the number of firms and in dollar volume. Because of good roads, communication improved considerably between the country town and the city. With the universal use of the automobile as a means of travel, the residents in a small town could visit the city easily and purchase ready made garments in stores that carried a wide selection of clothing. When ready made clothes were bought, there was no waiting period of several weeks, which was the case when special order garments were purchased. Moreover, the average store usually carried many price lines, and did not restrict itself to the styling and quality of only one wholesaler. Another industry development that caused a shrinkage of tailoring volume was the introduction of special order departments by ready made suit manufacturers, whereby styles might be ordered according to individual customer measurement by their regular retail accounts at only a small extra charge.

By the 1960's, the relative importance of the tailors-to-the-trade as a branch of the industry had dwindled to an estimated four to five per cent of total clothing production. The specialty tailoring houses that remained now catered mostly to those consumers who needed individually fit garments because of physical handicap, or required individually made clothing suitable for their profession (such as extra pockets), or else sold to that element of the public that desired extraordinary style features not to be found in the usual models featured by the industry. During the years of decline there were mergers and then mergers of the merged. The largest tailoring house in the country liquidated. Only those manufacturers continued who recognized that conditions had changed and that it was necessary to change with the times. Retailers that desired to carry a well rounded line in their special order department, not merely suits, but outercoats, sport coats and slacks as well, became customers of the tailoring houses. Merchant tailors who were still anxious for made-to-measure business also used the style and swatch books of the tailoring houses. At all events, by carefully watching sales trends, the tailors-to-the-trade have managed to maintain their limited foothold in the industry. Currently, however, the greater part of the made-to-measure volume is in the hands of the larger ready made clothing manufacturers who sell higher priced garments. To cite the importance that special order departments have assumed, it has been reported that individual orders represent up to 15 per cent of total dollar volume of many manufacturers making the higher priced suits. Medium priced clothing houses have also established special order departments as a service for their accounts. With such strong competition coming from the ready made clothing firms, it seems doubtful whether the tailoring houses will ever assume a more significant role in the production of men's clothing.

Fashion Evolves Slowly

In the course of the years, men's clothing fashions have changed, as might be expected, but the changes evolved slowly since this evolutionary process was dependent upon changes in the economic and social factors that influenced society as a whole. This could be readily observed during the gradual urbanization of our population which resulted in a substantial increase of the white collar class, employed in the stores, banks and offices of the expanding cities. Consequently, the demand for clothing suitable for work and city living increased. Then, as the work week was reduced over the years from six days to five and a half days, and more recently to only five days, resulting in more leisure time, clothing which was practical for wear in active sports participation or proper for spectator use was required. So sportswear sales zoomed. The demand for informal clothes also increased when the middle class moved to the suburbs in large numbers. It was a truism that changes in men's fashions over the decades were not designed in isolation but were prompted primarily by altered conditions of living within the social and economic state of our society.

Thus, in the 1890's, with businessmen setting the standard, the average male considered himself well dressed when he wore a coat, vest and trousers made of different fabrics and colors. The coat was a semi-cutaway, indicating the transition stage from the regular formal cutaway towards the future suit model to be. During this period of change, the tailess jacket (the tuxedo), first worn in Tuxedo Park in 1886, became popular. At first it was acceptable solely for stag affairs, but later it was recognized as suitable for general evening attire. The formal coat with tails continued in use, although considerably less popular and worn only for most formal type of social event.

At the turn of the century, the popular model in sack coats was short in length, with the shoulders wide and bulging unnaturally. This was the heyday of the manly "broad chester." Still, the frock coat maintained its special niche as a symbol of affluence and social status. Photographs of the day showed that men of prominence, and most public officials, wore, as a rule, the regular frock coat with striped trousers plus a fancy silk vest, or a white vest, or at least a vest edged with white piping. And the cutters of the clothing industry, habitually wearing frock coats to work, were determined to prove to the lowly shop operators that they really were superior persons.

While admittedly the cutaway represented social standing, still it was somewhat uncomfortable. It also gave the average man of portly proportions the appearance of a pouter pidgeon. Clearly, the sack coat of a suit was more practical for business wear. Moreover, with central heating growing in use, even the affluent recognized that the frock coat was a physical nuisance, and soon was discarded for every day wear. The suit (matched coat, vest and pants), as we know it generally, became the ordinary daily garb for the average businessman, for the professional man and for all engaged in other white collar occupations.

During the years immediately following 1900, the dominant fabric used in suits was serge, and the most popular color was blue. It was estimated at the time that 70 per cent of all cloth used in men's suits was blue serge. For the factory managers this was indeed a period of blissful contentment. With one fabric and one color so prevalent, there was a minimum of plant upset due to variety of pattern or color. Years later, when elderly factory managers met at industry functions, invariably the talk reverted to the good old days of blue serge. There were sighs of regret that plaids and checks were now worn in its place, with olives, browns, grays, and other shades in countless numbers bedeviling production schedules.

During the decade of 1910–1920, the natural shoulder model was introduced and widely adopted. The ungainly oversized "broad chester" look was now discarded, and the sharp, slim silhouette became the suit to wear. The popularity of the silhouette was caused partly by the growing awareness that a slim form implied youth and athletic vigor, while the portly form did not signify dignity any longer. It was merely proof of a hearty appetite and lack of exercise. With greater leisure time now available, participation in sports was growing. Golf was no longer an old man's game, but the popular pastime of the country club set. So fashions changed in accordance with changes in ways of living.

The turning point in men's clothing, stressing comfort in model and in fabric weight, came in 1919 when the soldiers returned to civilian life after the first World War. The experience of men in uniform profoundly influenced post-war fashions in all categories of men's apparel. The watchword now was wearing comfort. We can cite the decline of the starched collar as an outstanding example, because it was generally discarded in favor of the soft, attached collar as a consequence of the khaki shirt worn by the troops. Lightweight tropical worsted suits now made their appearance in quantity. The relatively heavyweight fabrics, light in color only, which had been favored previously for summer wear, began a steady decline in popularity.

As new models evolved, certain elements of the buying public sought, as always, an extreme version of the garment. It had to be "sharp, outstanding and eye catching." The buyers of such clothes were, for the most part, young men with low income who had need to prove, either to their friends or to themselves, that they were "somebody" not at all ordinary but really unique. Perhaps such clothes were bought to project visually to the world a personality that needed reassurance. At all events, when the narrow shoulder, slim silhouette grew in demand, an extreme model of this garment, called the "jazz suit," was produced in large quantities for such young men. This phase in dress died quickly, for its exaggerated style features brought more jeers than cheers for its wearers. Interestingly, Disraeli, as a young man, followed this very principle of bizarre dress to gain attention, but it was not his dress that made him a great man, rather his ability, if not his genius, as a political figure.

With more leisure time available in the 1920's, the first tailored clothing that could reasonably be considered as sportswear made its appearance. "Plus fours," which were knickers that hung below the knee were worn by young and old during the weekend. A sales unit ordinarily consisted of a sack coat, long trousers, knickers and perhaps a vest, made of tweed or other heavy wool fabric. Since the knickers were often uncomfortable, for they tended to slip, slacks came into use in place of the "plus fours" in the 1930's.

As a reaction to the silhouette model which emphasized the slim form to a somewhat extreme degree, the English drape model gained popularity. This suit had broader shoulders, although it had a definitely nipped-in waist in front and sides. The drape was favored by the average businessman, but the younger generation had its own ideas on style.

As the country was in a prosperous period, an increasing number of young men now entered the Ivy colleges from relatively high income homes. Such youngsters were far more conscious of clothes than their predecessors. The favorite pose of a student sitting on a fence, wearing a turtle neck sweater with the college letter prominent on the chest, was considered passé . . . a mere rah, rah boy. Now it was the four-button, natural shoulder Brooks model that was the suit to wear. Although there were considerable variations of the approved style, still Ivy League students, who were generally acknowledged as the national leaders of college dress, considered themselves to be properly attired only if they wore a four-button suit (a well known store label sewn on the inner pocket), extremely heavy brogue shoes which limited walking to a shuffle, an overcoat with collar turned up to the ears even though there was no need to do so, and a battered hat which may have been really brand new. Once clothed in this manner, every young man could be classified as genuine Ivy, although he attended a "cow" college in the Midwest or on the Coast. In addition, if perchance, a raccoon coat covered the four button suit, then the dress uniform was entirely complete.

This was the time when President Coolidge summarized popular thought by laconically noting that "the business of America is business," and his predecessor, Harding, had called for a time of "normalcy." As part of American society, the young collegian reflected this thinking, for it was the aim of the ambitious college graduate to join the ranks of business or preferably enter Wall Street. We can therefore understand why there was a trend towards the business suit for college wear, since many hoped to become young executives shortly, and the hopefuls dressed accordingly. It was the general feeling that good times would last forever, stocks would go still higher, jobs were plentiful, and very lucrative positions indeed awaited each college graduate. It was the heyday of follow the leader. In this instance, the leader was the Wall Street broker.

Chapter 11

Depression and Recovery

The Depression

When the speculative bubble burst on the New York Stock Exchange in October, 1929, the men's clothing industry was enjoying a fairly good year. While many manufacturers lost heavily in the stock market, the industry as a whole was not really perturbed. Just as a matter of course, the usual statements were immediately issued by the prominent clothing manufacturers assuring one and all that "conditions were fundamentally sound," assertions which resembled similar affirmations made during the deflationary period of 1920–1921. Saying something of an optimistic nature to the trade press in times of difficulty was an old industry tradition, practiced previously in periods of stress, and faithfully followed in the years to come. Such statements though were recognized as merely whistling in the dark. To many, it was a certain signal that danger was ahead and that times would really worsen.

Despite such hopeful affirmations that all was well, and that the financial storm would soon blow over, the depression struck the industry with the force of a hurricane. Numerous banks failed shortly thereafter, never to reopen. Then, on December 30, 1930, the Bank of the United States in New York, closed its doors. This was particularly hard on the clothing industry. One of the largest clothing manufacturers in the city was a director of that institution. The financial strength of this bank had been considered beyond question. Many clothing manufacturers who were substantial depositors lost a greater part of their ready cash, and their usual resource for business loans was no longer available. At the same time, during 1930, sales were declining and profits were turning into losses. It was a year of increasing gloom. Therefore, when Max L. Holtz, the president of the Rochester Clothiers Exchange, and an outstanding manufacturer in that city, announced that "1930 was a disturbing year," he was understating conditions to a remarkable degree. "Moreover," continued the ever-hopeful Mr. Holtz, "the upswing is in prospect for 1931," which was obviously intended to inspire confidence among manufacturers and nervous retailers. But a note of absolute certainty came from Chicago, when Mr. Alex M. Levy, the new president of Hart, Schaffner & Marx, informed his stockholders on January 26, 1931, that "we are looking forward for that revival in business which usually has followed each depression in the past." It was only a month later when the *Daily News Record* reported that retail stores were causing the dual distributors (including Harts) to suffer huge losses, and that Harts had set aside one million dollars as a reserve for such a forseeable deficit. Dual distributors in fact continued to encounter very rough weather, for one year later, on January 9, 1932, the trade paper reported that retail stores were heavy burdens and that Society Brand was closing its stores. "Astute observers," according to the trade paper, "were using their privilege of hindsight, and proclaiming that manufacturers owning stores had made a serious error in business judgment." Grave fears were expressed that some firms could not sustain the losses long. Despite this news, Dun & Bradstreet issued a statement on January 21, 1932, informing the trade as Holtz and Levy did only a year previous, that "there is gain in general confidence." In modern terms, there was somewhat of a credibility gap between statements and facts.

During the many years of the depression, all branches of the industry suffered severely. Only by detailing actual statistical data for the years of the crisis, could the hardships of manufacturers, and the retailers, and the human suffering imposed upon the clothing workers be accurately depicted. The tables that follow set forth the dire economic conditions that confronted the industry at the time.

Men's Clothing Industry in 1933 Compared with 1929
1929 = 100%

CITIES	1933 DOLLAR VOLUME	1933 NO. OF ESTABLISHMENTS
New York	57.0% of 1929	59.3% of 1929
Chicago	30.6% of 1929	54.1% of 1929
Philadelphia	53.6% of 1929	71.5% of 1929
Boston	64.1% of 1929	86.4% of 1929
Cleveland	51.9% of 1929	48.8% of 1929
St. Louis	51.7% of 1929	50.8% of 1929
Milwaukee	39.7% of 1929	78.5% of 1929
Cincinnati	41.7% of 1929	80.3% of 1929
Baltimore	52.8% of 1929	98.5% of 1929
Rochester	28.8% of 1929	38.5% of 1929
Other Cities	49.5% of 1929	37.5% of 1929
United States	49.4% of 1929	60.1% of 1929

Source: Bureau of the Census, U.S. Department of Commerce

The Rochester market suffered the greatest loss in dollar volume and more than 60 per cent of its establishments discontinued operations since 1929. All markets showed startling reductions in sales, but in some cities the number of liquidations or bankruptcies was relatively small, whereas in other cities more than half of the clothing plants operating in 1929 were closed by 1933. Chicago lost its place as the second largest market during the depression which was never regained. Philadelphia replaced Chicago and it has since maintained this position.

According to a Dun & Bradstreet analysis of financial statements issued by clothing manufacturers for 1931 operations, (median figures used), the loss on net sales incurred by manufacturers for the year was 1.42 per cent, rising to a 3.3 per cent loss on net sales in 1932. In that year, the net worth of the manufacturers declined by 11.45 per cent. Because of the enactment of the National Industrial Recovery Act (NIRA), the sudden late rush in business, a steep upsurge in prices, and consequent upward revaluation of inventory, in 1933 the industry actually operated on a net profit of 1.70 per cent on net sales.

Manufacturers were encountering great difficulty merely to stay in business. According to Sidney Hillman's biographer, at that time even the firm of Hart, Schaffner & Marx seriously considered liquidating the company. This crisis was soon overcome. The ACWA permitted a reduction in wages, calling it a "loan." The firm continued operations and later repaid the "loan" to its employes.

With the manufacturers finding their capital depleted, many firms simply could not afford to lose more money. Often they became insolvent. The table below, compiled by the National Credit Office, details the financial difficulties of the industry during this period:

Men's Clothing Industry
No. of Business Embarrassments
(Bankruptcies, Assignments, Trustees)

YEAR	TOTAL NO.	% OF TOTAL IN INDUSTRY	AMOUNT OF LIABILITIES (000 omitted)
1928	85	3.8%	$3,935
1929	58	2.8%	3,480
1930	132	7.0%	8,510
1931	153	8.0%	7,002
1932	168	*	8,455
1933	60	*	1,364
1934	34	*	980

* No data available

During the years of 1930, 1931 and 1932, the clothing industry was in dire straits, with an increasing number of firms in financial hot water.

By 1932, the economic status of the clothing workers, beset by such industry conditions, had become quite desperate. From 1928 to 1932, weekly wages had declined by 41 per cent, yet the cost of living had dropped only 25 per cent. Hillman estimated that 60 per cent of the ACWA members were unemployed in the summer of 1931. During the following year, Hillman stated that the clothing industry was operating at merely 30 per cent of capacity. Such a loss of employment was reflected in a reduction of union membership which had declined by 50,000 since 1929. The unemployment fund of the ACWA could not possibly cope with the magnitude of the needy workers who required relief, and thus the clothing workers were faced with insuperable conditions of hardship.

Retailers were also in great difficulty. Their sales reflected only too well general economic conditions throughout the country. Dun & Bradstreet analyses of financial statements issued by clothing stores disclosed that in 1931, retailers had suffered a loss of 2.44 per cent on their net sales, and in 1932 it rose to the fantastic height of 5.10 per cent of net sales. In the latter year, retailers' net worth had been reduced by 14.26 per cent. All through the years of depression, the columns of the trade paper were crowded with news that the largest and best known stores in the country, and nationally famous chains as well, were calling meetings of their creditors, seeking settlement of their debts. In order to move merchandise, many clothing manufacturers shipped goods on consignment. In that way, the retailers assumed no debt for merchandise, and the manufacturer was guaranteed payment if the clothing was sold. In other instances, where retail credit was shaky, manufacturers requested that their retail accounts give them the power of attorney, so that income and expenses of the stores might be carefully supervised by the creditor. One manufacturer was reported at the time to hold such powers of attorney for more than 100 stores. The traditional methods of trade were therefore completely disrupted by a general loss of confidence in the credit standing of even the best known accounts. It was a time of general uncertainty which often reached hysteria as credit losses mounted steadily. The retail credit structure was obviously tottering.

Such was the economic condition of the men's clothing industry at the end of 1932, the nadir of the depression. Then on March 4, 1933, Franklin Delano Roosevelt was inaugurated as President. Now started the "Hundred Days" of New Deal legislation. The first ray of hope for the industry was on the horizon.

Forming Two National Associations

With Roosevelt as President, steps were soon taken in Congress with the intent of creating order out of the economic chaos rampant throughout the country. Congressional committees immediately held hearings in order to determine the best means of raising wages, of reducing hours and of permitting the individual industries to establish trade practices that would stabilize business. As might be expected, panaceas were offered freely from all sides. There were suggestions of reducing the work week to 30 hours with the aim of spreading employment to the millions needing jobs. There were recommendations that a 40-hour week would be most feasible. In addition to a shorter work week, there were widespread demands that a minimum wage provision was necessary, though the actual amount of such a wage scale suggested was dependent upon the radical or conservative coloring of the proponents.

On the whole, it was a field day for the theorists, practical or impractical, and the manufacturers in the clothing industry had no inhibitions in proclaiming their individual opinions in the columns of the trade paper, or at the luncheon tables. Some foresaw fascism or worse if the government determined hours of work or established an enforced hourly minimum. The possible dangers to the "American way of life" and to "free enterprise" were mentioned frequently. Nevertheless, the overwhelming majority of the clothing manufacturers recognized that a fundamental change in the relationship of government and business was about to take place. As a means of preventing cutthroat competition at the expense of the workers, they favored shorter hours and a minimum wage scale. All of these suggestions, recommendations, or novel theories offered, were indicative of the new spirit of hope pervading the country. Now there was a possibility of escape from the depths of business despair.

If Congressional committees were to hold hearings on legislation with regard to wages and hours, which would clearly affect the clothing industry, then it was essential to have a national spokesman representing the manufacturers at the hearings. In turn, such a leader could speak only on behalf of the whole industry if there were a nationally organized body that determined policy. But there had been no such organization since the 1920's, when the National Association of Clothiers had ceased to function. Admittedly, in 1933, there was in existence a small group of manufacturers headed by William Goldman, called the Clothing Manufacturers Research Bureau, consisting of approximately 25 of the larger firms located in the various markets. This organization was started shortly after the former national association had folded, so that prominent manufacturers might gather and discuss mutual problems. Nearly half of the membership was non-union. This small, highly selective group was most interested in matters such as the need for proper cost accounting, mill problems, credit conditions and related subjects of importance.

Therefore, when William Goldman appeared on April 29, 1933, before the Congressional committee members studying the proposed wage and hours legislation, he spoke on behalf of the only organized existing national group of clothing manufacturers. Goldman informed them that he favored a 40-hour week, although his plant was operating 44 hours weekly, and he indicated that a national hourly minimum was desirable. The Rochester market promptly announced in the trade press that it favored a 36-hour week, but wanted a 40-hour week during the busy season. Mark W. Cresap, president of Hart, Schaffner & Marx; Bertram J. Cahn, president of B. Kuppenheimer & Co.; and Jeremiah G. Hickey, president of Hickey-Freeman Co., also appeared at the hearings. All recommended a shorter work week and an enforced hourly minimum wage. Cresap pointed out that over the years the unionized portion of the industry had reduced hours, and cited the experience of his own firm as an example of a steady decline in scheduled working hours. He presented the following data:

May 1913	54 hours reduced to 52 hours
May 1916	52 hours reduced to 49 hours
May 1917	49 hours reduced to 48 hours
May 1918	48 hours reduced to 44 hours

Cresap also informed the committee that while the minimum weekly wage in his company had been $15 on October, 1931, at the time of the hearing, which was May 6, 1933, the weekly wage minimum had been lowered to $12.15, and he strongly recommended a national floor for wages.

By this time, it was evident to all that there was no recognized single clothing industry spokesman, even though many manufacturers had testified in Washington. It was essential to establish promptly national leadership and unity of policy. Thereupon a series of events occurred in rapid fire order that permanently determined the direction of the industry. In bald terms, it was a battle for industry control. Who would become the authorized spokesman in Washington? Who would determine the character of the new association about to be formed? Who would control any administrative industry agency provided for in the pending Wagner bill? The significance of this struggle for power and control was clearly understood by all factions concerned.

On the tenth of May, William Goldman took the initiative when he publicly urged the formation of a national association. Goldman undoubtedly realized that the Research Bureau, consisting of a mere handful of firms, was not the proper body to deal with matters that were under consideration by Congress. Because in the past he had been the industry spokesman on occasion, he obviously considered himself its leader, and so announced that he was "willing to call the manufacturers together to start a national association." The Philadelphia market immediately fell in line, calling Goldman the "man of the hour." Other markets were equally enthusiastic. For the moment, it seemed that Goldman's leadership without any visible opposition, would be unquestioned for there was no outspoken objection. But Goldman was hardly the man to lead the clothing industry which was now 70 per cent unionized, even though his ability, experience and integrity were acknowledged by all. It was remembered that, as president of the Clothing Trade Association of New York, Goldman had spearheaded the New York strike of 1920–1921. During that strike, Cohen, Goldman & Co., had left the city and remained non-union until 1932. The past record of Cohen, Goldman & Company as viciously anti-union was not easily forgotten, even though the company was now a union shop. Moreover, as president of the Research Bureau, Goldman necessarily had acted on behalf of non-union firms as well as union firms. It seemed very likely, therefore, based upon precedent, that non-union as well as union manufacturers would be cordially welcome as members of any association sponsored by Goldman.

Then, as though to pour oil on the fire of suspicion, the trade press reported that Goldman had consulted with the United States Chamber of Commerce on ways and means of forming a national organization. The Chamber was blatantly anti-labor, and insofar as some markets were concerned, this did not help the cause of Goldman. Perhaps, in the minds of many manufacturers, and very probably in Hillman's mind as well, an association such as Goldman projected, might well be formed along the lines of the defunct National Association of Clothiers. This organization had fought labor bitterly prior to World War I through its affiliate, the National Labor Bureau.

At the same time, Hillman recognized early that the new legislation affecting wages and hours would be of utmost concern to the Amalgamated. If any national association of manufacturers was to be formed in the clothing industry, it was essential to the union that it be kept in friendly hands. The urgency of forming an association at the earliest moment that would fully cooperate with the ACWA was heightened when Goldman announced on May 13, that he had once more consulted with the Chamber of Commerce. He told the trade paper reporter that a meeting of the industry would be called shortly for the purpose of forming a national association.

David Drechsler and Sidney Hillman were determined to circumvent Goldman by "beating him to the punch." On May 14, the day following Goldman's announcement, Hillman let the industry know (not too subtly) via the trade press, that it would be excellent if the local unionized markets came together and formed a national association. The full implications of Hillman's suggestions were well understood by all manufacturers. In the same issue of the trade paper, it was reported that Cresap, Hickey and Jaffee, who were representing the Chicago, Rochester and New York markets, coincidently had been in Washington. While there, they had conferred with Hillman. The inference was clear. Quick action was being planned to bypass Goldman by organizing an association as soon as possible.

The pace quickened considerably when Goldman announced on May 17, that his meeting was being called for June 6–7. On that very day, Jaffee informed the press that the three markets of New York, Chicago and Rochester, plus Philadelphia and Baltimore would soon meet to form a national association. Now, striking while the iron was hot, on the following day Hillman said that he had been in contact with seven of the important unionized clothing markets, urging them to attend the forthcoming meeting called by Cresap for May 22, in the Mayflower Hotel in Washington. The markets contacted were Philadelphia, New York, Chicago, Rochester, Baltimore, Cincinnati and Indianapolis. Thus Hillman, Drechsler and the three manufacturers who had met originally in Washington, had taken the initiative away from Goldman. He had been clearly outmaneuvered. With the seven most important markets pledged to honor Cresap's call, the only ones who might presumably attend any later meeting arranged by Goldman would be the non-union houses. But Goldman, as head of a now unionized firm, could not place himself in the position of organizing an association of non-union manufacturers. Accepting reality gracefully, Goldman announced that his firm would accept Cresap's invitation to attend the May 22 meeting, and that Victor S. Riesenfeld, his manufacturing head, would be the company representative.

The agenda for the May 22 meeting was well prepared by the planning committee. Nothing was left to chance. Thirty-five clothing manufacturers from all the clothing markets attended. As a sort of footnote, the trade paper noted that Hillman and Blumberg also attended this meeting. By May 24, only two days after the initial organizing session, a lengthy and detailed policy report of the Clothing Manufacturers Association of the U.S.A. (CMA), was printed in the trade paper. It was questionable whether such a policy statement could have been prepared within 48 hours. Of even greater interest, a most comprehensive "articles of agreement" was prepared and approved on May 22. These "articles of agreement" of necessity required much prior thinking and careful preparation. And, on May 24, the association was incorporated in the District of Columbia. In short, the meeting on May 22 was merely a ratification session of a well-prepared agenda.

Cresap was elected president, Raymond H. Reiss of the International Tailoring Company became treasurer, David Drechsler was named counsel, and representatives of Philadelphia, New York and Rochester were elected vice presidents. All of the important markets were represented, and the association was truly national in scope.

Victor S. Riesenfeld then returned to New York, and as he told the story later, he informed Goldman, "It's all over. We must join them, we can't lick them," and Goldman agreed.

On May 26, the CMA placed a full page advertisement in the trade paper as an "open letter" to the industry. It was now duly launched as a full fledged association, complete with by-laws, articles of agreement, elected officers and directors from all markets who immediately issued a long and comprehensive statement of industry policy. All supposedly done in a matter of four days!

The executive committee of the CMA was formed on June 2. It included Cresap, Cahn, Hickey, Jaffee, Holtz, Makransky, Reiss and Riesenfeld (thus preventing any further action by Goldman). The CMA was now safely in the hands of men who were unionized and on friendly terms with the ACWA. It was a triumph for the unionized manufacturers and the ACWA.

When the "articles of agreement" were published on May 24, it was quickly recognized that while the membership was supposedly open to all firms "without restriction," union or non-union, yet the

FIRST ANNOUNCEMENT OF THE ASSOCIATION ORGANIZATION

Reprinted—Daily News Record, Friday, May 26, 1933

ASSOCIATIONS AND FIRMS REPRESENTED AT THE WASHINGTON CONFERENCE

NEW YORK

Representing New York Clothing Manufacturers' Exchange

Charles D. Jaffee, Jaffee-Cohen & Lang, Inc.
William P. Goldman, Wm. P. Goldman & Bros., Inc.
Simon Ackerman, Simon Ackerman Clothes, Inc.
Isidor Grossman, Grossman Clothing Co.
Charles Douglis, Chas. Douglis Co., Inc.
Joseph Levy, Crawford Clothes, Inc.
Samuel Kappel, Howard Clothes, Inc.
Jos. Politz, "Sampeck" Clothes, Inc.
Jerome I. Udell, Max Udell Sons & Co.
David Drechsler, Drechsler & Leff

CHICAGO

Bertram J. Cahn, B. Kuppenheimer & Co., Inc.
Sylvan W. Kahn, Chicago-Kahn Bros.
A. W. Meyer, J. B. Simpson & Co., Inc.
Mark W. Cresap, Hart Shaffner & Marx
Alfred Decker & Cohn
M. Born & Co.
Ed V. Price & Co.
Scotch Woolen Mills

ROCHESTER

Representing Rochester Clothiers' Exchange

Max Holtz, Louis Holtz & Sons, Inc.
J. G. Hickey, Hickey-Freeman Co.
Braeburn of Rochester, Inc.
Fashion Park
Levy Bros. & Adler-Rochester, Inc.
Stein-Bloch Co.
Walter Morton, Inc.

PHILADELPHIA

Representing Philadelphia Clothing Manufacturers' Assn.

Louis Daroff, H. Daroff & Sons, Inc.
Harry Makransky, S. Makransky & Sons, Inc.
R. Lipsky, Goodimate Co.
Louis Sussman, Middishade Co.
Jos. N. Gutman, E. Gutman & Sons
N. J. Ettelson, Max Fine & Co.

BALTIMORE

Bernhard Mackover, Baltimore Clothes, Inc.
Wm. A. Katzen, Harry Panitz & Co.
Joseph Ginsberg, S. Ginsberg Sons & Co., Inc.
M. L. Snyder, Cambridge Tailoring Co.

INDIANOPOLIS

Henry Kahn, Kahn Tailoring Co., Inc.

CINCINNATTI

W. H. Albers, A. Nash Co.

BOSTON

Joseph Barron, Barron Anderson Co.
M. Gordon, Trimount Clothes

Victor S. Riesenfeld, Cohen-Goldman Co. (New York)
Raymond H. Reiss, International Tailoring Co. (Chicago-N.Y.)
Rudolf Greeff, General Manager of Greater Clothing Contractors Association, Inc.

Thirty Years Ago

An Open Letter To The Clothing Manufacturers Of The United States

On Monday, May 22nd, in the City of Washington, representatives of the leading clothing markets met to organize a National Association that would apply to terms of the proposed National Industrial Recovery Bill to the Clothing Industry. Under the proposed Bill, the government, as President Roosevelt has expressed it, will become a partner in industry to aid management and labor in working out a code of standards and practices that will make for rehabilitation and stabilization.

We feel it to be highly desirable that every member of the industry should have a voice in drawing up the Code of Practice required of each industry by the Government under the proposed National Recovery Act, which will fix maximum hours and minimum wages, as well as such other standards as will form the law of our industry.

No action has as yet been taken by the association with respect to the preparation of the Code. of Practices, such action is intended to be taken in the next few days and it is hoped that when it is written it will be with the advice and assisance of every representative firm in the industry.

For these reasons, as well as a genuine desire to have you sit in with us in our labors to place the industry in which we have a mutual interest in the positon to which it rightfully belongs, we invite you to become a member of this association and participate in drafting a code of practices before it is submitted to the President of the United States for his approval.

Application for membership should be submitted at once to the secretary of the association.

Mark W Cresap
President

CLOTHING MANUFACTURERS ASSOCIATION OF THE UNITED STATES OF AMERICA

DAVID DRECHSLER, Secretary
225 Fifth Avenue, New York

Vice Presidents CHARLES D. JAFFEE—J. G. HICKEY—HARRY MAKRANSKY
Treasurer RAYMOND H. REISS

CMA operating statement which each member had to sign bound such members to conform implicitly in every respect to any policy approved by the directors of the association. Colonel Shelby H. Curlee of the Curlee Clothing Company of St. Louis, an outstanding and vocal opponent of trade unions, recognized at once the challenge implied by the formation of the CMA. If non-union firms were to have any spokesman at the hearings to come, or if they were to have any representation on an industry body when the Wagner Act was passed, it was necessary to gather at once the non-union houses into an organized group. Therefore, Curlee called a meeting of the non-union group quickly, and on June 3, the Industrial Recovery Association of the Clothing Manufacturers (IRA) was formed. It was admittedly an anti-union open shop organization.

The industry was now split into two factions, the union and the non-union firms. The CMA membership employed 84,571 workers according to its own reports, of whom 47,204 were employed in contract shops, and 37,367 in inside shops. The IRA had 111 members, who employed, according to their reports, some 35,000 on July 1, 1933. In addition, in 1933, it was estimated that approximately 35,000 clothing workers were totally unemployed. With the split wide open between the organized and non-organized firms, the two associations were to be pitted against each other during the entire life of the National Industrial Recovery Act (NIRA). This caused innumerable industrial and personal disputes, with much ill will accruing that took years to disappear. Now the stage was set for the formal hearings to be held in reference to the provisions that would govern the clothing industry during the NIRA.

The NIRA (later called NRA)

The National Industrial Recovery Act became effective June 16, 1933. It created an agency, the National Recovery Administration (NRA), which was to formulate codes of industry practice with the purpose of restoring the economic health of the country. This was to be accomplished by raising the workers' living standards from

Sidney Hillman, president ACWA
(Courtesy of ACWA)

the existing sub-standard conditions, and also by aiding the separate industries to establish proper and equitable trade practices. General Hugh S. Johnson was the administrator of the NRA, and he appointed deputy administrators who held hearings on the codes proposed by the interested trade associations. They also supervised the administration of such codes once they had been approved. Professor Lindsay Rogers of Columbia University, who was the deputy administrator for the men's clothing industry, held the code hearings in Washington on June 26–27, 1933. It was hoped that once the hearings were over and the issues publicly aired, the differences between the CMA and the IRA would be resolved so that an industry code satisfactory to all would be approved.

Actually, the hearings merely stressed the cleavage existent between the two groups. The fundamental fact that underlay all differences openly argued, was the obvious knowledge that the union houses paid higher wages than the non-union houses. According to the Bureau of Labor Statistics, the hourly earnings in 1932 of the clothing workers in the different markets were as follows:

MOSTLY UNIONIZED MARKETS		MOSTLY NON-UNION MARKETS	
Boston	69.5¢ an hour	Baltimore	45.4¢ an hour
Chicago	90.0¢ an hour	Cleveland	57.5¢ an hour
New York	79.9¢ an hour	Eastern Penn.	32.7¢ an hour
Rochester	71.1¢ an hour	St. Louis	49.5¢ an hour
Average	77.625¢ an hour	Average	46.275¢ an hour

There were lengthy and eloquent statements made by the IRA that the right of workers' freedom was trampled in the dust if and when they joined a union, whereas the CMA defended stoutly collective bargaining. The "American way of life" was duly praised by the IRA, while the CMA stressed the need to raise the living standard of workers in all clothing factories. No one could possibly object to either argument, for who would oppose patriotism or the

David Drechsler, counsel CMA

Mark W. Cresap, President CMA 1933–1939
(Courtesy of CMA)

humanitarian view of industry? But, one observer there noted later somewhat realistically, "It all boiled down to competition between union and non-union firms selling a retailer." The ACWA, as might be expected, fought on the side of the "angels," although Hillman favored somewhat higher wages and shorter hours than recommended by the CMA manufacturers. Because the philosophy of the NRA was New Deal oriented, and because the CMA recommendations conformed to such thinking, the final decision of the deputy administrator, for the most part, favored the position of the CMA. In a scholarly study of the Code made by Robert H. Connery, it was noted, "in the end the Industrial Recovery Association was in the position of having the code imposed on it. The principal reason that the association did not appeal to the courts was doubtless the unpopularity which would have resulted from such a step and the resulting difficulty of obtaining markets for their products." So, Mr. Curlee announced that the IRA "would comply with the code, not reluctantly, but in the spirit of full cooperation."

The code as finally approved by the deputy administrator included the following salient provisions:

- 40¢ an hour for the North, and 37¢ an hour for the South
- Wages for week workers $14.00 in the North and $13.00 in the South
- The working week was to be 36 hours; a maximum of 8 hours a day
- The manufacturers were not permitted to sell below cost
- Consignment selling by manufacturers was forbidden
- Cut, make, and trim by manufacturers or contractors was forbidden
- A label was to be sold by the Authority and had to be sewn on all garments produced in the clothing factories.

As later related by Drechsler, there were some interesting sidelights in writing the code. That section which prohibited cut, make, and trim was strenuously opposed by the chains and mail order houses. As might be expected, the manufacturers demanded that such a prohibition be inserted in the code. This would then force the chains and other large users to buy the completed garment directly from the clothing manufacturers, rather than have the work performed on the basis of cut, make and trim, which was really a form of the contract system. Hearings were then scheduled, so that both sides might be heard. One contractor testified that he had worked for a large mail order house for 20 years without any slow season intervening. He was entirely satisfied in his relationship with the mail order house. As Drechsler told the story, this contractor seemed to be in sheer ectasy when he described his pleasure as a cut, make and trim contractor. So Drechsler asked, "Why, after 20 years of hard and steady work, do you not become a manufacturer? It is more profitable you know." "Mr. Drechsler," exploded the contractor, "I have no money." That clinched the argument against cut, make and trim.

Drechsler also told how the 40-hour week, originally agreed upon, became 36 hours in the code. One night, during the hearings, at two in the morning, Drechsler received a phone call from Hillman, excitedly telling him that the women's wear group had just inserted a 35-hour week in their code. Could Hillman be far behind? He asked for consideration by the manufacturers. Thereupon, Drechsler phoned the committee immediately and most of them thought the hotel on fire. Drechsler asked them to meet in his room within an hour. It was urgent that action be taken before the early morning hearings when the weekly hours were to be discussed. The committee decided then and there to recommend a 36-hour week, returning to their rooms to continue an interrupted sleep. And Drechsler always ended the story with the question, "Could we, the clothing industry, let coat and suiters be more progressive?"

On August 26, 1933, the President signed the Clothing Industry Code. Under its provisions, the Code Authority acted as a board of directors might in any organization, determining general policy. The Authority consisted of 23 members, with ten chosen by the CMA, five were to represent the IRA, although only two of its members consented to serve, two additional clothing manufacturers

Jeremiah G. Hickey
(Courtesy of Hickey-Freeman)

were to be selected who did not belong to either association. Labor had five representatives, and a NRA official also served as a member of the Authority. At its first organization meeting, held on September 6, 1933, Mark W. Cresap was elected chairman; vice chairmen were Frank C. Lewman and Charles D. Jaffee; Victor S. Riesenfeld became treasurer; and Drechsler was secretary and general counsel.

George L. Bell, a vice president of the Caterpillar Tractor Company, who had once been a labor arbitrator for the New York market, was chosen as executive director. He was an unhappy choice because he felt that the position called for complete independence from the industry, which in turn made the manufacturers feel that they had selected a czar to rule rather than an administrator to accept orders. Bell's position became untenable when he showed partiality by taking a stand contrary to policies favored by influential

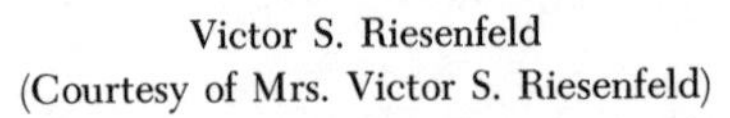
Victor S. Riesenfeld
(Courtesy of Mrs. Victor S. Riesenfeld)

members of the Authority. As a consequence, Bell resigned on February 6, 1935, and Morris Greenberg, an executive with the NRA, became the executive director. Greenberg was highly articulate and quite brash. He knew the industry thoroughly, understood the problems of labor and management, and enjoyed the complete confidence of all. He proved to be a most able administrator, serving until the NRA dissolved.

The IRA, led by Curlee, was a constant thorn in the side of the Code Authority. While Curlee had announced publicly that he would fully comply with the code, he evidently meant that in the spirit of full cooperation he would act the part of the "loyal opposition." This he did, for the Authority or its staff were regularly criticized by Curlee. He fully obeyed the code however, and his criticism was often constructive, even necessary at times.

The matter of properly defining the clothing industry was complicated because manufacturers producing work clothing such as separate trousers using cotton cloth, claimed to be subject to the Cotton Garment Code, which had a different set of work standards. After lengthy conferences, the clothing industry was finally defined as follows:

> The manufacture of men's, boys', and children's clothing, uniforms, single knee pants, single pants (except work pants or single pants made in work clothing factories), and men's summer clothing (except men's work suits of 100 per cent cotton content when made in work clothing factories in conjunction with work clothing) . . .

Within a few years, the cotton garment firms began making wool trousers. Because they were non-union in the majority of instances, and located in the South, they were able to undersell the single wool pants houses of the North. These manufacturers were determined to keep their advantage in work standards permanently, and at the hearings of the Fair Labor Standards Act held some years later, they were able to remain within the cotton garment group. Sectional political strength, rather than economic facts, finally determined their classification.

As early as April 21, 1933, the *Daily News Record* reported that mills, suppliers and clothing manufacturers were in the midst of a sensational inflationary movement. This was, to some extent, a rebound from the sharp drop in prices that had occurred since 1930. But with prices beginning to rise, buying accelerated. Production of men's clothing began to climb steadily. In 1933, according to the Bureau of the Census, production of men's suits had increased 20 per cent over 1932, and by 1935, production increased 29 per cent compared with 1933.

The number of workers employed in the industry and their wages showed a substantial rise during the period as the following table discloses:

PERIOD	WORKERS EMPLOYED	WEEKLY WAGES PAID
March 1929	154,135	$24.82
March 1933	109,601	12.62
March 1935	148,507	22.04

Source: U.S. Depts. of Labor & Commerce

There is no doubt, though, that some suppliers and mills serving the clothing industry raised prices unduly. It was generally agreed at the time, that while the codes, as written by the respective industries, forbade former trade practices which had reduced profits and prices, still the provisions in the approved codes created, if not encouraged a definite inflationary trend. We cite as an outstanding example the American Woolen Company, the largest producer of wool goods in the United States, and the bellwether of price trends in its field. In 1932, the company lost $7,269,822, while in 1933, it showed a profit of $7,053,088. This was the first profit the company had made since 1927, and the highest enjoyed since 1919, the year of wild inflation. In turn, of course, the clothing manufacturers passed on their increased costs plus profit to their retailers. Due to the highly competitive nature of the industry, Dun & Bradstreet data showed manufacturer profits during the years of 1933–1935 to be relatively reasonable, for in 1933, median net profit on net sales were 1.70 per cent; 0.78 per cent for 1934; and 0.94 per cent for 1935.

Through all of this economic upheaval, the Code Authority continued to function efficiently and effectively. The sale of labels was the source of its funds and the staff was capably supervised by Greenberg. As counsel, Drechsler had an able corps of assistants in the legal department, while the investigations of code infringements were carried on without undue harassment. Admittedly, some manufacturers balked at the code and went to court, fighting the restrictions. When the Supreme Court declared the NRA unconstitutional on May 27, 1935, this cut short the life of the Code Authority and its offices were immediately closed. The CMA ceased to function as well.

If it were asked whether the NRA had any permanent effect upon the clothing industry, the answer would be affirmative. The NRA did establish a shorter working week. Even though the clothing industry returned thereafter to an actual 40-hour week, nevertheless

William Goldman
(Courtesy of Mrs. H. Carlebach)

this was less than the 44 weekly hours that had prevailed prior to the NRA. The NRA also established the principle that hours and wages ought to be regulated nationally by the Federal government. In 1938, the Fair Labor Standards Act was passed. The provisions of the code encouraged the formation of the Clothing Manufacturers Association of the U.S.A. During the years of the NRA, the national association afforded manufacturers in the various markets an opportunity to meet each other personally. The hostile feeling formerly prevalent between the competing centers of clothing production was lessened considerably. Manufacturers now realized that there were many common problems that could be resolved only on a national basis. Whereas previously the clothing industry had been fragmented into many separate markets, the NRA was the catalytic agent that cemented the industry into a national body by means of the CMA. There was general recognition that the CMA had served well as a spokesman for the industry, so that the possibility of reactivating the association in the future was considerably enhanced. Meanwhile, it remained merely a paper organization, hibernating as it were, until the industry awoke once more to the need for a national organization.

Chapter 12

From Chaos to Stability

The Clothing Crisis of 1937

The Year of 1936

The clothing crisis of 1937 never should have happened. It was caused by sheer ineptitude on the part of labor and management in conducting their first industrywide wage negotiations. It was caused also by rank cupidity on the part of manufacturers and retailers who then suffered disastrous losses during the years of 1937 and 1938.

Even though the NRA was declared unconstitutional by the U.S. Supreme Court in 1935, bringing uncertainty, the clothing industry enjoyed a moderately prosperous year. The financial statements of the manufacturers at the year end disclosed that median net profits on net sales after taxes were 0.94 per cent, about normal. The trade paper of the industry, the *Daily News Record,* reported that clothing concerns were entering the year of 1936 in a mood of optimism, and that plans were being made for a 10 per cent increase in production for the first six months as compared with the same period in 1935.

The over all trend within the industry was towards higher prices of piece goods and clothing. This encouraged the expectation that substantial inventory profits might be made as the value of merchandise would inevitably rise in the months to come. Such sentiment received confirmation when the price of wool cloth rose 25¢ a yard for fall 1936, as compared with the past spring, and was 45¢ a yard higher than for the previous fall. Under these circumstances, when the manufacturers' lines opened for fall, 1936, the price of clothing rose. There also was widespread talk about the possible impact of pending bonus payments to veterans, and what it would mean in greater suit sales. Because of such optimism, and steadily higher prices, retailers recognized quickly the need of placing orders early. They came into the market prior to the usual time, buying 10 per cent more than previously. Business was good in 1936.

With a prosperous year past, the financial statements of manufacturers for 1936 showed that median net profits after taxes, were 1.28 per cent on net sales, which were excellent, somewhat higher than usual, and a 36 per cent increase over the previous year. There was possible danger, however, lurking in the manufacturers' statements, for they disclosed that 80.1 per cent of their working capital was tied up in inventory. Nevertheless, this was not a matter of concern to the accountants, the mill credit men, nor to the bankers, for with prices on the way up, the higher the inventory, the greater the potential profits accruing in the months to come. Nor were the retailers immune from possible danger. According to the financial statements of retail clothiers, inventories in their stores were 102.5 per cent of their working capital. This placed them in a most vulnerable condition should their sales decline, although with the price trend up, merchandise on hand seemed indeed to be a very safe and very profitable investment.

The Amalgamated, as might be expected, was carefully watching this upward spiral in manufacturers' production, prices and profits, and arrived at the conclusion that this offered an excellent opportunity to ask for a wage increase. Therefore, on December 7, it was "rumored" in the trade press that the manufacturers would be asked to confer on the matter of higher wages; such an increase would become effective May 1, 1937. This was the usual procedure of preparing the manufacturers psychologically that a wage demand was in the offing. Then, on the following day, Hillman confirmed this well placed rumor, stating that wage negotiations would take place sometime in February, 1937. Still, he gave no hint as to possible union demands. Because of buoyant conditions already existing in the industry, this ACWA announcement considerably accelerated the tendency of manufacturers to load up on piece goods and on made up clothing, while retailers were encouraged to buy far more than previously. With labor costs going up, all wanted to "beat the gun." On the whole, the manufacturers were surprisingly complacent about Hillman's statement. Their reaction was mild, without the expected indignation ordinarily expressed in terms such as "ridiculous," "a catastrophe for the industry," and the inevitable "now is not the time." Instead, in the trade paper of December 23, manufacturers were quoted as saying "that a 10 per cent wage increase was not unduly excessive." Naturally, the union could not permit such expectations of a puny 10 per cent wage boost to go unanswered. Strategy required an immediate rebuff by labor. So once more an "astute observer" publicly observed that the union would really request a 20 per cent wage increase. Such an "observation" served two purposes. First of all, it aimed to shock the manufacturers so that industry reaction could be gauged. Secondly, when the union would demand the actual wage increase, which would certainly be lower than 20 per cent, it might seem very reasonable in light of previous predictions.

Furthermore, the trade paper reported, Hillman had made a careful wage survey prior to asking for any labor increase, and his survey disclosed that a 20 per cent raise would be a feasible and a justified demand. It would have been somewhat astonishing had Hillman's survey proved otherwise. Following up this campaign of "softening up" the manufacturers, the clothing reporter (who seemed to have an extraordinary source of information) wrote on the following day that Hillman was putting the finishing touches on a letter asking for a national conference of manufacturers to consider the union's demands. In that manner, the stage was set for the labor-management meeting. The preliminary efforts of notifying, none too subtly, what might be expected by means of "rumors," "astute observer," and trade sources were now complete. So the year of 1936 ended on a note of comfortable complacency both for labor and management.

The Year of 1937

Then, on January 6, it was formally announced that the ACWA was asking for a conference to be held January 25, demanding a 15 per cent wage increase to become effective May 1. Actually, the initial joint meeting of the union and representatives of all the clothing markets did not take place until February 1. This meeting was an historic occasion, for it was the first national bargaining session ever held between labor and management in the clothing industry. After two days of discussion, the conferees adjourned so that the manufacturers might report the proceedings to their respective markets. At the later conference, which was held on February 13, it was agreed that a wage increase of 12 per cent, effective May 15, would be granted to all clothing workers. The wage increase was to be national in scope, and all unionized manufacturers (95 per cent of the industry) would be affected. At this time, there was no discernment by the conferees of the serious consequences that might follow by setting the effective date on May 15. The industry had been warned in December that labor costs would rise for fall of 1937. As previously noted, initial plans were already made by manufacturers to increase production at the current wage scale. Now manufacturers and retailers had been put on formal notice that three months hence, labor costs would rise, and the wholesale clothing prices would go up about four per cent, or perhaps even more. During this three month interval, no restrictions had been placed by the union which forbade manufacturers to produce fall merchandise at the existing wage level. This lack of foresight was disastrous to all branches of the industry.

No sooner had the labor agreement been reported, than the Howard Stores raised their prices from $19.50 to $22.50; Crawford Clothes announced that its $18.75 suits would be $21 thereafter; and Richman Bros., although non-union, went up from $22.50 to $24.50. The reasons given for such new prices were recent piece goods costs. But even though the higher wage rates were not to be paid for another three months, the pending labor rise was undoubtedly taken into consideration.

The wide publicity that a new wage agreement had been reached, effective at a later date, sparked a boom reminiscent of the 1919 buying spree. During the three months between February 15 and May 15, business conditions were hectic. Despite heavy inventories, and substantial purchase orders already outstanding, retailers rushed in and bought every available garment offered. In order to produce before the increase went into effect, manufacturers cut every yard of piece goods they could lay their hands on. Merchandise was rushed through the plants and hurriedly shipped to the stores. Then, on May 15, industry activity ground to a near halt. Whereas in 1936, the decline in cutting from April to May was 26 per cent, which was the seasonal pattern in those years, now there was a 43 per cent decline in units from April to May. It was only too evident that the manufacturers were highly successful in "beating the deadline," cutting and producing garments at a lower wage scale. The retailers were likewise very successful in buying clothing at unchanged prices. This artificial boom ended May 15. Soon after, repercussions followed.

With manufacturers producing at capacity, and retailers buying in quantity, but consumer sales showing no comparable increase, inventories in stores grew steadily. For example, according to a New York Federal Reserve Bank report, in January 1937, retail inventories of men's and boys' clothing in the New York district were 21.3 per cent higher than the previous January. By July though, retail stocks of clothing climbed to 40.9 per cent higher than the same month in 1936, while sales for the month were merely 6.9 per cent greater than last July. Based upon news items in the trade paper, clothing retailers in other areas of the country found themselves approximately in the same inventory condition as the New York stores. With retail sales showing only small gains, and inventory extraordinarily heavy, at the end of June Crawford Clothes reduced the price of summer suits from $21 to $17.50. Immediately, this was widely denounced as "rocking the boat" and "highly destructive." The other chains quickly followed Crawford's example, for they too had an excess of garments. Such a price trend was most distressing to the manufacturers and independent retailers, because the hoped for profits could easily turn to losses.

Now all retailers realized they had purchased wildly in order to avoid paying future higher prices. They had committed a grave error in overbuying. This was painfully brought home, for the national economy showed signs of weakening instead of expanding. Due to the excessive inventories, the financial position of many stores was now truly critical. Sales were widespread. Clothing prices were sharply reduced. Moreover, consumers were not buying as expected. In September, the trade paper mournfully reported that this was a month of uncertainty, and that retailers were cancelling their fall garments which they had blithely ordered months ago. Consequently, manufacturers found themselves loaded with heavy piece goods commitments, with racks full of made up garments and little probability of disposing of them in the near future. In the weeks that immediately followed, the traditional practice of whistling up courage in the dark was noticeable. The September 14 issue of the trade paper reported that prominent clothing leaders were caustic about industry pessimism. They categorically stated, with great emphasis, that prices could not drop because "prices were fixed by cost." Unfortunately, they were to learn shortly that prices were more often fixed by supply and demand.

Although spring, 1938 lines were ready by October, 1937, formal openings were delayed. Retailers were reluctant to buy. Stores were concerned about reducing their own inventories, purchasing fillins and sparingly at that. Manufacturers, in turn, bought 1938 spring fabrics merely to "sweeten up" their lines. As a result, there was a weakening in the price of piece goods, so that stock and staple fabrics were offered to manufacturers up to 50 per cent below list price. The trade paper pointedly commented that this automatically reduced the value of inventory on the shelves of the manufacturers. A period of liquidation for all branches of the industry now loomed ahead with heavy losses inevitable.

As usual, it was the manufacturer who received the brunt of the blame for conditions. According to the trade paper of October 19, one wrathful store owner berated a manufacturer by saying that "we do not care if your manufacturing plants shut down six months. We may not need you at all until next May when we start working on the fall, 1938 lines." The retailer then continued by complaining that he was extremely resentful of the way he had been loaded up by his suppliers with excessive amounts of clothing prior to the wage rise. Doubtless his own efforts to "make the extra buck" by trying to beat higher prices were forgotten in righteous anger that manufacturers had permitted him to buy their clothing!

Meanwhile, there were widespread rumors that mills would shortly cut the price of piece goods. This brought all transactions to a practical standstill. The axe fell on October 26, when some mills announced a 10–12.5¢ reduction per yard on all 1938 spring goods to be delivered. The American Woolen Company went further, by notifying the trade that it had reduced prices 17.5¢ a yard. Manufacturers glumly foresaw further depreciation of their top-heavy inventories.

In desperation, hope was now expressed that perhaps the union might be induced to rescind the recent wage increase, or possibly accept some compromise reduction. Maybe this might stimulate some buying. On November 9, the union categorically refused to reduce wages. The gloom deepened.

Because of declining values in piece goods, and the forced sale of distressed clothing, it was reported that accountants working on 1937 financial statements, which were to be issued shortly, considered a 20 per cent markdown on inventories as reasonable. When the manufacturers' year end statements were finally compiled, they showed a decline in median profits on net sales after taxes from 1.28 per cent in 1936 to 0.15 per cent in 1937, or a drop of 88 per cent, and that approximately 50 per cent of the manufacturers had sustained losses for the year. Likewise, retail median profits declined from 3.65 per cent on net sales after taxes in 1936 to 1.97 per cent, or a drop of 46 per cent for the year. So the year of 1937, which had started so promisingly, turned into a year of financial disaster.

The Year of 1938

Understandably, the new year began in a mood of deep pessimism, for the 1937 statements also disclosed that 84.6 per cent of the manufacturers' working capital was still represented by inventory (median figure), at the very time when prices were dropping steadily. Retailers' statements showed that their stock on the shelves were 101.1 per cent of their working capital. By this time, manufacturers were cutting prices to raise cash, and in the January 7 issue of the trade paper, it was noted that "some buyers refused to pay more than $14 for suits priced last season at $19 to $21." The 1938 spring season had been catastrophic, and there seemed little prospect for a better fall season.

The first ray of hope for the clothing industry came in June when the Works Progress Administration announced that it was ready to purchase ten million dollars worth of ready made clothing. This offer was the result of the efforts of Sidney Hillman to bail out the industry from an untenable position. He realized that only when the excess inventories had been moved from the racks of the manufacturers, could the situation ease, production begin once more and the workers return to their machines. At the same time, with a large number of destitute people in the country in need of clothing, this was a rare opportunity for the Federal Government to obtain, below actual cost, excellent garments for the poor. Under the existing circumstances, it was no surprise therefore that the trade paper reported in its issue of July 7, that "1800 clothing manufacturers were offering to sell clothing to the WPA, and the prices offered to the government were far below cost." A group of clothing experts was appointed to screen the garments offered, and it was the consensus that the values obtained by the government were extraordinary bargains.

This purchase of clothing by the Government was the turning point of the crisis. With the elimination of old inventories, manufacturers took heart once more and began producing again. Retailers now realized that distress merchandise at virtual bankruptcy prices was no longer hanging over the market, and that it was now time to purchase some new clothing in order to replenish the steadily diminishing store inventories. By November, the industry was optimistic once more. The trade paper reported that manufacturers expected a 10 per cent increase in dollar volume for 1939. Now there was talk of a rise in piece goods, with manufacturers calmly saying "that a 5–7.5¢ per yard was in order." In December, the trade paper reported that salesmen said "their orders increased from 20 per cent to 40 per cent, and that retail inventories were dwindling." Ever resilient, industry sentiment was again buoyant. Still, when the financial statements were finally issued for the year, the manufacturers had suffered a loss of 0.21 per cent on net sales (median figure), and retail median profits on net sales had declined to a mere 0.41 per cent. The year of 1938 had been a financial nightmare for the industry.

Why did the clothing crisis of 1937 happen at all? The announcement, three months in advance of the actual date, that a nationwide wage increase would be granted, was an open invitation for the manufacturer and the retailer to overproduce and overbuy prior to the effective date. This error was never repeated. Never again were national wage agreements reached and announced months in advance of the effective date. In future years, when a settlement was negotiated, it was usually concluded a month or less before the effective date. Again, in this instance, the union did not take the obvious precaution of forbidding the production of fall goods under the low wage scale. In future years, with a short period of time intervening between the final agreement reached and the effective date of the increase, such a restriction was unnecessary.

There was another cause for this crisis. Because the entire American economy was in an upward spiral, with all commodity prices rising, there was an air of general optimism throughout the country. Therefore, while under ordinary circumstances manufacturers would be wary of buying additional fabrics and producing clothing when their inventories were already excessive, they foresaw little danger to themselves with prices spiraling upwards and a wage increase pending. Hence they threw caution to the winds, bought more piece goods and made more clothing than they could sell. For the same reason, even though retail sales were becoming sluggish, stores did not watch their ratio of sales to inventory, accumulating an extraordinary quantity of clothing by July, 1937.

In summary, the clothing crisis of 1937 which caused widespread havoc in the industry was initially due to a case of misjudgment on the part of labor and management. In turn, this stimulated the extraordinary cupidity on the part of manufacturers and retailers who tried to save approximately $2 a garment, but eventually lost $5 or more in actually selling that garment.

The Stabilization Program-Grades

One of the immediate consequences of the "crisis" years of 1937–38, was a partial demoralization of customary labor practices and factory costs. Because substantial inventories made under the former wage scale were in the hands of manufacturers and retailers, there was strong resistance by store buyers to pay the higher prices for clothing produced under the new wage scale. It was for that reason that manufacturers had unsuccessfully endeavored to induce the union to rescind all or part of the wage rise. When this request was rejected, the manufacturers then turned to the local union managers for relief.

Unemployment was rife in all clothing centers. Consequently, there was strong economic pressure on the average local union manager to encourage production by offering a wage concession to the manufacturers in his market. Within a short time, industry rumors were widespread that wage reductions were readily granted in certain clothing centers. Such rumors could not be easily verified, for the actual facts were obviously not publicized. There was no doubt though, that in many instances, wage concessions or other forms of discrimination had been granted. Clothing firms which received no concessions at all complained vociferously. They pointed out that some manufacturers were now able to upset the competitive relationships that had heretofore existed by offering clothing at lower prices because of a market or individual wage deal. Indignant denials were repeatedly issued by all concerned, although years later it was publicly acknowledged by a prominent manufacturer that this had really occurred insofar as he was concerned. Manufacturers in the eastern markets, particularly in New York, felt most strongly that their competitive position was undermined, and the union leaders in these clothing centers strongly concurred. At the same time, union managers in some clothing areas, taking advantage of this economic turmoil, endeavored to expand their respective markets at the expense of other clothing markets. If they were successful, this would result in an increase in membership of their local and enhance their standing as managers in the ACWA. It was understood that they offered special wage advantages to factories operating within their jurisdiction. The 12 per cent wage increase, the first granted on an industrywide basis, was in serious danger of being whittled away.

The spread of wage demoralization was quickly noted by the ACWA. It was clearly evident that the centralized power of wage determination, so recently initiated and acquired by the national office, was being directly challenged by managers in several of the clothing markets. If national bargaining was to become a reality, and the national office was to retain its authority, then it was vital for the general officers of the ACWA to halt immediately this growing deterioration of the wage rates. They had to reassert centralized control. When the general executive board of the Amalgamated met in Pittsburgh in November, 1938, this matter was a subject of a long and heated discussion.

It was then decided, according to a later account published in the *Advance* (the ACWA membership paper), to establish "in the Union's General Office a special department to cooperate in the determination and maintenance of standards . . ." In explaining this action of the board, the paper also reported that "the program outlined by the general executive board meeting . . . calls for a detailed study of labor costs in all clothing markets, the establishment of fair minimum rates on the basis of adequate information and enforcement through a central agency in the General Office."

In accordance with the resolution of the general executive board, a stabilization department was soon organized in the national office, with the basic objective "that workers, wherever located, will receive the same total compensation in terms of piece rates paid" for making a given suit or overcoat. "This would," in the words of the new department, "end labor cost competition between firms in the same grade classification within and between markets." In order to properly evaluate the labor rates as they actually existed at the time, the first task of the department was to survey manufacturing costs in all sections of the country.

Meanwhile, the protests of the manufacturers in some of the eastern markets were steadily rising. There were repeated calls for immediate action to remedy inequitable labor costs. Definite steps of a concrete nature were therefore urgent that would reestablish stability between the markets and within each market. When the union survey was completed, at a meeting of the ACWA general executive board, held April 19, 1939, steps finally were taken to carry out fully the stabilization program previously proposed in Pittsburgh. Now Hillman appointed four outstanding production supervisors from management to recommend specific labor standards within the various price lines. They were:

Morris Greenberg, Hart, Schaffner & Marx, Chicago
Adolph Rosenberg, William P. Goldman & Bros., New York
Thomas Tillona, Eagle Clothes, New York
Philip Fishon, S. Makransky & Sons, Philadelphia

By having industry representatives of such high caliber survey labor practices and costs, plus using the data compiled by the stabilization department, it was hoped that any conclusions reached would satisfy all segments of the industry. After a careful study, the industry panel recommended that all clothing factories be classified by grades in accordance with the operations included in the making of the garment. Six grades of workmanship were to be established, with number one as the lowest in quality, and number six as the highest in quality. A special grade of X was established for boys' wear; later this was also used as a standard for very low quality men's clothing. The panel recommended that all of the operations within each grade be specified. Therefore, in keeping with the objective of the program, the total labor cost for each grade would be set nationally. The union immediately accepted the panel's recommendations, and this was widely acclaimed as a forward step in stabilizing the industry permanently on a sound basis.

Now it became the function of the stabilization department to ascertain that each factory performed only those operations that were included in its respective grade of workmanship and paid the proper total labor costs for that grade. As the director and his staff were able and conscientious in their duties, supervision was strict. With greater stability established, charges of special wage concessions granted were silenced for the time. However, World War II started shortly after the stabilization program was established, and the industry now began manufacturing uniforms. The specifications set forth by the military were naturally standard and industrywide, applying to all firms making a particular model of a uniform. Temporarily, this tended to disrupt the entire theory of grades, which was based upon the principle of differentiating plants in accordance with the operations used in making a garment. The manufacture of uniforms, on the contrary, tended to level these factories to a more or less similar quality of workmanship. This affected the hourly earnings of the operators in shops producing the higher grade garments where productivity was usually lower, but piece rates higher, than in factories making lower grade garments. The union therefore endeavored to remedy this situation. It secured from the Philadelphia Quartermaster Depot higher prices for those shops that previously produced better made garments so that their hourly wage rates might be maintained at the former level. But grades as such, and their list of specifications were put in limbo for the duration of the war.

When the war ended, there were renewed efforts to reestablish the grade system as originally formulated. This was found to be a practical impossibility, for the specifications as determined by the industry panel had allowed for no change. The panel had frozen the operations in each grade for all time. Nevertheless, each year saw new machines introduced which changed or even replaced some of the operations originally included in specific grades; machines were now taking the place of handwork. Perhaps, had a permanent panel of production experts been established, with authority to revise each grade from time to time, the system might not have cracked under the pressure of new machinery and a desire for innovation. With some operations becoming obsolete, or radically changed as time went on, stabilization faltered, for the very principle of permanent stability in methods of production was an impossible aim in a period of progressive change. At the same time, for competitive reasons, some firms found it desirable to eliminate certain style features from their regular models, while other firms, for the same reasons, added operations in order to stress new model changes. This was done with the seeming consent of the local managers who recognized the need for continuous variation from season to season and year to year. There were immediate complaints that such changes were unfair and destroying the grade system, but the industry could not stagnate.

Within a short time, the stablization program was in a state of utmost confusion. There was a "good" grade one and a "bad" grade one, and similar variations within the other grades. Retailers advertised grade 6 to consumers who could not possibly know just what this meant. Actually, some of the operations that qualified a garment for such a grade were no longer used in many factories. The union soon recognized the impossibility of maintaining the system of grades. Within a few years, the very principle of grades was discarded as a means of establishing wage stability, and the stabilization department was abolished for all practical purposes. Quality of workmanship then became the sole criterion for labor costs in each factory.

There is no doubt that the creation of the grade system in 1939 did stop the chaos that existed throughout the industry as a result of the debacle of 1937–38. It did reestablish the authority of the national office of the ACWA as the authoritative body that determined wage rates nationally. It did create the basis therefore for further industrywide bargaining, because the grade system standardized labor costs nationally. Nevertheless, because it did not allow for inevitable change in methods of operation, the grade system could not withstand the pressure for innovation and was therefore necessarily discarded.

The CMA Revived

With the demise of the NRA in May, 1935, the Clothing Manufacturers Association of the U.S.A. (CMA), went into hibernation. As related in a previous chapter, the Association had been formed under the direct impetus of the NRA. It was then deemed necessary to have a national organization representing the industry at the hearings to be held for the purpose of formulating a Clothing Code. It was also deemed necessary that the manufacturers have a national spokesman who would act on behalf of the industry in future contacts with the NRA officials and the Code Authority as well. Under the leadership of Mark W. Cresap as president, and David Drechsler as counsel, the association had served its membership well. Representatives of the organization attended all NRA hearings, presented the consensus of manufacturer thinking in regard to the provisions of the code, and once the Code Authority had been established, the association dominated that body.

Nevertheless, when the United States Supreme Court declared the NRA unconstitutional, in the opinion of many manufacturers, the CMA had lost its prime reason for existing. As yet, manufacturers were not prepared to accept a national organization that would act on their behalf before government agencies and confer with mills or retailers when mutual problems arose. In addition, as relics of past history, there were some remaining sparks of antagonism between the markets. Moreover, industrywide bargaining, which would require the cooperation of all clothing manufacturers, was still some years away. So the CMA went quietly into a deep freeze, to be resurrected, if and when the need arose. In the meantime, it became merely a name on the door of Drechsler & Leff.

But these were the years of the New Deal, and problems affecting the entire industry arose periodically. Legislation was frequently proposed, which if enacted, would have a profound impact upon all clothing manufacturers. For example, the Fair Labor Standards Act of 1938 dealt with minimum wages and maximum hours. The Wool Products Labeling Act of 1939 required the labeling of all garments containing wool, and the Robinson-Patman Act set forth conditions of sale to retailers. Because it was the regular procedure for hearings to be held by Congressional committees prior to presenting legislation to the Congress, it was often a matter of great importance to appear and offer pertinent industry testimony. In such instances, Drechsler as counsel of the still dormant CMA, usually secured as witnesses various market leaders, with one manufacturer who was still serving as a director of the CMA, appearing on behalf of the association, and the others speaking as representatives of their local markets. Thus, at the March 3, 1939 hearing held on the Wool Products Labeling Act, Isidore Grossman as the CMA representative, objected to some of the provisions of the bill. Several officers of the various local markets supported Grossman's stand. In that manner, Drechsler usually carried the burden, gathering together from time to time, a small group of industry-minded manufacturers, if and when a problem affecting clothing arose. This was necessarily done on a temporary hit or miss basis. There could be no continuity of industry policy, nor necessary activity maintained once such legislation had passed. Far-sighted manufacturers appreciated these serious handicaps facing the industry. Nevertheless, they were apparently unable, or too apathetic, to take the necessary practical steps that would reestablish the association. The catalytic agents that brought about the revival of the CMA were a series of unexpected and urgent labor negotiations with the ACWA that could only be conducted on an industrywide basis. This, coupled with the start of World War II, brought matters to a head.

As related, the first industrywide wage agreement had catastrophic consequences. Notwithstanding, as the fundamental principle of national bargaining for the industry was generally recognized as sound by the manufacturers and by the union, there was every likelihood that such a procedure would be followed in the future. Meanwhile, the stabilization program was slowly reducing or entirely eliminating the concessions and discriminatory practices found prevalent in the shops, for Hillman's first task was to restore equitable labor costs after the debacle of 1937. So without fanfare, in June, 1939, wage agreements by markets were renewed without change for another two years. Industrywide bargaining was held in abeyance, to be revived when conditions warranted. Then suddenly, the international situation worsened and once more the shaky stability of the industry was threatened.

When war was declared in Europe on September 3, 1939, the manufacturers recalled with dread their sad experiences of World War I. At that time inflation ran wild only to be followed by severe deflation and there were unhappy memories of those years. But the woolen mills had learned nothing from the chaotic years of 1919–1920. Insofar as they were concerned, war meant profits. Now there was the opportunity of quickly garnering really big profits, for raw wool imports from overseas might be subject to possible interruption. If such was the case, shortages would arise, and prices at a later date inevitably go up. Anticipating such a future contingency, the mills lost no time in raising prices. On September 12, only nine days after war had been declared, there were reports in the trade paper that piece goods prices were rising. Shortly after, the American Woolen Company, the perennial price leader, announced a 25¢ per yard increase in worsteds weighing 13 ounces or more and a 15 per cent rise in lighterweight cloth. This gave the mills an immediate profit by inflating the value of their inventories, with the prospect of perhaps still greater gain to come. The possible effect of such unwarranted mill action upon the industry and upon the economy as a whole apparently received no consideration. The mills simply followed a shortsighted policy of sheer avarice, interested solely in immediate profits. This action by the mills soon created widespread fear of inflation among manufacturers, portending possible speculation in fabric purchases. It also raised the possibility of excessive retail buying. Would there be a repetition of World War I practices?

Inspired by Drechsler, who quickly recognized this potential threat to economic stability, a meeting of the clothing markets was held in New York on September 26, with the aim of combating "undue speculation and profiteering." The manufacturers appointed Raymond H. Reiss of the International Tailoring Company as chairman of an industry committee to meet with the mills, the union and the retailers, so that all might join in a move to prevent undue price rises. On the following day though, Hillman publicly warned the clothing industry of a possible wage boost if the cost of living went up. This was an unforeseen bombshell, heightening further fears of wild inflation. It was now imperative to prevent unreasonable panic from spreading. Therefore, Drechsler, Reiss and Cresap met with Hillman immediately after his statement was issued. As Reiss told it later, they "persuaded the ACWA to delay a demand for a wage increase pending more opportune conditions." For the moment, a semblance of price steadiness had been attained.

But it seemed impossible to prevent this inflationary volcano from erupting. Manufacturers were now informing their trade that prices for spring would necessarily go up due to higher fabric costs. As it happened though, consumers were not at all excited about shortages in clothing and did not rush to buy. In turn, retailers were slow in placing spring orders. For the moment, the price hysteria stimulated by a fear of shortages had fizzled. Therefore the trade paper reported on October 23, that because of a lack of enthusiasm by retailers buying spring garments, "a feeling of conservatism was taking hold in the clothing market." But there were forces within the economy that could set off, at any moment, a bandwagon rush towards uninhibited inflation. The CMA committee, headed by Reiss, knew only too well that such a real danger existed, which was the reason why Reiss announced that his committee would meet with mills, retailers and the union on November 8, "to discuss the price situation."

By this time, the immediate need for a national association had become only too obvious to many clothing manufacturers. A united industry policy on prices became most urgent. In reality the ACWA had been conferring with the manufacturers on an industry-wide basis, but a truly national organization of clothing firms was lacking. Prodded by many, the CMA called a meeting of industry leaders for November 8. This meeting was to be held prior to the general conference on price trends called for the same day. It was the clothing reporter of the trade paper who expressed the sentiments of many manufacturers when he wrote the following article on October 30, 1939:

TIME SEEN RIPE FOR NATIONAL GROUP
WITH ABLE LEADERSHIP

* * *

MEETING NOV. 8, AT HOTEL BILTMORE TO CREATE VOLUNTARY NATIONAL ASSOCIATION HELD FACING OPPORTUNITY TO GIVE INDUSTRY INVALUABLE SERVICE UNDER CURRENT CONDITIONS—OUTSTANDING PERSONALITY AT HEAD BELIEVED ESSENTIAL TO SUCCESS OF UNDERTAKING

* * *

By Marshall M. Jacobson

Never before have leaders in the Clothing Industry faced a grander opportunity to create a voluntary national association than that which is proposed for the meeting of the Clothing Manufacturers Association of the U.S.A. at the Hotel Biltmore on Wednesday afternoon Nov. 8th, but in order to obtain a trade wide rally behind the movement, there must be proved a genuine sincerity of purpose, to help manufacturers, large and small, to do a better and more stable job, to establish equitable rules of practice and procedure, and to select an individual of unquestioned integrity, character and ability to manage the executive affairs of such an organization . . .

* * *

On the morning of November 8, the CMA group met as planned, and concrete steps were taken to reorganize the association. There were 30 manufacturers present on behalf of the various markets. A board of directors was selected, representing the New York, Philadelphia, Rochester, Chicago, Boston, Baltimore, Cleveland and Cincinnati clothing centers. The CMA was now reactivated.

That afternoon, according to schedule, Reiss and his committee of manufacturers met with the union, the mills and the retailers. As might be expected, all publicly deplored at great length the danger of higher prices. Then Hillman warned the group that he could not pledge to hold down wages. This warning revived immediately the hidden fears of inflation. Despite brave words about holding the line expressed at the meeting, it adjourned on a most disquieting note.

As told later by men who participated in the many conferences with Hillman, at that time he was seriously considering a wage increase effective January 1, 1940. He was under strong pressures from the local market managers to obtain an immediate raise in wages. Still struggling to maintain price stability, Drechsler, Reiss and the newly appointed labor committee of the CMA met with Hillman in his office on November 29. They told him that "the consuming power of the public has not reached the state where an increase in the price of clothing can be absorbed." Trade paper reports of consumer reluctance to buy confirmed the manufacturers' statement. Hillman recognized the cogency of this argument. He also recognized that a period of time was still required for the ACWA stabilization wage program to function according to plan, for only after the national labor costs had been equitably set by the stabilization department, could an industrywide wage increase be truly effective. Therefore, Hillman suggested that the CMA committee confer with the ACWA general executive board which was to meet in Atlantic City on the following day. The committee promptly left for Atlantic City. On December 1, the CMA representatives discussed all aspects of the wage problem with the national officers and the general executive board of the ACWA.

At the conclusion of the conference, it was agreed that no wage increase was feasible at this time. The postponement was hailed as an achievement of the association, and among the manufacturers throughout the country there was a notable rise of enthusiasm for the CMA. Industrywide agreements were now recognized by all as the most practical means of resolving labor-management problems. It was also readily acknowledged that the industrywide Atlantic City decision could never have been made through piece meal market conferences.

After the joint conference with the union, the CMA directors (all of whom were members of the labor committee), met to elect officers of the Association. Raymond H. Reiss became president, succeeding Mark W. Cresap who resigned after serving as head of the CMA since the formation of the association in 1933. Reiss, a vice president of the International Tailoring Company and a man of widespread business interests, was undoubtedly one of the most able executives in the industry, as well as a man of learning and great charm. He was an engineer, had earned his doctorate in philosophy, and had thorough knowledge of labor management relations. His ability to conduct labor negotiations in a calm and reasonable manner was considered outstanding. In time, Reiss not merely engaged in the manufacture of clothing, but became prominent in banking, real estate, shipping and many other commercial enterprises. In later years, Reiss was chairman of the president's council of Georgetown University and chairman of the advisory board of St. Vincent's Hospital in New York City. As an outstanding citizen, he was the recipient of honorary degrees from several universities. Despite his many business and community interests, Reiss devoted considerable time to the policy and direction of the CMA, laying the foundation of its many activities in the years to come.

Victor S. Riesenfeld was elected treasurer of the CMA. He was born in Chicago and began his clothing career as an office boy for Rosenwald and Weil of that city. In 1915 he joined Cohen, Goldman & Co., to take charge of production, later becoming chairman of the board of his company. Riesenfeld had also been a director of the CMA since its inception. He was soon appointed chairman of the CMA national labor committee, and during World War II, was active in all industry matters affecting government regulations.

Riesenfeld was a small, intense person, highly intelligent, very articulate, ever active, and ever ready to serve the industry. In 1950 he retired from the industry upon the liquidation of his company.

Now that the CMA had a slate of able officers, it was necessary to select an executive secretary. The usual practice at that time was to seek an industry czar, a so-called national figure, which was interpreted by some to mean a politician out of office needing a job. On the other hand, Reiss, Drechsler and the CMA directors as well, felt that a thorough knowledge of the industry, plus ability to understand fully the problems of the membership, were the most important qualifications for an executive secretary. They recalled the unhappy experience of the NRA when Bell had been executive director of the Code Authority. After carefully reviewing all possible candidates, they selected Frank P. Zurn of Philadelphia. He was a clothing manufacturer, had extensive experience in all phases of production and management, and had been prominent in all industry activities. However, Zurn's clothing business in Philadelphia did not permit him to devote sufficient time to his new position, so he resigned within a few months. His assistant, Harry A. Cobrin, became executive secretary and remained in that office for nearly 28 years, retiring on December 31, 1967, when Robert A. Kaplan, then the clothing reporter of the *Daily News Record*, succeeded him.

Shortly thereafter, the manufacturers in the New England area realized their need for a local association such as existed in Philadelphia, New York, Rochester and Baltimore. They therefore organized the New England Men's and Boys' Clothing Manufacturers Association, which immediately affiliated with the CMA. Abraham Saxe, a young attorney, was appointed executive secretary. He soon established his group as an active organization, participating in all industry affairs. Saxe, an able administrator, continues to serve as executive secretary to date.

It was a stroke of good fortune that the affairs of the clothing industry were on a relatively even keel now. The CMA had opened its offices in 220 Fifth Avenue on March 4, 1940 and began to function once more on an active basis. The stabilization program was quietly resolving intermarket and within market disputes in regard to wage differentials. Therefore, when the United States entered the war in December, 1941, the problems of labor were minimal, and now there was a fully organized trade association prepared to assume the burdens of leadership during the years of national emergency.

Chapter 13

The Industry and World War II

The Defense Program

When the war in Europe was declared in September, 1939, the clothing industry was primarily concerned about its possible impact upon the price structure of clothing. Hence, there were repeated meetings with the union, the mills and the retailers, reflecting the fears which were aroused because of memories of World War I and its aftermath. The Neutrality Act, as well as other legislation, confirmed our nation's determination to keep clear this time of involvement in any European conflict. Then, in May, 1940, there was a sudden and fundamental change in the status of the war. Hitler had defeated France and was in possession of its Atlantic ports. Britain apparently was helpless and in danger of invasion. The implications of the French surrender, and the prospect of Britain's destruction were of great concern to Washington. The possibility of eventual American involvement loomed on the horizon. Now it was necessary to bolster the defenses of the United States, for were the British fleet to become the German fleet, Hitler would be a direct and potential threat to this country. Steps were taken quickly to augment the defenses of the country.

Within a month, in June, 1940, President Roosevelt formed the National Defense Advisory Commission with Sidney Hillman as a member of that body. Initial plans were prepared for a huge increase in military armament, and the armed forces were to be greatly increased. When the procurement activities grew complex, necessitating an expanded administrative body, in December, 1940, the Commission became the Office of Production Management (OPM) with increased powers. Then, in January, 1942, the OPM was reorganized as the War Production Board (WPB), headed by Donald Nelson of the Sears Roebuck Company. Its functions were to supervise and control the total productive facilities of the country in order to fulfill the requirements of the military. In addition, it was to channel equitably that proportion of the nation's output still available for civilian needs.

To organize initial production of military supplies took time. During 1940 and 1941 it might well be said that the preparedness program was at the planning stage. Matters moved swiftly however after the Japanese attacked on December 7, 1941. Severe shortages for civilians were in prospect as an ever-increasing proportion of the nation's productive capacity was to be devoted to the war effort. If we were to avoid unlimited inflation, price control of civilian goods was necessary. To prevent a repetition of the World War I experience, in January, 1942, the Emergency Price Control Act was passed, and the Office of Price Administration (OPA) was organized with Leon Henderson as administrator. Now the OPA and the WPB began operating under full steam.

Orders immediately were issued by both agencies with the purpose of controlling prices and establishing a scale of priorities in all scarce items needed for military and civilian use. Inevitably, there was an overlapping in the activities of the WPB and the OPA.

Often a pricing order which allowed little or no profit influenced the supply of an item, creating an eventual shortage. Likewise, the imposition of a high priority rating frequently reduced civilian supply, necessitating severe price control. For the purposes of clarity though, we shall discuss the activities of the WPB and the OPA separately, indicating when the overlapping of pricing orders or issuance of priorities occurred, which were of major importance in affecting the manufacture of clothing. Because procurement of uniforms was handled directly by the armed forces, this will be treated separately in the chapter that follows.

The War Production Board

The WPB was headed by Donald Nelson, a former businessman, and for the most part it was staffed by businessmen. Under an elaborate scale of priorities, this board allocated all scarce materials used by the military as well as by civilians. If and when a contract bid for the manufacture of uniforms was accepted, the Quartermaster Depot in Philadelphia supplied the fabrics directly, although some component parts were usually purchased by the bidder from his regular suppliers. High priority ratings were granted by the WPB in such instances, and there was usually little difficulty in obtaining the necessary supplies. Fabrics, trimmings, machinery and machine parts that were required by manufacturers who operated solely for civilian use were granted lower priority ratings, and often there was great difficulty in obtaining a specific item.

At times, due to sudden changes in the comparative price relationship between two products, caused by two diverse pricing orders, the suppliers eliminated the least profitable product, concentrating on the more profitable product. Serious and unexpected shortages would then develop. The OPA officials apparently followed a general policy that prices and profit limitation were of greater importance than sufficient civilian supply. This created confusion and conflict of aims between the WPB and the OPA. One agency wanted prices and profits to receive the highest, if not sole consideration, while the other wanted adequate production to receive paramount emphasis.

Immediately after Pearl Harbor, the WPB asked the Clothing Manufacturers Association whether it would assist in supplying industry data, because the research and economic sections of the WPB were still understaffed and not fully organized. The association naturally agreed. Shortly thereafter, in January, 1942, the executive secretary of the association received a request from the WPB asking the organization to make a survey of suit production by model types. As a probable shortage of wool cloth was in prospect, there was an immediate need of simplifying civilian garments and so reducing fabric yardage per garment. A survey was promptly made, which disclosed that:

In Men's Suits—1941 Production

12% were sold as 2 piece units (coats and pants)
49% were sold as 3 piece units (coats, pants and vest)
39% were sold as 4 piece units (coat, 2 pants and vest)

and also that:

57% of the suits were in single breasted models
43% of the suits were in double breasted models

On January 21, 1942, a committee representing the association met with the WPB officials to discuss the facts disclosed in the CMA survey. The committee recommended that specific style features be eliminated in the suit, as well as the vest in the double breasted suit model, and the extra pants in the 2 pants suit. It was incomprehensible to many in the industry how the elimination of the 2 pants suit could possibly save wool cloth. The 2 pants sales unit had originally been introduced as an economy measure to prolong the life of a suit. The coat of a suit usually received less wear and tear than the matched trouser; hence 2 pants really meant a double life for the suit coat. If anything, more suits (and more wool cloth) would be needed for civilian use if the 2 pants suit were to be eliminated. Still, there was no vocal objection to this provision in the committee's program for cloth conservation. The recommendations of the committee were accepted by the WPB and officially approved when the style simplification order was issued on March 2, 1942, known as General Conservation Order M373A.

From time to time, at the request of the WPB, the association continued to collect and supply additional industry data which were not available from regular government departments. Close cooperation between the manufacturers and the WPB was maintained throughout the war years.

The Men's and Boys' Clothing Division of the WPB was headed by Morton J. Baum of the Hickey-Freeman Company of Rochester, New York. Baum was a most conscientious and able executive. He commuted from Rochester to Washington on a part time basis, supervising the proper allocation of the numerous components necessary for the manufacture of civilian clothing as well as establishing priorities for military requirements. Because of a lifetime of industry experience, Baum was able to perform his duties in a magnificent manner. He was highly praised by knowing government officials in Washington, by the military in Philadelphia and by the manufacturers as well, for he accomplished the nearly impossible task of allocating the limited supply of fabrics and components on a most equitable basis.

In performing its functions, the WPB had to issue regulations, interpretations of the regulations, then amendments to the initial regulations, followed usually by additional interpretations of the new regulation. It would be somewhat of an understatement to say that such a procedure did not make for the manufacturers' peace of mind. These changes in regulations though, often were necessary as the flow of supplies varied from month to month.

Naturally the WPB dealt with hundreds of thousands of items, granting priorities that often caused misunderstanding and frustration. An excellent example of such unhappy moments was the supply of rayon linings, and its use and misuse due to unforeseen results when certain industries were granted high ratings. This brought about some bizarre incidents. For obvious reasons, the coffin industry secured a very high priority for the component parts of the coffin, and rayon linings were considered by these manufacturers to be a necessary part of the coffin. A lustrous rayon lining in a mahogany box was eye appealing to the relatives of the deceased who saw their beloved laid out peacefully on the attractive fabric. But rayon was badly needed for civilians, and the WPB really had not meant to include rayon linings as the vital part of a coffin. This matter was brought to a head when one clothing manufacturer went to a funeral and saw the deceased permanently resting on the very scarce rayon fabric. He called the association at once, screaming, "Call Washington. They're giving linings to the dead ones, not to the live ones." The WPB was immediately contacted, and this lining was removed from this high priority list, even though, according to one official, there were complaints that it would "affect morale." A similar complaint was successfully lodged with the WPB when it was discovered that toy rabbits were covered with rayon, despite objections raised that children loved rabbits best when so covered.

So the WPB met problems, large and small, as they arose. As practical businessmen, they reviewed the situation regularly and then took whatever steps were necessary to remedy the supply crisis, be it in wool fabric, rayon linings, cotton goods, or badly needed machine parts. All things taken into consideration, the WPB performed its duties well under intense pressure, and maintained a reasonable flow of materials and garments for civilians after allocating to the military all that it required.

The Office of Price Administration

When Leon Henderson became Price Administrator of the OPA, he recognized the immediate danger of inflation. In order to prevent an upward price spiral following Pearl Harbor, a general maximum price regulation was issued in April, 1942, rolling back all prices as of March, 1942, and then freezing them. Once the national price structure was stabilized for the time being, the OPA immediately proceeded to formulate and issue individual industry pricing orders. It was highly impractical to have the same over-all provisions of a general price control order apply to thousands of diverse industries.

Theodore Rothschild of Michaels, Stern and Company of Rochester, New York, was appointed to be head of the clothing industry division, and he proceeded to write a pricing order for clothing that took into consideration usual industry methods of computing costs, although establishing strict price controls. An industry committee met with Rothschild while the order was being written, and when the document was issued as Maximum Price Regulation No. 177, it set forth detailed guidelines for the pricing of men's and boys' clothing. The regulation admittedly consisted of some 17 printed pages, but it was not difficult for the average clothing manufacturer to understand, because it was written in layman's English, and the commercial terms used were usually in "clothing language." The close interrelationship between pricing the finished garment and the cost of fabrics and labor was carefully considered in MPR 177. When Rothschild resigned to return to his company, Nathan L. Schwartz of Julius Schwartz & Sons of New York, assumed charge of the division. Schwartz followed the general policies initiated by Rothschild. At all times, both men were available for visits by clothing manufacturers who were confronted with individual problems, and it was relatively easy to receive a prompt answer from them, either by telephone or by mail.

There were widespread changes of personnel after Schwartz left to return to New York. The succeeding OPA officials did not come from the industry and lacked the basic knowledge necessary to supervise properly a clothing price control order. As the replacements were totally inexperienced, they were prone to suspect all suggestions made by industry representatives. They looked with a jaundiced eye towards any effort made to simplify the complicated procedures that were required in accordance with the provisions of the numerous OPA regulations. David Drechsler and Herbert Ferster of Drechsler and Leff, counsel to the association, and Victor S. Riesenfeld, then chairman of the CMA committee on price control, found themselves confronted with agency officials who were fearful of making decisions, because they obviously did not know what decisions to make. If the inexperienced "price executive" turned to the "economist" of the division for advice, he found a man who did not know the economic structure of the industry, while the agency's legal department could only cite the law, offering no practical solution. As for the higher echelon of the OPA, they were men who seemed more interested in rolling back prices which created favorable publicity for the agency, even though such action frequently hampered production. Such a policy encouraged black markets in linings and in other components used in the making of a garment. As a consequence, there was a minimum of proper communication between the industry and the OPA with impractical pricing regulations periodically issued that defeated the very purpose of maintaining price stability.

In time, the relatively simple MPR 177 Clothing Order had to be revised due to changing economic conditions. After a prolonged period of gestation (including several meetings with manufacturers), the OPA issued a new pricing order for the men's and boys' clothing industry known as MPR 607. This Order consisted of 83 printed pages and weighed nearly half a pound! The 83 pages necessitated an unlimited number of interpretations, followed by amendments. Inevitably, interpretations were again needed to cover up the errors discovered in the most recent amendments.

Extreme shortages were frequently caused by the effect of a pricing order upon production of an item. The most outstanding example of such a growing shortage as time went on was the supply of rayon linings, which in turn compelled the WPB to issue a highly restrictive priority rating for the fabric. In accordance with general policy, the OPA had approved a pricing order for rayon linings which allowed little or no profit for the weaving mills. Thereupon, many mills reduced sharply, or even eliminated entirely the weaving of that fabric, finding, for example, that curtain materials were far more profitable under another OPA pricing regulation.

Soon the clothing industry faced a critical shortage of rayon linings. Immediately some textile firms who converted the unfinished cloth purchased from weaving mills into properly dyed fabrics, brazenly entered the black market in linings, obtaining unconscionable prices. The largest weaver of rayon linings was the Hathaway Manufacturing Company of New Bedford, Mass. An official of the company, Otis Stanton, was in charge of sales. He was horrified at the chaos created by the OPA regulation and immediately increased his mill production of rayon linings by 15 per cent, even though such a fabric offered little profit. Stanton was determined to break the black market. The CMA office arranged with Stanton to notify him when a manufacturer was short of linings. In turn, he then promptly told one of his converter accounts to ship linings to that manufacturer, and the converter received a correspondingly greater yardage allotment. Due to the unselfish act of Stanton, who considered the effects of the black market as detrimental to the war effort, the men's clothing industry was able to supply clothing to civilians without undue deterioration of product.

The shortage of cotton pocketings and sleeve linings was also the end result of a series of OPA pricing orders which limited profits unduly and so caused a reduction in yardage. J. P. Stevens and Company came to the rescue by offering a special lot of goods to the industry. The association office handled this distribution, allotting the scarce material to manufacturers who were in need of the piece goods. Civilian production was maintained.

Nevertheless, the OPA made no change in its pricing policy for cotton goods, and supply was chronically short. When the troops began returning to civilian life after the war, the demand for suits rose sharply. There was a consequent need of increased yardage in cotton goods. But the OPA was still in control of pricing, and the supply remained low. To facilitate the rapid return of veterans to civilian life, General Graves B. Erskine, who participated in the capture of Iwo Jima, had been put in charge of apparel supply for returning soldiers. He called a meeting of clothing manufacturers in Washington and wanted to know why there was a slow down in producing suits. The manufacturers informed him that there were shortages due to pricing orders and cited the pocketing situation as most acute. One clothing man said that he was using potato sacks for pocketings! The general then called the OPA officials to the meeting. They were asked to explain their pricing policy. The OPA replied that the cotton goods regulation was in accordance with the over-all pricing policy of the agency. The general demanded that his veterans must be well clothed! The OPA could not oppose a general who helped capture Iwo Jima. They unconditionally surrendered and promised immediate price relief for the mills. Then one of the clothing men rose and announced that "you are the best general I ever saw," and all left happy.

Due to such incidents, the OPA fell into utter disrepute. It was primarily the price agency that caused the greatest amount of discontent among manufacturers who had need to meet with government officials. When the manufacturers said that Washington was a "madhouse during the war," they generally referred to the OPA.

Clothing Prices and Profits

Was price control effective? Despite confusion and frequent ineptitude, did the OPA directives which governed prices succeed in maintaining clothing prices at a reasonable level? Did price control prevent an inflationary spiral comparable to that rampant during World War I? Did the OPA pricing avoid a period of disastrous deflation comparable to the 1920 decline in prices?

It may be recalled that Hickey-Freeman reported in its pamphlet on price changes during World War I, that retail prices of clothing had risen 135 per cent from 1915 to 1920. During World War II, the data for the price index of apparel and clothing were carefully compiled by the Bureau of Labor Statistics, U.S. Department of Commerce, which showed as follows:

YEAR	ALL APPAREL		MEN'S WOOL, ALL YEAR ROUND SUIT	
1939	100%		100%	
1940	101%		101%	
1941	105%		107%	
1942	123%		128%	
1943	130%		133%	
1944	138%		137%	
1945	145%	last full year of price controls	139%	last full year of price controls
1946	160%	price control lifted	153%	price control lifted
1947	185%		176%	
1948	197%		205%	
1949	189%		204%	
1950	186%		203%	

According to the Bureau of Labor Statistics, men's suits at retail rose merely 39 per cent during the years of World War II when price control was in full force; retail prices had risen 135 per cent during the five-year interval ending 1920. However, the Bureau did have some qualification about prices in general about the above data. Although it did not specifically refer to men's clothing, the reservations made in the paragraph that follows could well apply to some men's clothing manufacturers, based upon the knowledge of those who were in the industry at that time. The Bureau noted that:

> . . . Attempts by sellers to circumvent the effects of price control led to substitution of inferior for standard goods, elimination of lower-priced lines, curtailment of services, and outright black market transactions at illegal prices. It was estimated that the combined effect of these, if they had been fully reflected in the price indexes would have been to raise the Consumers' Price Index by 3 to 4 per cent by the end of 1943. By 1945, the accumulated understatement was estimated at 5 percentage points, . . . but since VJ day, most of it has been cancelled out by a reverse trend toward improvement of quality . . .

Despite this qualification, it can be said that generally clothing prices held the line in a fairly responsible manner during the years of the OPA. When price control was lifted in August, 1946, there was a sharp price rise, reaching its peak in 1948. The veterans were returning to civilian life and the demand for suits was far greater than immediate supply. While the uncontrolled prices rose, yet considering the strong economic pressures exerted by inflationary forces at that time, including higher labor and fabric costs, the rise in clothing prices was relatively moderate. In the years that followed, the prices remained stable, even though demand declined. This indicated that the higher prices were primarily based upon higher costs although greater profit margins were apparent.

There was no period of deflation in clothing prices after World War II. During the conflict, particularly as the war neared its end, many economists had predicted that a post-war depression was inevitable. Such prophecies usually were based upon the experience of 1920. Deflation did not occur in 1949, partly because the labor unions were far stronger than in 1920 and were now able to force a round of wage increases rather than accept wage reductions. In addition, the Employment Act of 1946 passed by Congress, declared that the government favored full employment of the national work force. Hereafter, Washington policy, fiscal and monetary, was directed to accomplish that aim.

If price control was fairly effective, did it seriously affect the profits of the manufacturers and retailers? Were profits maintained, or even increased during the war? The financial statements of clothing manufacturers and clothing retailers during the decade of peace and war, as analyzed by Dun & Bradstreet, showed as follows:

Median Net Profit After Taxes on Net Sales

YEAR	MANUFACTURERS	RETAILERS
1939	0.88%	2.39%
1940	1.07%	3.33%
1941	2.04%	4.02%
1942	2.13%	3.87%
1943	2.59%	3.92%
1944	2.77%	4.57%
1945	4.05%	6.47%
1946	5.01%	8.06%
1947	3.19%	5.76%
1948	2.47%	4.06%

The manufacturers of clothing and the clothing retailers made high profits during the war years, far higher than normal. The peak in profits was reached in 1946 when price controls weakened and finally were abolished. Despite complaints by manufacturers and retailers that price control was throttling their sales and "was putting them out of business," it just was not so. The OPA and related agencies did throttle production due to unrealistic pricing orders which caused shortages and, at times, black markets. But on the whole, not withstanding the barrage of regulations, manufacturers operated at capacity or near capacity, producing uniforms and civilian garments, had no closeouts, and even disposed of old inventory at regular prices. The retailers likewise cleaned out their old stocks at a profit, and there were no markdowns during the period. With no losses suffered due to deflation, the industry entered the 1950's in good financial condition.

The Government Regulations

To fully comprehend what is meant to conduct a clothing business under strict government control during World War II, the list detailing some of the 54 salient regulations issued by the OPA and WPB affecting the production of men's clothing from 1941–1946 may be of interest. In addition, each pricing order and each amendment, was usually followed (for so-called clarification purposes), by several interpretative bulletins, plus numerous sheets of instructions telling manufacturers how to fill in the necessary forms required to be filed in Washington. Some manufacturers were positive that "Washington" (generally referred to in unfavorable terms), was deliberately issuing orders to keep bookkeepers, accountants and lawyers busy, while manufacturers teetered on the verge of a breakdown.

The Year of 1941

4/22/41	Preference Rating Order, P22, detailing order of priorities
11/18/41	Preference Rating Order 22 amended
12/30/41	P-100 replaces Order 22
	PDI issued, priority to obtain wool cloth for officers' uniforms

The Year of 1942

2/9/42	WPB Rating Order 10, under P100 for factory supplies
	OPA Price Schedule 58, Wool Rags
	WPB M73, allocation of piece goods
3/2/42	WPB M73A, Style Simplification Order
3/31/42	OPA amends pricing of wool rags
4/14/42	WPB restricts use of zippers
4/27/42	WPB amends Style Simplification Order
5/2/42	WPB lifts ceiling on wool rags
5/2/42	WPB amends Style Simplification Order

6/5/42	WPB lifts ban on zippers, new order to be issued
6/8/42	WPB Preference Order P131, cloth for officers' uniforms
6/18/42	OPA issues PR 163, ceilings on wool cloth
6/30/42	OPA issues MPR 172, ceilings on clothing contractors
7/11/42	OPA issues MPR 177, tailored clothing ceiling
7/31/42	OPA amends MPR 163, ceilings on wool cloth
8/7/42	OPA amends MPR 157, pricing on government contracts
9/2/42	OPA amends MPR 172, ceilings on clothing contractors
9/9/42	OPA amends MPR 177, tailored clothing order
9/25/42	WPB amends PO Order 131, cloth for officers' uniforms
10/16/42	OPA issues forms for clothing order MPR 177
10/26/42	WPB issues L224, new Style Simplification Order
11/7/42	OPA issues MPR 127, new order for wool rags

The Year of 1943

1/11/43	OPA amends MPR 163, wool fabric ceiling
3/11/43	WPB issues PO 139, priorities for factory supplies
3/31/43	OPA issues pricing order governing leggings and snow suits
5/15/43	WPB amends PO 131, cloth for officers' uniforms
6/4/43	WPB amends Style Simplification Order, L224
7/31/43	WPB amends PO 131, cloth for officers' uniforms
10/17/43	WPB issues Order L317, limiting supply of shipping boxes
11/1/43	WPB issues amendments to L224, Style Simplification Order

The Year of 1944

1/6/44	WPB issues M317, cotton pocketings priorities
4/18/44	OPA amends MPR 163, ceiling for wool goods
10/14/44	WPB amends L224, Style Simplification Order
12/16/44	WPB issues Order M325, restricts civilian production

The Year of 1945

1/10/45	WPB Order 328, restricts production of civilian trousers
2/15/45	OPA announces new price order, Maximum Average Price (MAP)
2/19/45	WPB issues Order 388, priorities of low priced goods
4/2/45	WPB issues M328B, fabrics for children's wear
4/14/45	WPB amends Order 388
4/19/45	OPA issues MPR 108 (protested because of too many forms)
6/15/45	WPB issues M388, directive No. 4, knitted clothback
8/22/45	WPB replaces M388 with M328B
9/28/45	WPB order M328B amended, new forms to be filed
10/3/45	OPA issues MPR 578, ticketing low priced garments

The Year of 1946

1/3/46	OPA amends M328, new forms to be filed
4/5/46	OPA issues MPR 607, new pricing order for tailored clothing
5/13/46	OPA amends MAP order
5/23/46	OPA amends MPR 607, clothing order
7/17/46	OPA amends MPR 578, pre-ticketing order
7/18/46	WPB amends Schedule K of order M328B

AND SHORTLY THEREAFTER—GOVERNMENT REGULATIONS WERE ABOLISHED!

Chapter 14

Military Procurement in World War II

The Year of 1941

As related in the previous chapter, the various government agencies in Washington took all steps they deemed necessary during the war to maintain an adequate production of clothing for the armed forces. Admittedly, their steps were often quite faltering. There were even frequent missteps due to a lack of knowledge about the industry, its methods of production, or even just ordinary business practice. Notwithstanding, the war effort was accelerated to the utmost with a minimum of delay, causing the clothing industry to operate its factories under intense stress.

The first authoritative and direct information to the clothing manufacturers which outlined what might be required of them came on Thursday, July 31, 1941, when the board of directors of the CMA met in Washington with Sidney Hillman, then associate director of the Office of Production Management. A wage agreement had been signed with the ACWA effective April 1, 1941, and one of the points of the settlement called "for the establishment of a fund to provide health and life insurance" for the union membership. Hillman, because of his official position, had not participated in the actual wage negotiations, and the directors of the CMA desired to discuss with him many of the fundamental problems that would be raised in establishing such a welfare fund. Accordingly, a dinner meeting was arranged at the Wardman Park Hotel.

After a general exchange of views in regard to the labor-management problem at hand, Hillman was asked about the pending program for military procurement. As a high official, with a thorough knowledge of government policy, Hillman's opinion was most important. As the clothing manufacturers were to be the producers of uniforms, the interest of the directors was understandable. Hillman told them that the preparedness program was just getting under way, and that large quantities of uniforms would be required shortly. The government was undertaking a greatly expanded program to meet the expected military needs; this would eventually affect every industry in the United States. Because the number of men in the armed forces of the country would total in the millions, the manufacturers of men's clothing would necessarily be in the forefront of such a preparedness program. He then pointed out that civilian production would probably be curtailed due to a lack of factory capacity, and shortages might develop so that rationing might even be introduced. Admittedly, the details of the program were still in the blueprint stage, but Hillman warned the directors that the industry must prepare for drastic changes in the near future. In summary, he painted a most somber picture of the months ahead. Incidently, as a good union leader, Hillman closed his remarks with the advice to the manufacturers that they be liberal in their attitude towards establishing the welfare fund for the ACWA members, so as to give the workers a greater stake in their country.

There was foreboding among the directors that the country was facing a period of great danger. On the train, returning to New York, the full implications of Hillman's warning about "things to come" were quietly discussed by very worried men. One of the directors summed up the matter in typical clothing language by saying, "We'll all be making a new line of merchandise soon . . . uniforms . . . and have a new account, a big one . . . Uncle Sam, but I hope to God the consumer . . . the soldiers . . . won't have to use our clothing in a war . . . " Before long, the only sons of two directors died in battle, and other sons were soon casualties during the years of conflict.

In view of the situation, Harry A. Cobrin, the executive secretary of the CMA, went to Philadelphia and met with Colonel Thomas Jones, the procurement officer of the Quartermaster Depot of the Army (QM). He offered the Colonel the full cooperation of the association and told him that the organization was ready, in all ways possible, to serve the QM. Because the CMA membership included the overwhelming majority of manufacturers who produced the wool clothing, Jones gladly accepted this offer. During the years to come, there was close cooperation between the association office and the military. The fact that William B. Flickstein was the executive secretary of the Philadelphia Clothing Manufacturers Association was of inestimable assistance in establishing such a close working relationship. Flickstein had a thorough knowledge of the industry as well as close contacts with the officers at the Depot. He often acted as a liaison between the CMA office in New York and the military in Philadelphia. Thanks to Flickstein, if and when a difficulty in production arose, it was quickly settled and the flow of uniforms was unimpeded.

Government contracts came slowly at the start, but there was considerable acceleration in each succeeding quarter of the year. By December 31, 1941, the industry had cut the following under government contracts:

WOOL UNIFORMS	
Uniform Pants and Breeches	1,687,944
Uniform Coats	3,041,376
Uniform Long Overcoats	1,114,766

Source: Bureau of Census, U.S. Department of Commerce

The manufacturing time for a uniform usually required 50 per cent or more man hours than for ordinary civilian garments. Therefore, the impact upon factory production was far greater than the data might indicate. Despite substantial contracts for uniforms, by working at full capacity, plus considerable overtime, the industry managed to produce 25,327,274 suits, the highest number made in many years, in addition to 1,940,000 sport coats and 7,360,000 overcoats and topcoats. It was particularly fortunate that such a large number of garments was made. It filled the racks of the retailers and the closets of the consumers as well, in preparation for years to come when, due to the steadily growing requirements of the military, civilian production would decline sharply.

The Year of 1942

Japan attacked on December 7, 1941, and now we were actually at war. The dire foreboding of the directors of the association had come to pass. Immediately the QM was under increased pressure to secure an increased number of contractors for the manufacture of uniforms. The Army quickly requested the aid of the industry in properly designing new types of uniforms that were deemed necessary because of changing conditions in warfare. These uniforms were so designed that only minor changes in established methods of usual manufacturing were required. Consequently, a minimum of time was lost in the flow of production, which facilitated scheduled delivery.

Now the industry devoted its prime energies to the war effort. The association was in constant contact with the Philadelphia QM, issuing bulletins quickly when additional uniforms were required, listing each new contract bid as announced by the procurement officers. Thanks to the combined efforts of all, in 1942 the clothing industry produced the following under government contract:

WOOL UNIFORMS	
Uniform Pants and Breeches	5,879,381
Uniform Coats	6,592,188
Uniform Long Overcoats	4,454,644

Source: Bureau of Census, U.S. Department of Commerce

The ever-growing production requirements of the military were reflected in a corresponding decline in factory output of civilian garments. The clothing plants were unable to increase their productive capacity because of a lack of skilled tailors, coupled with insufficient time to properly train new operators as replacements. Therefore, the Bureau of the Census reported that production of civilian suits declined approximately 22 per cent in 1942 as compared with 1941, and overcoat production for civilians dropped 20 per cent as compared with the previous year. The industry was now geared to fully clothe the armed forces.

The Year of 1943

It was fortunate for the effective planning and production of uniforms, that practical clothing men served as procurement officers. Their experience was invaluable in properly allocating contracts to those manufacturers who were most capable of making the desired garments. Men such as Major David Levine and Captain Irwin Weitzenhoffer had been top clothing executives in civilian life, and they performed near miracles in procurement because they spoke in "clothing language" to the industry. They knew well the problems encountered in the various plants. They also knew the ways and means of solving such problems, and they took an approach in giving out contracts that was direct, reducing red tape to a minimum. By cutting corners in bureaucratic procedure, they got quick results. These men were indefatigable in badgering the contractors of uniforms, persevering to obtain the greatest possible number of units for delivery in the shortest practical time. Manufacturers could see them in Philadelphia without difficulty, ask questions and get answers promptly. The country was well served by the clothing executives who entered the armed forces and put their know-how at the service of the military. For example, in one instance, there were two bids for an overcoat. One of the firms had made a few coats some years back, while the other was one of the top producers in the field. Despite the fact that the relatively inexperienced firm was 25¢ lower in its bid per garment than the experienced manufacturer, Levine gave the contract to the higher bidder. Such procedure was contrary to regulations. But Levine obtained excellent coats instead of possibly poorly made coats. And as the Major used to tell the story, by paying 25¢ more, the Army received coats that were worth $10 more in workmanship. Still, said his superiors in the QM, the price was high; it should have gone to the lowest bidder. There were threats that Levine would be held financially responsible for "overpaying." Levine was ready to assume that risk too.

To a great extent, clothing men wearing uniforms were permitted to get such results, and they did get results, because their superior was probably the ablest procurement officer in the Army, namely, Colonel Thomas Jones. The Colonel, a professional soldier, was a dynamo at the Depot, who drove his command to the utmost. He was extremely able, a fine administrator, and if he felt that he was doing the correct thing, he was afraid of no man, nor of criticism. Jones permitted no politics to enter into consideration in allocating a contract. As a good officer, he performed superbly under intense pressure. The services of Colonel Jones to his country during the war years were outstanding, and it was unfortunate that they were not suitably recognized when the conflict ended. The Colonel had stepped on too many toes, top brass and political, in performing his duty.

Thanks to the close cooperation between the industry and the QM, for the year the industry produced under government contract the following:

WOOL UNIFORMS	
Uniform Pants and Breeches	18,056,020
Uniform Coats	5,272,958
Overcoats	5,505,094

Source: Bureau of Census, U.S. Department of Commerce

But shortages of skilled labor were growing. More men were leaving for war service and replacements were few. Supplies of every item were becoming acute, from machinery parts for repairs, to paper and twine for shipping. It was becoming increasingly difficult to maintain production schedules.

The Year of 1944

Then, for reasons best known to the Washington defense officials, for the greater part of 1944, there was a gradual slowdown in new contracts. This was a startling development. Yet, there had been considerable talk about the war ending soon, for France was quickly liberated by the Allied forces, and it was generally hoped that the war would end before the year was over. Suddenly, in the late fall of the year, the military situation in Europe changed drastically. The Germans were now resisting strongly at their borders, and the likelihood of the war extending for a year or more seemed possible. Because of such a reversal in the military prospect, once more the QM began issuing bids for extremely large uniform contracts. By November, 1944, the supply situation became truly critical. Extraordinary military needs had to be met. When the QM informed the association of its dilemma, the executive secretary, after consulting with industry leaders, went to Philadelphia and recommended to the procurement officers that QM top brass meet with the CMA board of directors. They were to explain to the Board the sudden change in procurement plans, "laying it on the line." As experienced clothing men, the directors would be able to advise the best course of action to follow. After a lengthy conference, the QM agreed to come to the New York office of the association and meet with the board. In the CMA Bulletin of November 24, the details of this meeting were sent to the membership, so that they too would be fully aware of the critical supply situation facing the armed forces. This bulletin read as follows:

ARMY REQUIRES MORE UNIFORMS IMMEDIATELY

November 24, 1944

Directors Confer with Army Officers

On November 21, 1944 the Board of Directors and high Army officers met at the association office, for the purpose of expediting necessary production of Army uniforms.

The Army officers pointed out that its current and impending program of procurement was such that a large number of manufacturers who had never before made uniforms would necessarily have to begin immediate production of such garments. In particular, the Army officers were most concerned about the current and impending contract on field jackets. It was pointed out that the current contracts are delinquent up to 2,000,000 garments, and that there was an additional contract for 3,100,000 pending for completion by the end of April 1945.

The following is a list of current and impending Army needs which indicate the extreme need for every suitable manufacturer to enter into immediate production of uniforms:

Current Contracts

1,000,000 pair *short,* of wool serge trousers on present outstanding contracts
2,000,000 field jackets *delinquent* on present contracts by December 31st, 1944.
345,000 officers trousers *needed*
50,000 officers jackets *needed*
54,000 officers tropical worsted uniforms *needed*
15,000 officers short overcoats *needed*

Pending Contracts

3,100,000 new contract for field jackets . . . needed for completion by April 30th, 1945
200,000 officers trousers . . . contracts will be forthcoming shortly
475,000 enlisted men's overcoats . . . bid open now
IN ADDITION IT IS ANTICIPATED THAT MORE OFFICERS UNIFORMS WILL BE NEEDED.

* * *

Decision of Meeting

It was the consensus on the part of those present at the meeting that if a sufficient number of firms do not voluntarily accept government contracts, then mandatory and directive orders be issued upon each and every clothing firm in the United States, compelling each firm to make a required number of garments.

Harry A. Cobrin,
Executive Secretary

It was at this meeting, after the discussion was over, that one of the directors asked the officers present as follows, "May I ask why you reduced contracts on uniforms during the greater part of the year, so that you are now in such a jam?" One of the brass replied, somewhat abashed, "If the generals in Europe made a mistake, giving us the impression that the war was nearly over, why can't we, the lower echelon also make a mistake?" It was remarked later that this was the first time that any Army officer had admitted a miscalculation in procurement plans.

In accordance with the recommendations of those present at the meeting, the War Production Board (WPB) issued an order dated December 16, which restricted the production of all coats, suit jackets and overcoats, from January 1, 1945 to April 30, 1945. The manufacturers were ordered to accept contracts from the U.S. Army on or before January 1, 1945, which practically tied up all available production in overcoat factories, and absorbed an estimated 50 per cent of the total suit production capacity. Only those firms whose plants were not suitable for the making of uniforms, mainly very small factories, were exempt.

The Year of 1945

The WPB soon recognized that the ever-mounting overcoat requirements could not be met by April 15, and so it extended the freeze to August 31. The full impact of military requirements upon the clothing industry could best be evaluated by recapitulating the status of garment production in the factories during the first half of 1945:

Overcoat production	total factory capacity to be devoted to the military until August 31, 1945.
Suit production	QM estimated at the time that at least 50 per cent of available suit productive capacity of all grades were operating on uniforms.

Then, in face of this tight situation, the QM informed the Association that it would soon issue a bid for an additional five million overcoats, because they were needed badly. To quote a procurement officer, "It was an emergency of the very highest priority." The amount was staggering, far beyond the capacity of the manufacturers to produce such a quantity within a reasonable time. The regular overcoat houses were already frozen 100 per cent until August 31, and suit manufacturers were already operating 50 per cent of capacity on uniforms. So the harassed executive secretary of the association once again hurried down to Philadelphia. He informed the procurement officers that "you can not pour water in a keg already full." He stressed that an impossible burden which could not be carried, was being placed on the backs of the industry.

Anyway, the executive secretary pointed out, the QM had already bought or had bids outstanding for approximately 13 million overcoats, and the war practically over in Europe, therefore why so many heavy garments? He was then told, in a quiet whisper, "A military secret. Washington won't talk," with implications that the Army would not get caught short again as in November, 1944. So the bewildered executive secretary left Philadelphia certain that the United States would shortly invade Japan via cold Siberia! And the Army did actually get some firms to accept contracts amounting to a million or more additional overcoats, although not the usual specialty overcoat houses. The new contracts were let out shortly before Japan surrendered on VJ Day. Overcoat piece goods in the hands of the manufacturers were already cut for sewing but now the Army did not need them any longer. In fact, they had recently discovered an excessive amount of overcoats stored in the warehouses. After a somewhat hectic time by the QM looking for someone, for anyone, to buy the extra coats at any price, they were finally sold to department stores at a price even less than labor cost.

When the war ended, it could be well said that the clothing industry had fulfilled its function as a producer of uniforms. The military had received their requirements, even though there were times when it seemed likely that shortages might actually develop. Despite a reduced labor force, not only were the manufacturers able to keep the civilian population adequately supplied with clothing, but they were also able to produce additional garments for the newly liberated peoples of Europe. Had the war continued for any length of time though, we would certainly have witnessed definite shortages of civilian clothing, for the possibilities of further expansion in the labor force had reached its limits. It had been a close call for all concerned.

Chapter 15

The Union and the Manufacturers

Labor Arbitration

Arbitration machinery for settling labor disputes in the men's clothing industry was first established in 1911. At that time, an agreement which provided for ways and means of resolving labor differences was signed between the workers and the management of Hart, Schaffner & Marx. An arbitration committee of three members was set up, consisting of employe, employer and an impartial person. This committee was authorized to "fix the method for the settlement of grievances, if any, in the future," and furthermore, "the findings of such committee or a majority thereof" were to be binding upon both parties. Soon the employe and employer members of the committee were dropped, reducing the possibilities of a conflict in personalities, and the impartial member became the sole arbitrator, called the impartial chairman.

Because the Hart, Schaffner & Marx arbitration machinery proved successful, this same principle of settling labor disputes was included in the Chicago market agreement of 1919. Then, as each clothing area was organized in later years, a clause was usually inserted in each agreement providing for the appointment of an impartial chairman.

Customarily, the labor contract was negotiated between union and management representatives without the services or presence of any third party. Once the agreement had been signed, then the impartial chairman was appointed. This chairman had the power of adjudicating all matters of labor controversy, basing his decisions upon his interpretation of the labor agreement then in force. As time went on, in accordance with the ruling of the impartial chairman, a mutually satisfactory code of labor relations was formulated, which actually became an informal body of labor law for the clothing industry. In political terms, the collective agreement was the constitution; the impartial chairman was the judge who decided matters of dispute as he interpreted the provisions of the agreement. The decisions became the precedents that governed future labor relations between the union and the manufacturer.

To a great extent, in the early years of unionization, the industry was able to operate with a minimum of discord disturbing production because of the high calibre of men who were appointed as impartial chairmen, such as J. E. Williams in Chicago, William M. Leiserson in New York and Rochester, and George W. Taylor in Philadelphia. Their decisions covered all possible matters of dispute which could arise in a clothing factory, and their interpretations of the labor agreements were deemed fair and equitable. They truly established the fundamental principles which have since been followed in conducting peaceful labor relations between union and manufacturer in the clothing factories.

Soon, both labor and management found it feasible to settle disputes directly in accordance with prior decisions of the impartial chairman. The day-to-day disputes which had been formerly brought before the chairman were now settled between the union's business agent and the factory supervisor. There was less need for the frequent use of the impartial chairman. After some decades, in several of the markets, especially where only a few large firms operated, the office of the impartial chairman was ultimately abolished. In these instances, union and management had become fully confident that differences arising in labor relations could be expeditiously settled directly between the two parties concerned. However, in the larger markets, such as Philadelphia and New York, because of the number and diversity of firms, and the consequent multiplicity of disputes, the impartial chairman has continued to function actively.

When national bargaining first began in the clothing industry, the question of providing for an arbitration procedure had to be resolved. Therefore, in a paragraph of the national agreement stating that all matters of dispute between union and manufacturer were subject to the usual arbitration proceedings, a sentence was inserted which read that, "The details of the grievance and arbitration procedure thus provided are expressly reserved to each of the said market associations, if any, and/or individual employer and each joint board or local union for negotiation and joint agreement." There is no provision for arbitration on a national basis.

Industrywide Bargaining

A most important fact of life in the men's clothing industry, for the manufacturers and for the workers, is the pervasive, if not overpowering influence of labor-management relations which are conducted by means of industrywide bargaining.

The employes in the men's clothing industry can be sub-divided into factory workers and office personnel who are unionized, all belonging to the Amalgamated Clothing Workers of America (ACWA), and the non-union employes, consisting of the sales force, the miscellaneous employes such as piece goods buyers, office managers, designers and factory supervisors. In our discussion of national

A conference in 1950
Hollander Tells His Story
(Left to right) J. Potofsky, D. Drechsler,
L. Hollander, R. Reiss.

bargaining in the industry, only unionized workers will be considered, for only they bargain collectively for wages, hours and fringe benefits.

Prior to 1937, collective bargaining was on a regional or individual firm basis. This was highly unsatisfactory both to the national office of the ACWA and to the industry. There was a constant shifting of factories from one locality to another in a desperate race to seek lower wage levels, with the consequent loss of job security for workers and utter chaos at the industry level. This trend encouraged competition on the basis of shaving labor costs, rather than on the basis of increased efficiency and progressive methods of merchandising and selling. It therefore became increasingly desirable to remedy this intolerable condition.

It was the judgment of many manufacturers that national bargaining would eliminate such an objectionable form of competition in the industry. Again, when bargaining was on a market or individual basis, it had been the experience of the clothing firms that the union sought out the manufacturer or market that was most able, in the opinion of labor, to pay the highest possible wage increase. The union then reached an agreement with that manufacturer or that market. Once an individual or market agreement had been completed and announced, particularly if it was with a well known company or an important clothing market, the national floor for the labor increase was firmly set. Therefore, when the other members of the industry subsequently met with the union, the wage demands were not subject to negotiation. Proper wage bargaining was hampered or made impossible because of the wage increase already announced. The position of the manufacturers who were still to make a settlement with the union was weakened. The ACWA benefited considerably in market bargaining, since it could call a strike in the factory of one manufacturer or group of manufacturers located in any one clothing center which did not grant a wage increase and permit manufacturers located in other clothing markets to operate. Thus competitive pressure was exerted upon those firms whose plants were closed. If the struck plants did not settle quickly, their competitors would surely take away the customers of the firm or firms unable to deliver merchandise.

Despite this apparent advantage, the national office of the ACWA found that market or individual agreements were detrimental to the maintenance of orderly collective bargaining and affected the functioning of the ACWA as a national organization. It had been found that these piecemeal market or individual settlements tended to encourage a competitive drive among the local union managers. When market wage contracts were to be drawn, each local leader often sought extra benefits for his members which other locals in

A serious moment in negotiations—1950.
(Left to right) D. Drechsler, R. Reiss, J. Potofsky,
F. Rosenblum, H. Blumberg.

the union did not obtain. This increased his standing in his own market and perhaps also raised his national reputation as an aggressive leader within the ACWA. So, over the years, sharp differentials between the markets developed in the number of holidays granted, in permissible methods of cutting, in plans for unemployment insurance benefits, and similar matters granted locally when the wage contracts were written at the market or individual level.

Recognizing that bargaining by markets was highly unsatisfactory, both labor and management concluded that national negotiations were preferable. Accordingly, in 1937, as related, the first industrywide settlement was reached. From the standpoint of an organizational setup though, it was merely a matter of temporary expedience, possibly a "one-shot deal," for the manufacturers had no formal organization that could deal collectively with the ACWA on a permanent basis. Once the 1937 settlement had been made, each market went its own way. As already related, within two years after the agreement, in many clothing centers the basic principle of a nationwide wage settlement applicable throughout the country was utterly disregarded.

The chaotic condition in the national wage structure following the 1937 industrywide wage agreement was a direct blow to the authority of the national office of the ACWA. Metaphorically, the local union managers had thumbed their noses at their national office when they had granted wage concessions to the manufacturers within their markets. The move towards wage stabilization was an obvious effort to restore the authority of the national office as the sole power that determined changes in the national wage structure. It should be stressed that this authority, assumed by the ACWA, was a recent assertion of increased centralized power by Hillman and the other national officers. They apparently felt that only in that way could they eliminate the evil of inter-market competition based upon labor costs.

Drechsler, counsel of the dormant CMA, also served as counsel of the New York Clothing Manufacturers Exchange. He observed that his market was at a distinct disadvantage, for the terms of the 1937 wage increase were rigidly adherred to in New York City.

Rochester Labor-Management Conference—1950
(left) A. Chatman, ACWA,
(right) M. J. Baum, Hickey-Freeman

Drechsler therefore saw the revival of differentials in labor costs between markets as not merely harmful to the industry in general, but to the New York market specifically. He strongly favored permanent industrywide bargaining as a lasting form of labor-management procedure, and this could be accomplished only when the majority of the manufacturers were members of a permanently organized national association. Then the association directors, representing all of the clothing markets, could negotiate with the general executive board of the ACWA and agree upon a formal and written settlement applicable to the entire country. When pressure of national events practically compelled the revival of the CMA in 1940, industrywide bargaining really came into its own.

The wage settlement of March, 1941, was the result of many heated conferences held between the general executive board of the ACWA and the board of directors of the CMA. It was not a cut and dried affair, nor did the discussions last merely one or two days as in 1937. Now the manufacturers were members of a national association, and they had ample opportunity to determine policy prior to the joint labor-management conferences. They were meeting with the ACWA as a highly organized group of manufacturers.

There was opportunity for each demand to be carefully weighed and its implications well considered. Contrary to the previous settlement of 1937, this new agreement was not hurriedly completed. Once both sides agreed upon the terms of the settlement, the legal staffs of the union and the association put the wage agreement in writing.

Immediately thereafter, in April, 1941, this written contract was sent to all members of the association, giving them formal notice of the pending wage increase. The exact language of the national settlement was then inserted in all wage agreements signed by the local affiliated organizations of the CMA, and where there was no local organization, by the individual manufacturer. This national agreement did not disturb the special market practices or traditions currently in force. The agreement merely imposed changes that were industrywide, for the settlement did not cover the problems that ordinarily arose in local markets due to local conditions. Hence, if one market had paid for more holidays to their cutters than the other markets, and an additional holiday was granted as a result of national bargaining, the extra holiday was applied to all markets regardless of the number of holidays already paid for.

The basic principle that the national settlement serve primarily as a master agreement for the entire industry has remained unchanged to this day. Therefore, when an agreement is signed by the markets or individual manufacturers, it contains matters of local concern as well as all of the provisions of the national settlement.

Once established, industrywide bargaining as conducted by the ACWA and the CMA received the immediate approval of manufacturers. It became the basis of future labor-management relations. There have been no serious difficulties over the years as to method of bargaining, nor has there been any desire expressed either by the union or by the manufacturers for a reversion to negotiate by market or by individual firm. Some years ago, Morton J. Baum, then president of the association, in a statement to a Congressional committee, set forth the considered opinion of clothing manufacturers in reference to industrywide bargaining. He said in part:

> . . . As a result of industrywide bargaining, we find that competition which resulted from under cutting of the wage scales has practically

stopped, and that greater efficiency in factory operations and progressive merchandising methods have become the important factors in determining the success of a clothing business.

. . . Now, opponents of industrywide bargaining have said the industry meets with the Union, agrees upon a wage increase, and then the manufacturers uniformly raise prices at the expense of the consumer. Obviously, such a situation is entirely fantastic, at least in the Clothing Industry. We have about 900 manufacturers in our industry, located in all parts of the United States, and general agreement to increase prices would not merely be illegal, but physically impossible.

. . . Competition is probably stronger amongst the manufacturers than it has ever been. The profits of the industry are certainly no greater than they have been in the past. However, competition now is on a socially desirable level. It is not based upon lowering wages, but rather upon efficiency and merchandising skill . . .

Weinstein discusses problems with manufacturers—1950
(Left to right) L. Markin, C. Weinstein, M. Daroff, W. Flickstein.

An important reservation might have been added by Baum when he endorsed industrywide bargaining—namely—that it must, under all circumstances, be enforced by the union on an industrywide basis. If a local leader imposes changes in the settlement of his market contrary to the national agreement, it is the duty of the union to compel compliance by the local leader within the terms of the industrywide settlement.

In view of Baum's statement indicating industry approval, what have been the fundamental reasons for the continued success of national bargaining in the men's clothing industry? A most important reason is the fact that the same general type of garments are made by all members of the industry. The general method of manufacturing these garments (cutting, sewing and pressing) are fundamentally similar, so that the labor problems encountered in production are common to all. Admittedly, the quality varies from

New York Confers with Boston—1950
(Left to right) I. Grossman, J. Levy,
W. P. Goldman, M. Schapiro.

firm to firm, but all make either suits, sport coats, outercoats, slacks, or else several of these garments and, as noted, the operations in manufacturing are similar if not identical. Therefore, the manufacturers find themselves on a mutually common ground when they decide upon industry policy to be pursued in labor negotiations, and the union officials can likewise consider the problems of labor as industrywide, covering all types of clothing. If the clothing industry were, for example, to bargain for retailers and manufacturers at the same time, it would obviously be impossible to arrive at any common settlement that could be applied to the operators in a clothing factory and to retail salesmen as well. The recent efforts of the labor unions to compel total industrywide bargaining in the copper field, failed because they sought one settlement that would apply to the mines, to the refining plants and to the other branches of the industry as well. The diverse conditions of labor, and diverse labor costs were insuperable obstacles in granting the union's over-all demands. Only when an industry is generally homogeneous in product, and has a common method of manufacturing, can national bargaining succeed; the clothing industry fulfills these requirements.

A Case Study in Collective Bargaining

This is a case study of the wage negotiations that took place between the CMA and the ACWA during the early months of 1965. It is given in detail, so that the reader may have an opportunity to follow the actual proceedings as they occurred during labor negotiations in the industry. The format of industrywide bargaining might well be compared to the script of a well constructed and well rehearsed drama. There is the prologue (preliminary announcement that a wage increase will be demanded); then there is an unfolding of the plot (the labor-management conferences); followed by dramatic action (threats to "take steps"); the emotional prelude to the climax (when both parties say *no, but definitely!*); and the satisfactory culmination in the last scene (when both labor and management shake hands before photographers, and live happily ever after, at least until the next round of wage demands).

The series of events that took place in 1965, when the association and the union conducted industrywide negotiations were fairly typical of the previous occasions when labor and management met to revise the national labor agreement. By setting forth these events as reported in chronological order in the industry trade paper, the *Daily News Record*, and in the Association bulletins, we see a gradual unfolding of the proceedings, that led as in the past, gradually but surely, to a peaceful settlement in the clothing industry.

Collective bargaining in the clothing industry is not a cut and dried affair as sometimes seen by outside observers. It is in fact a highly complex process, wherein diverse and conflicting interests are involved, each group seeking a solution that will be most beneficial to itself. The factory workers are members of their respective union locals which belong to regional or city-wide joint boards that are affiliates of the Amalgamated Clothing Workers of America. The general executive board of the union, which consists of the more important market managers, is the bargaining agent for the workers. On the employers' side, hundreds of clothing firms belong to the local associations that are affiliated with the Clothing Manufacturers Association of the U.S.A. If there is no local organization in any particular clothing center, the individual firms join the CMA directly as members. The board of directors of the association, consisting of manufacturers chosen from all of the larger clothing markets, represents the employers in labor negotiations. Therefore, when the ACWA and the CMA confer, it is a joint labor-management meeting of the entire industry.

At these national conferences, problems that are the cause of dissatisfaction in the individual local markets are presented, such as, methods of work, excessive absenteeism, or else a necessary change in the days set for holiday pay. Often, many of the underlying economic and psychological complaints first seen at the local level, uncover a problem that has national significance. Therefore, ordinarily, all complaints, either by manufacturers or by the local unions are thoroughly aired at the joint meetings. Usually though, many are not resolved and revert to the particular clothing market for "further study" or "local action," which is really a diplomatic burial of the subject, much to the dissatisfaction of the complainants.

The first rumblings indicating the possibility of a new wage demand to come, are customarily heard in the local markets, and when these initial tremors, as it were, are reported in the trade paper, they are usually dismissed, hopefully so, as mere rumors by the industry. They are not taken too seriously by most manufacturers, perhaps on the theory of "read no evil, learn no evil, and all will pass in the night." In the labor negotiations we are now reviewing, the earliest of such publicized rumors (probably planted) took place during the latter months of 1964. This was the initial shot in a bitter battle that ended in a three-year labor agreement, effective June 1, 1965.

It should be understood that there was a three-year national labor agreement already in force from June 1, 1963 to May 31, 1966 between the CMA and the ACWA. When this contract had been signed in 1963, substantial benefits had been granted to the workers in the form of wages and fringe improvements. In that agreement however, there was a paragraph giving each party the right to reopen the contract as "relating to wages, hours, or working conditions, by serving written notice of such request on the other, on or before February 1, 1964, or February 1, of any subsequent year of the term of this agreement." Therefore, this was a three-year contract subject to reopening after the first year, either by the ACWA or by the CMA.

On November 25, 1964, the trade paper reported that the Rochester manufacturers were waiting to hear whether the ACWA would reopen the contract by February 1, 1965, for this would create uncertainty in regard to labor costs at the time when fall lines were to open in March. The contents of the Rochester news article were most unusual. Ordinarily, such reflections on the part of manufacturers were not publicized because there was the ever-present fear of "giving ideas to the union." Evidently someone, for very good reasons, deemed it desirable to stir up discussion about a possible wage rise. This story with a Rochester dateline was perhaps a trial balloon, or else it may have been a deliberate leak of an off-the-record luncheon meeting between one or several manufacturers and several leaders of the local union. During the meal, there may have been some general talk about the possibility of the ACWA reopening the contract. At all events, a seed had been planted, and this was duly printed for all manufacturers to read, to ponder and to worry.

Then, on December 24, 1964, now under a New York dateline, the trade paper reported that the "ACWA may reopen contract talks on wages and benefits" and the story then disclosed that "rumbles," "reports" and other so-called "unsubstantiated rumors" indicated that there was an excellent likelihood of wage demands to be made by the union on or before February 1, 1965. Evidently, New York was not going to lag far behind in its discovery of "rumbles" and "reports" which uncovered a widespread demand by the workers for higher wages. But as yet, no national action had been taken by the ACWA, nor had any written demands been made. By this time though, it was most likely that there had already been informal conversations at the local level between some manufacturers and some local labor officials. In military terms, this was preliminary skirmishing of the advance scouts to feel out the enemy

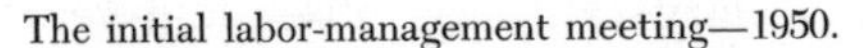
The initial labor-management meeting—1950.

strength, each side seeking the weak links in its opponents, thus revealing what items would meet with stubborn resistance, and what items will yield to pressure if forcibly applied.

It would be a mild understatement to say that the overwhelming majority of manufacturers were vehemently opposed to reopening the contract. In the showrooms, this rash of publicized rumors created a great deal of excitement, consternation and anguish, because wholesale clothing prices were soon to be determined for the fall selling season. Now, with wage negotiations probable, actual costs would not be definitely known until the selling season was over, not until May perhaps. The hazard of uncertainty in labor costs became a manufacturer's nightmare, for this meant that fall merchandise would have to be offered at prices "subject to a labor increase."

Soon, concrete evidence accumulated that many leading manufacturers and numerous top union officials had conferred informally, talking about the actual possibility of the contract being reopened upon demand of the union. By this time, amid a great deal of smoke and definite symptoms of fire, there was no doubt in the minds of many that the general executive board of the ACWA had made its decision. It was clear that the union would notify the association on or before February 1, 1965, that it would request a reopening of the contract in accordance with the terms of the national agreement. A special meeting of the board of directors of the CMA was called for January 25, 1965, to provide for such a contingency.

The chronological recital of events that follows represents a bare outline, a skeleton as it were, of conferences, of special meetings held at all hours, with hundreds of sandwiches hastily swallowed at the association office during long, emotional and heated discussions. There were angry harangues by the more belligerent members of the labor committee, demanding that the manufacturers should fight, should reject any union demands. In their calmer moments, they stressed the need to reduce the demands to a minimum, with a *quid pro quo* if anything were granted to the ACWA. They wanted a change in cutting methods which were restricting production in some markets, and a national agreement to permit the use of stencilled patterns in cutting. Often, several spoke out loudly that this was the time to "stand firm, and not to give an inch." One committee member, particularly strident, reiterated at all times the refrain, "Let'em strike. No reopening of the contract! Are we mice or are we men?" This was loudly applauded whenever repeated, although later, second thoughts came. Undoubtedly there were corresponding meetings within the general executive board of the union, just as long, just as heated and just as emotional. Committee meetings were the time to let off steam.

We now record the events as reported in the trade press and in the association bulletins:

Jan. 11: ACWA action expected in "two weeks" to reopen the contract, and several manufacturers never to be left behind, claim that they have already been "alerted and tipped off" to expect a three-year contract for higher wages and improved fringe benefits.

Jan. 25: Special meeting of CMA board of directors. Great indignation expressed that the union wants to reopen contract. CMA to stand firm . . . to oppose the reopening of the contract prior to June 1, 1966 . . . preparations are made for the forthcoming negotiations. . . . Richard H. Adler, president of Joseph & Feiss Company of Cleveland, who proved to be a most able negotiator, is appointed chairman of the national labor committee. The committee members represent all markets and are empowered to conduct labor negotiations with the ACWA. At the same time, the board votes to notify the union that the association also desires to reopen the contract. It is more of a case of "tit for tat" on the part of the manufacturers. In reality, it is a legal device which will enable the CMA to ask for changes in production practices that are considered objectionable.

There is no question that the manufacturers will gladly forego the doubtful pleasure of notifying the union that the CMA also wants to reopen the contract if only the union will also remain quiescent and promise not to mail the traditional registered letter prior to the dreaded day of February 1. In the opinion of the board however, if the die is to be cast, let the manufacturers not be caught napping. And the mood that evening is one of crisis. Now is the time to demand changes in manufacturing procedures and bring forth all other complaints that apparently hamper a smooth flow of work. So the stage is set for the regular industrywide negotiations to be carried on in accordance with the traditional pattern that had been followed for some decades.

Jan. 26: The registered letter from general president Jacob S. Potofsky of the ACWA is received by John D. Gray, president of the CMA, asking for a meeting to "be arranged at a time and place mutually to be agreed upon" in order "to modify certain terms and provisions" of the existing collective bargaining agreement.

Jan. 27: CMA membership is immediately notified that the expected letter from Potofsky has actually been received. This Association bulletin is considered by some to fall in the same category as a hurricane warning, an omen that rough times are ahead. In turn, the *Advance* (the ACWA paper) tells its readers that a just and reasonable demand for a wage increase is in the offing. Publication of such information in the union paper is intended to incite the natural desire of the workers for higher wages. This enables the union officials to maintain stoutly at future conferences that "our membership wants an increase . . . it is coming from our people . . . it's a *must!*" (a favorite union word in conferences).

Jan. 28: New headline—"Is it chaos or planned confusion?" Reporter predicts that fall prices will go up, a rather obvious prediction.

In another article of the same day, the unhappy clothing reporter finds out that he really does not know what the ACWA will possibly want, but guesses are that "the union will request a three year contract, wage and fringe benefits," while "it is known" that manufacturers will ask for a firm three year settlement with no reopening clause and cutting room changes to satisfy those markets where special restrictions are now enforced. Now retailers begin worrying about possible price rises. They insist that the harassed manufacturers quote firm prices immediately.

Jan. 29: Paper reports that union demands are still vague, with no settlement on either side. Actually, the two sides have not even met, and will not meet for another eight weeks.

Feb. 1: Reporter reiterates—The association will seek to negotiate on cutting room practices. The reporter might have added without any exaggeration that such a demand had been made upon the union since industrywide bargaining began, and to date no satisfaction had been obtained. The adamant position of the cutting locals in some markets had stymied any progress in cutting methods for a generation. In fact, the national office of the ACWA has been helpless, unable to obtain the cutters' consent to change. "However," says one "well-known manufacturer" in a moment of unusual optimism, "this time we will pin the union down!"

Feb. 9: In an interview, a "prominent manufacturer" who desires to remain anonymous but not silent, informs the clothing reporter that "a complete fresh approach and an objective re-examination of the basic concepts that have governed our relations with the union must be inaugurated." This merely discloses some of the wishful and cloudy thinking that habitually occurs prior to the actual confrontation between the union and the association.

Under the same dateline, the New York manufacturers absolutely "find no call" by the workers for the ACWA to reopen the contract . . . and they further claim that the reopening clause in the agreement should be used only for emergency purposes, maintaining there is no emergency now . . . anyway, this is not the time to raise wages. On the basis of this strong New York statement, some manufacturers, naïvely disregarding the possibility of a wage increase by June 1, 1965, sell at firm prices.

Feb. 15: The general executive board of the ACWA announces that it will meet in Miami the first week in March, and wage negotiations will start during the fourth week of the month.

Feb. 19: The association distributes a "fact book" to the national labor committee, which includes statistical data regarding production, a history of wage increases, hourly earnings, and profits in the industry. This book is to be used for the purposes of rebuttal when the joint conferences are held with the ACWA. Some optimists think that this book may be of assistance in obtaining concessions from the union. Unfortunately, as always, economic muscle, not economic fact, is the controlling element in wage negotiations.

March 2: Preliminary reports from Florida indicate that the ACWA looks to a huge package, with a "grand total cost of 35 to 40 cents" an hour. This news item, obviously an authentic leak, is a way of preparing the industry for "things to come."

March 3: The ACWA officially unwraps a 36¢ package deal at the Florida meeting. Manufacturers react with shock, saying "this is an astronomical hike," and predict "catastrophe" for the clothing industry.

March 4: Clothing manufacturers are reported as still "gasping," for industry reaction is one of "non-belief." One manufacturer hopefully claims "it can't be so," while another, in a fighting mood, repeats the traditional, "Never a cent."

March 9: There are reports that retailers are still insisting on firm prices and want delivery on time as well. Actually, most clothing firms will sell "subject to a labor increase," except those who blindly follow the leadership of the New York market.

March 11: The New York Clothing Manufacturers Exchange informs the clothing reporter that it will insist on no change until June 1, 1966, and predicts "fireworks" at the forthcoming meeting of the CMA Board. This usually implies a threat by New York to leave the association, which occurs fairly regularly whenever an agreement is to be negotiated.

March 12: Philadelphia manufacturers laud New York stand, although one pessimist says realistically, "I hope we can make it stick."

March 15: Large manufacturer boastfully reports that he is 70 per cent sold up. This is hardly helpful, for it informs the union that manufacturers will have to settle because of substantial bookings that await production.

March 23: CMA directors meet and vote once more to oppose any wage increase prior to June 1, 1966, and will so inform ACWA on following day.

March 24: The day of the big initial meeting! This is usually attended by all directors of the CMA (some bring their partners as well), and the entire general executive board of the ACWA plus their aides, assistants, etc. . . . After the usual amenities, with each side lauding the other for a "reasonable and realistic" approach to labor matters in the "spirit of Hillman and Drechsler," the union unfolds its demands. The ACWA wants a wage increase, greater fringe benefits, a full third week for vacation, plus such perennials as severance pay etc. . . . etc. . . . The manufacturers recoil with shock, for such demands are neither "reasonable nor realistic," and the conference breaks up with a minimum of the usual social amenities.

Some years ago it was the practice at the joint conference which unveils the union's demands, to have each member of the general executive board and each director of the CMA rise and give his opinion why or why not a raise should be granted. This permitted each speaker to return to his market and inform the membership, "did I tell the bosses" or "did I tell the union." At times, there were as many as forty speeches, long and repetitive. During one lengthy marathon of speeches which took place in Atlantic City, some thirty-odd speeches of varying fervor had already been made. All present were bored and tired when a fiery union manager rose. There was little that he could say that had not been said many times that day. But he had to speak! So, with deep emotion in his voice, he asked, "When the worker comes home, what does he find? I ask you. A wife, one baby, two babies, three babies, four babies . . . what does he need. What I ask you . . ." One manufacturer fearful of a further count by the speaker, rose and pointing his finger shouted, "Condoms, that's what he needs Joe, condoms." The meeting broke up then and there.

March 25: The clothing reporter of the *Daily News Record*, apparently experienced in such matters, sagely writes that "while the situation seems to have reached an early impasse at yesterday's session, veteran observers are confident that an eventual compromise will be worked out."

March 26: Potofsky having been rebuffed on March 24, warns John D. Gray, president of the CMA, in a publicized letter that "serious friction" may develop unless the CMA reconsiders its stand against any labor increase before June 1, 1966, and furthermore, that the board of the ACWA will meet March 30 to determine "future action." This letter immediately brings results. Both parties agree to meet March 31. Now the tempo quickens considerably towards a final settlement.

March 31: CMA and ACWA labor committees confer.

April 1: News headline—"ACWA and CMA deadlock Continues on Pact Date" . . . although the reporter carefully hedges by writing that "two encouraging signs were a statement from CMA expressing the hope of further meetings, and that the CMA labor committee was setting up smaller negotiating committees, which usually means the parties are getting down to brass tack bargaining."

April 2: New York once more announces it will stand firm for the June 1, 1966 date, and assures the industry that New York will not weaken under any circumstances. All manufacturers applaud such firmness.

April 6: Somewhat more realistically, small CMA groups start analyzing ACWA terms, and four sub-committees are appointed to meet with respective sub-committees of ACWA.

These sub-committees will discuss:

1. Wages and hours
2. Technical Productivity
3. Insurance and Welfare
4. Made-To-Measure firms.

April 8: Wages and hours sub-committee meets with corresponding ACWA group in Warwick Hotel.

April 9: There are reports that negotiations are still at "feeler" stage, and further meetings will be held.

April 25: Reporter hears that CMA may now actually give the increase as of June 1, 1965. Meetings have been held all week, but reporter finds that New York is still firm for June 1, 1966 date, . . . also rumors that manufacturers have offered 17.5¢ raise, but received a cool response from ACWA.

April 15: Subcommittee on productivity meets in CMA office . . . little progress reported.

April 22: Then, like a bombshell, clothing reporter writes that a prominent manufacturer, hitherto the leader of the group within the committee vehemently opposed to any wage increase prior to June 1, 1966, has written to his retailers that he expects the wage rise to go into effect June 1, 1965, and therefore he is now raising his fall prices. The CMA labor committee members are stunned, for they received no prior notice of his unprecedented action. Somewhat dazed at this about face, opposition to June 1, 1965 date collapses completely.

April 28: Contract held near, and report that a 25 to 27¢ package is in the works at a meeting held in the Warwick Hotel.

May 5: Best sources available say that the package will be effective for three years

May 6: New headline— Today may be the day for ACWA-CMA pact!

May 7: A 30¢ wage package announced in a joint CMA-ACWA press release which states in part:

> . . . Mr. Jacob S. Potofsky, General President of the ACWA declared, 'This contract is the best in the history of negotiations between the Amalgamated and the CMA, and is a fitting tribute to the many years of peaceful negotiations between the two parties'. . . . Mr. John D. Gray, President of the CMA and also head of Hart, Schaffner & Marx, stated that 'he joined with Mr. Potofsky in paying tribute to the ability of the negotiating parties to achieve a firm three year settlement without industrial strife', . . . He pointed out 'that the 30¢ package represented a real cost to the manufacturers of at least 36¢ an hour because of fringe costs'. . . .

The foregoing recital of rumors, meetings, and the eventual settlement, gives a bare outline of clashes in personalities, conflicts in business interests, and of the numerous problems affecting the individual markets which had to be ironed out (not always to the satisfaction of manufacturers), before the national agreement could be settled. To a great extent, on the part of the manufacturers, this was accomplished because of the ability of Richard H. Adler to mold the often diverse interests of the local markets and the competitive rivalry of the manufacturers, into a more or less harmonious unified policy. It was evident that the chairman of the labor committee during these negotiations had to be endowed with the patience of Job, the thick skin of a rhinoceros, the diplomatic touch of a Metternich, an extensive knowledge of the industry, and above all, common sense. Fortunately, Adler fit this concept.

Despite the usual manufacturer comment that "they gave what the union wanted and didn't fight," the facts speak for themselves. National bargaining was not a "pushover" in the men's clothing industry, nor was it a love feast. Hard bargaining was the rule, with the basic understanding by both parties, that after all was said, a settlement had to be reached before June 1, 1965, and such settlement had to be viable for the employers and satisfactory to the union.

Chapter 16

The Clothing Manufacturers Association of the U.S.A. (CMA)

Reorganization of the CMA

Since it was reactivated in 1940, the CMA, as the trade association of the clothing manufacturers, has been in the very center of all organized activity within the industry, for its membership includes the overwhelming majority of firms in all of the important clothing markets. The CMA board of directors is a cross-section of the industry by region, size of company and type of garment made. The association has been recognized as the national spokesman for the manufacturers by all government departments, by the mills and by the retailers. Therefore, to describe the activities of the CMA is to record since 1940, for all practical purposes, the history of the industry and its organized activities. Because the association's activities have been so varied, covering every facet of the manufacturers' interests, it will be necessary to divide the CMA story of nearly three decades into two chapters of the volume.

When the association offices were reopened on March 4, 1940, with Frank P. Zurn as executive secretary and Harry A. Cobrin as his part-time assistant, a multiplicity of industry problems required immediate attention. The Wage & Hour Division of the U.S. Department of Labor was in the process of organization. It was busily preparing regulations covering learners, exemption rules for supervisory employees, and was formulating record keeping procedures for hours worked. The Wool Products Labeling Act of 1939 needed considerable clarification by the Federal Trade Commission, so that

Raymond H. Reiss—1939–1952
(Courtesy of CMA)

the provisions of the Act might be properly enforced. The Robinson-Patman Act, governing the terms of sale to retailers, a matter of prime importance to the industry, had not as yet established proper guidelines for the sale of merchandise. The war in Europe had already begun, and the union was most anxious to secure a wage increase at an early date. All this and much more for an association office staff that consisted, on that March day, of Zurn, Cobrin and a lonely stenographer! There was obviously much to do, and it had to be done quickly in order to serve the membership. David Drechsler, as counsel, was always nearby, and his advice and judgment helped immeasurably in initiating activities that would establish the CMA as an energetic and well-rounded trade association.

When the CMA was formed in 1933, there were several local associations already in existence, namely, in Rochester, Philadelphia, New York and Baltimore. The tailors-to-the-trade in Chicago and Cincinnati also had their local organizations. Therefore, in forming the national association, it was set up somewhat similar to the plan

Morton J. Baum—1952–1959
(Courtesy of CMA)

Leo Ullman—1959–1962
(Courtesy of CMA)

of the Federal government. The local associations became affiliates of the national association, and the membership of each local organization automatically became members of the national organization. If there was no market association in any area, the individual manufacturers joined the CMA directly. Once the national framework had been established, each market organization appointed its alloted number of directors to the board; such allotment was made on the basis of the relative importance of the market within the industry. The made-to-measure houses were represented by single directors from Baltimore, Cincinnati, Chicago and New York. A half-dozen prominent manufacturers who did not belong to any local market group became directors on behalf of the "independent" firms. On the whole, the board was a fair representation of all unionized clothing manufacturers in the United States.

It may be recalled that the CMA was formed and organized on May 22, 1933, with the by-laws hastily drawn and quite vague in language. This posed no difficulty however, for during the NRA years the association really acted as an unofficial arm of the Clothing Code Authority. Its apparent principal function at the time was to prod the Authority officials in promoting the interests of the manufacturers as the CMA directors thought best. By 1940 though, the situation had changed entirely. The NRA disappeared, but the CMA by-laws remained. Because they were so vague, they were left undisturbed, and were considered for many years as loose guidelines rather than exact rules of procedure. The association frankly operated on an entirely pragmatic basis, resolving each situation as seemed best at the time. For example, the by-laws did not limit the term of service nor provide for the regular election of officers.

It should be emphasized that the office of the association president of the CMA, has not been, and is not, a sinecure, a mere honorary or figurehead position. Based upon resolutions passed by the board of directors, the president usually directs policy through the executive secretary and counsel who are in frequent communication with him. As noted, one of the prime functions of the organization is to conduct industrywide bargaining. This requires officers who are thoroughly experienced in dealing with the ACWA on a national basis. Because the president's term had been indeterminate until 1967 (when the by-laws were changed), the many years of office had given him the opportunity to acquire the experience and the know-how so necessary in matters of national bargaining. Therefore, he has been an invaluable advisor to the labor committee when it negotiated the industrywide wage settlement. At the same time, in instances when necessary, the president often has appeared on behalf of the association before government bodies. Manifestly, only a man of stature in the industry, who has the complete confidence of the manufacturers, can serve as president of the association.

Fortunately, the men who have served as presidents of the association have possessed these qualifications. Mark W. Cresap, president of Hart, Schaffner & Marx, and a community leader in Chicago, was entirely devoted to the welfare of the industry. During the hectic period of the NRA, and in 1939–1940 when he revived the association, Cresap took a leading role in creating the feeling of common purpose among the manufacturers. Previously, they

John D. Gray—1962-1969
(Courtesy of CMA)

thought of themselves only as individuals, or merely as members of a local market. It was Cresap who cemented the separate regional fragments into a national clothing industry.

His successor, Raymond H. Reiss, who headed the reactivated organization, was a man of enterprise and industry foresight. Reiss stressed the need for the association to serve the membership in every possible way. During the years of war, and the years of peace that followed, Reiss directed the association policy towards that end. As a result, by the time Reiss resigned as president in 1952, the CMA had become outstanding as a trade organization.

Morton J. Baum, president of the Hickey-Freeman Company, the successor of Reiss, was a quiet person who was most conscientious as president, and directed association policy with care. Reserved in manner, Baum was a most warm-hearted and thoughtful person. His tact in handling difficult moments at a meeting, particularly during labor negotiations, often reduced mounting tension that might have hampered the settlement. However, his community interests, as well as the association activity, proved too much of a burden when added to his duties as president of his company. Because of ill health, Baum resigned in 1959.

Leo Ullman, of Joseph H. Cohen & Sons, Inc., succeeded Baum. Ullman was thoroughly versed in all matters concerning labor, having had many years of experience in dealing with the ACWA. As Ullman was also most interested in the effect of Federal regulations upon the industry, he often appeared in Washington before various government departments. Leo Ullman served the industry well as president. In 1962, because of pressures of business, he resigned, and John D. Gray, president of Hart, Schaffner & Marx, was elected head of the CMA.

Gray followed the tradition of his predecessors in his direction of the CMA. He maintained proper relations with the Amalgamated, and expanded the activities of the association. In February, 1969, Richard H. Adler of Joseph & Feiss, Inc., succeeded Gray as president of the association.

In August, 1955, David Drechsler died, and Herbert Ferster, a partner of Drechsler & Leff, assumed his duties as counsel to the association. Ferster had spent his entire law career as an associate and later partner of Drechsler, so he was fully acquainted with the policy and the activities of the association. He followed in the Drechsler tradition, offering his advice and judgment as needed by the association officers. He has been successful in continuing the close relationship that had been originally established by Drechsler between the law firm and the CMA office.

By 1967, it was obvious to all that the by-laws were entirely out of date and should be completely reviewed. Accordingly, a committee of manufacturers in cooperation with the counsel and the executive secretary, prepared a revised set of by-laws. The board of directors approved the committee's report, and currently the CMA is organized on the following basis: There are 28 directors

Richard H. Adler—1969—
(Courtesy of Fairchild Publications, Inc.)

in all, seven of whom are appointed by the New York Clothing Manufacturers Association; five by the Philadelphia Clothing Manufacturers Association; two by the New England Men's and Boys' Clothing Manufacturers Association; and two by the Rochester Clothiers Exchange. The manufacturers who are not members of any market organization elect nine directors, and three directors are elected by the made-to-measure houses of Baltimore, Cincinnati and Chicago. In actual practice, because there may be prominent firms in some of the markets where the allotted number of directors has already been appointed, a number of firms are invited to attend the board meetings as "alternates" of their market representatives. One of the important changes in the by-laws is the provision that the national officers of the CMA are to be elected for a term of two years, and may serve only two consecutive terms.

Services to the Membership

Within a few months after the office opened, Zurn resigned due to pressure of personal business, and Cobrin became the executive secretary. In order to establish a means of communication between the membership and the CMA office, a bulletin service was immediately started. For a short time, it was sent bi-weekly, but when the war came in 1941, with government regulations so frequent, it was issued weekly until 1950, when it once more reverted to a bi-weekly basis.

The usual contents of the current association bulletins are information about government regulations, interpretations of such regulations, a merchandise exchange section which enables members to buy and sell excess piece goods or supplies without charge, and an employment service for the benefit of the members in the industry who are out of work. In addition, at regular intervals, manufacturers are asked to file their trade names for the purpose of preventing any duplication by competing manufacturers. The CMA files now include some 4,000 trade names, with more added each season.

At times, the bulletin has been used as a means of avoiding embarrassment, for often the association office has been called upon by members to solve matters that are somewhat outside the province of regular industry activity. There was the clothing manufacturer who informed the executive secretary that he had a daughter of marriageable age. Could the executive secretary recommend a nice husband for the young lady, preferably "a good clothing man?" This duty was tactfully evaded by suggesting that "maybe such a notice can be inserted in the association bulletin." The father took the recommendation in good grace. Nothing further was heard of this incipient effort to expand the association's activities.

Economic Reports

Since the inception of the association, the members receive each month industry production statistics, including detailed analyses of the data. In addition, special reports such as the year-end financial statements of manufacturers and retailers, as well as economic studies on merchandising and sales trends are frequently sent to the membership.

Because the association issued numerous economic studies, it was bruited about that the CMA office kept every variety of economic information. This caused an obvious misconception by laymen as to the type of data actually compiled by the organization. For example, in one instance, a young man sought a complete financial dossier about one of the manufacturers. Obviously the association did not keep such facts. However, the curiosity of the executive secretary was aroused, and he asked this young fellow why he wanted to know the exact financial status of this manufacturer. "I'm taking out his daughter," was his immediate reply. He was referred to Dun & Bradstreet as an aid in advancing the budding romance.

Technology

Within recent years, there have been annual seminars of problems concerning productivity. Several hundred factory executives have usually attended each season. In cooperation with industrial engineers, the CMA has been sending to the members numerous studies dealing with specific problems of manufacturing.

Traffic Department

The association employs a traffic consultant who carefully oversees the freight rate structure of the industry. This has resulted in reducing transportation costs to the manufacturers and to their retailers.

Relations With Government Agencies

Over the years, the executive secretary and the counsel to the association, have established a close working relationship with the various government departments. The U.S. Department of Labor, and its numerous bureaus are of particular concern to the association, because the Fair Labor Standards Act as well as other legislation are within the province of that Department. Cobrin, the executive secretary, because of his knowledge of economics, was a member of the Business Research Advisory Council of the Bureau of Labor Statistics of the Department of Labor for 16 consecutive years; upon retirement from the association, he resigned as a member of the Council.

From time to time, numerous hearings are held by the various government agencies due to frequent changes in the Fair Labor Standards Act, the Walsh-Healey Act, the Wool Products Labeling Act, and other pieces of legislation that vitally affect the interests of the manufacturers. It is important to the industry that all approved legislation be enforced in a practical manner. Thus the CMA met with the Federal Trade Commission some years ago and recommended the substitution of the registered number on the garment label rather than the manufacturer's name. This recommendation was accepted by the Commission, so reducing the complications arising in enforcing the Act. In another instance, the clothing industry recommended a code of proper advertising allowances to the Commission in accordance with the provisions of the Robinson-Patman Act; this recommendation was adopted by the Commission as a guide line for the clothing manufacturers.

Invariably, special problems arise not usually within the province of routine Association activity that are of vital importance to manufacturers, such as dealing with the military, or a dangerous increase in foreign garment imports.

Dealing With The Military

The activities of the CMA during World War II were fully described in a previous chapter of this volume. It was fortunate that the association had acquired this experience, for the Korean incident began June 25, 1950, and once more problems of producing uniforms arose. As on the previous occasion, the association office immediately offered its cooperation to the Quartermaster Depot which had been transferred to New York City, but now there was no Colonel Jones in charge. The industry was brusquely repulsed. Army contracts were given to many firms that were entirely incompetent to make uniforms. The so-called Industrial Mobilization Plan, prepared by the Army at a cost of many millions just to meet such a contingency, was brazenly discarded. Vainly, the executive secretary of the CMA issued statements to the press decrying this situation. David Drechsler, as counsel, met with the top officials of the Department of the Army and the Defense Department, protesting the procurement policy. It was seemingly impossible to convince the proper officials that military purchases were being outrageously mishandled. Within a year or so, the problem of procurement became an open scandal. Several civilian employes and army officers as well were indicted on criminal charges. Only then did the Defense Department realize that it had been misled, and now it sought the cooperation of the association in an effort to resolve this malodorous mess.

At their special request, the executive secretary of the association met with high officials in the Pentagon, and he recommended the establishment of a Qualified Bidders List. He even prepared tentative forms that should be filed by the contractor prior to bidding. Properly filled out, this information would establish the financial worth of the firm, the ability of the company to produce uniforms, and the moral character of the controlling stockholders of the uniform maker. In the beginning, there was very strong resistance by the QM towards initiating such a program. Conditions in the QM did not improve despite complaints, and widespread protests grew steadily. The ACWA also vigorously protested the character of the firms that were obtaining contracts. All to no avail. Then the newspapers began reporting the court proceedings which disclosed serious maladministration of Army purchases. Because of such unfavorable publicity, Congressional hearings were finally held in 1957. At the hearings, the CMA revealed the information about procurement that had been previously given to the Department of the Army. The hearings were long and thorough. At their conclusion, the Congressional sub-committee issued this devastating statement:

> This sub-committee finds from consideration of testimony and documentation presented, that bribery, inefficiency, and other improprieties existed in the Government's procurement of millions of dollars of military clothing, including Army and Air Force coats, jackets, and headwear. A substantial amount of this clothing was purchased from a particularly nefarious group of contractors, who through connivance obtained improper favors . . .

Now, at last, the Department of Defense took action and established a Qualified Bidders List for uniforms. Since 1958, the date when the List was first used, there has not been any scandal in procurement such as frequently occurred in prior years. In fact, this method of securing information from contracting firms was so satisfactory, that the Department extended the basic principle of a Qualified Bidders List to many other items purchased by the military. Belated recognition came to the CMA for its unrelenting efforts to establish proper standards of industry experience, financial responsibility and moral standing, when on September 28, 1961, Cobrin personally received a Certificate of Merit from the Quartermaster Association for his effort in establishing the list.

However, it was not all drama in dealing with the Army, for oftimes it was absurdity, or even comedy. There was the time when, shortly after the Korean War, a general in Washington decided that the morale of the soldiers needed a booster shot. His solution—that they dress more smartly. Included in the panacea for smarter dress was—have the button holes hand sewn rather than machine sewn on all uniforms worn by privates. The association immediately pointed out that hand button holes, while excellent as such, were sewn only on the higher priced suits, and that the number of handsewers was limited. To prove this point, a special survey was made. But the general could not be moved. He was adamant, and he even came to New York to meet with the union and a committee of the CMA in order to put his idea across. At the conference, after a lengthy and entirely unsatisfactory discussion, the top brass was bluntly asked, "How will you justify to a Congressional Committee your hand sewn button holes as a morale booster, which will cost a million dollars or more, in terms of increasing the combat efficiency of a soldier?" The question was not answered, but the idea of hand sewn button holes on uniforms for privates was shelved permanently.

At another time, an Army general decided that all manufacturers, regardless of quality, should be able to make a garment at the same price, regardless of the fact that some companies produced suits selling at $100 or more, and others sold suits at $25 each. Said this officer, "When I give specifications, that's all I have to do." He was told that a Rolls Royce, even though the specifications were the same, made in a Ford plant would be somewhat different, and the cost would differ sharply from one made in the Rolls Royce factory. The general probably had never made automobiles, and certainly he had never made clothing, so he would not budge. Finally, a test was agreed upon. Four garments were to be sewn. All were to be made with the same specifications, but were to be produced in four different shops, ranging from a factory of the lowest quality to one of the highest quality. The purpose of the test was to prove the differences in fit between the four garments and the variations in quality of workmanship, even though the specifications were the same. The lowest quality maker, who was given a coat to sew, manufactured suits solely for a very cheap basement trade. However, when the four coats were returned, it was found that this low priced maker had sent in the finest coat of the four, all hand tailored, an excellent custom-made garment! There was consternation in the association office. So the manufacturer was called in and asked if that was the way he usually made his regular clothing. He replied, "Certainly not. But for Uncle Sam . . . nothing but the best . . . it was only one coat, so I sent it to a Fifth Avenue custom tailor. Let me tell you, it cost me a fortune. What's the matter, is it a bad coat?" It took a lot of fast talking by the executive secretary of the CMA to convince the general that one test coat was not available, and that the association would gladly pay for the fabric used. Moreover, the three garments presented to the general did prove CMA's point, and so matters remained quiescent for a few years. Then came the war in Vietnam.

It was a quiet Friday afternoon, about 4 P.M. on December 3, 1965, when Flickstein called the CMA office from Philadelphia. The Defense Personnel Supply Center (formerly the Quartermaster), needed uniforms badly and wanted the executive secretary to come to Philadelphia quickly. It was an emergency, and there was danger that the military would issue "rated orders" under the Defense Production Act of 1950. This was the Act that gave the government the power to require manufacturers to produce uniforms, and if necessary, reduce civilian production. On the following Tuesday, Cobrin, Flickstein and Ferster as counsel, were at the offices of the Center. They were informed that millions of uniforms were needed in a hurry, and what would the industry do about it? Arrangements were then made for the military to confer with the CMA board of directors on the following week. At this special meeting, held on December 13, the board discussed the problem of procurement with the officers, and an association committee was appointed to cooperate with the military.

Numerous meetings were subsequently held in New York and in Philadelphia. Urgent bulletins were sent to the membership informing them of the emergency. Now, this was the time of the year when the industry had the shops full of garments in work for the spring trade. Piece goods purchased many months ago were on hand to be cut. Retail orders taken in August had to be delivered during the early months of 1966. Despite substantial civilian orders, the majority of firms made immediate plans to take care of the military requirements. Some firms were somewhat reluctant to endanger their civilian business, promising to accept contracts later on. But there was a shortage of uniforms, and so "rated orders" were placed on these manufacturers. There was a hectic period for six months or more. Nevertheless, as the industry gained experience in handling contracts for uniforms, civilian production gradually was reduced. Within a short time, the dilemma was solved, and no further "rated orders" were necessary. Another unexpected crisis was overcome. There still remained the problem of foreign garment imports which could not be resolved so easily.

Foreign Garment Imports

Prior to World War II, the manufacturers of men's clothing encountered little competition from foreign clothing firms. Ready made, tailored clothing was ordinarily produced and sold in the industrialized countries where there was a substantial urban middle class. Outside of western Europe, there were relatively few centers of population that fell into such a category. In South America, the average middle-class businessman, executive, and professional, had his suit made by a custom tailor. To an extent, this was due to tradition, and also due to snob appeal wherein the consumer was able to boast of "my tailor." This same tradition was widespread in Europe as well, and even in England. In that country ready made clothing ("off the peg"), was far less important than made-to-measure garments. There were large retail chains in the British Isles that sold only individually tailored suits, even to the lower middle class. On the whole, the ready made clothing industry, outside of the United States, was relatively unimportant. Consequently, the American clothing manufacturers faced no competition of imports from foreign countries. A few garments did come in from England, but they were sold primarily on the basis of sheer snobbishness. The weight of the English fabric was more suitable for foggy London rather than New York, and the cut of the coat was usually far different from the American model.

After World War II, the CMA office had carefully analyzed the potential possibilities of export, and it was then found that there was no prospect of selling tailored clothing to foreign countries. The usual tariff laws were prohibitive, and in South America, for all practical purposes, no wool clothing was permitted to enter. Even in western Europe, the tariff walls were deliberately high in order to protect domestic clothing firms, and frequently their imports were limited because of the problems caused by balance of payments.

With the war ended, in an effort to rebuild Europe, our government encouraged west European manufacturers to visit the United States and study our methods of production and merchandising.

Every west European country sent productivity teams which were cordially welcomed by the industry. Within a few short years, it was estimated that fourteen such teams had thoroughly inspected the domestic clothing plants. They prepared careful analyses concerning our methods of production which were then distributed throughout their respective countries. The welcome mat was suddenly withdrawn however, when one outstanding leader of an English team, somewhat tactlessly, announced upon his arrival in London, "Now that we know how the Americans make clothing, and how they style, we will be able to make the garments and sell them in quantity to the United States." The CMA office received calls from members denouncing such visitors, and thereafter our manufacturers were reluctant to have their plants examined by foreigners. The industry took the position that if it could not sell in foreign lands because of tariff laws, the foreigners should stay in their own back yards.

Meanwhile, a threat to our American clothing industry was gradually developing in Japan. Due to bombing, we had completely destroyed the woolen mills in that country as well as other industrial plants. General MacArthur was most anxious to help Japan get on its feet once more in order to reduce unemployment and eliminate the danger of communism. He therefore secured the services of American textile engineers who went to Japan and helped build modern worsted mills. Labor in Japan was cheap, and the price of their cloth was far below American prices. The engineers immediately saw the possibility of exporting worsteds to the United States at a price that would undersell the mills in this country. Some engineers even became sales agents for the Japanese mills they had helped build and equip with the most modern machinery. As thoroughly experienced textile experts, the Americans taught the Japanese how to style fabrics that would be acceptable in this country. The Japanese were apt pupils and quickly learned their lessons. They had found a large market for wool fabrics in the United States and soon developed an extensive export business selling their piece goods to the American clothing manufacturers. In turn, it should be acknowledged that the clothing firms in this country encouraged such sales, for the price of foreign fabrics were far lower than the price of comparable domestic piece goods. It was merely a question of time, however, before the Japanese would consider the possibility of converting the cloth that was so acceptable for American made clothing into suits sewn and produced in Japan for export uses. These suits could be manufactured at low wages and then sold to American importers at prices far below the sale price of domestic suits.

By 1958, the threat became real. Here and there, department stores offered Japanese made clothing, considerably underselling the domestically made garments. This was to be expected, for the earnings of a clothing worker in Japan then averaged about 16¢ an hour, whereas the American clothing worker then earned approximately $2 an hour. Fringe benefits in Japan were from 30–50 per cent of hourly earnings; the total wage cost to the Japanese manufacturer was merely 24¢ an hour. The total wage cost to the American clothing manufacturer was $2.50 an hour, for fringe benefits in 1958 were about 25 per cent of hourly earnings. In addition, Federal legislation compelled the Americans to pay overtime after 40 hours worked, whereas there was no such limitation in Japan. The American industry was in danger of destruction.

The clothing manufacturers though, took immediate notice of this threat. Al Lerner, president of Phoenix Clothes, was appointed chairman of the special committee on foreign garment imports, and by 1959 steps were taken to discourage low priced foreign made clothing from flooding this country. Herbert Ferster, counsel of the CMA, and Frank Rosenblum, secretary-treasurer of the ACWA, visited Japan and endeavored to secure assurances that the Japanese would not send men's and boys' tailored wool clothing into the United States. The Japanese were vague in giving such assurances, and little of practical value was accomplished.

Meanwhile, the committee on foreign garment imports realized that it was necessary to alert the industry and the interested government agencies that the clothing industry was in imminent danger. Thereupon, a special group was formed, called the Men's Clothing Industry Import Committee, separate and apart from the CMA organization. A public relations counsel was hired. Efforts were made to inform all interested departments within the government that not merely were hundreds of manufacturers in danger of losing their business, but well over 100,000 clothing workers as well were in peril of losing their jobs. The government officials were sympathetic, but they were confronted with the necessity of keeping a friendly relationship with Japan. It should be pointed out as well that many of our officials had their economic training under free trade professors in college, who in turn, had studied Adam Smith and similar economists at the start of the century. It was obvious that our government could not, or would not, offer relief. Meanwhile, one U.S. Senator, a professed liberal, coming from a state that included thousands of clothing workers, informed the manufacturers at a meeting that they should not oppose imports. He lectured to them, pointing out that this stand was contrary to the very principle of free trade. The solution he offered was simple and direct, namely, that if the manufacturers had to go out of business because of foreign made clothing, then they should enter another line of endeavor, and perhaps the government might assist them. And as for the clothing workers, it was his considered opinion that they would undoubtedly be employed elsewhere. His suggestions were not accepted either by employer or by employe. Then Potofsky, as president of the ACWA, took action. In a statement published on March 1, 1961 in *Advance,* the union paper, he announced:

> The General Executive Board of the Amalgamated Clothing workers of America is deeply disturbed by the Japanese Government's repeated rebuffs of all efforts to work out a reasonable solution to the problem raised by Japan's export of men's and boys' suits to the United States . . .
>
> However, if the Japanese Government persists in its refusal to recognize the problems affecting our Industry, the Union will have to take appropriate action.
>
> The Union's general officers have recommended that, in self defense, the union cutters stop cutting imported Japanese fabrics received by the United States manufacturers after May 1st, 1961. The General Executive Board supports this recommendation of its general officers, and has authorized them to take any action in the developing situation which they deem necessary to protect our membership.

The reaction was immediate. In a press conference published in the New York *Times* on March 9, 1961, President Kennedy strongly opposed this boycott. The New York *Times,* in a ringing editorial, was certain that such a boycott would harm our relations with Japan. Finally, when the President of the United States himself requested that the ACWA rescind the boycott order, Potofsky complied, notifying the President that this was done "in the national interest." By this time though, the Japanese got the message clear and loud. They now realized that their very profitable and growing export business in worsted fabrics was in imminent danger. They also knew that the quantity of suits they were sending into the United States was, as yet, relatively few. At the same time, Japan was making great industrial strides. Her cities were growing, and the demand for ready made clothing was expanding. Under the circumstances, the Japanese judged that it would be wise to concentrate their efforts, for the time being at least, in supplying their own domestic market and send a relatively modest quantity of suits into this country. To date, they have continued this policy.

But, this was merely setting up one dam to halt a potential flood from all directions. There was always the ever present possibility of large quantities of foreign made garments entering the United States from a low wage country that would simply overwhelm our domestic clothing industry.

The reasons for this statement can be seen on page 276. Wage data are subject to qualification in regard to the hourly earnings of the workers in the United States. As the work week is only 40 hours by law, overtime is paid, whereas the other countries have had no such regulation. As the average hourly earnings of the clothing workers in 1967 were $2.37, it should be noted that the most recent collective bargaining agreement between the CMA and the ACWA, effective June 1, 1968, provided for a 25¢ an hour increase effective immediately, an additional 17.5¢ an hour on June 2, 1969, and a further wage increase of 15¢ an hour on June 1, 1970, a total of 57.5¢ an hour.

Obviously, wages in the clothing industry of the United States far exceed wages paid in the foreign countries listed on page 276. It is of prime consideration that the wages paid to the American clothing

Estimated Average Hourly Earnings
The Men's Clothing Industry in the U.S.
and the Apparel Industries Abroad

(expressed in United States dollars)

COUNTRY	YEAR OF DATA	AVERAGE HOURLY EARNINGS
United States	1967	$2.37
Italy	1966	46¢
Japan	1966	35¢
Jamaica	1964	29¢
Mexico	1966	26¢
Hong Kong	1966	20¢
Spain	1966	20¢
Portugal	1964	17¢
Egypt	1966	13¢
India	1966	13¢
Pakistan	1966	13¢
China (Taiwan)	1966	13¢
South Korea	1967	8¢

NOTE: The figures do not take into account earnings of cottage workers; *i.e.*, industrial home workers. Their numbers, however, are significant in many countries. Their wages are but a fraction of the earnings of apparel factory workers in the same countries.

workers represent 36.6 per cent of the wholesale price of clothing. Therefore it is relatively easy for the foreign clothing manufacturers to export unlimited quantities of garments produced in the factories operated under sweat shop conditions, frequently paying workers less than 10 per cent of the American wage scale. The current tariff on wool clothing is 37.5¢ a lb. plus 21 per cent ad valorum duty. Because of the lopsided comparison between labor costs in foreign countries and labor costs in the United States, even a considerably higher tariff would be of slight assistance in damming a possible flood of foreign made clothing. And higher tariff rates are strongly opposed by the free trade theorists.

The theory of free trade as we know it today, originated in England in the 18th century, at a time when no other country was industrialized. Obviously, it was to England's advantage to export manufactured products to foreign lands that had no tariff restrictions. There was no danger that these countries might possibly reciprocate by perhaps shipping products into England that would jeopardize the domestic products of England. So England gloried in proclaiming the virtues of her free trade policy. Then, during the second half of the 19th century, when other countries also became industrialized and began to send into the markets of England products that were priced lower than English-made goods, the British Government became strongly protective in theory and in practice.

Frankly, free trade is beneficial to a country only if it has a competitive advantage, or at least no obvious disadvantage. It is disastrous however to a native industry that requires protection. Due to the low wage scale in the lands of the Far East, where sweated labor is widespread, American clothing manufacturers cannot possibly compete and still pay a wage scale that will permit decent living standards. For that reason, Congress has been petitioned recently by the labor unions of the apparel industries that there is "the need to develop and implement programs to regularize international trade in apparel of all fibers, preferably through international agreements which is an essential and desirable objective of national and international policy. . . ." Undoubtedly, the Congress and the Administration will have to take some concrete action in the near future, in order to protect the American standards of living for its citizens.

Somewhat naïvely, and always short sighted when a quick dollar comes on the horizon, a few clothing manufacturers in this country have established licensing arrangements with Japanese firms. The Americans give them their cutting patterns and show them their latest models. They have even sent their factory managers to Japan in order to teach American methods of production. All this is done with the understanding that the garments so produced shall be made and sold only in Japan. As the contracts are ordinarily for a limited number of years, what will happen after that period is a matter of conjecture. But one thing is certain;—if the Japanese begin sending in large quantities of American type clothing into the United States once the contracts have expired, it will be too late for the domestic clothing firms to wail that they have committed an error in their anxiety to make a relatively small sum from royalties.

Chapter 17

The CMA and Further Industry Activities

The First Convention

When the CMA was reorganized in early 1940, the subject of holding industrywide conventions was soon broached. This was to be expected, for it was a normal trade association activity that ordinarily received enthusiastic membership support. Such affairs cemented the industry socially, and from a business and public relations standpoint, they were invaluable. In addition, the "image" of the association was usually enhanced and favorable publicity was obtained for the industry as well. Trade conventions imposed no burden upon the association's budget for they were ordinarily financed by featuring supplier exhibits, such as fabric mills and machinery firms interested in displaying their most recent products. Despite the benefits to be derived from holding a convention, in the opinion of the CMA directors, there was an immediate need to organize first the more basic activities which were detailed in the previous chapter. Thus the entire subject was shelved for the time being. Shortly thereafter, military preparedness became the focal point of activity, and the desire or even need for a convention diminished. In December, 1941, with the advent of the war, all thought of industrywide conventions was set aside.

With the war over in 1947, there was renewed interest and further discussion about the possibility of holding an industry "get together," although nothing of a concrete nature occurred until more than two years had passed. Finally, in 1949, the board of directors approved plans to hold the first CMA convention of the men's and boys' clothing industry. The date set was October, 9–11, 1950, and the place selected was the Waldorf Astoria Hotel in New York. The actual convention, as originally planned, had a two-fold purpose; namely to benefit the manufacturer by holding an exhibit of the most recent products in machinery and textiles, and secondly to conduct a series of meetings and panel discussions which would encompass all phases of industry activity. Because the timing of the convention coincided with the opening of the spring lines, retailers were invited to attend, and they came in large numbers. Isidore Grossman, of Grossman Clothing Company, was appointed convention chairman, and Louis H. Bloom of William P. Goldman & Bros., was association chairman.

In a desire to please everybody from piece goods buyer to production supervisor, plus the sales force and office management as well, each day several breakfasts, morning meetings, luncheons, plus afternoon seminars were held. For the top industry executives a special breakfast was arranged with the Mayor of New York attending. There were separate seminars for accountants, for credit managers, for sales managers, for piece goods buyers, for boys' clothing firms, and for tailors-to-the-trade. For the special benefit of retailers, an alteration and busheling clinic was held, while the factory supervisors conducted their own panel discussion in conjunction with the designers.

As if the convention's exhibits plus a plethora of meetings were insufficient to keep the manufacturers busy, labor negotiations were simultaneously conducted in the same hotel. Then, to make certain that industry activity really reached fever pitch, a public relations firm that had been hired to promote greater consumer purchases of clothing, entered the scene. They saw the large clothing crowd in the Waldorf, and so held their own special promotional meetings there. It was truly an industry "get together" in every sense of the word!

To the surprise of all, despite the many breakfasts, luncheons, panel discussions, seminars, labor meetings, plus public relations hoopla, there was a minimum of chaos. The sessions were well attended and fruitful. One of the direct results of the seminar conducted by the accountants, chaired by Leo Ullman, was the issuance by the CMA of a book entitled, "Methods of Accounting and Office Procedure in the Men's and Boys' Clothing Industry." Some 4,000 copies were printed and later sold to the majority of clothing firms in the United States. Many firms in foreign countries also bought this book. For years it was the standard accounting text for the industry.

The Industry Dinner

The climax of the Convention was the dinner held in the grand ballroom of the hotel, with over 1,000 guests present. In spite of lengthy speeches, preceded by a long introduction to each speaker, the evening was considered a success.

It was then that the association office first experienced the heartaches and headaches that usually accompany the planning and organizing of an industry dinner. Every prominent member, or any member who thought he was or should be prominent, requested a seat on the dais. In one instance, a jealous partner called the association office, and his phone conversation went as follows: "Am I a good member? Didn't I buy a table? Do I pay dues? How will it look if my partner sits on the dais and I don't? What will they say in the industry? I'm an equal partner in the business and I want equal treatment." He got equal treatment. That is one of the reasons why there were 60 guests on the dais. Necessity made it advisable to have three rows of tables on the stage. This brought complaints from those placed in the last row of the dais, and one gentleman put it bluntly when he growled, "You put me in with the garbage."

Little did the association office realize that every industry banquet had its own series of crises, its own special list of complaints from dissatisfaction because of seating arrangements (the most common sore spot) to a member's anger that a competitor had "stolen" as guests the very retailers who should have sat at his table. If the roast beef were rare, or if it were well done, or if the soup were cold or too hot, or the music loud or too soft, the usual threat followed, "I won't buy a table again, absolutely not. You have my word for it." At times, a manufacturer would refuse to buy dinner tickets because of a family party. Suddenly, a well known buyer would arrive the day before the dinner with a number of assistants. Naturally they wanted to attend the industry affair. So the member would call the association for a table, but, "It must be in front; this is a big account." When told that the only tables left were near the kitchen, a cry of deep anguish could be heard on the phone. At one dinner, the harassed association office received an urgent call from a member who wanted a "personal favor." He just had to be placed next to Potofsky who was seated on the dais. Said this excited manufacturer, "I got labor trouble. I got to talk things over with Potofsky but fast. I need his immediate answer." This "personal request" was not granted. In that manner the executive secretary made enemies for life, or at least until the next affair. Life was not easy for those in charge of dinner arrangements.

Later Conventions

Because the convention entailed an enormous amount of planning and work, it was decided to hold the affair bi-annually. In October, 1952, another industrywide convention was held, and there were seminars as in 1950, covering all phases of activity. Prior experience had shown that if the convention was to be successful, it must be geared towards entertaining the retailer, plus stress upon the new selling season. This was confirmed when it was found that the most favored events were those that were interesting to retailers. If the buyers were present at a meeting, the manufacturers were there, hence, good attendance. Still learning from experience, the bi-annual convention held in October, 1954, was officially called the National Market Week. It was primarily a selling event, with emphasis upon entertaining retailers in the form of a social get together, a fashion show (very unsuccessful due to a lack of experience), a manufacturer-retailer panel, and finally, the big industry dinner. The machinery and textile exhibits were eliminated, mainly because there had been complaints that the CMA was infringing upon the activities of the International Association of Clothing Designers who also featured a similar supplier exhibit. With large retail attendance at the convention, the industry appetite had been whetted in conducting two market weeks, one for each season. Complying with the manufacturers' requests, in 1955, there were meetings, panel discussions and a banquet for the fall and the spring selling season respectively. This meant expensive entertaining for each season for the manufacturers. By this time the members were certain that retailers would come into the market anyway and why incur expense? In their opinion, there was no further need of Market Week, and from 1956 to 1959, the CMA held no industrywide seasonal events.

By 1959, however, the manufacturers found that retailers were reverting to their old habits of coming in late to buy the season's requirements because there was no set date for the opening of the lines. Once again a committee was formed, with Louis H. Bloom as chairman. An entirely new format was projected and wildly acclaimed at the time.

The Musical Shows

The seasonal opening of the lines was renamed Clothing Market Action. Now emphasis was on breakfasts where musical shows were given, promoting the new styles for the coming season. After an early breakfast, the buyers were free to go into the manufacturers' showrooms to view the lines. This meant that there was no interference with the buying hours, and yet retailers had an opportunity to enjoy a lively, witty musical performance early in the morning, with music which promoted the latest in clothing. At first, the shows were enormously successful, for they were novel. The formula of a young actress singing about "blazers are blue, we have'm for you . . ." etc . . . amused the audience.

After the first show, one of the members thought that this would be an excellent opportunity to have his own musical numbers included in future performances. Unsolicited, he sent his original lyrics to the association office. The executive secretary diplomatically showed them to the producer, a most excitable fellow, who said in no uncertain terms that the manufacturer should stick to suits and not try to become an Irving Berlin. The member was informed, somewhat more diplomatically, that his songs would probably be considered at a later date, certainly not for a season or two. This did not cement friendly relations with the member.

Clothing Market Action was strenuously promoted by sending attractive style books to 10,000 retailers. Hordes of buyers came to the market, and the season was a success. There was no doubt now that Clothing Market Action had become a fixture in the industry, and would be an important activity of the association.

Nevertheless, the musical fashion shows tried the patience of the association office in a way that could not be foreseen. As one officer said, "It had to be experienced." And it was an experience. The producers were "artistic," at least in their opinion. They considered clothing men to fall into the category of lowly "squares," if not worse. They raged with unbelievable fury unless their demands, frequently most unreasonable, were not immediately met. They often wrote the show script only the day before rehearsals began. In one instance, the producer did not finish the script until midnight before the first show went on at eight in the morning. Rehearsals went on all night. Hotel rooms had to be hired to provide for cold showers to keep the weary actors awake and fresh when they danced in the morning. The piano player was on the verge of physical collapse due to a lack of sleep, so smelling salts were placed at his side. Soon, musical breakfast shows lost their novelty. They necessarily ran into a set format, and there was a steadily declining interest on the part of the industry. They became old hat. Certainly, the association office had no objection to a change because of its bizarre experiences with the theatrical folk. In fact, one producer had an apparent mental block in completing his script due to a fight with his wife. It was with utmost difficulty that this show went on at all. So the association committee met once more, discussed things as they saw them, and changed the format.

This time it was to be a night club, which was located in a cellar. The emphasis that evening was to be on uninhibited gaiety. An excellent musical was planned. An elaborate dinner was to be served. Unfortunately, on that September night, the temperature was some 90 degrees or more outdoors. The club was jammed to the walls. Then the air conditioning system went out of order! The guests left hurriedly before dinner and the show, in an effort to escape rapid suffocation. The association office never heard the end of this unhappy experience.

Thereupon, the committee met again and decided that the format had to be changed once more. Clothing Market Action, despite the unfortunate setback, did bring in the retailers, so it was extended for two weeks each season. In cooperation with the American Institute of Men's and Boys' Wear, an elaborate motion picture, stressing new fashions was presented at the breakfasts. It was very well received, and the following season another motion picture was produced. Once more a new format was wanted. The motion picture did not present "live" actors. It was merely a movie short in the opinion of the manufacturers, and so, unsatisfactory.

Now the industry felt that it was best not to have too many affairs during each selling season, for they did interfere with early morning selling. Therefore the committee decided that the CMA would hold only one dinner a year, in the fall when the spring lines open, and issue two style books to 10,000 retailers, forecasting spring and fall models. This formula was highly successful, and it has been continued from 1963 to date.

In 1965, Louis H. Bloom, who had served as chairman of Clothing

Market Action since its inception, died suddenly. He had been most conscientious in making this event a permanent success. The industry was greatly indebted to this kindly, quiet man who had devoted many hours promoting the welfare of the manufacturers. William Mendelsohn, of Louis Goldsmith, Inc., was then appointed chairman by the president of the association. Mendelsohn, a most likable person, has been a dynamo as chairman, at all times seeking ways and means of enhancing the value of Clothing Market Action to the manufacturers and to the retailers.

Evaluating Clothing Market Action

Because Clothing Market Action has become an integral part of the industry—the main focal point of each selling season—we have given a brief history of this event since its inception, which began because retailers did not know when all lines would open. Heretofore, they came into the market from early September through October, and often drifted in even during November. When the buyers did come to New York early, they found that not all of their manufacturers' lines were ready. If they came later, then some firms had already sold out their best numbers. Moreover, when salesmen went on the road, they frequently found that many store owners were visiting the New York market. Time was lost and traveling expenses wasted. Hence, Clothing Market Action was planned with the aim of informing retailers of the date when all lines would be open, that salesmen would be awaiting the buyers in the New York showrooms, and that during this two-week period, selling would be carried on to all intents and purposes mainly in New York.

It will be recalled that at the start, spring lines opened in October, and fall lines opened in the middle of April. Over the years, these dates were set earlier gradually, so that currently, Clothing Market Action occurs in February and in August. Because the opening of the lines have been advanced in time, there has been a levelling in the seasonal pattern of production, which had been the bane of the industry in prior years. When manufacturers opened their lines in October, they began cutting spring merchandise in December. As they usually finished production of their fall garments in October, the month of November was a relatively slow period in the factories. The same seasonal pattern repeated itself for spring. May was usually considered a poor production month when fall lines opened in April, because cutting did not begin until June, while the spring goods had been completed by the end of April.

By opening lines in February and August, which is the current practice, the manufacturer is in a position to go immediately into production on the first of May or earlier, and on the first of November or sooner. There is no slowdown in the plant operations. This is one of the direct benefits of Clothing Market Action to the manufacturer and to his employes. The dreaded bi-seasonal lull with factory layoffs has been blunted, if not eliminated.

Admittedly, many retailers, particularly the large ones, come to the market prior to the regularly announced openings. This affords them an opportunity to examine all of the lines that are ready, to shop around, and to purchase without fear that some firms may be sold up, or particular fabric ranges withdrawn. However, if there had not been Clothing Market Action as the focal point, which is the very peak period of retail buying, there would be a continuation of the chaos that existed in the years gone by. Still it is difficult to satisfy all. Some manufacturers have begun complaining recently that too many retailers arrive when the lines open, and that it is impossible to handle the numbers that crowd the showrooms. But there are some who say, "That is just what we like. The more, the merrier." One thing is certain: Clothing Market Action is the sparkplug creating seasonal excitement every six months, with emphasis on new styles and widespread publicity to the retailers of America by means of elaborate style books, articles in the consumer press, and frequent items in the trade papers.

Past experience, often sad, shows that it is best to eliminate a dais at an industrywide dinner, and so maintain the ego of many. The so-called head table has been placed in the back, so that everyone at this dinner is seated in front! Another lesson learned as a result of unhappy moments, is the fact that fashion shows of men's clothing are not practical at big dinners. It is extremely difficult to distinguish the relatively staid clothing models at a distance. Glens, plaids and stripes are mere blurs on the far-off stage. It should be remembered that the manufacturer and retailer have viewed garment lines all day long, and they are in no mood to see still more suits at a dinner which essentially serves a social function. There always have been some though, who have favored the hard sell approach at all times. They have insisted that the dinner must have a message in the form of a sales talk. This idea has been discarded after unfortunate experiences. It has been found that a social evening, merely getting together, with light entertainment, is the most desirable formula for a satisfactory industrywide affair. And so it now rests until there will be new calls for "something different," a "dynamic affair", whatever it may be, which will "improve the image," or any other stray thought or cliché that may enter the mind of an articulate committee member while eating his corned beef sandwich at a luncheon meeting.

Relations With Mills

The past history of the relationship between the woolen mills in the United States and the clothing manufacturers includes many episodes which tell of unhappy experiences on both sides. In recent years though, there has been an appreciable improvement in this relationship. Nevertheless, there are still many remaining areas of disagreement which apparently cannot be resolved because of basic differences of economic interest.

In the early 1900's, when the manufacturers of clothing had recently organized the National Association of Clothiers, they felt that the mills could now be approached by a united industry for the purpose of conferring on matters of mutual interest. Previously, there had been an obvious lack of proper communication between the buyers and sellers of wool piece goods. Possibly this was due to ethnic differences between the manufacturers and the mill executives. The Yankee families of New England, in control of the mills, seemed to look down on the German and Russian Jews who owned most of the clothing factories. At least that was the feeling of the manufacturers who perhaps suffered from a fear of rebuff because they were relatively small firms and many were recent immigrants. But, with a national organization of manufacturers in existence, in 1906, the manufacturers appointed a committee to consider several complaints against the American Woolen Company, the outstanding giant among mills. As related in a previous chapter, the president of the mill curtly refused to meet with this committee. The National Wool and Worsted Manufacturers Association however, was in a more cooperative state of mind, for in 1908, at the convention of the National Association of Clothiers, there were reports of joint meetings held between the mills and the clothing firms. In the following year, Marcus M. Marks, president of the Association, reported at the annual convention that there had been further joint conferences and "the establishment of such close cooperation between buyers and sellers opens a new era in merchandising, the value of which cannot be overstated. Let us be patient and fair in working out the problems of this department for the best interests of cloth and clothing trades." It is appropriate to remark that greater emphasis might well have been placed on the word patience in Marks' glowing report, for nothing further of a concrete nature occurred. An unhappy relationship continued for decades, and discontent among the manufacturers simmered.

An important reason that hampered rapport between mills and manufacturers was the absence of a permanent organization whereby both parties could regularly meet on a common ground if a dispute arose, and then and there settle their differences. It was a constructive step to resolve buyer and seller disputes, without rancor or law suit, when the Mutual Adjustment Bureau was organized shortly after World War I. In 1937, William Goldman, of Cohen, Goldman & Co., reported that conditions had been chaotic prior to World War I, but with the formation of the Bureau, there had been a noticeable improvement. He stated that manufacturers had been in the habit of returning goods to mills without good cause, and in turn, mills did not "string" their piece goods properly, thus reducing the number of acknowledged damages. With the establishment of the Bureau, Goldman declared, there was now an organization that examined all goods in dispute, setting standards of quality acceptable to buyer and seller. If either party refused to accept the Bureau's verdict (where impartial experts had judged the quality of the fabric), the dispute could then be arbitrated. Undoubtedly, the formation of the Bureau was a definite advance in better mill-manufacturer relationships, as Goldman contended. Still, there was considerable dissatisfaction so far as the clothing firms were concerned. It was their complaint that the mills had imposed harsh terms of sale which were usually printed in small type on the back of the sales contract. However, this was outside of the province of the Bureau, which judged only quality of fabric and did not rule on terms of sale.

Under these circumstances, despite Goldman's optimism in his 1937 statement, shortly after the CMA was reorganized in 1940, the directors authorized a thorough survey of mill relations. The topics they wanted studied were enlightening, for they disclosed the areas of complaint. The manufacturers were to be asked about allowances for damages, delivery of imperfect goods, lack of standard widths, insufficient dating of bills and better terms of sale. Accordingly, such a survey was made, and its conclusions were "that present conditions are not at all satisfactory to the manufacturers of the clothing industry in regard to existing trade practices between mill and manufacturer." At the same time, the recent effort of the woolen mills to gain quick and excessive profits at the start of the war in Europe did not augur well for future friendly relations between buyer and seller. There was a definite feeling of antagonism between the two groups.

We went to war in December, 1941, and an acute shortage of wool goods was felt immediately. Despite War Production Board (WPB) priorities and directives, requiring shipment of goods on an equitable basis in proportion to pre-war purchases, there were numerous complaints that mills were playing favorites among manufacturers. The association found that a substantial number of these complaints were entirely justified. In such instances, the CMA reported the matter to the authorities in Washington, requesting that an inventory be made of the mills in question, for invariably there "were no goods to ship." Naturally this aroused the mill men to fury, for it might be interpreted as a lack of integrity, an indication of favoritism, unpatriotic, perhaps an effort to profiteer when the country was at war, and most important, there was the ever-present danger of bad and widespread publicity. Unfortunately, as the WPB investigations revealed, only too often many mills had incorrectly reported their inventories. Initially, the National Association of Wool Manufacturers (NAWM), the trade association of the mills, had avoided entering into this situation, feeling perhaps that the clothing manufacturers would have to bow down to the mills as in the past, take whatever goods were offered no matter how slight the yardage, and just keep quiet. But with the association active, a steady stream of complaints were filed in Washington. Some mill agents soon informed the members of the CMA that the executive secretary was *persona non grata* so far as they were concerned, and even talked about "getting him out of the industry." Notwithstanding, complaints went forward to Washington, the WPB acted promptly and secured immediate redress for the complaining manufacturers.

The unhappy mills then informed the NAWM that the manufacturers' association was creating trouble for them. Thereupon Arthur Besse, the president of the NAWM, contacted the CMA and suggested that his organization be informed first if a complaint was to be filed, and "perhaps it would be possible to settle matters without running to Washington," as he put it. This was entirely agreeable to the CMA, for then the disputes could be settled more quickly, and there was always the possibility of final recourse to the redoubtable WPB. Thanks to the ever-present threat of ultimate appeal to the government agency, there was never any need to ask for any directive again from Washington so far as equitable distribution was concerned. Henceforth, the CMA and the NAWM co-operated in a most harmonious manner to the great satisfaction of manufacturers, and perhaps to the mills as well.

But, at all times there was the great ogre of the woolen mills in the background, the American Woolen Company. This company was considered as the leader of the industry solely because of size, for at no time was it outstanding in manufacturing technique, styling or fabric research. And the public relations policy of this company could be described best in the succinct sentence, "The customer be damned." The attitude of the American Woolen Co. in 1908 has already been told, but the height of the mill's arrogance was reached when, towards the end of World War II, at the very time when wool goods were extremely difficult to obtain, it changed terms of sale. It now introduced a clause in its sales contract which stated in practical terms that the goods purchased were to be shipped with no time limit set on delivery date. Actually, the manufacturer would have to accept delivery at the pleasure of the mill. The clothing industry revolted. A CMA committee of prominent manufacturers met with the top executives of the mill, seeking to eliminate this delivery clause. Knowing that they owned the piece goods in a time of extreme shortage, the American threatened to punish committee members for even daring to complain publicly about the new contract. Retribution came to the mill in good time. It was not long after the war when manufacturers showed an expected reluctance to purchase piece goods from the American. After taking heavy losses in the post-war years, the mighty American Woolen Company, that had been formed for the very purpose of creating an industry monopoly, was forced to shut its doors forever.

With the elimination of the American Woolen, and some other mills that had followed a "take-it-or-leave-it" sales policy, there was more of a desire evident on the part of manufacturers and mills to arrive at a set of mutually satisfactory procedures in doing business. For example, there was no industrywide uniform sales contract when wool fabrics were purchased. Each mill contract varied widely. On the back of the order sheets, there were always numerous paragraphs of fine print that tied up the manufacturer completely. The purchase contracts were usually one-sided and written in legal language that was incomprehensible to the layman.

Of necessity, the manufacturers ordinarily signed such contracts blindly. Therefore, to warn the unwary of hidden clauses, in an entirely unconventional form of bulletin issued by the CMA, the following doggerel was printed on December 12, 1956:

BEWARE!

Mill contracts were not read by Sam,
He bought goods, then he signed,
One day he was in a very bad jam,
'Cause the fine print had clauses that bind!

SO BEWARE!

As might be expected, this outburst of "poetic" warning had little effect.

Understandably, the manufacturers were most anxious to establish a mill sales contract that would be industrywide and fair to both sides. This prompted the CMA to establish a mill relations committee. In turn, the NAWM readily appointed a corresponding group. For a moment there was a gleam of hope that perhaps something constructive might finally be accomplished in improving mill-manufacturer relations. The meetings were frequent. The committees worked assiduously. Corrected drafts of ideal contracts were presented at each meeting, but concrete results were agonizingly slow. In February, 1958, the committee chairman reported "progress" to the board of directors. In the same mood of sheer optimism, the same chairman reported to the board on January 19, 1960, some two years later, that the sales contract was "nearly ready." Unfortunately, there never was any final agreement. To date, each mill goes its own way, inserting clauses in its contract that are understood by no manufacturer but obviously enforceable in court. There the matter rests at the present time.

Terms of sale inserted in the purchase contract were only one of the problems worrying clothing manufacturers when buying wool fabrics. There was need of clarification in exactly defining trade customs, spelling out clearly standards of fabric quality. Only then would there be a minimum of disputes in reference to damages, allowances, shrinkage and color fastness. Ever hopeful, the CMA once more appointed a mill relations committee for the purpose of establishing proper standards in judging wool piece goods. The NAWM was contacted as usual, and they appointed a representative committee of mill men. Following past practice, the committees conferred, and said the committee chairman, "matters look hopeful." Optimists even predicted that a new era in mill-manufacturer relations was unfolding (somewhat similar to the statement issued in 1910 by the National Association of Clothiers). Then, one large mill refused to accept the definitions of trade customs agreed upon by its own representative at the joint conference. The NAWM withdrew its tentative approval. Once more all efforts of industry cooperation came to naught.

Thereupon the CMA board of directors voted to send the "Definitions of Trade Customs" etc., as originally approved, to the association membership. The manufacturers were informed the "Definitions" were to be considered by the clothing industry as the basis of business practice between mill and manufacturer. To this day, if and when a clothing firm has difficulty with a mill, the manufacturer uses the "Definitions" as his yardstick, and gradually even the mills have come to recognize unofficially the equity of the manufacturers' position. Nevertheless, in a CMA bulletin issued on August 30, 1968, the association once more sought information regarding problems of delivery of piece goods and quality control performance of the mills. After 58 years of study, conferences, surveys and further study, little concrete progress has been made in mill-manufacturer relations. In one way, during recent years, the power of the woolen mills has increased immeasurably. Due to industry conditions, such as mills moving South, lack of initiative of family-owned mills in New England, and recent mergers into giant textile organizations, the woolen mills, particularly those making worsteds, are now few in number. They are in a strong economic position in dealing with the clothing industry. These advantages of economic power though are counter-balanced, to an extent, by the large clothing firms of today who also wield great economic buying strength. Another fact to be considered, is the strong countervailing muscle of foreign fabric imports which are steadily growing since World War II. It is estimated that at least 50 per cent of the worsted cloth used in men's suits is imported, and the percentage is increasing steadily. The domestic mills realize that they face strong and very successful competition from the foreign mills, particularly from the Asiatic countries. The old idea that Japan made only low quality goods has become a myth. Italy, England and several other European countries also offer strong competition to the American mills. To that extent, we are witnessing a standoff in economic strength between the domestic mills and the American clothing manufacturers.

Nevertheless, when clothing manufacturers are asked about the status today in regard to their relations with domestic mills, they usually reply, "The same as it has always been. The sales contract has been unfair, and is still unfair. Trade definitions of quality are still subject to argument. But, the top executives in the mills today are much greater men of understanding than the men of 20 or even 10 years ago. They are an entirely different breed. In some respects, they really try to remedy the situation. Surely they are not the old crowd. Why, they even talk to us now!"

Relations With Retailers

The relationship over the years between the respective associations of the clothing manufacturers and the retail clothiers, might well be characterized as a perpetual talk fest upon the need for "cooperation, but only if the other side is reasonable." In instances where economic interests differ, each organization has often accused the other of reluctance to "cooperate," which, simply translated means a refusal to grant an advantage now possessed either by the manufacturers or by the retailers. Nevertheless, in matters of mutual concern, both sides have worked closely together, for there has always been an obvious recognition that manufacturers and retailers are merely two sides of the same clothing coin—essentially, one makes and the other sells. In clothing terms, it has been said that,

"We can't live without them, they can't live without us, so let's make the best of the bargain."

When the National Association of Clothiers (NAC) was officially notified in September, 1910, that the retailers were planning to form a national organization, President Marks of the NAC sent a letter extending his best wishes for the success of the future National Association of Retail Clothiers (later "and Furnishers" was added, hence, NARCF). However, it was not until November 17, 1914, that the retail organization was formally set up, with Charles E. Wry as executive secretary.

Shortly thereafter, in February, 1915, Mr. Louis M. Meyers of Springfield, Illinois, the first president of the newly-organized retail association, was invited to address the convention of the manufacturers. As reported in a previous chapter, his topic was "Cooperation," which was applauded loudly with the expected prediction that "it would result in a new era of retail relations." Coincidentally, it was at this same convention that Jacob L. Freeman of Hickey-Freeman, made his lengthy explanation why manufacturers did not deliver their orders on time. It should have occasioned no surprise that "cooperation" and "poor deliveries" were the highlights of the 1915 convention. These two topics were, and have always been, the perennial subjects for discussion when manufacturers and retailers meet. To date, some 50 years or more later, a rousing talk on cooperation is still a good and safe standby, an inocuous subject for a rip-roaring speech hurting the feelings of no one. And a detailed explanation to assembled retailers telling them why delivery of clothing can be late, or why it is not sent in complete shipments, has undoubtedly been heard by thousands of skeptical store owners since Freeman first recounted his frustrations in February, 1915. There is no doubt that retailers do have a serious complaint when shipments are incomplete. Sizes are missing and not all shades are shipped. Consequently, the retailers cannot offer a complete line of clothing to their customers. Despite manufacturer excuses, and they are entirely legitimate usually, and eloquently put forth, retailers, nevertheless are hampered in selling because of this industry practice.

Charles E. Wry, the first executive secretary of the retail association, was a most enterprising official. He edited an association-owned magazine which was then reputed to be the largest trade publication in the industry. Wry organized the Apparel Industry Committee in the middle 1920's, which was a most ambitious effort to coordinate the activities of the manufacturers and retailers in the men's apparel field. The stated purpose of this committee was the "general improvement of methods and the establishment of better practices and policies in the trade." Bertram J. Cahn of B. Kuppenheimer & Co., was chairman of the committee. Other clothing members were Jeremiah G. Hickey, Louis J. Jaffee, Paul Feiss and William Goldman. Certainly this was a group of top industry executives in the clothing field. Equally as important, were the committee members who represented the other branches of men's apparel. Well-known retailers were likewise members of the committee.

The program of planned activities included every facet of interest to the industry. There was a joint board of arbitration for disputes between manufacturers and retailers. The board of trade division endeavored to arrive at equitable and satisfactory solutions on matters of cancellations, returns, discounts and terms of sale. The educational division made studies of proper budgeting, stock control methods, traffic and rate adjustments, and all other matters of importance to retailers. Then there were sub-committees for each branch of the apparel industry which recommended delivery dates each season, proper standards for sizing of garments and also quality standards of workmanship. The publicity division promoted men's and boys' dress in a campaign of "Dress Well and Succeed." On the whole, it was truly the greatest effort that had ever been made by any organization to establish a comprehensive program that would benefit manufacturer and retailer in the industry. Unfortunately, the committee was active only for a short period of time, because this program had disclosed imagination, enterprise and excellent knowledge of the industry problems.

But the depression of 1929–33 came soon thereafter, and there was no further contact between organized groups of manufacturers and retailers until after World War II. By that time, Louis Rothschild had been appointed executive director of the retail organization, and the NARCF once more became an active and influential association. The CMA had been reactivated in 1940, and therefore it was now possible to re-establish formal relations between the two organizations.

Since that date, there have been numerous meetings between the two groups. Mutual problems have been discussed and analyzed in detail, but concrete results have been meager. For example, in 1953, the CMA board of directors approved the creation of a retail relations committee. It was understood that its initial effort was to seek an agreement from the retailers for an approved uniform sales contract. All seemed to go well during the preliminary conferences, but the entire project collapsed because the retailers refused to accept the usual arbitration clause. They demanded that all matters in dispute be adjudicated in the courts of the retailer's city. This hope for a fair and equitable sales contract never died, being revived from time to time. Thus, on the agenda of a joint conference between the two groups, held in February 19, 1967, an item was listed as "Report of Respective Sub-Committees on Uniform Sales Contract." There it rests to this very day, with no further advance made, although joint conferences continue, some 17 years or more after the topic was first broached.

Frankly, there has been little or no progress in any practical solution of the many problems that are encountered in the usual relationship between manufacturer and retailer. The committee chairmen report "progress," which has become a synonym for unfulfilled hope of things to come. The only controversy that has been settled in recent years, to the mutual satisfaction of both sides, has been the determination of the dates of future MRA conventions and their sites. The NARCF was recently renamed the Men's Wear Retailers of America.

Despite this paucity of concrete results, the joint conferences have been helpful in establishing a rapport between the two groups. They have learned to discuss matters amicably, know each others' problems, and understand why it is difficult to agree upon a mutually satisfactory solution. And that is real progress. (*Note:* The National Retail Merchants Association, the department store organization, has not been mentioned in this chapter because there has been little contact over the years between the CMA and this retail group. In the infrequent instances when there have been matters of mutual interest, such as motor carrier rates, the cooperation between the two organizations has always been excellent.)

Chapter 18

Merchandising and Sales Trends

In previous chapters, we have read the history of the industry during the past two hundred years. Economic and social trends have been detailed as they have occurred, and their impact upon the manufacturers of clothing has been told. In this chapter, merchandising and sales trends in recent years shall be described, and such pertinent data that influence the sale of clothing. Based upon this information, the reader will be enabled to draw a conclusion with regard to the patterns of distribution that seem probable, perhaps even inevitable in the years to come.

Who Will Buy Clothing?

All manufacturers are naturally most interested in knowing who will be the customers in future years, who will enter the retail stores to purchase men's clothing. The relative importance as well as the numerical size of each age group is the vital information desired. Only when a clothing executive knows the growth potential, short and long term for each classification by age group, can proper merchandising plans be made in reference to styling, to sales approach and to advertising appeal. Hence the estimates and projection of population growth supplied by the Bureau of the Census, U.S. Department of Commerce, are of value, for they disclose the relative magnitude of each segment in the male population up to the year of 1990. The most recent projection issued by the Bureau is detailed in the Table below.

Estimates and Projection of Male Population of the U.S. by Age 1970–1990

(In thousands, including Armed Forces overseas)

AGE GROUP	1970	1975	1980	1985	1990
All Ages	102,542	111,993	123,186	135,305	148,157
Under 5	10,887	13,898	15,857	17,008	17,893
5–9	10,507	10,958	13,958	15,910	17,059
10–14	10,500	10,580	11,030	14,024	15,972
15–19	9,694	10,555	10,634	11,084	14,065
20–24	8,711	9,741	10,596	10,674	11,222
25–29	6,935	8,758	9,779	10,626	10,705
30–34	5,674	6,971	8,778	9,792	10,633
35–39	5,464	5,674	6,959	8,748	9,753
40–44	5,825	5,408	5,617	6,882	8,645
45–49	5,919	5,684	5,282	5,489	6,725
50–54	5,344	5,663	5,444	5,065	5,269
55–59	4,789	4,974	5,278	5,081	4,735
60–64	3,957	4,293	4,467	4,747	4,577
65–69	3,123	3,341	3,635	3,794	4,043
70–74	2,230	2,439	2,624	2,869	3,011
75 years and over	2,983	3,056	3,248	3,512	3,850

NOTE: Last digit of totals rounded.

Source: Bureau of the Census, U.S. Department of Commerce

For the purposes of clarification and simplicity, these data have been rearranged into the two tables that follow. The age categories have been grouped in accordance with the usual merchandising practices of the industry.

This analysis is, of course, purely quantitative. It deals with numbers of men, and does not indicate what type of clothing they will seek. That will depend upon the social and economic conditions of the times, which will influence, as always, fashion trends and model changes.

Numerically we find as follows:

Estimates and Projection of Male Population by Merchandising Age Group

(in thousands)

AGE GROUP	1970	1975	1980	1985	1990
Boys (14 and younger)	31,894	35,436	40,845	46,942	50,924
Young Men (15–24)	18,405	20,296	21,230	21,758	25,287
Young Executives (25–34)	12,609	15,729	18,557	20,418	21,338
Executives (35–44)	11,289	11,082	12,576	15,630	18,398
Top Executives (45–64)	20,009	20,614	20,471	20,382	21,306
Seniors (65 and over)	8,336	8,836	9,507	10,175	10,904

Percentagewise we find as follows:

Relative Importance of Each Merchandising Age Group in Projection

AGE GROUP	1970	1975	1980	1985	1990
Boys (14 and younger)	31.0%	31.7%	33.2%	34.7%	34.4%
Young Men (15–24)	17.9%	18.0%	17.2%	16.1%	17.1%
Young Executives (25–34)	12.2%	14.1%	15.0%	15.1%	14.6%
Executives (35–44)	11.1%	9.9%	10.3%	11.6%	12.3%
Top Executives (45–64)	19.7%	18.4%	16.7%	15.0%	14.3%
Seniors (65 and over)	8.1%	7.9%	7.6%	7.5%	7.3%

Based upon the above tables, we can conclude that:

Boys: This group will continue to be the largest single segment of the male population in the future, percentagewise and numerically. This augurs well for population growth and the consequent increase in potential buyers of men's clothing in the future years.

Young Men: While showing no significant change in relative importance, and even showing a decline at times, nevertheless as the boys' group enters into this age category, there will be a steady increase in numbers throughout the decades.

Young Executives: This age group will show a steady rise, relatively and numerically, for by 1975, it will include the babies born during the population explosion in the years immediately following World War II.

Executives: This age group will include, for the most part, the births that occurred during the depression years of the 1930's. Not until the births that took place in 1947 and later are included within this classification will any substantial increases be noted.

Top Executives: This age group will decline in per cent and will barely hold its own numerically despite the rise in total population.

Seniors: This age group will decline in per cent and will show but a modest increase in numbers in the later years of this century.

So far as the manufacturers of clothing are concerned, it is evident that the emphasis in the forthcoming decades will be on the young men and the younger executive age groups. It will be among these categories that the population will show the greatest growth potential for the sale of clothing. Model styles, advertising programs and sales efforts will necessarily have to be geared to entice this segment of the population to think in terms of proper grooming and style consciousness.

Where Does Clothing Sell Best?

In planning a sales campaign, the manufacturers are most interested in knowing which are the best clothing markets, where should the greatest effort be made for concentrated selling to retailers, and in what areas is the largest amount of clothing sold per potential retail customer. The following table (most recent data available), shows the area percentage of the total U.S. population, the per cent of total U.S. men's and boys' wear sales within each area, the per capita sales in the area, and the per cent of urban population living there. An analysis of the data discloses not only where clothing sells best, but indicates a possible cause for such sales:

Comparison-Area Population in the U.S. and the Respective Proportion of Men's and Boys' Wear Sales In 1963

AREA	% OF POPULATION	% OF MEN'S & BOYS' WEAR SALES	PER CAPITA SALES	% OF URBAN POPULATION IN 1960
Middle Atlantic	18.8%	21.5%	1.14	81.4%
Pacific Coast	12.4%	13.6%	1.09	81.1%
New England	5.8%	6.2%	1.07	76.4%
E. No. Central	19.7%	20.9%	1.06	73.0%
W. No. Central	8.3%	7.9%	0.95	58.8%
Mountain	4.1%	3.8%	0.93	67.1%
W. So. Central	9.7%	8.7%	0.90	67.7%
South Atlantic	14.6%	12.9%	0.89	57.2%
E. So. Central	6.6%	4.5%	0.68	48.4%

Source: Bureau of the Census

The above table discloses that men's and boys' wear sales per capita are relatively high in the Middle Atlantic, Pacific, New England and East North Central States. We also find a direct correlation (with the exception of the West North Central Area) between the proportion of per capita sales of men's and boys' wear in an area and the per cent of urban population living there. Men's tailored clothing, as noted in a previous chapter, is purchased mainly for city and for suburban use. It is bought least in rural areas. The correlation between tailored clothing and urban areas has been historic, and the evidence indicates that there has been no change in the trend to date.

What Stores Buy Clothing?

In 1964, the Market Planning Service, a division of the National Credit Office, made a careful study of the distribution pattern of men's clothing by category of garment. The dollar volume for each category has grown since then, but the relative importance of each product has remained approximately the same in regard to the avenues of retail distribution. Therefore, the data are still highly pertinent, indicating where manufacturers sell their products.

Men's Suits

The manufacturers of men's suits produced a variety of garment types as shown in the table that follows. While suits were their main line, sport coats were a most important item. In fact, the producers of suits manufactured 82 per cent of the total dollar volume of all sport coats sold at wholesale. Topcoats, overcoats and slacks were usually produced by some suit manufacturers to round out their lines when selling their retail accounts. The manufacturers reported that approximately 61 per cent of their volume sold as branded merchandise (sold under the manufacturer's own label) and 39 per cent was sold unbranded.

Relative Proportion of Garments Made by Suit Manufacturers

GARMENTS	% OF TOTAL DOLLAR VOLUME
Suits (including formal wear)	73.8%
Topcoats & Overcoats	5.5%
Sport Coats and Blazers	16.8%
Separate Tailored Trousers	3.3%
Other Garments	.6%
	100.00%

The suit manufacturers distributed their products as follows:

TYPE OF RETAIL OUTLET	% OF TOTAL DOLLAR VOLUME
Department Stores	19.3%
Specialty Stores	68.6%
Chains and Mail Order Houses	7.1%
Discount Houses and Others	5.0%
	100.00%

Specialty stores were the main outlets for the sale of clothing made by the suit manufacturers. This fact was important, for dual distributors were buying specialty stores with an undoubted effect upon the sales volume of some "independent" clothing firms. In a later chapter of the volume, this very matter will be discussed in greater detail.

Sport Coat Specialists

As noted, the manufacturers who specialize in producing sport coats sell approximately 18 per cent of the total dollar volume of all sport coats produced. There is very little product mix among these specialists, for we find that:

Relative Proportion of Garments Made by Sport Coat Specialists

GARMENTS	% OF TOTAL DOLLAR VOLUME
Sport Coats	89%
Suits	9%
Other Garments	2%
	100.00%

It is likely that the "other garments" may have shown a recent trend towards greater importance, because some firms have begun making slacks for the purpose of merchandising co-ordinates (sport coats and slacks). Nevertheless, when a sport coat house specializes, it really specializes. The manufacturers indicated that 68 per cent of their volume was sold as branded, and 32 per cent was unbranded. They distributed their products as follows:

TYPE OF RETAIL OUTLET	% OF TOTAL DOLLAR VOLUME
Department Stores	35.0%
Specialty Stores	49.0%
Chains and Mail Order Houses	13.0%
Discount Houses and Others	3.0%
	100.00%

While department stores were more important as sales outlets for the sport coat specialists than for men's suit houses, nevertheless, the specialty stores still dominated as the prime source of retail distribution.

Men's Tailored Slack Specialists

Relative Proportion of Garments Made By Slacks Specialists

GARMENTS	% OF TOTAL DOLLAR VOLUME
Men's and Boys' Slacks & Shorts	92.7%
Women's Slacks & Shorts	3.1%
Men's Clothing	3.0%
All Other Garments	1.2%
	100.00%

These specialists distributed their products as follows:

TYPE OF RETAIL OUTLET	% OF TOTAL DOLLAR VOLUME
Department Stores	24.6%
Specialty Stores	48.0%
Chains and Mail Order Houses	23.5%
Discount Houses and Others	3.9%
	100.00%

While specialty stores were still the dominant avenue of distribution, and widely sold to department stores, the chains and the mail order houses were far more important relatively in selling slacks than in the other men's garments studied. The manufacturers reported that 72 per cent of their products were branded, and 28 per cent were unbranded.

As a group, we find that the three classes of manufacturers distributed their garments in the following approximate proportions:

TYPE OF RETAIL OUTLET	% OF TOTAL DOLLAR VOLUME
Specialty Stores	64%
Department Stores	21%
Chains and Mail Order Houses	11%
Discount Houses and Others	4%
	100.00%

The paramount avenue of distribution in the men's clothing industry is the specialty store, and the majority of such stores are relatively small or medium-sized businesses. Therefore, the average clothing manufacturer has been confronted with a merchandising problem when he sells a branded line, and the majority of clothing sold is branded. It is highly necessary to inform the consumer directly which local store carries the branded garment. Without the aid of his supplier, the average specialty store owner is in no financial position to give adequate prominence by means of advertising the branded line. Hence the importance and growth of co-operative advertising.

The Style Cycle

For the purpose of clarity, it is advisable to emphasize once more the sharp difference between the meaning of "fashion" and "style" as used in this volume. Fashion is a long term change, a change in type of garment worn, such as sportswear replacing the regular suit. It is influenced by social and economic conditions of the time. Style, on the other hand, is more ephemeral. A suit may change in style from a two-button to a three-button model, or a new fabric pattern may be introduced, or the cut of the coat may be shaped closer to the contours of the body than previously. That is style.

When the style committee of the CMA's Clothing Market Action meets semi-annually, all branches of the industry are represented. Conferences on style portend a lively session. To arrange such a meeting, a sense of diplomacy is required, extreme tact is advisable, and a thorough knowledge of the personalities involved is necessary. When the notices for the meeting are sent out, there are the inevitable phone calls, inquiring who will be present. All who are invited prefer to have their competitors attend. Once this is known, many of the committee will come to "get the thinking of the whole industry," which can be translated to mean, "what will my competitors promote next season?"

Each committee member considers himself to be *the* authority on style, and a strongly opinionated authority at that. His competitors, also committee members, likewise hold themselves to be *the* most knowledgeable. When a member enters the meeting room, he is determined to guard closely any information about his next season's lines. In fact, he plans to keep mum. On the other hand, it will be his bounden duty to induce the others who attend to disclose their new styles. Everyone plans to keep quiet, to listen carefully, and to learn much. This would not augur well for the meeting, except that these men will listen, and will learn, but as salesmen or former salesmen, they will certainly not keep quiet!

Recognizing the potential difficulty in obtaining the necessary information for the forthcoming style book, through experience the association has found it desirable to create an initial feeling of warmth, of hospitality, of good fellowship. Invariably, the CMA serves a fine lunch in the office. Every type of hot and cold beverage is available.

Once the amenities are over, the committee gets down to business. During the first half hour, there is verbal sparring about new style trends. Soon the conversation becomes heated. A definite statement has been made which must be contradicted at once. All thoughts of keeping mum are now forgotten. After all, these are men with strong opinions, and when they disagree, they are frank in saying so. Now tongues really loosen! Someone present will strongly urge, emphatically so, that a particular model must, under all circumstances, be featured in the forthcoming book. Not through sheer coincidence, it will probably be a garment which will be promoted in his new line. Others will have their own outspoken thoughts on the subject, telling in no uncertain terms what they think will sell best. So, inadvertently, the supposed style secrets are uncovered and the new models described in detail. In the course of this discussion, to the surprise, discomfort and chagrin of most attending, it develops that practically every member present will promote approximately the same model, fabric or color as the rest of the group. This is to be expected. All of the clothing firms buy from the same fabric mills, their designers meet regularly at conventions to discuss new styles, and most important, there are very few secrets, personal or business, that can be kept on the eight clothing floors of the Sperry Rand building.

Now that the supposed secrets are revealed, an industry consensus of the new style trend is possible. Thereupon, the editors are instructed to prepare the Style Forecast for the next season. And in that manner, regularly, every six months, 10,000 stores throughout the country are informed by means of the printed page, supplemented by photography, of the model, fabric or color to be highlighted when the new lines are shown.

But styles, though ephemeral, do not change suddenly. For some years, studies were carefully made by the association on this very matter, seeking answers to the following questions. Do styles burst forth in full force without warning? Do they rather gain in popularity gradually? Are style trends merely seasonal, or do they last over a period of years? And finally, does the popularity and acceptance of a style tend to decline slowly or quickly? Answers to these questions are fundamental to the manufacturer and to the retailer in his determination of promotion and merchandising policies.

These CMA studies were conducted over a period of time, and they revealed a definite pattern in the life span of a style. Data were compiled in reference to the changing importance of the two-button suit, the three-button suit, the growth and decline in popularity of the charcoal grey shade as well as other style changes, and most recently, the industry acceptance of the "shaped" suit. In the latter instance, we find that the term "shape," was first introduced in the discussion when the style committee met in January, 1965, in order to determine the contents of the fall Forecast. There was general agreement at the time that "shape" was something new, as yet barely born, but it did have potential growth. Therefore, the fall, 1965 book, issued to the 10,000 retailers in March of that year, stressed in bold type, "THE SHAPE OF THINGS TO COME FOR FALL/WINTER OF 1965." The committee had agreed that possibly five per cent of the suits might be bought initially in the new shaped model, but it was something new and a good "talking point." Retailers bought sparingly, as expected. Each succeeding season, though, there was a gradual increase in stress upon the importance of shape in the style book. And each season, the retailers bought a larger proportion of their suits in the shaped model. Some three years later, when the committee issued its semi-annual style book, it could truly say in the fall, 1968 Forecast, that "SHAPE MOVES INTO IMPORTANT VOLUME." The previous style cycle studies disclosed that it took approximately the same length of time for the charcoal grey, the two-button suit, and the three-button suit to reach peak popularity.

This does not necessarily mean that every style introduced and promoted will take hold, even though the industry may go to great lengths in order to "put it over." Hothouse promotion, pushing some out of the way color or model that does not conform with the generally accepted trend, or contradicts consumer standards of taste in good grooming, has been doomed to quick death. The burgundy shade in suits proved a dud. The recent ill-fated boom on "mod" and the still more recent "tunic" boomlet, are ample proof that style trends entirely alien to a normal conception of proper dress are fated, despite press hoopla, to quick failure. These styles are bought during a short period of time by the same sort of individuals who purchased the "jazz" model suit after World War I. The wearing of such clothing has been in reality a form of individual exhibitionism.

Because model or fabric changes are gradual, the obsolescence factor in men's clothing is not precipitous nor rapid. Admittedly, while this may permit retailers to dispose of their inventory with a minimum of loss in the form of markdowns, it may hamper a proper stress on a newly emerging style at the beginning of the retail selling season. How does this affect the manufacturer?

For the reason that style acceptance is cumulative in effect and not sudden, as our surveys have shown, the planning and merchandising of each season's lines take into consideration the relatively conservative buying habits of retailers. New models are not introduced in any one season to the practical exclusion of the old standbys, a practice we find existing in women's wear. At all times the manufacturer looks forward to a change in models, but of necessity he also looks backwards, showing the older models as well, though probably to a decreasing degree. Slowly, but surely, over a number of seasons, the old models fade, and the new models take the limelight.

In recent years, there has been considerable excitement in the industry due to the efforts of foreign designers to sell their garments, or else their models in the American market. Their influence has been good in that they have brought into this country garments that are not traditional in styling. Due to this influence, certain model features have been grafted on to the American made clothing. Therefore, foreign-designed garments, as such, have usually been viewed with considerable interest by most manufacturers. Still, there is industry reluctance as a whole, for reasons already given, to jump headlong into a new style; total acceptance is a slow process.

The American designers, as members of the International Association of Clothing Designers, have been criticized for not showing extreme originality in their style shows held during their semi-annual conventions. As employes of the manufacturers, they must necessarily confine their best efforts to please their employers. In turn, the employers must think in terms of selling the garments in volume, with a minimum of financial risk. Therefore, criticism of the IACD members does not take into consideration the economics of factory production, of volume sales, and the need for wide retail acceptance. The foreign designers, without any responsibility for selling a large number of garments, or keeping a thousand factory workers efficiently employed, are not hampered in presenting their "way-out" models. They need not think in terms of many thousands of units. On the other hand, the American designer must take these matters into consideration when drafting a new model. It should be recognized that the American designer has produced the styles that are required by the manufacturers, their employers. The very fact that these garments are well made, have been bought eagerly by the retailers, and are acceptable to the consuming public, is clear indication that, on the whole, the men's clothing industry has been fulfilling its function of dressing the American man in a satisfactory manner.

The "Consumer Dollar"

A perennial subject of discussion by the industry for many decades, has been the matter of getting a "proper share of the consumer dollar." Specifically, this has meant the need to promote tailored clothing in order to increase style consciousness, with a resultant greater sales volume. For years, at meetings, and in the trade press as well, the possibility of an industrywide advertising program that will bring this additional business to the manufacturer and to the retailer has been brought forth regularly. The efforts of Charles E. Wry and the men's apparel committee in planning a campaign of "Dress Well and Succeed" in the 1920's was indicative of the industry's desire to make men conscious of proper grooming. The magnitude of such talk rose and fell in inverse proportion to business conditions. Very often, an advertising executive in reciting his usual sales spiel at a convention, would stress the fact that the clothing industry was getting a gradually diminishing percentage of the consumer dollar, even though times were getting better. In view of this incontrovertible truth, no one looked behind the truth. The average clothing manufacturer who listened to such a persuasive talk, felt that the glib speaker "had something there," and that "there" called for action.

Actually, this steadily declining percentage of the consumer dollar spent for the purchase of men's and boys' apparel was to be expected as a long term trend, because, over the years the country grew more prosperous. It was mere common sense to recognize that when the country was in a depressed economic state, with wages low, such wages were used primarily for food, clothing and shelter. Little was left for luxuries, or even for needed services such as medical attention. Therefore, in bad times, clothing absorbed a very substantial part of the consumer dollar. When economic conditions improved and wages rose, the average consumer spent more on food, bought more expensive clothing, and moved to higher priced living quarters. However, the consumer spent a lower *percentage* of his increased wages than previously upon these necessities of life. With more money coming in, he now set aside a proportion to purchase a television set, perhaps visited his doctor more frequently, and may have even bought an automobile. What are usually characterized as services and luxuries now took a growing percentage of his enlarged income. The table that follows shows this tendency clearly during the years of depression and prosperity:

Disposable Personal Income (Excluding Taxes) and Consumer Expenditures For Men's and Boys' Apparel

YEAR	DISPOSABLE PERSONAL INCOME $ BILLIONS	EXPENDITURES MEN'S & BOYS' $ MILLIONS	% OF DISPOSABLE INCOME SPENT ON MALE APPAREL
1930	$74.5	$2,559	3.43%
1935	58.5	1,902	3.25
1940	75.7	2,387	3.15
1945	150.2	4,313	2.87
1950	206.9	6,026	2.91
1955	275.3	6,971	2.53
1960	350.0	7,976	2.28
1965	473.2	10,687	2.26
1966	511.6	11,814	2.31
1967	546.3	12,669	2.32
1968	590.0	13,780	2.34

Source: Survey of Current Business, U.S. Department of Commerce

We find that as disposable personal income increased, the amount of dollars spent on men's and boys' apparel rose, but it did not rise in direct proportion to greater income. The total dollars spent on male apparel were more, but the percentage of total income so spent became less. Thus, by 1968, the most recent data, disposable personal income, excluding taxes, increased by 692 per cent since the depression year of 1930, whereas the total expenditures for men's and boys' apparel increased a mere 438 per cent. Nevertheless, we do find a definite reversal in the trend for 1966 when the proportion of income spent on male apparel was higher than it had been since 1955. Perhaps a turning point has been reached, thanks to the intensive efforts made by the industry in recent years to really get more of the consumer dollar. There is no doubt that sufficient advertising, plus public relations, will create greater dress consciousness if social conditions are present to encourage greater purchases of clothing. There has been widespread unrest among the youth of the country in recent years, with a definite tendency for many of them to dress in a highly individual manner. The new mode of haircuts, the sideburns on young and old alike, and the growth of beards, all indicate a desire for individuality, a desire for personal adornment. Currently, it seems as if social conditions are ripe for a rising proportion of the income to be spent on men's and boys' apparel. Fortunately, the industry is presently engaged in making just such an effort by means of the American Institute of Men's and Boys' Wear. But, it would prove to be a veritable miracle, and contrary to the historic trend of past practice in consumer spending patterns, if the *percentage* of money spent on male apparel were to rise in the future in *direct* proportion to the rise in disposable personal income.

Promoting Clothing

When business grew slack in the late 1940's, after the returning veterans had replenished their civilian wardrobes, the movement for industrywide promotion gained momentum once more. Now manufacturers were seeking ways and means of increasing volume, and they watched growing automobile sales with envious eyes. Every time statistics were published, showing that many millions of cars had been bought, the CMA received calls that "they are buying expensive cars, but no suits. What is the industry doing about it?"

Now the time seemed ripe for a promotion program to get started. Jerome I. Udell, of Max Udell, Sons & Co., a director of the association, presented a comprehensive plan of promotion to the directors in March, 1948, detailing ways and means of financing such a project. He gave chapter and verse why there was need for such a campaign. The board approved Udell's concept and appointed a committee headed by Isidore Grossman. The association committee decided that before any plan could be implemented, facts regarding consumer attitudes about clothing must be obtained. Only if such information were available, could the project be successful.

The committee also deemed it advisable that all segments of the industry become part of this promotion plan. Thereupon the association group met with representatives of the National Association of Wool Manufacturers (NAWM) and the National Association of Retail Clothiers and Furnishers (NARCF), and a joint fact-finding group was formed. Twenty-five thousand dollars were obtained ($10,000 each from the CMA and the NAWM, and $5,000 from the NARCF). A prominent public relations firm was hired to supervise the project, and then the industry awaited results.

In turn, the publicity organization secured the services of academic social study teams who used methods of research that seemed somewhat far fetched to the practical clothing manufacturers. The consumers were psychoanalyzed as a group. The consumers, as individuals, were interviewed "in depth." The motivation of the unconscious urge of the American male was carefully charted. Clothed in sociological jargon, the conclusions completely bewildered the industry. Said the final report, "That one general check on buying that pervades every class in our typology of clothing behavior is Brummelphobia . . . the fear of being too well dressed, or the desire to be 'inconspicuous' is the greatest single factor in inhibiting increased purchases."

After reading the report, the committee met several times, and the manufacturers finally refused to go along with the program outlined by the public relations firm. The fundamental reasons for the refusal were the feeling that the program was not practical as outlined by the agency, and far too ambitious in terms of money. Once more, all plans for promoting the industry were held in abeyance.

Then, at the annual convention of the NARCF in Los Angeles in 1955, Willard W. Cole, president of Lyttons of Chicago, recommended another industrywide promotion program. His proposals were received with enthusiasm by the retailers and the manufacturers present. Immediate plans were made to carry out Cole's proposals. No time was lost. At a board meeting of the CMA, held April 20, 1955, Cole presented the retail plan for reaching the consumer, increasing the sales volume of clothing and creating greater style consciousness among men. The CMA board endorsed Cole's project and voted "to recommend to its members that they individually cooperate by joining the organizational committee" of the embryo American Institute of Men's and Boys' Wear (AIMBW).

Soon the manufacturers, retailers and fabric suppliers formed an industrywide committee in order to collect funds, secure a director of the budding organization, and hire a public relations and advertising counsel to set the project in motion. A large sum was raised. Industry enthusiasm was high. The stage was set for a real push towards greater clothes consciousness. In that way, the AIMBW was created.

During the first few years, the Institute had severe organizational problems, and floundered as to policy. There was the controversy whether it was best to reach the consumer by means of newspaper advertising, or whether it was best to stress public relations. Other methods of procedure were also unsettled. After trial and error, Louis C. Pfeifle, a former Sears Roebuck official, was appointed as the new directing head, and the Institute soon acquired a definite plan of activities. It now stressed public relations. It eliminated the expensive and seemingly bottomless financial pit of advertising to the consumer. The Institute had found itself at last.

Today, the activities of the AIMBW are many. It periodically conducts press showings of new styles in men's and boys' wear. It prepares a style column used regularly by hundreds of newspapers. It has an educational program in the schools promoting proper dress for boys. It has secured national recognition on radio and television as the authority when matters of style are to be discussed. Undoubtedly, the activities of the Institute have tended to make the American male more style conscious in the 1960's. Upon Pfeifle's retirement in 1966, his assistant, Norman Karr, became the executive director.

Advertising Clothing

National advertising of men's clothing began in the latter decades of the 19th century. Hart, Schaffner & Marx first promoted their brand name around 1890. They prepared advertising copy for use by their retailers, educating the stores in regard to the value of proper brand line promotion. The store owners soon recognized that a well-advertised national brand name was a definite asset. It became a mark of good value and excellent styling. It also helped the retailer sell clothing by predisposing the consumer to enter a store featuring the nationally branded clothes. Naturally, other manufacturers soon entered the field of national advertising. B. Kuppenheimer & Co. created an advertising department in 1890, and offered money back if the garment proved unsatisfactory. In 1901, Joseph & Feiss began a national campaign to sell "Clothcraft Clothes," which retailed at $10 and upwards for men, by telling the stores that "the wearer will be brought to you by judicious advertising. We pay for it." By 1908, many manufacturers were offering to pay one-half of the larger retailers' advertisements, and so cooperative advertising proved important.

Currently, cooperative advertising is widely used in the men's clothing industry for several reasons. It is well known that the national advertising rate in newspapers is considerably higher than the local retail advertising rate. It is therefore to the advantage of a manufacturer to cooperate with his retailer, and enjoy the benefits of the local advertising rate structure. By means of the newspaper ad, the consumer is directly informed where he may purchase the branded product in his locality. In that way, the manufacturer secures the active support and good will of his retail account, for cooperative advertising is aimed at increasing the sales volume of the store in its locality. This is to the advantage of the average small retailer, as previously noted, for with limited financial resources, he ordinarily cannot afford the expense incurred in promoting adequately his merchandise by means of newspaper advertisements. With the manufacturer paying half the cost, the financial burden is then lightened considerably.

Because of the importance of cooperative retailer advertising, national advertising by manufacturers often plays a secondary role. This has permitted advertising agencies to proclaim that the industry is far behind other industries in spending a proper amount to "get the inevitable consumer dollar." But the agencies use only national advertising expenditures of the manufacturers to prove their point. Only if the cooperative advertising total were included (and it is practically impossible to obtain such data), would the total amount be known that is actually spent by the clothing industry to reach the consumer. It can be taken as a fair statement of fact that retail advertising of men's clothing in the daily press reaches practically all of the potential customers of clothing. This does not mean that the character of the advertisement layout is such that it gets the attention of the newspaper readers, nor does the advertising copy often act as an inducement to buy. By means of cooperative advertising, the reader coverage is usually ample, but at times the quality of the advertisement itself may be mediocre. Nevertheless, though, cooperative advertising seems to be the most practical means of reaching the consumer and directly benefiting the local retailer as well.

Chapter 19

The Clothing Workers Today

The men's clothing industry of today can be viewed only in its proper and total perspective if the importance of its labor force is recognized as a significant influence in determination of industry policy and practice. The successors of the immigrant workers employed in the sweat shops at the turn of this century have become highly-organized members of a powerful union. Factory conditions in many of the clothing shops are now comparable with the most progressive industry plant layouts throughout the country. The clothing manufacturers of today are no longer employers of immigrant labor, because large scale immigration stopped for all practical purposes after World War I. Currently, the industry employs mostly American born workers who are far different, ethnically and culturally, from the machine operators described in the previous chapters of our history. It would be correct to state that the present clothing worker is no different from the usual employe to be found in the other neighboring factories. And, most important, the overpowering and pervasive influence upon the lives of the clothing workers of today is their union, the Amalgamated Clothing Workers of America (ACWA).

The Union

The analysis of the ACWA is made by the author of this volume, who was executive secretary of the Clothing Manufacturers Association of the U.S.A., for 28 years, certainly no impartial post. It reflects an objective evaluation of the union, based upon his observation over the many years.

The Amalgamated represents approximately 95 per cent of all workers engaged in the manufacture of suits, sport coats and outer coats. The larger manufacturers of separate trousers are located mostly in the South, and it is estimated that the majority of the garments made there are produced in non-union shops. The ACWA probably represents a minority of the total number of workers employed in the separate trouser industry for the country as a whole. But north of the Mason-Dixon line, the Amalgamated is the paramount labor organization including those plants that make separate trousers.

While the products of the clothing industry are an obvious necessity, still the manufacture of clothing is not truly basic in our complex economy, such as for example, steel construction, automobiles, or transportation. The unions representing the workers in these heavy industries are far larger in membership than the ACWA, and their impact upon our economy is infinitely greater than the production of clothing. The Amalgamated is a relatively moderate-sized union as unions go, consisting of some 400,000 members who produce clothing, cotton garments, sell in retail clothing stores, or work in laundries. Yet this union has a national reputation second to none in the trade union field, regardless of size or economic power.

One can correctly say that the high standing of the Amalgamated among the unions in this country is primarily due to the personal stature of its national and local officers. It is also highly regarded because of its innovations in activities and services to its members. Sidney Hillman and his associates of 1914 first set the precedent, which has been followed by the succeeding ACWA officials. Certainly Hillman did not become associate director-general of the Office of Production Management during World War II because of the relative industrial importance of the clothing industry, for the industry employed less workers than any one of the large automobile corporations. It was a personal tribute to Hillman when President Roosevelt appointed him as the top representative of all labor during the war. Joseph Schlossberg, August Bellanca, later Louis Hollander and Vincent La Capria in New York, Sam Levin and Murray Finley in Chicago, Abraham Chatman in Rochester, Jack Kroll in Cincinnati, Joseph Salerno in Boston, and Charles Weinstein in Philadelphia (to mention merely a few) were, and some still are active and acknowledged as outstanding labor leaders in their communities. They were not prominent because the clothing industry was the largest employer in their respective cities, for usually this was not the case, nor was the manufacture of clothing vital for the welfare of the community, such as for example the employes in public utility services. These ACWA men made their mark locally, and often nationally, simply because they displayed innate ability and enterprise far above the usual labor official; they had social vision. They were, and they are today, not only efficient union officers of the Amalgamated, but leaders in the affairs of the community outside of the labor field.

As a trade union, the ACWA is, of course, primarily interested in the welfare of its membership. As such, it has not been merely a "bread and butter" organization, seeking only higher wages and extended fringe benefits. In its effort to service all aspects of a member's life, the union has become, in the words of Wall Street, a "conglomerate." The ACWA is engaged in housing, owns a bank, controls a life insurance company, runs health centers, conducts day nurseries for working mothers, and in one market, even offers

ACWA National Officers Confer
(Left to right) J. Potofsky, H. Blumberg, F. Rosenblum.

scholarships for all children of the members who are planning to enter college. Looking at the ACWA objectively, in the year of 1969, the union is a veritable empire of services for the benefit of the clothing worker, from the birth of his child through all the mortal days of the member himself. This is a far cry from the strife-ridden ACWA organized in the rather dingy Webster Hall in December, 1914.

The present national officers of the Amalgamated were clothing workers when the union was first organized and have risen from the ranks, so they fully understand the problems that confront the average member. Jacob S. Potofsky, the present general president, succeeded Hillman upon the latter's death in July, 1946. As a close associate of Hillman, Potofsky was in sympathy and in full accord with the policy of pragmatism favored by Hillman. Accordingly, he has generally followed in that tradition in the conduct of the union's affairs. A soft-spoken man of impressive appearance,

Potofsky has proven himself extremely able in conducting the affairs of the ACWA. Under his leadership, the union has made notable progress, particularly in the field of social welfare for its members. Frank Rosenblum, the present general secretary-treasurer, who, it may be recalled, took an active part in the founding of the union, is known to be an aggressive and hard-hitting negotiator in all wage settlements. In his early years, he was the directing head of the organizing campaign in the Midwest and is still most influential in that area. Hyman Blumberg was the third member of the national triumvirate as executive vice president until his recent death. Blumberg was the leader of Baltimore in his younger days, and he also helped organize the eastern markets. More recently, he showed great ability in dealing with management, as well as supervising the ACWA's national welfare program.

It should be recognized that the same group of men who founded the union more than 50 years ago, are for all practical purposes still the leaders and are in complete control of ACWA policy. During the half-century, there have been fundamental changes in the union membership. Men have been replaced by women. The immigrant workers have been replaced by American born workers. In many operations, automation has replaced hand sewing. The small tailor shops have been replaced by large, air-conditioned factories. New ethnic groups are now entering the industry and may soon demand full representation as officials. The methods of approach to labor-management problems are vastly different today from methods favored in former years. The large clothing firms are often controlled today by outside organizations with huge financial resources. Many of these conglomerates have had no prior experience in labor negotiations. Certainly, they have little knowledge of the industry traditions that have kept employer and employe relationship on an even keel. The old bosses have been replaced by financial tycoons who may control railroads, steel mills, and incidently also be in the clothing business. This may require a future re-evaluation of labor relations as they have been conducted in the past. The industry has profoundly changed.

Admittedly, the present officers have also changed with the times, as the list of wage increases, fringe and welfare benefits prove. Nevertheless, in view of the changing labor scene, what has the ACWA done to meet this challenge of the future?

Ordinarily, an organization the size and complexity of the Amalgamated, has made suitable provision for a regular line of succession, so that there may be no hiatus in union policy and practice. Surprising as it may seem, this has not been done by the ACWA. The industry is therefore confronted with complete uncertainty about the future of the Amalgamated. Who will be the next leaders of the ACWA, and what sort of men will they be? This is a matter of grave concern to the industry, for a poorly-run union might well be a calamity for employer and employe. While the vice presidents have shown ability as local labor leaders, to date they have not been tested as leaders at the national level. Will they have the tact, the personality and the power to keep all markets in line when a national wage agreement is signed? Will they be able to control maverick local managers? While at the present time the ACWA is apparently all powerful, led by able officers, still the future of the union needs clarification.

The Amalgamated has now become a "welfare union," comparable in a way, because of the extent of its activities, to the modern welfare state. The ACWA has steadily sought to initiate projects that would enable its members to enjoy a fuller life outside of the factory walls. For that reason, the housing program of the Amalgamated has been of national interest. In an effort to remove the clothing workers from the slums of New York's East Side, in November, 1927, the union opened its first cooperative housing development in the Bronx. Since that time, this activity has grown so that nearly 20,000 people are now living in four cooperative projects in New York City, all directly sponsored by the ACWA. This housing development program has been expanded to other cities as well. Recently, the Joint Board of Chicago has established a moderate income cooperative project for some 600 families. In Philadelphia, the local union, as a joint venture with the Philadelphia Clothing Manufacturers Association, has sponsored the Sidney Hillman Apartments of the Elderly, a 17-story building near the medical and geriatric center of the union. Judging from plans recently announced, cooperative housing sponsored by the ACWA will be greatly expanded in New York City. The clothing worker who lived in rat-infested tenements in the 1900's, as described in this volume, suffered from illness and died early. The present union member need have no fear of tuberculosis, the former industry scourge, and many workers may now live in light airy apartments built by the Amalgamated.

Another activity of the ACWA is banking. Recognizing the need for a financial institution that would cater to small loan clients who had need to borrow at low interest rates, in 1920 the union organized the Amalgamated Bank of New York. In 1967, this bank reported resources of over $200,000,000, serving some 59,000 customers. In 1922, the union founded the Amalgamated Trust and Savings Bank in Chicago. Although the controlling interest in this bank was sold in 1966, for the time being the ACWA still retains a share of this bank stock.

Going even further afield, a far cry from ordinary union activities, is the Sidney Hillman Foundation. It was started in 1946, after Hillman's death, "to honor and perpetuate the ideals of Sidney Hillman in order to explore the common concerns of labor and the community at large." Lecture programs are organized in the various universities of the country. It grants scholarships in various educational institutions, and honors authors for journalism and books written that usually favor the cause of liberalism. This encouragement in the intellectual field is in keeping with the union's declared ideal, that men do not live by bread alone.

But, wages and fringe benefits are, as might be expected, the prime interest of the ACWA at all times.

Wages

In Chapter 12 of this volume, we told of the experience of the industry when the first national wage increase became effective on May 15, 1937. As noted, it was a meeting of a number of prominent clothing firms from the various markets, called together by the ACWA, and after several days of bargaining, a settlement raising wages by 12 per cent was agreed upon. It was not a written agreement between the two parties, for the manufacturers had no national organization. Rather, it was verbally understood that the increase was to be put into effect throughout the industry by means of supplemental additions to the local market agreements. The ultimate consequences of such a procedure were entirely unsatisfactory to the union and to the manufacturers. The first formal industrywide bargaining occurred after the reactivation of the CMA in 1940. Each side appointed a negotiating team, which then met jointly in Atlantic City in March, 1941. After a series of meetings, a written agreement was prepared, effective April 1, 1941, which granted a 10 per cent wage boost to all workers making garments above Grade I, and a 13 per cent wage boost to all workers producing Grade I clothing.

The table that follows gives the salient points of all wage settlements reached since the first national agreement was put in writing.

Wage and Fringe Benefit Payments Given Under Collective Bargaining

DATE	WAGE CHANGE	PAYMENTS TO INSURANCE FUND	VACATIONS & HOLIDAYS
April/1941	13% Grade I 10% all others		
July/1942	10¢ an hour	2% of Payroll	
Nov/1943			One Week
Dec/1945	15¢ an hour	3% of payroll added—5% total	6 holidays hereafter—New Year's Day, Labor Day, Decoration Day, Thanksgiving, 4th of July and Christmas
Nov/1946	12½¢ an hour		
Nov/1947	12½¢ an hour		2 weeks vacation (during summer months)
Nov/1950	12½¢ an hour		

DATE	WAGE CHANGE	PAYMENTS TO INSURANCE FUND	VACATIONS & HOLIDAYS
Dec/1952		1% of payroll added—6% total	
June/1953	12½¢ an hour		
June/1956	12½¢ an hour		
June/1957			Additional holiday 7 days in all
Dec/1957		6½% of payroll	
June/1960	17½¢ an hour		
June/1963	17½¢ an hour		
Dec/1964			4 day vacation during Christmas week
June/1965	12½¢ an hour		5th day vacation during Christmas week
Aug/1965		2% of payroll added—8½% total	
June/1966		1% of payroll added—9½% total	
June/1967	10¢ an hour		
June/1968	25¢ an hour	reduced to 8.7% of payroll	
June/1969	17½¢ an hour		
June/1970	15¢ an hour		

A comparison of the increase in wages since April, 1941, and the rise in the Consumer Price Index, discloses the following:

Consumer Price Index (CPI)—1957–59 = 100

March, 1941: The CPI was 49.3 and the clothing workers were earning 60 cents an hour

May, 1968: The CPI had risen to 120.3 and the clothing workers were earning $2.48 an hour

Source: Bureau of Labor Statistics, U.S. Dep't of Labor

The Consumer Price Index has gone up 144 per cent from March, 1941 (the month before the April, 1941 increase) to May, 1968 (the month before the recent labor increase), while wages in the industry have increased 313 per cent during the interval. Obviously wages in the clothing industry have far exceeded the rise in the Consumer Price Index. Thus the standard of living for the clothing workers has improved considerably over the years. The ever expanding fringe benefits have further supplemented the rise in living standards of the workers.

Until December, 1952, it was the practice to detail the wage agreement in relatively few paragraphs, describing the wage change and whatever new fringe benefits that were perhaps granted. Such memoranda were called Supplemental Agreements and were signed by the officers of the CMA and the ACWA. These agreements were supplemental to the local market agreements that were to be signed either by the local market organization, or else by the individual manufacturer if he did not belong to a local association. The national wage agreement of December 31, 1952 was the first all inclusive agreement. It was a lengthy document which covered, in a comprehensive manner, all matters considered of industrywide importance, such as the learning period, the hours of work, the numerous fringe benefits, and the wage changes. Printed as a booklet, it was distributed to the entire CMA membership and to the union officials as well. Since then, all national agreements are printed, and they now include in even greater detail not merely the new wage settlement, but the existing fringe benefits and all agreed upon industry practices. The national agreement, though, contains a restrictive clause which hampers the introduction of technological change in the cutting department, for it forbids the use of perforated or duplicated patterns without the consent of the general executive board of the ACWA. This is in keeping with the conservative tendencies of the cutters in several of the markets who strenuously oppose any change in cutting methods. Technological improvement in the sewing department, however, has always received the full cooperation of the Amalgamated.

The most recent labor negotiations were completed just under the wire on May 17, 1968, with the current contract expiring May 31. These negotiations were considered to be the longest and most difficult ever held. The union asked for a far higher wage increase than ever before, and the manufacturers strongly resisted the wage demand. They objected strenuously to some of the other "must" demands of the union. The procedure in negotiations generally followed the same format related in the case study in Chapter Fifteen. Thus, on October 17, 1967, the trade paper reported that Potofsky had announced "major demands by union due in February." The opening blast was somewhat earlier than on previous occasions, but then the ACWA was going to ask for more than in the past, and the softening up process might take longer. In informal conversation, Potofsky told members of the industry that the demand would be "high, the highest ever." Quite casually, he remarked that "a $1 an hour is a fair increase, on the order of the automobile raise recently granted." This was routine needling—a series of hints and "off the record" information, mentioning a greater amount than the initial actual demand to come. When the authoritative news would finally be publicized, and it would be less than rumored, it

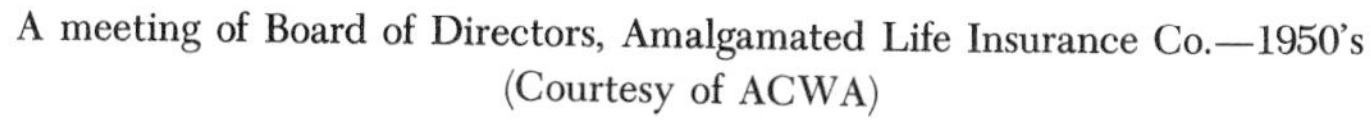

A meeting of Board of Directors, Amalgamated Life Insurance Co.—1950's
(Courtesy of ACWA)

was hoped, that the industry would gladly grant the union's "low" demand with a sigh of relief. Actually, this had never happened, for the manufacturers never gave an increase without stubborn resistance.

On January 5, 1968, Potofsky wrote to John D. Gray, president of the CMA, giving formal notice "of our request to modifying certain of the terms of the aforesaid agreement." The first joint meeting between the CMA board of directors and the general executive board of the ACWA took place March 5, and bargaining continued without letup until the wage settlement was finally reached on May 17. The sessions were long and at times acrimonious. The union demanded a three-year contract, 75¢ an hour increase during the life of the agreement, changes in fringe benefits, a guarantee of minimum payment when employes were called to work for the day, and payment for time lost when machinery broke down. The final settlement was reached when the union accepted 57½¢ an hour over the three-year period, several changes in working conditions were also granted, and fringe benefits were substantially improved because higher wages meant greater income to the Amalgamated Insurance Fund. Gray's statement to the delegates at the Amalgamated convention in Miami on May 28, 1968 (given in part), was enlightening, for it disclosed the state of mind of the industry after the settlement had been made. There was widespread uncertainty what effect such a substantial wage boost would have upon the price structure of clothing. The trade paper reported as follows in its May 29 issue:

MODERNIZE YOUR OUTLOOK ON CUTTING,
GRAY ASKS ACWA

Miami Beach. "Antiquated practices must be eliminated from the cutting room," John D. Gray told the Amalgamated Clothing Workers of America convention here. . . .

"Your officers have successfully negotiated the highest settlement in the history of the Apparel Industry. Your high demands and other factors made the negotiations most difficult. Your leadership has always demonstrated a high degree of responsibility for the welfare of its members and of the Industry. . . ."

Gray said that the new contract would "increase the price of our products, and could very well cause a sharp decline in the demand for clothing. This has happened before. Widespread unemployment resulted, and we had a sick Industry on our hands."

He asked the Union to accept its share of the responsibility for the settlement. "You must do everything possible to encourage increased employe productivity and help us decrease our costs."

"All antiquated and uneconomic practices must be eliminated, particularly in the cutting room."

This was relatively a strong statement, indicating concern for the future of the industry. Industrial peace was assured for another three years, but there was worry among many manufacturers whether low priced sportswear would not make further gains because of the rising price of suits. In reality, both the union and the industry were on the horns of a dilemma. The union recognized that it was necessary to keep members satisfied. It was also aware that since other unions were obtaining substantial settlements, the Amalgamated could not be far behind. And the local managers undoubtedly stressed the point that the wages of the clothing workers within their respective areas had to be competitive, comparable to other industries, otherwise the shortage of workers would be even more acute than at present. Very likely, the union was aware of possible danger that unemployment might occur if clothing prices were sharply higher as a result of an extraordinarily high wage rise. This was a risk though that had to be faced by the clothing industry every time a wage increase was granted.

The manufacturers agreed with many of the arguments put forth by the union. The industry did need new workers, and it was necessary that ACWA members receive take-home pay comparable to the pay envelopes of workers in other industries within the same area. Nevertheless, if clothing prices went up too high, then consumers would surely balk. Obviously it was to the interest of both the union and the industry that a wage increase be granted, but the amount of such increase was a matter of difference of opinion. The union naturally gave first priority to satisfying the membership. The manufacturers gave first thought in keeping clothing prices to a minimal rise. Hence the long and stormy sessions before the settlement was made, and Gray's warning of possible danger to come.

The Social Benefit Program

By 1968, the social benefit program of the ACWA became all inclusive, covering the member, the spouse, and their dependents in all of the ordinary incidents and accidents of life. The Chicago market was the first to inaugurate life and health insurance for the union members. The market organized a separate insurance company, and the first payments to members were made in April, 1940. Therefore the Amalgamated had some experience when it launched a life insurance and health benefits program for the membership on an industrywide basis. In the national settlement of April, 1941, a paragraph was inserted which read, "In addition, we agree that a joint committee should be appointed to confer upon the establishment of a Fund to provide health and life insurance to our members. We are about to designate eight members of our organization to serve upon this committee." As a result of this committee's recommendation, the October 10, 1941 agreement specified that 2 per cent of the payroll was to be contributed by the employers, effective July 1, 1942, to be used for life insurance payments and for health benefits.

The Amalgamated Insurance Fund was then formed to act essentially as the collection agency, and the Amalgamated Life Insurance Company was organized under the laws of the State of New York to issue life policies and grant health benefits to the union members. The charter provided for twenty five directors as members of the board for the insurance company, thirteen of whom were union officials, and twelve manufacturers. On February 1, 1944, the first insurance policy was issued by the company. This provided for $500 life insurance, accident and health insurance amounting to $12 a week for men, and $8 for women, to be given for the duration of thirteen weeks in any calendar year.

Since 1944, there were gradual increases as the program expanded, so that in time, benefit coverage included not only members, but the entire family of a member as well, all receiving hospital and surgical expense money. In January, 1947, retirement pensions for the elderly workers were first paid by the Fund, which were an addition to the regular social security payments. The 1968 agreement provided that life insurance for the members would hereafter be $3,000, and that retirement pensions were to be increased. A basic amount of $75 would be paid monthly to retirees after 20 years of industry employment, plus additional amounts, depending upon length of employment after 20 years and salary earned during the working years. The maximum payment could not be in excess of $160 a month, plus the regular social security payments of course. The June, 1968 settlement also granted reduced pension payments for those employed from 10–20 years. These workers were not hitherto eligible for industry retirement pensions. Surgical and hospitalization benefits were also considerably liberalized as a result of the 1968 wage agreement.

To indicate, to some extent, the impact that the extensive benefit program has had upon the clothing workers, we cite the sums of money expended over the years for these benefits:

Retirement Benefits: The Amalgamated Insurance Fund has paid out $219,013,778.43 in retirement benefits since its inception in 1947 to the end of 1967. At present, there are 25,650 retirees receiving payments. In January, 1951, total and permanent disability retirement was first provided, and at present there are 1,526 retirees of this nature receiving payment.

Assets: The assets of the Insurance Section of the Clothing Fund amount to $18,760,236.

The assets of the Retirement Section of the Clothing Fund amount to $73,302,981.

Other Social Benefits

For the year of 1967, the claims paid for benefits, excluding retirement pension payments to the clothing workers, were as follows:

TYPE OF CLAIM	NO. OF CLAIMS	AMOUNT PAID
Death	1,847	$ 1,572,152
Employe Disability	19,842	4,009,162
Employe Hospital, Surgical & Maternity	38,613	7,673,935
Dependent Hospital, Surgical & Maternity	20,819	3,143,807
	81,121	$16,399,056

By 1968, not merely were the clothing workers receiving liberal life insurance coverage and health benefits, but all of the other members of the union, such as cotton garment workers, the laundry workers and the retail clothing salesmen, are likewise covered by somewhat similar programs. Because the insurance has been purchased almost entirely by the union-industry controlled insurance company, with no brokers' fees or agents' commissions given, and has been a completely non-profit operation, 94 per cent of each dollar contributed by the employers has been used for the benefits and necessary reserves. Investments of the funds have been confined primarily to government securities. James J. Shoaff has been the executive director of the Company and the Fund since their inception, and he has administered both divisions in an extremely able manner.

We have given in detail the data about the social benefits program of the ACWA so that the reader may judge how far the clothing industry has advanced insofar as the welfare of the workers is concerned since the dark days of the early 1900's. From a sweatshop industry, it has become a modern, socially conscious industry.

The Work Force

The composition of the work force in the men's clothing industry has shown a radical shift over the years. With large scale immigration sharply reduced after World War I, the type of worker entering the clothing factories has changed considerably since 1920. The foreign born Jews and Italians, hitherto the majority of the workers, have practically stopped coming into the factories, particularly as machine operators. Therefore, the manufacturers have had to recruit replacements from the native born within the respective cities. Currently, we find that the members of practically every racial group of our population are employed in the manufacture of clothing. It is interesting to report that the union paper, the *Advance,* has been printing a Spanish page for the benefit of its newly admitted Spanish reading members.

Of great significance has been the ever increasing proportion of women entering the factories, so that today the sewing machine operators and finishers are almost all women. Currently, most men are employed in the cutting and shipping departments. The table below details the gradual shift in the relative importance of the sexes employed:

Sex of Workers—
Clothing Industry

YEAR	MALE	FEMALE
1922	56%	44%
1950	40%	60%
1960	33%	67%
1966	30%	70%
1967	29.1%	70.9%

SOURCE: Bureau of Labor Statistics, U.S. Department of Labor, and Industry sources

As more and more women have entered the industry, the comparative hourly earnings data for the workers have become distorted, even misleading. A 1967 survey made by the Bureau of Labor Statistics, disclosed that the average hourly earnings of women in the industry were approximately 73 per cent of the average hourly earnings of the men when both worked on the same operation, with no differential in piece rate because of sex. Therefore, as more women have entered the plants, there has been a downward bias in the average hourly earnings of industry statistics. Under the circumstances, it would be incorrect to compare the average hourly earnings of the industry from year to year, without due recognition that the increasing number of women has been forcing downwards the average hourly earnings for the industry as a whole. For the same reason, a cautious approach must be applied in comparing the average hourly earnings in the men's clothing industry with other industries. Only those that employ approximately 70 per cent women can be compared properly with the average hourly earnings of the clothing workers, otherwise the bias of higher wages earned simply because of higher proportion of men employed (such as in steel), will distort the entire basis of comparison.

An analysis of the age composition of the work force, and its distribution by age groups, is of particular importance, especially in disclosing the percentage of workers who are liable to retire from the industry and so receive industry pensions plus social security payments. This is a matter of concern, for the manufacturers now find that a chronic shortage of workers is prevalent in the shops.

In 1967, an industry survey was made on this very matter, which showed the following:

AGE GROUP	CLOTHING WORKERS	% OF TOTAL
Under 30 years	29,178	23.7%
30–39	23,787	19.3%
40–49	27,120	22.1%
50–59	26,555	21.6%
60–64	8,910	7.3%
65 and over	7,403	6.0%
	122,953	100.0%

SOURCE: Industry Survey

According to the Bureau of Labor Statistics, in May, 1968, of the total civilian work force employed in the United States, 4.1 per cent were 65 years and over. As an industry, the overall percentage of workers 65 and over in the clothing factories was higher than for the country as a whole. A further analysis by sex of clothing workers revealed a most disquieting situation. A breakdown by sex of the previous industry table showed:

Clothing Workers

AGE GROUP	MALE	% OF MALE	FEMALE	% OF FEMALE
Under 30 years	8,646	24.1%	20,532	23.6%
30–39	6,823	19.0%	16,964	19.5%
40–49	7,073	19.7%	20.047	23.0%
50–59	7,351	20.5%	19,204	22.1%
60–64	2,804	7.8%	6,106	7.0%
65 & Over	3,205	8.9%	4,198	4.8%
	35,902	100.00%	87,051	100.00%

SOURCE: Industry Survey

According to the Bureau of Labor Statistics, in May, 1968, 4.5 per cent of the men, and 3.5 per cent of the women in the civilian labor force of the country were aged 65 and over. In the clothing industry, we find that 8.9 per cent of the men, and 4.8 per cent of the women were 65 years and over. Of particular importance to the manufacturers was the relatively significant proportion of men in the clothing factories who have reached the retirement age. Because pension payments from the Amalgamated Fund were increased considerably recently, and because the length of service in the industry had been reduced as a requirement for pensions, the clothing factories may soon be confronted with a serious labor shortage, particularly of men employes. Clothing workers can now retire with greatly increased pensions, and many can now retire who were not eligible before. We can reasonably expect that there will be a greater inducement than ever for the older workers to leave the industry. Since the 65 and over age group is an important segment of the entire labor force in the clothing plants, such an occurrence can seriously hamper production, especially at a time when the industry is already suffering from a lack of experienced workers. By making retirement far more attractive to the elderly than previously, both the union and the industry may have unwittingly reduced the number of essential clothing workers to an extent that will be detrimental both to labor and management.

The clothing industry now competes, and will continue to compete in the future for its labor with other industries that can easily raise wages regularly because of their steady increase in productivity. Under such circumstances, the union and the industry in future years will be subject to pressure in maintaining the momentum of improving working conditions and paying even greater monetary wages for work performed. Only if productivity in the clothing industry keeps pace with rising clothing wages will the potential danger of consumer resistance to higher prices be averted. This will require the full cooperation of the union and the industry in improving present methods of production. In itself, though, this will not suffice.

It was the introduction of the sewing machine that revolutionized the manufacture of clothing in the 1850's. This invention created the opportunity of producing ready made clothing in volume. Now another complete change in making clothing has become a necessity. The industry requires a radical innovation in the system of manufacturing. This may occur because of developments in new machinery, or new chemical processes such as fusing the parts of the garment. There is no doubt that the clothing manufacturer faces two fold competition. He competes for the consumer dollar with other types of garments that are lower in price and can be worn in place of tailored clothing. He also competes for the consumer dollar with practically every other possible item of use that may be purchased by the average family. Therefore, the price of clothing must be kept within reasonable limits, and still the wages of the clothing workers must be on a competitive level with other industries. That is the dilemma now facing the men's clothing industry; hence the urgent need for a never-ending stress on increasing productivity in the years to come.

Chapter 20

The Clothing Manufacturers Today

The Industry Moves

This chapter will deal with the industry of today. It will describe the economic pressures that the clothing manufacturer is subjected to under current conditions. Only by evaluating the diverse forces that are apparently powerful in formulating manufacturing, merchandising and selling policies, can we fully understand why and how the average manufacturer of men's clothing conducts his business in 1969.

During the first half of 1963, the salesrooms of the clothing firms whose factories were located out of New York City moved en masse from their location in 200 Fifth Avenue at 23rd Street, to 1290 Avenue of the Americas, called the Sperry Rand Building. This move was initiated by a committee of manufacturers headed by Elmer Ward Sr., the president of the Palm Beach Company. Because of the concentration of buyers that would certainly be visiting the Sperry Rand, several of the larger New York City clothing houses also rented sales space there, although the bulk of the city firms remained below 23rd Street.

In the opinion of the industry, it was a wise move, for it removed the salesrooms away from a somewhat dreary area of the city to the up and coming section of New York. Hotels, where buyers stopped were now close by, and the theatrical district was not far off. Admittedly, the rents were considerably higher, and large sums of money were necessarily expended in fixing up the new offices. It was generally agreed however, that the image of the industry had been improved considerably, for it was now situated where other large industries were currently locating.

Some of the newly furnished showrooms were decorated on an elaborate, if not lavish scale. One firm even placed a Giacometti statue in its vestibule and hung valuable paintings on the walls. Another clothing manufacturer built his sales room as though it was a Dutch living room. Some of the professional decorators, who were hired to supervise the construction of the showrooms and executive suites, planned them on a scale and style that might be best described as a wild Hollywood conception how a big business man's office should look. And, at times, they succeeded in their conception only too well! Nevertheless, the majority of the offices were strictly functional, decorated in good taste and suitable for the business on hand, namely, to sell clothing.

Today, approximately 125 clothing manufacturers are located on eight floors of this enormous glass tower. These firms produce about 75 per cent of all clothing made in the United States.

Manufacturers' Volume

The clothing industry thus has become an important segment of the American economy. It is really big business, with all of the problems, present and future, that confront most other industries, plus several that are inherent to the production and sale of clothing. Industry statistics are impressive, showing that the clothing manufacturers in the 1960's have advanced far from the small one-room shops of the early 1900's.

In 1966, (latest data available), the men's clothing industry, classified by prime product made, accounted for the following volume:

Men's Clothing Industry

CATEGORY	NO. OF FIRMS	$ VOLUME AT WHOLESALE PRICES
Suit Mfrs.	257	$1,216,820,000
Outercoat Mfrs. (Topcoat & Overcoats)	27	$51,741,000
Sport Coat Mfrs.	33	$66,221,000
Tailored Slack Mfrs.	144	$400,910,000
	461	$1,735,692,000

Source: Market Planning Service, a division of the National Credit Office

At the retail level, in 1966, figuring approximately 42 per cent markup on the store selling price (often much higher), about three billions of dollars of clothing were sold to the consumers. Because the dollar volume of the manufacturers has risen appreciably since 1966 due to higher clothing prices, there is little doubt that the total dollar sales at the manufacturing and retail level are considerably greater today. The wage settlement of June 1, 1968, which meant an increase in labor cost of more than 20 per cent over a period of three years, is certain to boost further the dollar volume by at least 7 per cent or even more, provided production does not decline because of higher garment prices. The manufacture of clothing is now truly a multi-billion dollar industry.

An analysis of the manufacturers by size of volume reveals how the industry was constituted in 1957, and the change that took place within a decade. For the sake of clarity, two tables are presented, one dealing with men's suits, sport coats and outercoats, and the other dealing with men's tailored slacks.

Over the 10-year interval, there was a decline of 31 per cent in the number of firms, and this decline was primarily due to the disap-

Manufacturers of Suits, Sport Coats & Outercoats
1957–1966

	NO. OF FIRMS		% OF TOTAL INDUSTRY SALES	
$ VOLUME	1957	1966	1957	1966
Under $500,000	175	78	3.5%	1.6%
$500,000–1 million	102	48	6.2%	2.5%
1–2.5 million	91	87	11.9%	10.4%
2.5–5 million	39	35	11.5%	8.7%
5–10 million	28	38	17.4%	21.2%
10–25 million	24	21	49.5%	24.9%
Over 25 million	—	10	—	30.7%
	459	317	100%	100%

Source: Market Planning Service, a division of National Credit Office

pearance of those manufacturers whose volume was less than one million dollars annually in 1957. The table also showed that 10 per cent of the manufacturers sold 55.6 per cent of the total dollar sales in 1966. This situation was similar to a general pattern that was common to many American industries, namely, the already large firms were getting larger, and the smaller firms were disappearing in substantial numbers.

The table that follows, compares the firms making men's tailored slacks during the years of 1958–1966.

Manufacturers of Men's Tailored Slacks (see note below)
1958–1966

	NO. OF FIRMS		% OF TOTAL INDUSTRY SALES	
$ VOLUME	1958	1966	1958	1966
Under $250,000	88	—	4.6%	—
$250,000–500,000	47	—	5.9%	—
$500,000–1 million	46	71	11.0%	8.9%
1–2.5 million	33	37	19.5%	15.4%
2.5–5 million	19	18	24.4%	17.0%
Over 5 million	11	9	34.6%	16.7%
$10–25 million		7		23.1%
Over 25 million		2		18.9%
	244	144	100%	100%

Source: Market Planning Service, a division of the National Credit Office

NOTE: According to the Service, "tailored slacks" manufacturers are defined as those firms that make slacks wherein "the finished garment usually requires fitting and alteration by the retailer, and purchased by the unit rather than by the dozen at the wholesale level."

The preceding table reveals that there was a decline of 41 per cent in the number of tailored slack manufacturers during the nine year interval, primarily caused by the disappearance of those firms whose dollar volume was less than one million in 1958. It also shows that 6 per cent of the manufacturers produced 42 per cent of all slacks sold in 1966.

* * *

It was evident that the larger firms in the clothing industry received the greatest benefit of the increase in dollar volume that had been enjoyed by the industry during the years studied. The smaller clothing houses were unable to compete with the larger companies due to economies of size. The latter had the advantage of more favorable purchases of piece goods in quantity and price, more efficient factories that had been well engineered, and adequate financial resources.

Often, the average small manufacturer was rather a jobber

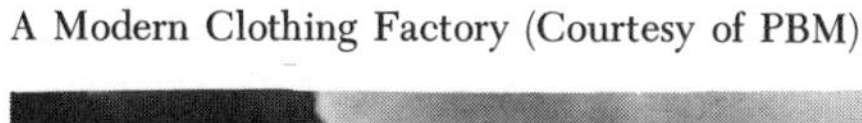

A Modern Clothing Factory (Courtesy of PBM)

A Modern Cutting Room (Courtesy of PBM)

than a producer of clothing. He bought piece goods in limited quantities, cut the goods on his premises, had a contractor sew the garments as best he might, and then disposed of his product usually to marginal stores. Many of the smaller firms had little or no conception of true cost. They frequently figured a $1 or so profit a garment, regardless of cost rising or falling. Their knowledge of the manufacturing processes was limited, so they were at the mercy of the contractor. If the firm was a partnership, one was ordinarily the salesman, and the other had probably been a cutter. Their understanding of proper merchandising a line was often hazy at best. At a time when fabrics and colors were more or less standard, such a firm was able to operate, for imagination and initiative in buying and selling were at a minimum. Originality in styling was not required. Price was the sole criterion.

But, when in recent years, the necessary ingredient in successfully conducting a business became an intuitive sense of style and flexibility to change with the times, then the average small firm fell behind. At one time, some of the smaller manufacturers even refused to produce sportcoats, for "it was not their line." They stayed and died with staple suits. However, when the small firm did posses enterprise in merchandising, good factory management, and aggressive salesmanship, that firm became highly successful, even though it was a small clothing house only two decades ago. Thus we find clothing manufacturers today with a dollar volume of many millions who started in business no longer than twenty years ago. Apparently it was not of great importance whether the manufacturer was located in New York as Brookfield Clothes, or in Philadelphia as Stanley Blacker, Inc., or in a small Pennsylvania town as Phoenix, Inc., or in any other clothing center. As in all success stories in the clothing industry, ability . . . sheer ability, was, and had always been the reason for the small clothing firm becoming the large manufacturer. This took place despite the ever looming handicap that many good sized firms were making comparable garments and were supposedly already controlling the field. The formula for success had not changed.

Price Levels and Profits

As costs have regularly increased over the years, the wholesale price line of men's clothing has been climbing gradually. Low priced garments have become a relatively less important factor of production because manufacturers have been offering and selling more higher priced clothing. As already noted, it is very possible that many of the consumers who previously purchased suits have turned to the wearing of sport coats and slacks solely for economic reasons. As a consequence, the clothing manufacturers have probably been losing such customers permanently to their strongest competitors, the sportswear houses. According to the Bureau of the Census data, the manufacturers have produced the following relative proportion of suits by price lines since 1959 (the first year this information was collected):

Production Trend By Price Line in Men's Suits
(a coat and one trouser)

	1959	1960	1961	1962	1963
Under $33.00	59%	57%	57%	55%	53%
$33–49.99	33%	35%	34%	35%	35%
$50.00 and over	8%	8%	9%	10%	12%

In 1964, the Bureau of the Census changed the classification by price lines, and reported as follows hereafter:

	1964	1965	1966	
Under $28.00	30%	25%	16.3%	
$28.00–34.99	25%	28%	18.7%	
$35.00–49.99	31%	32%	31.6%	
$50.00 and over	14%	15%	12.6%	
			20.8%	No price line specified by manufacturers.

The trend is unmistakable—higher priced suits are becoming more important in relation to total production of men's suits. This tendency can be understood, because labor costs, always a very important item, have been rising steadily due to regular wage increases, fabric costs have gradually inched forward, and in general, overhead expenses have mounted regularly from year to year. The question then may well be asked, are clothing prices therefore out of line today with the increase in the consumer price index of all items, and more specifically, how have retail prices of clothing behaved over the years?

If we take 1950 as our base year of 100 per cent, according to the data published by the Bureau of Labor Statistics we find:

The price of a man's worsted suit has kept pace with the general consumer price index (CPI). However, the retail price of a worsted suit, and it is the retail price that the consumer pays, has exceeded the general price level. It is likely that the need for an increased markup by retailers, due to the higher cost of doing business, has been the reason for retail prices going considerably higher than the wholesale price index of clothing, and the price level for all items

YEAR	WHOLESALE PRICE INDEX (a medium grade worsted suit)	RETAIL PRICE INDEX (an all year round worsted suit)	CONSUMER PRICE INDEX (all items)
1950	100%	100%	100%
1955	106%	112%	111%
1960	116%	122%	123%
1961	118%	125%	124%
1962	119%	126%	126%
1963	123%	130%	127%
1964	126%	137%	129%
1965	130%	141%	131%
1966	133%	148%	135%
1967	135%	153%	139%
1968 (before wage increase)	137%	158%	142%

bought. There is every prospect that clothing prices at wholesale, and at retail, will make a great jump in the second half of 1968, and that this rise will *continue* its upward climb during the two following years due to the recent wage settlement. Because prices have been gradually going up for years, what has been the trend in manufacturing and retail profits during the period? Have higher clothing profits been closely related to higher clothing prices? The table that follows shows the profits during the period:

Median Net Profit on Net Sales after Taxes

YEAR	CLOTHING MANUFACTURERS	MEN'S & BOYS' CLOTHING STORES
1950	2.09%	5.48%
1955	1.14%	3.91%
1960	1.05%	1.71%
1961	0.65%	2.60%
1962	0.80%	2.78%
1963	0.88%	2.34%
1964	0.70%	2.46%
1965	1.15%	2.63%
1966	1.41%	3.22%
1967	1.55%	2.47%
1968	1.72%	2.77%

Source: Dun & Bradstreet, Inc.

While the wholesale and retail price indices of clothing have risen steadily since 1950, the profits have wobbled, with no clearcut correlation between higher prices and greater profits after taxes.

Production

In the table on page 349, the production of the industry during the past 20 years is detailed, as compiled by the Bureau of the Census. The manufacture of suits has been at a rather stationary level, showing little or no progress over the two decades. Several reasons for this condition have been offered by the industry. It has been said that the age group that might now wear suits has not increased appreciably because of the low birth rate in the 1930's and early 1940's. It has also been said that sport coats and slacks have replaced the wearing of suits by many men even during business hours, and that suburban living has encouraged the wearing of informal garments. These reasons are entirely valid. Nevertheless, these reasons are the outward manifestations of more fundamental causes which underlie the dormant status of the suit.

As we have repeatedly stressed, fashion is based upon social and economic conditions of the time, and there has been a definite change in the social structure of our society. Within the last 20 years, we have witnessed an enormous growth of the middle class, as the economic status of the workers has steadily improved. The white collar man, even the so-called blue collar worker, has increased his income to an extent whereby he can afford to move from the crowded tenements of the cities to the suburbs. The reduction of the work week to 40 hours because of the Fair Labor Standards Act, has practically made the five-day week mandatory, leaving the weekend a time for rest and enjoyment. This has given the average man a holiday feeling of freedom, encouraging less formality in clothing. Even churchgoers on Sunday have been considered well dressed when they wear a sport coat and slacks. This has been the social revolution.

Economics has obviously played an important role in the declining birth rate during the depression, with its impact upon the extent

Production of Men's Suits; Outercoats (topcoats & overcoats); Sport Coats; Separate Trousers (dress and sport); 1948–1967

(in thousands)

YEAR	SUITS	OUTERCOATS	SPORT COATS	SEPARATE TROUSERS
1948	23,412	6,194	4,865	37,742
1949	19,497	5,628	5,767	38,533
1950	23,695	6,550	7,039	46,998
1951	19,559	5,540	6,328	39,010
1952	19,336	5,318	8,212	45,785
1953	21,665	5,694	7,510	56,267
1954	18,797	4,627	6,018	56,088
1955	20,280	5,672	7,932	67,355
1956	20,827	6,150	8,909	72,087
1957	19,943	5,053	9,021	71,666
1958	17,932	4,841	8,470	73,405
1959	21,111	6,038	9,853	90,923
1960	21,316	5,293	10,237	105,923
1961	18,797	4,695	9,711	103,285
1962	20,315	4,483	11,339	123,964
1963	20,561	4,269	11,183	125,307
1964	20,377	3,969	10,827	135,625
1965	21,855	3,980	12,291	142,348
1966	20,495	4,052	13,446	147,246
1967	19,719	4,770	13,726	138,571
1968	21,748 (1)	4,183 (1)	14,087 (1)	156,439 (1)

(1) preliminary

Source: Bureau of the Census, U.S. Department of Commerce

of consumer demand in later years. Economics also has played an important role in the rise of sportswear at the expense of the suit specifically. Normally, the trousers of the matched suit wears out first, and so the relatively usable jacket has to be discarded. The two pants suit, (approximately 40 per cent of total suits sold in 1940), was eliminated during World War II on the strange reason that it saved cloth. Of course it didn't, because it compelled a man to buy an additional suit which would have been unnecessary if he had originally been able to buy the two pants sales unit. In fact it really created an increase in demand for suits rather than lessened demand. Be that as it may, the two pants suit has never returned

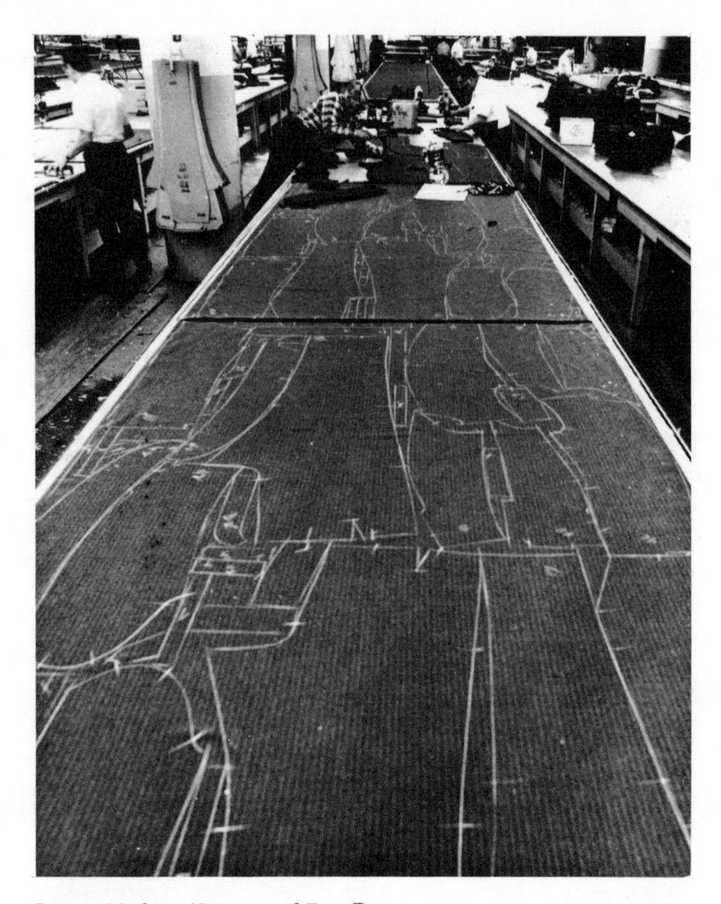

Pattern Marking (Courtesy of Daroff)

in importance, nor has the single pants suit grown in greater demand as a consequence. The low income customer, rather, has turned to the purchase of the sport coat and the separate pants.

As a matter of dollars and cents, the average consumer can readily purchase a sport coat plus slacks at a price usually less than the comparable price of a well made suit. When the slack wears out, another can be bought easily at a reasonable price, and the sport coat continues as a part of the ensemble. That this is a widespread practice, the prior data discloses by the tremendous rise in the production of separate pants during the period studied. To a degree, this is one economic cause for the stagnation of suit production.

Often, when the non-existent increase in suit production is the topic of clothing conversation, the rate of population growth is brought into discussion. It should be recalled that the most rapid growth in population has occurred in the relatively mild climates of California, the Southwest, and in Florida. In these sections of the country, for many months of the year, any sort of a jacket is entirely superfluous, with resultant lessened demand for suits.

Belatedly, the manufacturers of suits who are now the major producers of the sport coats as well, have awakened to the inroads made in displacement of suits by sport coats. They have attacked the problem in two ways. They have begun stressing color and style in the formerly staid suit models. They promote the color of the fabric and the cut of the garment. The body silhouette, known as the shape, is being talked about in the consumer press, hopeful that it will make the average man more style conscious and encourage greater wearing of the suit. At the same time, in order to regain the added pants business which was lost when the two pants unit was eliminated, the manufacturers have featured the co-ordinate (sport coat and slacks in contrasting or related shade), with the aim of inducing the consumer to buy this ensemble as one sales unit. To date, it has been an uphill battle with only slight success realized.

The outercoat houses (topcoats and overcoats) have been reduced to less than 30 specialty firms. Years ago, many suit manufacturers produced substantial quantities of outercoats, and it was an important part of their total sales volume. The production of the outercoats has dropped sharply during the years studied. From 1948 to date, unit production has declined 32 per cent. There are several reasons for this decline. Some years ago, the outercoat manufacturers, with little foresight, introduced the removable woolen liner in the topcoat. The consumer merely had to purchase one garment that served the purpose of a topcoat as well as an overcoat, depending upon weather conditions. At this very time, the raincoat industry introduced highly styled garments which usually sold at a considerably lower price than the wool outercoat. Then, the raincoat houses, sensing a trend, also included the warm removable liner in their raincoat so that it might be worn in cold weather. Raincoat business zoomed, wool outercoat business dropped. The outercoat branch of the clothing industry soon became a mere shadow of its former self. Suit houses discontinued making outercoats. Many specialty coat manufacturers liquidated. Drastic steps had to be taken to halt the downward trend in outercoats.

The outercoat firms that have remained in business, are making their garments more colorful, sharply veering away from the usual staple black. However, they have a difficult task to overtake the raincoat manufacturers and so regain their former dominance. While the price differential has somewhat narrowed, as raincoats have added style features that are costly to produce, still there is as yet a substantial price differential between the two garments. Then, the wearing habits of many men are difficult to change. To date, production figures show that there has been only slight progress, if any, in wool outercoats replacing raincoats.

The moral to be drawn in studying the trends in suits and outercoats is clear. The consumer *does not* have to buy a suit or outercoat if the price is too high, or if the style does not conform to consumer preference. There is usually an alternative garment or garments that may be purchased, perhaps at a considerably lower cost. It cannot be stressed too strongly that the clothing industry is not merely competing for the elusive consumer dollar with items such as television sets, or automobiles, but it is competing directly with other types of men's apparel as well. The men's clothing industry does not enjoy a monopoly by any means in supplying proper garments for men.

Dual Distribution

Dual distribution (selling part of manufacturer's total production to own stores) has been no new phenomenon in the clothing industry. As related in previous chapters, it was the common practice, prior to the Civil War, for northern manufacturers to own several retail outlets in southern cities. Again, with business excellent after World War I, manufacturers either opened their own retail outlets, or else bought several stores that had been their accounts. Times were good, and many firms felt that they had gained a built-in insurance policy, which guaranteed the distribution of a definite percentage of their total production. Then there was talk of double profits to be made, wholesale and retail. After the stock market break in 1929, however, and with retail sales falling sharply, the clothing manufacturers suffered two-fold losses. They lost from their retail operations, for the stores were burdened with high rents and long leases. They also lost from the decline in their wholesale business as well. It will be recalled that in the 1930's, Society Brand Clothes, Fashion Park Associates, and other dual distributors either discontinued their retail stores, or else dissolved their ties between themselves and their controlled outlets. The bonanza of double profits turned into a nightmare of double losses. Obviously, dual distribution was not always a profitable venture.

Nevertheless, when times are good, the lure of dual distribution is strong. Retailers are prosperous, and the manufacturer seeks, as always, to expand his guaranteed and assured volume. The average men's wear retail store consists of about 50 per cent clothing and 50 per cent furnishings and accessories. Therefore, control of a store means an excellent opportunity of obtaining a very substantial proportion of its business. The purchase of a retail store is considered to be a sure-fire method of growing in volume and profits. This is particularly attractive if the purchase can be made by means of stock transfer, for then the cash position of the manufacturer is not weakened. With business conditions booming after World War II, dual distribution has once more grown in popularity as in other days when times have been good. The purchase of stores by manufacturers has been in full swing in recent years.

According to the *Daily News Record* of Nov. 14, 1968, Hart, Schaffner & Marx owns some 190 stores, and projects the ownership of 206 retail outlets by 1970. Botany Industries, essentially a clothing manufacturer, owns 101 stores. Eagle Clothes, a relative newcomer in the acquisition field, controls 39 stores, and is looking towards further expansion. Phillips Van Heusen, initially a shirt concern, controls Joseph & Feiss, Inc. and Brookfield Clothes and owns 75 stores, prophesying that it will continue to expand. Cluett, Peabody, another shirt manufacturer that also owns J. Schoeneman, Inc., reports that it controls 58 stores, and Genesco, with interests in all categories of apparel including two clothing manufacturers, Phoenix and L. Greif & Bros., owns 52 stores that sell men's clothing. Obviously dual distribution is very profitable, for the financial statements of each corporation shows steadily rising sales, steadily rising profits, plus glowing reports of greater things to come. Why are retailers selling now, if their stores are profitable ventures?

The average retail store is usually family owned, or may be a partnership of two individuals. After a number of years of successful retailing, many store owners find that they are growing old and want some one to take over the reins of management. If there is a son, or close relative who is interested in the retail business, then the problem is solved. Often however, there is no near relative either desirous or capable of assuming charge. That is when it is advisable to sell. Again, the retailer may be thinking in terms of estate taxes as he grows older. The store's cash position may be depleted badly, its very existence possibly endangered, if there is a sudden withdrawal of a substantial proportion of capital. By selling the store, the retailer obtains cash, or else stock that can easily be converted into cash, so that his estate will not suffer unduly when death occurs. Then there are the innumerable personal reasons why a retailer may deem it desirable to retire.

Frequently, the manufacturer has been selling such a retailer for many years. If the products of the clothing firm are nationally branded (as they usually are), then it has a real stake in the future welfare of this store. Consumers in the locality know that this retailer is where the manufacturer's line can be bought. If the store goes out of business, the good will of this store, that took years to build up, will be lost. To keep this store as an outlet for the line, the manufacturer will probably buy the store. In that way, he also prevents his competitor from gaining a foothold if the store ownership were to fall into "unfriendly" hands. Again, perhaps the

Modern Sewing Room (Courtesy of PBM)

retailer may be falling behind the times due to a lack of capital to modernize, or fail to open a number of branches in nearby shopping centers. By turning over the store to a manufacturer with ample capital, there will be an increase in retail volume and greater profits, an obvious temptation to the clothing manufacturer. At all events, it is apparently good business for many retailers to sell, and for many manufacturers to buy. How does this affect the industry?

From the standpoint of retailing, the effect of dual distribution should not be too severe. Usually, the manufacturer does not open new stores in an already settled community, but rather buys a store that has probably been his account. The ownership may change but the competition has not been increased numerically. With greater capital resources though, the newly acquired store will be in a position to open branches in the surrounding areas, but that does not affect the existing stores that are already in business and ordinarily located in the central part of the town. The main problem confronting the independent retailer who finds himself in competition with a manufacturer owned store, is the liklihood that the competing store will have greater capital available for modernization and expansion, or there may be new and more aggressive management. On the whole, it has been the experience of the independents that stores owned by manufacturers are good competitors, give fair values at fair prices, and offer no threat to enterprising independents. How does this affect the independent manufacturers?

If an independent manufacturer has been selling his line of merchandise to a store that is taken over by a competing firm, he may well find that his orders in the future will be reduced, or entirely eliminated. That is to be expected, because the store has been acquired for the very reason to increase the volume of the dual distributor. At times, even if the independent firm is not directly competitive with the dual distributor's own product, he may shortly find that the dual distributor has merged with a higher or lower price line of clothing than his own, or bought an outercoat firm, or a separate trouser concern. It is logical for a store controlled by a dual distributor to give full preference to the organization that is in control. Doubtless, independent manufacturers have lost accounts or else have found their sales reduced if and when the ownership passes into the hands of a dual distributor.

It is a frequent complaint of the independent clothing manufacturer that the best stores in many cities, with prime location, are usually the very ones taken over by the dual distributor. If a manufacturer seeks increased retail volume through ownership of stores, it is understandable that he will hardly make an effort to buy the second rate or low volume outlets. For that reason, it is doubtful whether more than one or two clothing stores on Fifth Ave, in New York City, are independently owned at the present time. And, according to industry sources, in many of the largest cities of the country, usually the most prominent and largest clothing stores are owned by dual distributors. Admittedly, there are some 30,000 retailers in the United States who are reported to sell men's wear, so the relative proportion owned by manufacturers is numerically infinitesimal. Nevertheless, as one manufacturer put it, "They have skimmed off the top cream." The average independent clothing manufacturer is then left with the choice of selling other retailers in the area who may not be top rated, or else put greater effort in expanding his volume in the department-store field. It is the clothing firms that sell high priced clothing that are placed in a most difficult position. Of necessity, there are only a limited number of stores, located usually in the larger cities, that are able to sell expensive clothing. If a prestige store of this character is absorbed by a dual distributor who also has a line of high priced garments, the possibilities are ordinarily dim of the independent clothing house finding another retailer in the city who will be able to take the place of the lost account.

The future of dual distribution depends upon several factors that are uncertain at the present time. If economic conditions are favorable, then profits will roll in, both from the wholesale and from the retail divisions. If times are poor, or if a serious depression were to strike the economy for a long period of time, then the dual distributor would face the prospect of double jeopardy as in the

Modern Sewing Room (Courtesy of Hammonton Park)

1930's. Another factor to consider, is the matter of management personnel, always of prime importance in the industry. The manufacturer who buys a retail store buys good will developed by the store owner who has displayed an active civic spirit, has been well known in his community, and has acquired thorough knowledge of local conditions. Under ordinary circumstances, the original owner stays on as a manager for a term of years. Inevitably, new management will be necessary to take over, and that is where the danger may lie. If just mediocre men are put in charge because of a desire to keep expenses down, or no excellent men are available, it is likely that the original enterprise and initiative that made this store such a success will soon disappear. It will be recalled that the threat of the $22.50 retail chains in the 1920's declined once the successors of the founders assumed charge. In short, it will be a matter of maintaining momentum, and that will not be fully tested for a decade or more.

Conglomerates or Diversified Corporations

The conglomerates, or diversified corporations, have one thing in common, they have not been clothing manufacturers originally and have little knowledge of the intricate phases of the clothing business. They are really stock holding companies that have bought clothing firms that, in some instances, may even be dual distributors. The conglomerate may be interested in other apparel firms, may control a chain of variety stores, and perhaps has substantial stock holdings in organizations that have no relationship whatsoever with the men's clothing industry.

The entrance of the diversified corporation into the clothing field is a relatively recent development that has taken place within the last decade. It has been caused by many clothing manufacturers seeking to dispose of their businesses for the same reason that the retailers have sold out to the manufacturers, such as age of owners, estate taxes to be considered, and perhaps no successors available to continue the firm. In turn, the outside interests have found that it has been a good investment to purchase a prosperous clothing manufacturer. While the profits are not sensational at any time, they are steady if the management is capable, and there is always the prospect of expanding volume by means of purchasing stores.

The future of these organizations in the clothing industry is somewhat similar to the situation we found among the dual distributors. If they secure proper management to run their clothing interests, they will have no difficulty. Will they be able to do so, especially after the present management retires? There already have been several unhappy experiences because the conglomerates have chosen inexperienced executives to take charge of their clothing subsidiaries.

Of Influence in the Industry

Publications

The dominant trade paper in the men's clothing industry is the *Daily News Record,* a Fairchild publication. Its news reports about clothing have been the most frequent sources of information in preparing this volume, as the reader is aware. The *Record* was started by the Fairchild brothers as the *Daily Trade Record* in 1892, and later changed to its present name. As a publication covering all activities of the industry, it has become a news medium that is practically required reading by all manufacturers and retailers of male apparel. It reports not merely clothing news, but covers all other categories of men's apparel as well as textiles and machinery used by the industry. Until lately, it has been a newspaper primarily covering the actual events of the day. In recent years, it has given greater coverage to men's fashions and styles, giving stress to foreign as well as domestic trends in apparel. This activity has created expected controversy, for not all readers have, at times, approved the garments sketched and vigorously promoted in the *Record.* Nevertheless, because it does encourage the creation of new models, it has great influence throughout the entire men's wear industry.

Men's Wear magazine, begun in 1890, was the first publication started by the Fairchild family. It is issued semi-monthly, and points up style through liberal use of photographs and sketches. Of great interest to its retail readers as well as to the manufacturers, it is most influential in emphasizing what the clothing houses are actually showing in their lines, as well as disclosing the new models for the future. *Men's Wear* has received wide acceptance by the retailers and is thought to carry considerable weight when stores buy the new lines.

Apparel Manufacturer is a monthly magazine devoted to problems of production in the men's wear industry. It is primarily of interest to production men and designers, for it covers the field of factory management and style changes thoroughly.

Clothes Magazine is a monthly devoted to news about the entire apparel industry, men, women and children. Its articles are of a general nature, and of interest to consumers as well as manufacturers and retailers.

In 1931, an advertising man of imagination and initiative, named William H. Weintraub, started *Apparel Arts,* a monthly magazine that created intense excitement in the industry. The layout of the publication was elaborate, with emphasis upon color. New fashions and style trends were given space priority. It was a far cry from the ordinary run-of-the-mill black and white trade publication. *Apparel Arts* was an immediate success, and although aimed primarily at the manufacturing and retail trade, consumers who saw the issues in the stores were intrigued by the colorful presentation of the garments. Evidently, there was an opportunity for the offering of a magazine to the men in the country that carried fashion and style trend news in men's apparel. Shortly thereafter, in 1932, the publishing house that issued *Apparel Arts* started the publication of *Esquire,* a monthly magazine for the consumer public. While it promoted men's fashions extensively under the guidance of Oscar Schoeffler, a most knowledgeable stylist, there was equal, if not greater emphasis upon girlie sketches, plus stories and articles of interest to the average man. Circulation boomed, and in time it became the prototype of a magazine of a particular sort, that is, one that carried plenty of sexy illustrations as well as stories and articles of the type that would appeal to its male readers. In an effort to create consumer inclination and get the attention of the average reader interested in attire, *Esquire* often promoted the extreme, the "out of the way" garments and colors that were not usually worn by the majority of male consumers. Although this may not have directly promoted any specific clothing sold by the majority of manufacturers, still it did create interest in dress consciousness on the part of the American male. To that extent, the influence of *Esquire* upon the industry has been beneficial.

After a time, *Apparel Arts* discontinued publication for interest languished, and in 1957, *Gentlemen's Quarterly* (actually printed more frequently), was started, with Bernard J. Miller as titular publisher, although in fact it was an affiliate of the Esquire publication group. The magazine aimed at the consumer as well as the manufacturer and retailer. In a way, it was a successor to *Apparel Arts,* plus stories, articles, and also there were sketches and photographs of models of a more restrained nature than found in *Esquire.* Miller made this magazine not only an outstanding commercial success, but also aesthetically a publication of good taste, which promoted proper grooming in the best sense of that word. At the present time, *Gentlemen's Quarterly* has become influential as a recognized fashion and style authority by the industry.

Other publishing houses obviously noted the commercial success of *Esquire* as a magazine for men, and have since entered the field. If sex is a formula for circulation, then the road to greater success and greater circulation is simply more sex, and still more sex. The outstanding example of such a magazine is *Playboy,* which highlights sex in a plethora of illustrations. In addition there are stories and articles of popular interest. *Playboy* promotes men's fashions regularly, and Robert L. Green is the men's wear fashion editor. The phenomonal success of *Playboy* has brought forth numerous other monthlies that have tried to go one better than *Playboy* in concentrating on girlie pictures. They also carry some style news of men's apparel in order to attract the advertising income from the clothing manufacturers.

So far as the clothing industry is concerned, the consumer-oriented magazines have had a practical and definite influence upon the average man, particularly the young man. They have made him more clothes conscious. They have shown him the latest models in clothes, and the most recent garments worn by men in the public eye. Admittedly, they have often stressed the extraordinary rather than the ordinary in apparel, but that in itself has been helpful because it attracted the attention of the reader. Unquestionably, one of the reasons for the increasing interest in dress by the American male has been this proliferation of the type of magazine which has candidly made sex the come on as a means of obtaining wide readership. At the same time though, due to their large circulation, these publications, by promoting fashion in clothes as well, have been of benefit to the men's clothing industry.

Educational Institutions

In 1967, the Michael Mutolese Apparel Research Center had its official opening in the Philadelphia College of Textiles and Science, primarily an institution of industrial training in textile technology. This project was initiated by Michael Mutolese, a man entirely devoted to the welfare of the industry, who is the production manager of H. Daroff & Sons of that city. Mutolese had the active cooperations of the foremen of Philadelphia as well as the manufacturers of the city in financing the project. The Center is located in a new modern building, and is emphasizing, at the present time, problems of research affecting production. To date, the full possibilities in the potential use of the Center have not yet been realized. It has shown activity in matters of a technical nature concerning the manufacture of clothing. As yet, the Center has not branched out in conducting research in other matters of interest to the clothing industry, such as efficient office management, executive training and merchandising. Probably, as the Center develops, its activities and research projects will widen. The possibilities for the Center to aid the industry are really without limit, for there are a multitude of problems that might well be resolved through adequate research.

The Fashion Institute of Technology in New York City is a

two-year community college devoted to training young men and women in factory production technique and fashion design in the apparel industry. The overwhelming majority of the students are women, and there are relatively few men attending at the present time. Some of the male graduates enter the men's clothing field each year, usually as future factory foremen, with the hope that they will eventually become production supervisors. The Clothing Manufacturers Association recently tried to encourage the college to establish an Institute of Management for budding executives in the clothing industry. The college, however, was apparently in no position to assume the sponsorship of such a program, so the proposal had to be abandoned.

There is great need for an educational institution in the city which will emphasize the training of young men in all branches of the clothing industry. The college is magnificently equipped to do this. It is hoped that in the near future it will take steps to initiate day and night courses that will cover not merely factory supervision, but merchandising, selling and office management as well, specifically geared for prospective members of the clothing industry and those already employed by clothing manufacturers.

Chapter 21

The Clothing Manufacturers of Tomorrow

Clothing Is Big Business

In the 1960's, the men's clothing industry reached the status of big business. Hart, Schaffner & Marx, Bond Stores and a few clothing chains had been listed on the New York Stock Exchange for many years. The shares of some of the other large firms had been traded for several decades over the counter. As a general rule though, publicly owned clothing firms were the rare exceptions. A manufacturing concern in the clothing industry was either a closed corporation, or else a partnership, or perhaps individually owned. With increasing volume, and a good history of stability in profits, a number of the larger manufacturers in the industry "went public," or were sold to publicly owned organizations. Outside interests, usually conglomerates, gained control of some dual distributors as well as a number of large manufacturers who were "independents." Wall Street had discovered the men's clothing industry and liked it as an investment.

Therefore, we find today that not merely Hart, Schaffner & Marx, Bond and a few clothing chains are traded on the New York Stock Exchange, but that many of the conglomerates now in control of large clothing firms are also listed on the various exchanges or traded over the counter. Currently, the industry closely watches the stock quotations for Phillips Van Heusen, Genesco, Glen Alden, Rapid American, Botany Industries, Cluett Peabody, Eagle Clothes, Palm Beach, B.V.D., Kayser Roth, and even Woolworth, all of whom are either clothing manufacturers, or else own clothing firms.

The very fact that there are many shareholders in each of these corporations that supposedly have a permanent existence, is most beneficial for the economic welfare of the industry. The danger of a well-established company liquidating due to a lack of executive succession, or for any other reason, is gone. The possibility of a prominent firm, such as Cohen, Goldman & Co., closing its doors, despite its size and affluence, is unlikely. Under current conditions, it would have been taken over by some conglomerate, gone public, or else would have merged with another clothing manufacturer.

When a large firm goes out of business, numerous personal tragedies take place. Employes who have been with the company for many years, and are middle-aged, cannot find any employment easily or else are offered salaries less than half they had previously earned. Factories are closed. If the plant is the only one in a small town, then the workers have no other means of employment. Unfortunately, this has occurred in the past. Therefore, the fact that a portion of the industry is now publicly owned, means that the possibility of liquidation, because of death or old age of the owners, has been reduced to that extent. The clothing industry has acquired greater stability. It has now arrived at the stage of big business, and we can expect the industry to follow the trend of mergers and public ownership to an even greater degree in the years to come.

The Leaders of Today and Tomorrow

The clothing industry is rapidly changing in type of executive as well as in type of labor force employed. Many of the old timers have passed away, and their heirs, usually sons or close relatives, are now in charge. Even though some firms are now controlled by outside interests, still there has been no substantial change as yet in the top executives who have previously managed their respective companies. The typical member of the older generation has usually been a self-made man, perhaps an immigrant, a youth who made good. He came up from relatively low circumstances to affluence and became the head of a large organization. William P. Goldman, now well past 90, started his firm of William P. Goldman & Bros. in 1895, and amazingly, he is still actively in charge of his very successful company. The late Joseph Barron of Barron Anderson, the prominent outercoat house in Boston, went into business in 1901, and was active in his company until recent years. There are others, well in their 70's or more, such as Isidore Grossman of Grossman Clothing Company, Emanuel Weinstein of West Mill Clothes, and Elmer Ward Sr. of the Palm Beach Company, who are still the top executives in their organizations.

These old timers apparently fall into a general pattern, and their contemporaries who passed away in recent years were of a similar character, energetic, extremely able as business men, and also men who had been most interested in humanitarian affairs within the community. They organized the Philanthropic Fifty in New York City, were trustees of hospitals, they headed charity drives in their cities, and they were liberal contributors to the local educational institutions. This older generation is passing, and the second, and even third generation has now assumed charge.

The younger group is usually college educated, highly articulate, alert to all methods of production and merchandising. The outstanding prototype of the new clothing man of the future, although not an heir to any clothing firm, was the late Meyer Kestnbaum, president of Hart, Schaffner & Marx. Immediately after graduating from Harvard, he entered the employ of the company. He rose steadily to important executive positions and finally became president. He was not only a clothing manufacturer, but was also on the Board of Overseers of Harvard, the head of the Committee for Economic Development, prominent in community affairs, and assistant to the late President Dwight D. Eisenhower.

Who will be the industry leaders in the future? Undoubtedly, men little known today will rise to high executive position and become most active in industry affairs. But there are already many who stand out not merely because of business ability, but primarily because of their interest in the welfare of the industry. We can necessarily cite but a few. Many of them are members of the second and third generation of well-known clothing families. In upstate New York, we have the members of the Hickey family of Hickey-Freeman Co.; Lester Frankenstein of Michaels, Stern & Co.; and the Gunzberg brothers of M. Wile & Co. In New York City, there are the Goldman brothers of Eagle Clothes; the Grossman brothers of Grossman Clothing Company; Chester Kessler of Hammonton Park Clothes; the Goodstein family of Goodstein Brothers; Harvey Weinstein of West Mill Clothes; and the Hilton brothers of the Hilton clothing family. In Philadelphia, there is the Ettelson family of V Line Clothes; the Seitchik family of W. Seitchik & Sons; the Pincus brothers of PBM Clothes; the Rudofker family of After Six; Alfred Goldsmith of Louis Goldsmith Inc.; the Daroff family of H. Daroff & Sons; the Cohen family of Joseph H. Cohen & Sons; and Steve Lerner of Phoenix Inc. In Boston there is the Barron family of Barron Anderson; and the Picariello brothers of Trimount Clothing Company. In Cincinnati, there are the Ward brothers of the Palm Beach Company; Arthur Bowman of H. A. Seinsheimer Co; and Thomas Simon of Schaeffer Tailoring Co. In Chicago, we find John B. Foreman of M. Born & Co.; and Michael Roth of B. Kuppenheimer & Co., with his father, Harry, still a relatively young man, heading the combined Louis Roth-Kuppenheimer organization; and the top executive group of Hart, Schaffner & Marx. Then there are the Haspels in New Orleans. In Baltimore, we have the Haas family of Haas Tailoring Co., and Sidney Snyder of Cambridge Tailoring Co. And in Cleveland, there is Richard H. Adler of the Joseph & Feiss Co., a descendant of many generations of clothing men.

With this roster of young men at the helm of their companies, located in all of the important clothing markets (and very many not cited), the industry has no lack of present and coming leaders. These young executives fully understand the problems of the clothing industry, and the ways and means such problems can be attacked and possibly solved. In many instances, they have been active in labor negotiations. They have participated in all industry activities. They have served on committees that have met with government officials, with retailers and with mills. And they have usually followed closely the footsteps of their elders by participating in all communal affairs. These men, and the many others who could not necessarily be listed, will undoubtedly maintain the men's clothing industry at its present level of prestige. They know the clothing business thoroughly and are men of character. Therefore, the interests of the industry are in capable hands for many years to come. And, on that note of reasonable optimism, this volume closes the history of the men's clothing industry as of the year of 1969.

Bibliography

BOOKS & PERIODICALS

The Advance. Amalgamated Clothing Workers of America.
Apparel Arts. Esquire, Inc.
Apparel Manufacturer. Haire Business Publications.
Best, Harry. *The Men's Garment Industry, Strike of 1913*. Union Settlement Studies, Union Settlement Society, 1914.
Birmingham, Stephen. *Our Crowd*. Harper & Row, Publishers, 1967.
Bookbinder, Hyman. *History of AWCA*. Amalgamated Clothing Workers of America, 1950.
Boys' Outfitter. The Boys' Outfitter, Inc.
Braun, Kurt. *Union-Management Cooperation*. The Brookings Institute, 1947.
Budish, J. M. and Soule, G. *The New Unionism*. Harcourt, Brace & Howe, 1920.
Clothes. Prads, Inc.
Clothier & Furnisher. George N. Lowrey & Co.
Commons, John R. *Trade Unionism and Labor Problems*. Ginn and Company, 1921.
Connery, Robert H. *The Administration of an NRA Code*. Social Science Research Council, 1938.
The Daily News Record. Fairchild Publications, Inc.
Drake & Glasser. *Trends in New York Clothing Industry*. Institute of Public Administration, 1942.
Ervin, Charles W. *Homegrown Liberal*. Dodd, Mead & Co., 1954.
Feldman, Egal. *Fit for Men*. Public Affairs Press, 1960.
Gentlemen's Quarterly. Esquire, Inc.
Josephson, Mathew. *Sidney Hillman*. Doubleday & Co., 1952.
La Mar, Elden. *Philadelphia Clothing Workers*. Philadelphia Joint Board, Amalgamated Clothing Workers of America, 1940.
Lowe, Boutelle Ellsworth. *Unionism in an American City*. W. D. Gray, 1912.
Men's Wear Magazine. Fairchild Publications, Inc.
Methods of Accounting & Office Procedures. Clothing Manufacturers Association of U.S.A., 1951.
Monthly Labor Review. U.S. Department of Labor.
Muir, Ross L. and White, Carl J. Over the Long Term, Story of J. & W. Seligman & Co. J. & W. Seligman & Co., 1964.

Nash, Arthur. *The Golden Rule in Business.* Fleming H. Revell Co., 1930.
The New York Clothing Manufacturers Exchange, 1924–1949. The New York Clothing Manufacturers Exchange, 1949.
The New York Times. The New York Times Co.
Pope, Jesse E. *The Clothing Industry in New York.* University of Missouri, Social Science Studies, Vol. I, 1905.
Projan, Ben. *Grass Roots Retailing.* Fairchild Publications, Inc., 1962.
Seidman, Joel. *The Needle Trades.* Farrar & Rinehart, 1942.
Solinger, Jacob. *Apparel Manufacturing Analysis.* Textile Book Publications, 1961.
Soule, George. *Sidney Hillman, Labor Statesman.* MacMillan Co., 1939.
Survey of Current Business. U.S. Department of Commerce.
Twomey, Jerome R. *Financing the Men's Clothing Industry.* Bankers Trust Co., 1958.
Wilcox, R. Turner. *Five Centuries of American Costume.* Charles Scribner's Sons, 1963.

PAMPHLETS AND RESEARCH REPORTS

Amalgamated Clothing Workers of America Reports

Amalgamated Insurance Co. Reports, 1967.
Chapter in Labor History, Pennsylvania Joint Board, 1958.
The Chicago Workers, 1910–1922, Chicago Joint Board.
Convention Proceedings, 1920, 1922, 1944, 1946, 1968.
Constitution of Amalgamated Clothing Workers of America, 1955.
50th Anniversary Souvenir History of N.Y. Joint Board, 1914–1964.
Sidney Hillman Health Center, New York City, New York Joint Board, 1952.
La Mar, Elden, Sidney Hillman Health Center of Philadelphia, 1951.
Needle and Thread, 1915–1960, New York Joint Board, 1966.
Samuel, Howard D., *Panorama,* 1960.
Samuel, Howard D. and Rhodes, Lynne, *Profile of a Union,* May 1958.
30 Years of Amalgamated Cooperative Housing, 1927–1957, Amalgamated Housing Corporation, 1958.

Miscellaneous Industry Pamphlets and Research Reports

American Clothing Contractors Association, National Convention, 1933.
American Institute of Men's and Boys' Wear, Reports, 1963–1966.
Associated Clothing Manufacturers of N.Y., Bulletins, 1925–July 1927.
Brooks Brothers, Inc. One Hundred Twenty-five Years, 1818–1943.
Business History Review, Harvard University Graduate School of Business Administration, Spring-Summer 1963.
Clothing Manufacturers Association of the U.S.A., Reports and bulletins from 1940 to date.
A Conceptual Analysis of Motivation in Men's Clothing Behavior, Columbia University, 1949.
Dubofsky, Melvyn, *Organized Labor & the Immigrant in New York,* 1900–1918, Spring 1961.
Dun & Bradstreet, Inc. Financial Reports, 1931 to date.
Fairchild Publications, Inc., Reports, Research Department.
Fried, Milton and Teper, Lazare, *Domestic Apparel Industry,* May 1968.
Hart, Abraham, *Hart, Schaffner & Marx,* April 4, 1937.
The Invention of the Sewing Machine, The Singer Company.
Jackendorf, Ruth, *The Wool Bureau,* Industry Reports.
Jewish Social Studies, Vol. II, No. 1, Jan. 1940.
McKelvey, Blake, Rochester Public Library, *History of the Clothing Industry,* July 1960.
Market Planning Service, Division of the National Credit Office, Research Reports.
National Clothiers Association of the U.S., 2nd Annual Convention, Proceedings, 1885.

Bibliography

Jacob Reed's Sons, Philadelphia, Pa., History 100 Years Old, 1925.
Rieman, L. Neville, *The Men's Suit Industry,* 1947.
Robbins, Barber & Baer, National Men's and Boys' Apparel Committee, 1950.
Rochester Clothiers Exchange, Minutes of meetings, June 11, 1920–December 21, 1925.
Rogers Peet Co., History of Stores, issued 1942.
Roos Bros., Inc., Story of Stores, 1948.
Stitches in Time, L. Grief & Bro., Inc., 1862–1962.

Miscellaneous Reports on Work Force

Causes of Industrial Peace under Collective Bargaining, Case Study # 4, National Planning Association, issued 1949.
Cincinnati, Board of Education, Vocational pamphlet, # 3, issued 1924.
The Clothing Industry, Sweatshop Evil, Commissioner of Labor Statistics, Maryland, issued 1901.
Hickman, Mildred M., *The Clothing Industry in Cleveland,* Educational Research Bureau, 1929.
Homework in the Men's Clothing in New York and Rochester, N.Y. State Labor Department, Bulletin # 147, issued 1926.
Imberman, A. A., *Report on Men's Clothing Industry,* Maryland State Planning Commission, issued 1936.
Murtland, Cleo, *Garment Making Industries,* Cincinnati Chamber of Commerce, 1916.
National Wage Agreements between CMA and AWCA, 1941–1968.
Rochester, N.Y., *An Investigation of the Condition Existing in the Clothing Factories,* Rochester Chamber of Commerce, 1912.

U.S. Government Reports

Bureau of Census, U.S. Department of Commerce
  Men's Factory Made Clothing, 1916, Foreign and Domestic Commerce.
  Production Reports of Men's Clothing, 1922 to date.
Bureau of Labor Statistics, U.S. Department of Labor
  Bulletins Covering Hours and Wages
    # 161—for years of 1911–1913.
    # 187—for years of 1911–1914.
    # 16—Training Bulletin of Clothing Workers, 1919.
    # 265—for year of 1919.
    # 329—for years of 1911–1922.
    # 387—for years of 1911–1924.
    # 503—for years of 1911–1928.
    # 594—for year of 1932.
    Report # 140—Wage Structure, March 1958.
    # 1424—Wage Structure, October 1963.
    Survey of Wage Structure, April 1967, Clothing Industry.
Di Dalle, Michael V., *Price Stabilization Data,* May 1951.
Federal Trade Commission—Reports and Regulations:
  Wool Products Labeling Act
  Robinson-Patman Act
Men's Preferences among Wool Suits, etc., U.S. Department of Agriculture, Bulleting # 64, September 1951.
Military Clothing Procurement, Reports 1168 and 1166, 85th Congress, First Session, 1957.
Price Control Laws & Executive Orders as Amended, August 1946.

Index

Abramowitz, Bessie, 106
Adler, L., Bros. & Co., 48, 119, 126
Levi, 48
Mortimer, 119
Richard H., 48, 248, 254, 262, *263*, 368
Advance, 195, 249, 274
After Six, 367
Amalgamated Clothing Workers of America (ACWA), 4, 8, 9–10, *65*, *68*, *70*, *71*, 98–99, 108–110, 111–112, 114–115, 127–142, 165–166, 170–172, *174*, 177, 186–188, 195–196, 199–200, 202, 203, 204, 224, 235–240, 243–254, 260, 262, 267, 273–275, 320–334
Bank of New York, 325
General Executive Board, 274
General Office, 195–196
Insurance Fund, 330, 332–333, 337
Joint Board of Chicago, 324
Life Insurance Co., *329*, 332
Trust and Savings Bank, 325
American Federation of Labor, 90, 100, 103, 112
American Institute of Men's and Boys' Wear (AIMBW), 11, 284, 314, 316
American Revolution, 16
"American way of life," 167, 176
American Woolen Company, 93, 117, 121, 123–124, 126, 182, 191, 201, 288, 291
Annual Reports of Commissioner-General of Immigration, *63*
Apparel Arts, 360, 361
Apparel Industry Committee, 296
Apparel Manufacturer, 360
Arbitration, 235
Associated Boys' Clothing Manufacturers, 138
Associated Clothing Manufacturers of New York, 139

Baker, R. B., 151
Bank of the United States in New York, 163
Barron, Anderson, 366, 367
Joseph, 366
Bashowitz Brothers, 123
Baum, Morton, J., 212, *239*, 240–242, *258*, 261–262
Beauharnais, Josephine de (1763–1814), 17
Bell, George L., 180–181, 206
Bellanca, August, 321
"Benevolent Society," 77
Benjamin, Alfred, and Co., 84
Bennet, Colonel Joseph, 22–23, 31
Berlin, Irving, 283
Better Business Bureaus, 154
Blacker, Stanley, Inc., 345
Bloom, Cohen & Co., 85

Bloom, Louis H., 279, 282, 284–285
Blooston, Max, *85*
Blumberg, Hyman, 110, 172, *237*, *322*, 323
Blumenthal Bros., 85
Bonaparte, Napoleon (1769–1821), 17, 113
Bond Stores, 149, 364, 365
Born, M., & Co., 367
"Boston System," 76
Boswell, James (1740–1795), 14
Botany Industries, 12, 353–354, 365
Bowman, Arthur, 367
Brandeis University, 10
"British lounge," 14
"Broad chester," 158, 159
Broadstreet, 147
Brookfield Clothes, 140, 345, 354
Brooks Bros., 23–24, 161
Brooks, H. & D. H.,
    see Brooks Bros.
Brooks, Harry Sands, 23
Browning, John H., 35
Browning, King & Co., 35, 61
Brummel, George Bryan (Beau Brummel) (1778–1840), 17
    Brummelphobia, 315
Bureau of the Census,
    see U.S. Department of Commerce
Bureau of Labor Statistics (BLS),
    see U.S. Department of Labor
Burkhardt, Andreas, 135
Burton, Mansfield & Co., 85
Buyers Market Week, 118, 121–122
B.V.D., 365

Cahan, Abraham, 109
Cahn, Bertram J., 168, 172, 296
Cambridge Tailoring Co., 368
Canals, 28
    construction in 1850's, 37
"Capitol Clothing House, The," 49
Capps, J., & Sons, Ltd., 39–40
    Robert, 40
Carlebach, Mrs. H., *183*
Carney and Sleeper, 31
Caterpillar Tractor Company, 180
Chatman, Abraham, 137, *239*, 321
Chicago Association of Labor, 91
Child labor, 66–67
Chirnside, Adam, 19
City College of New York, 141
Civil War, 25–26, 28, 31, 36, 37, 41, 46
"Clothcraft Clothes," 317
Clothes Magazine, 360
"Clothier," 19
Clothiers and Haberdashers Weekly, 84, 85, 86
Clothiers Association of New York, 83, 85, 92
Clothiers Association (of Rochester), 83
Clothing, defined, 5, 6
Clothing Industry Code, 7, 174–179, 199
Clothing Industry Code Authority, 179–181, 183, 199, 206, 259–260
Clothing Manufacturers Association of New York, 119, 138–139, 140
Clothing Manufacturers Association of the United States (CMA), 4, 6, 93, 95, 126, 139, 140, *144*, 156, 172–177, 179, 183–184, 199–200, 202–206, 211, 214, 216, 223–225, 229–231, 238–240, 243–245, 247–249, 251–254, *257*, *258*, *259*, *261*, 264–280, 282, 284, 289–293, 297–298, 307–309, 314–316, 320, 324, 326–328, 330, 363
    Board of Directors, 229
    Bulletins, 229, 244, 249, 251, 264, 293
    Clothing Market Action, 282–287, 307
    Convention of 1950, 279–281
    "Definitions of Trade Customs," 293
    Reorganization, 256–263
    Services, 264
    Style Forecast, 309
Clothing Manufacturers Research Bureau, 168, 170
Clothing Trade Association of New York, 138, 170

Cluett, Peabody & Co., 12, 52–53, 354, 365
Cobrin, Harry A., 206, 225–230, 257, 258, 266, 268, 270
Cohen and Lang, 123
Cohen, Goldman & Co., 47, 92, 125, 150, 168, 205, 288, 365
Cohen, Joseph H., & Sons, Inc., 262, 367
"C.O.D. One-Price Clothier," 49
Cole, William W., 315–316
Commercial Economy Board, 116–117
Committee for Economic Development, 367
Committee of Fourteen, 93
Commons, Professor John R., 74–75
Conant, F. J., 29, 30
Connery, Robert H., 177
Consumers' Price Index (CPI), 218, 326–327
Coolidge, President Calvin (1872–1933), 161
Cooperative advertising, 317–318
Cotton Garment Code, 181
Court of Special Sessions, 77
Crane, Irving, 131
Crash of 1837, 31
Crawford Clothes, 149, 189–190
Cresap, Mark W., 168–172, *177,* 180, 199, 202, 205, 260–261
Crosman, Brevet Brigadier General G. H., 46
Curlee Clothing Company, 174
Curlee, Colonel Shelby H., 174, 178, 181
Cutaway coat, 27, 158–159

Daily News Record, 6, 120, 121–123, 163, 181–182, 185–186, 206, 244, 252, 353–354, 359
Daily Trade Record, 359
see also Daily News Record
Daroff, H., & Sons, 143, 144, *350,* 362, 367
Daroff, Michael, 144, *241*
Samuel H., 143–144

Defense Personnel Supply Center, 270
see also Quartermaster Depot of the Army
Defense Production Act of 1950, 270
Delmonicos, 92
Disraeli, Benjamin (1804–1881), 160
Division of labor, 61
Dodge, Rev. John Adams, 43
Douglis, Charles, 139
Drechsler and Leff, 139, 140, 200, 214, 262
Drechsler, David, 139, 140–142, 170–172, *176,* 178–179, 180, 183, 199, 200, 202, 204, 206, 214, *237,* 238–239, *246,* 252, 258, 262, 267
Drury Lane Theatre, 14
Dun & Bradstreet, 163–165, 182, 219, 265, *347*
Dun, R. G., and Company, 31
Dun, Robert G., 31
Duroy, 16

Eagle Clothes, 196, 353–354, 365, 367
Eastman, George, House Collections, *66*
Education Research Bureau, 69
Eisenhower, President Dwight D., (1890–1969), 367
Eisner, Jacob, 139
Electric needle, 10
Emergency Price Control Act, 209
Employment Act of 1946, 219
Emporium, The Buffalo, 77
Erie Canal, 25, 32
Erskine, General Graves B., 216
Esquire, 360–361
Ettelson, Albert, 144
Ettelson family, *143,* 367
Ettelson, Henry J., 142–144

Fabrics, historical, 13, 15, 16, 159–160
Fairchild Publications, Inc., *263,* 359, 360
Fair Labor Standards Act, 181, 184, 200, 266, 348

Index

Fashion Institute of Technology, 362–363
Fashion Park, 57, 58, 150, 157, 353
Fashions, 157–161
Fecheimer, M. & L. S., & Co., 85
Federal Trade Commission, 152, 153, 257, 266
Feiss, Paul, 125, 296
  Richard, 119
Ferster, Herbert, 214, 262, 270, 273
Figg, Howard, 125
Finchley, 151
Finley, Murray, 321
Fishon, Philip, 196
Five Centuries of American Costume, 16
Fleisher Bros., 85
Flickstein, William B., 142, 144, 225, *241,* 270
Ford, 269
Foreign designers, 12
Foreman, John B., 367
Frankenstein, Lester, 367
Freeman, Jacob L., 115–116, 295
French Revolution, 15
Friedman, J., & Co., 57–58, 95, 119, 123, 125
Friedman, Max, 57–58, 95, 119, 125
Frock coat, 27, 158–159
Furnishings, defined, 5, 6

General Conservation Order M373A, 212
Genesco Inc., 53, 354, 365
Gentlemen's Quarterly, 361
Georgetown University, 205
Giacometti, Alberto (1901-1966), 340
Glen Alden, 365
Goldman, William, 47, 56–57, 92, 122, 123, 125, 147, 168–172, *183,* 288–289, 296
  Wm. P., 139–140, *242,* 366
Goldman, Wm. P., & Brothers, 139–140, 196, 279, 366
Goldsmith, Alfred, 367
  Louis, 53–54, 143
Goldsmith (*cont.*)
  Louis, Inc., 143, 285, 367
Goldstein, Isaac, 107
Goodstein Brothers, 367
Gray, John D., 249, 252, 254, 262, 330–332
Green, Robert L., 361
Greenberg, Morris, 181, 183, 196
Greentree, Meyer, 32
Greif, Alvin, 53
  David, 53
Greif, L., & Bro., 53, 84, 150, 354
Greif, Leonard, 53
  Levi, 52–53
  Simon, 53
Grossman Clothing Company, 139, 279, 366, 367
Grossman, Isidore, 139, 140, *144,* 200, *242,* 279, 314, 366
Gunzberg brothers, 367

Haas family, 367–368
Haas Tailoring Co., 368
Hall and Opdyke, 35
Hamburger, Isaac, & Sons, 85
Hammerslough Bros., 49, 50
Hammonton Park, *357,* 367
Hanford and Brother
  see Lewis and Hanford
Hanford, John E., 35
Harding, President Warren G. (1865–1923), 161
"Hard sell," 23, 287
Harry Hart and Brother, 50
Hart, Abt and Marx, 50
Hart, Schaffner & Marx, 9, 12, 23, 50–51, 105, 150, 163, 165, 168, 196, 233–234, 254, 260, 262, 316–317, 353–354, 364, 365, 366, 367
Harvard, 367
Haspel family, 367
Hathaway Manufacturing Company, 215
Heidelberg & Wolfe, 123
Henderson, Leon, 209, 213

Hickey-Freeman, Co., 94, 115, 117–118, 125, 168, *179*, 212, 217, 261, 295, 367
Hickey, Jeremiah G., 94–95, 125, 137, 168, 171, 172, *179*, 296
Hillman and Drechsler, spirit of, 3
Hillman, Sidney, 8, 9, 105–106, 109–112, 128, 134, 136, 142, 165–166, 170–172, *174*, 177, 178, 187–188, 192, 201, 202, 204, 209, 224–225, 252, 321, 322
  Apartments of the Elderly, 324–325
  Foundation, 325
  Mrs. Sidney,
  see Abramowitz, Bessie
Hillquit, Morris, 109
Hilton brothers, 367
Hine, Lewis W., *66*
"History and a Prophecy of the Clothing Trade, A," 47
Hitler, Adolf (1889–1945), 208–209
Hoffman, David, 139
Hollander, Louis, 107, *246*, 321
Holtz, Max L., 137, 163, 164
Hotchkiss, Professor W. E., 129–131
Hotel Biltmore, *203*
Howard Stores, 149, 189
Howe, Elias, Jr., 43–44
Hoyt, F. A., and Brother, 31–32
Hub, The, 150–151
"Hundred Days," 167

Industrial Mobilization Plan, 267
Industrial Recovery Association of Clothing Manufacturers (IRA), 174–176, 178–179, 181
Industrial Revolution, 17, 61
Institute of Management, 363
International Association of Clothing Designers (IACD), 282, 311
International Tailoring Company, 153, 172, 202, 205
Irish famine, 61
Ivy League style, 161
Iwo Jima, 216

Jacobson, Marshall M., *203*
Jaffee, Charles D., 139, 140, 171, 172, 180
  Louis J., 296
Japan, 272–276, 294
"Jazz suit," 160, 310
Jobbers, 343–344
  post-Civil War influence, 54–55
Johnson, General Hugh S., 175
  Samuel (1709–1784), 6, 14
Jones, Colonel Thomas, 225, 228, 267
Joseph and Feiss Company, 38, 48, 119, 125, 248, 317, 354, 368
Journeymen Tailors National Trade Union, 98–99
Juster Brothers, 151

Kaplan, Robert A., 206
Kappel, Marks and Langeman, 149
Karr, Norman, 316
Kayser-Roth Corp., 54, 365
Kennedy, President John F. (1917–1963), 275
Kessler, Chester, 367
Kestnbaum, Meyer, 9, 366–367
Kirschbaum, B., & Company, 125, 136
Kirschbaum, David, 125
Knights of Labor, 79–80, 83, 99, 103
Koch and Loeb, 38
Korean War, 9, 266–268
Kroll, Jack, 321
Kuhn, Loeb & Co., 39, 50
Kuhn, Nathan and Fischer, 85
Kuhn, Rindskoff & Co., 39
Kuppenheimer, B., & Co., 48, 119, 125, 168, 296, 317, 367
Kuppenheimer, Bernard, 48

Labor-management relations, 3–5, *et al*
La Capria, Vincent, 321
Lang, Meyer, 57, 58
Leiserson, William M., 234

Lerner, Al, 273
Steve, 367
Levin, Sam, 321
Levine, Major David, 227-228
Levy, Alex M., 163, 164
Colonel Fred, 125
Joseph, 149
Julius H., 139, 140
Moe, 124
Lewis and Hanford, 25, 35
Lewman, Frank C., 180
Light & Schlesinger, 123
Lincoln, President Abraham (1809-1865), 24
Lipmann, Dan, 151
London, Meyer, 109
Lyttons, 315

MacArthur, General Douglas (1880-1964), 272
McKelvey, Blake, 32, 69, 83
McKinley, President William (1843-1901), 82
Made-to-measure trade, 157
Madison Square Garden, 124, 125
Makransky, S., & Sons, 196
Manhattan Shirt Company, 120
Markin, L., *241*
Marks, David, 51
Marks, David, & Sons, 84
Marks, Marcus M., 50, 51, 86, 93, 288, 295
Martin, John T., 52
William R. H., 52
Massachusetts Bureau of Labor, 73
Maximum Price Regulation No. 177 (MPR 177), 214-215, 221
Mayer, Felix S., 38-39
Mayer, Scheuer & Co., 85
Mayflower Hotel, 171
Mayor's Court, 77
Mendelsohn, William, 285
Men's Clothing Industry Import Committee, 273-274
Men's Wear Magazine, 148-149, 360
Menswear Retailers of America, 95, 115
Mercantile Agency
see R. G. Dun and Company
Merchants' Vigilance Association, 31
Methods of Accounting and Office Procedures in the Men's and Boys' Clothing Industry, 280
Metternich, Prince Klemens Wenzel von (1773-1859), 255
Meyers, Louis M., 295
Michaels, Henry, 32, 83
Michaels, Stern & Company, 32, 83, 84, 126, 214, 367
Miller, Bernard J., 361
Mirror of Fashion, 28
"Mod" styles, 310
Moody, John, 120
Moody's Investors' Service, 120
Morgan, T. J., 69-70
Morse, Julius, 57
Morse, Leopold, Company, 31, 57
Munroe, Alfred, & Company, 34-35
Mutolese, Michael, 362
Mutolese, Michael, Apparel Research Center, 362
Mutual Adjustment Bureau, 288-289
Myers, Louis M., 115

Napoleon
see Bonaparte, Napoleon
Nash, Arthur, 136
Nathan, S. J., & Son and Company, 84
National Association of Clothiers (NAC), 47, 51, 56, 81-96, 106-107, 115, 119, 120, 123, 127-128, 131, 137, 147, 168, 170, 287-288, 293, 295
National Association of Retail Clothiers, 95, 135, 295, 297, 315
see also Menswear Retailers of America; National Association of Retail Clothiers and Furnishers (NARCF)

National Association of Wool Manufacturers (NAWM), 290–293, 315
National Credit Office, 165
Market Planning Service, 303–304, *341, 342*
National Defense Advisory Commission, 209
see also Office of Production Management
National Industrial Federation of Clothing Manufacturers, 128–131, 138
National Industrial Recovery Act (NIRA), 7, 165, 174–177
see also National Recovery Administration (NRA)
National Labor Bureau of Clothing Manufacturers of America, 88, 90, 95–96, 127, 138, 170
National Market Week, 282
National Organization of Manufacturers
see National Association of Clothiers
National Recovery Administration (NRA), 174–175, 177, 180–181, 183–184, 185, 199, 206, 260
National Retail Merchants Association, 298
National Wool and Worsted Manufacturers Association, 288
"Negro clothing," 37
Nelson, Donald, 209, 210
Neutrality Act, 208
New Deal, 167, 177, 200
New England Men's and Boys' Clothing Manufacturing Association, 206, 263
New York Association of Clothiers, 51, 138
New York Brotherhood of Tailors, 107–108
New York Bureau of Labor, *72,* 90
New York Chamber of Commerce, 26, 73
New York Clothing Manufacturers Association, 140, 263
New York Clothing Manufacturers Exchange, 139, 140, 238, 251
see also New York Clothing Manufacturers Association
New York Factory Laws, 71–72
New York Federal Reserve Bank, 189
New York *Herald,* The, 37
New York Labor Bureau
see New York Bureau of Labor
New York State, 104
New York State Legislature, 70–72
New York Stock Exchange, 162, 364, 365
New York Times, The, 4, 6, 275
New York University, 141

"Oak Hall," 22, 49
Office of Price Administration (OPA), 6, 209–210, 213–220, 321
Record of regulations, 220–222
Office of Production Management (OPM), 209, 224
Opdyke, George, 35–36, 38, 50
Osler, Sir William (1849–1919), 92
Outerwear, heavy, defined, 5

Palm Beach Company, 340, 365, 367
"Pants King,"
see Schoeneman, Jacob
PBM Clothes, *343, 344, 355,* 367
Pearl Harbor, 211
Peavy & Bros., 85
Peet, Charles B., & Co., 51
Penney, J. C., 150
Pentagon, 267
Pfeifle, Louis C., 316
Philadelphia Clothing Manufacturers Association, 142–144, 225, 263
Philadelphia College of Textiles and Science, 362
Philadelphia Quartermaster Depot, 46, 197, 210, 226
Philanthropic Fifty, 366

Phoenix Clothes, 213, 345, 354, 367
Picariello brothers, 367
Pincus Brothers, 143, 367
Pincus, Nathan, 143
Playboy, 361
"Plus fours," 160
Pope, Jesse E., 67, 72, 74
Potofsky, Jacob S., 8, 9, 110, *237*, *246*, 249, 252, 254, 275, 281, 322–323, 330
Prince Albert, 27
"Psalm of the Clothier," 87
Puritan Revolution, 15

Qualified Bidders List, 267–268
Quartermaster Depot of the Army (QM), 225, 226, 228–229, 231–232, 267

Railroads, 28
  extension of in 1850's, 37
Rainwear, 5, 351–352
Rapid American, 12, 365
Ready-made clothing industry, 5
  As result of urban development, 18
  Expansion and protection, 25–26
  Feasible, 18–20
  Market grows, 20–24
Reed, Jacob, 23
Reed's, Jacob, Sons, 23
  see also Hart, Schaffner & Marx
Reinhard, Samuel E., 95–96
Reiss, Raymond H., 172, 202, 204, 205–206, *237*, *246*, *257*, 261
Reynolds, A., *85*
Richdale, J. E., *85*
Richman Bros., 149, 189
Riesenfeld, Victor S., 171–172, 180, 205–206, 214
  Mrs. Victor, *180*
Robinson-Patman Act, 200, 258, 266
Rochester Clothiers Exchange, 83, 137, 163, 263
Rogers, Professor Lindsay, 175
Rogers (*cont.*)
  Marvin N., 52
Rogers, Marvin N., & Co., 51
Rogers Peet, 50, 51, 52
Rolls Royce, 269
Roosevelt, President Franklin Delano (1882–1945), 167, 179, 209, 321
ROPECO, 52
Rosenberg, Adolph, 196
Rosenblum, Frank, 108–109, 110, *237*, 273, *322*, 323
Rosenthal, Samuel, 84
Rosenthal, Samuel, & Company, 123
Rosenwald and Weil, 50, 205
Rosenwald, Julius, 49–50
  Samuel, 49
Rosenwald, S., & Co., 49
Roth, Harry, 367
Roth-Kuppenheimer, Louis, 367
Roth, Michael, 367
Rothschild, Louis, 297
  Theodore, 214
Rubin, Barney, 149
Rudofker family, 367
Ryan, Daniel Edward, 61

Sack coat, 28, 158–159
St. Vincent's Hospital, 205
Salerno, Joseph, 321
Saxe, Abraham, 206
Schaeffer Tailoring Co., 367
Schaffner, Joseph, 50, 105
Schapiro family, 10
  see also Trimount Clothing Company
Schloss Bros. & Co., 84–85
Schlossberg, Joseph, 109, 321
Schoeff, Oscar, 360
Schoeneman, Ansel, 53
  Jacob, 53
Schoeneman, J., Inc., 52, 354
Schwartz & Jaffee, 123
Schwartz, Julius, & Sons, 214
Schwartz, Nathan L., 214

Sears Roebuck, 49, 50, 105, 209, 316
Seinsheimer, H. A., Co., 367
Seitchik, Joseph, 144
Seitchik, W., & Sons, 144, 367
Seligman family, 50
Semi-cutaway, 158
Sewing machine, 10, 42–46
"Sewing Machine War," 44
"Shape clothing," 14
Sherrys, 86
Shoaff, James J., 334
Simmons College, 9–10, 22
Simmons, Cornelius, 22
 George W., 22
 John, 10, 22
  family, 31, 49
Simon, Thomas, 367
Singer, Isaac Merrit, 44
Singer, Isaac M., & Company, 45
Singer Machine Combination, 44
Slacks, 7–8
Smith, Adam, 61, 274
Snellenberg Clothing Co., 53
Snellenberg, Nathan, 53
Snyder, Sidney, 368
Socialist Party, 109–110
Society Brand, 126, 163, 353
"Society of Master Tailors in the City of New York," 78–79
"Soft sell," 23
Soifer, Herman, 140
Sperry Rand Building, 308, 339–340
Sport coats, 7
Sportswear, 158
Stanton, Otis, 215–216
Stein-Adler, 38
Stein-Bloch Company, 48, 84, 150
Stein, Ludwig, 119, 125
 Nathan, 48
Stephens, Uriah, 80
Stevens, J. P., and Company, 216
Strauss, Levi, 41
Strauss, Levi, & Company, 41
Strouse Brothers, 84, 123, 125
Strouse, Eli, 125
Survey of Current Business
 see U. S. Department of Commerce
Sweatshops, 65–72, 319

Tailors' Council, 107
Tailors' National Protective Union, 99
Tailors-to-the-trade, 154–157
Talmud, 141
Tappan, Louis, 31
"Task shop," 74
"Task system," 74–75
Taylor, George W., 234
Thimmonier, Barthelemy, 43
Tillona, Thomas, 196
Tirin, Louis B., 120
Tower Hall, 23
Trade Unionism and Labor Problems, 74–75
Trimount Clothing Company, 10, 367
 see also Schapiro family
Tuberculosis, 325
Tulane, Paul, 9, 36
Tulane University, 9, 36
"Tunic" styles, 310
Tuxedo, 158

Udell, Jerome I., 314
Udell, Max, Sons & Co., 314
Ullman, Leo, 259, 262, 280
Union Trade Society of Journeymen Tailors, 78
United Garment Workers of America, 88, 89–92, 99–112, 113, 114
United Hebrew Trades, 99
U.S. Bureau of Foreign and Domestic Commerce, 68
U.S. Census of 1860, 32
U.S. Chamber of Commerce, 168, 170
U.S. Commissioner of Labor, 104
U.S. Congress, 167–169, 219
U.S. Council of National Defense, 116–117
U.S. Defense Department, 267

U.S. Department of the Army, 267–268
U.S. Department of Commerce, *46, 164, 182, 225, 226, 228,* 300, *313, 349*
Bureau of the Census, 46, 63–64, 155–156, *164,* 182, *225, 226,* 227, *228,* 300, *303,* 343, 346, 347, 348, *349*
Survey of Current Business, *313*
U.S. Department of Justice, 119
U.S. Department of Labor, 6, *182,* 266, *327, 335*
Bureau of Labor Statistics, 6, 133, 176, 217–218, 266, *327,* 335, 336, 337, 346
Business Research Advisory Council, 266
Wage & Hour Division, 257
U.S. Patent Office, 43
U.S. Senate, 70
U.S. Supreme Court, 183, 185, 199
Universal Express Company, 92

Van Heusen, Phillips, 354, 365
Vietnam War, 9, 269
VJ Day, 218, 232
V Line Clothes, 367
Voronoff, Doctor
see Mayer, Felix S.

Wages, 73–74, 325–332
and benefits, 1969, 8, 327
Wagner Act, 169, 174
Waldorf Astoria Hotel, 279, 280
Wall Street, 161, 321
Walsh-Healey Act, 266
Wanamaker & Brown, 22
Wanamaker, John, 22, 23, 123
Ward, Elmer, Sr., 340, 366
Wardman Park Hotel, 224
War Production Board (WPB), 6, 209–213, 215, 220, 231, 289–290
Men's and Boys' Clothing Division, 212
War Production Board (WPB) (*cont.*)
Record of issue of regulations, 220–222
Warwick Hotel, 253, 254
Washington, President George (1732–1799), 16
Wealth of Nations, The, 61
Weber & Heilbroner, 151
Webster Hall, 322
Webster, Noah (1758–1843), 6, 7
Webster's New Collegiate Dictionary, 5
Weider, Sam, 121
Weil, Julius B., 50
Samuel, 125
Weinstein, Charles, 142–143, *241,* 321
Emanuel, 140, 366
Harvey, 367
Weintraub, William, H., 360
Weitzenhoffer, Captain Irving, 227
West Mill Clothes, 140, 366, 367
Whitmarsh, Thomas, 20
Wilcox, R. Turner, 16, 27
"Wildcat" banking system, 30
Wile & Brickner, 84
Wile, Sol, 83, 90
Williams, J. E., 234
Women, 335–337
Wood William, 93, 120
Wool Products Labeling Act of 1939, 200, 257, 266
Woolworth, 365
Worcester, Massachusetts, 16
Work clothes, defined, 5
Working week, 19th century, 72
Works Progress Administration (WPA), 192
World War I, 9, 64, 113–114, 208
World War II, 6, 7, 9, 114, 156, 200, 208–222
Military procurement, 223–232
Wry, Charles E., 295, 296, 312

Zaretz, Charles E., 70
Zurn, Frank P., 206, 257, 258, 264